MASTERPLOTS
FIFTEEN-VOLUME
COMBINED EDITION

Volume Fourteen
Supp-Unfo

MASTERPLOTS

15-Volume Combined Edition
FIFTEEN HUNDRED AND TEN
Plot-Stories and Essay-Reviews
from the
WORLD'S FINE LITERATURE

Edited by
FRANK N. MAGILL

Story Editor
DAYTON KOHLER

VOLUME FOURTEEN—SUPP-UNFO

SALEM PRESS
INCORPORATED
NEW YORK

This work also appears under the title of
MASTERPIECES OF WORLD LITERATURE IN DIGEST FORM

MASTERPLOTS
FIFTEEN-VOLUME
COMBINED EDITION

Volume Fourteen
Supp-Unfo

THE SUPPLIANTS

Type of work: Drama
Author: Aeschylus (525-456 B. C.)
Type of plot: Classical tragedy
Time of plot: Age of myth
Locale: Argos
First presented: c. 490 B. C.

Principal characters:
DANAUS, an Egyptian of Greek descent
HIS FIFTY MAIDEN DAUGHTERS
PELASGUS, King of Argos
THE FIFTY SONS OF AEGYPTUS, BROTHER OF DANAUS

Critique:

The Suppliants, although complete artistically, seems to be a part of a larger pattern, possibly a trilogy, which probably told the complete, tragic story of Danaus and Aegyptus and their sons and daughters. The value of The Suppliants to the student of drama lies in the fact that it bridged the gap between the purely lyric phase of Greek drama and that glorious phase in which character and situation were developed to almost unbelievable heights of artistic perfection. In this play the protagonist is the chorus of maidens; Pelasgus, in his timidity, is almost three-dimensional, thus foreshadowing the great characters of the classic drama written during subsequent decades.

The Story:

Danaus and his fifty maiden daughters fled from Egypt after Danaus' brother, Aegyptus, had decided that his fifty sons should take their cousins to wife. At last the fugitives reached the shores of Argos, the land of their illustrious ancestress, Io, a mortal who had been loved by Zeus.

Holding olive branches wrapped in wool, the maidens sought, before an Argive altar, Zeus' protection of their purity. Their supplications to the father of the gods included the wish that the sons of Aegyptus might meet disaster at sea between Egypt and Argos. In fear of being forced to marry Aegyptus' sons, the maidens also invoked the wretched Procne, who had been given in marriage to the perfidious Tereus, and who took the life of her child, Itylus, out of hatred for her husband. They repeated their supplication to Zeus to protect them from forced love; they invoked Artemis, the goddess of chastity, to be favorable to them. They declared that they would end their own lives before they would submit to the sons of Aegyptus.

Danaus, observing that someone approached, cautioned his daughters to stay near the altar and to conduct themselves with modesty. Meanwhile they invoked not only Zeus but Apollo as well, who himself was once an exile. They prayed to Poseidon, god of the sea, and to Hermes, the messenger of the gods. Danaus recalled that the gods were merciless to those who indulged in lustful pleasures.

A man, followed by servants and warriors, entered the sacred area. Seeing that the maidens wore Oriental clothing and that suppliant wands had been placed on the altar, he asked whence Danaus and the young women had come. Questioned in turn, he disclosed that he was Pelasgus, King of Argos. One of the maidens then told him that they were of Argive stock, descendants of Io, the Argive woman who had given birth to a son by Zeus. Pelasgus interrupted to remark that the maidens appeared to be North Africans, and akin to the Amazons, rather than Grecian.

The maiden then resumed her tale. When Hera, wife of Zeus, saw that Zeus loved the mortal Io, she transformed Io into a heifer, over whom she placed Argus, the many-eyed god, as a guard. Fur-

3661

ther, Hera created a gadfly which she willed to sting Io into a miserable, wandering existence on earth. When Io, in her wanderings, came to Memphis, in Egypt, by mystical union with Zeus—the touch of his hand—she gave birth to a son. She named him Epaphus, from the nature of his birth. Epaphus had a daughter, Libya, after whom a great stretch of North Africa was named. Libya had a son, Belus, who fathered two sons, Danaus and Aegyptus. Danaus was the father of fifty daughters—the king beheld the father and his daughters before his very eyes—and Aegyptus was the father of fifty sons.

Pelasgus, satisfied that they were of Argive stock, asked why they had left Egypt. The maiden explained that they had fled because they were threatened with forced marriage to their cousins; that it was not so much that they hated their cousins as it was that they wanted their husbands to love them. Pelasgus, observing that in the most advantageous marriages there was no aspect of love, was not sure he could support the maidens in their cause. The maidens pointed to the wand-decked shrine and asked Pelasgus to heed the sign.

All the sisters pleaded for assistance from Pelasgus, who feared that his meddling in the affair might bring war to Argos. Apprehensive, yet anxious to succor the maidens, he insisted that he would have to consult his people. The suppliants answered that he was an absolute ruler, that he could, if he so desired, make his own decisions. They warned him to beware of the wrath of Zeus, the god who took pity on humans in distress and who was merciless with those mortals who refused to assist others. Still Pelasgus insisted on consulting his people; he feared lest he bring disaster to Argos. Even after searching deeply into his soul for an answer, he declared that the problem was one with which he alone could not cope, that to resolve it would involve frightful sacrifices to the gods.

In despair, the maidens proposed that Pelasgus use their girdles to hang them to the statues in the sacred area. Deeply disturbed, Pelasgus suggested that Danaus gather up all of the wands and, in hopes of eliciting general Argive sympathy for the maidens, place them on altars in the city of Argos itself. Danaus accepted the suggestion after he had been assured of safe passage into the city.

Danaus then departed with the wands. When Pelasgus directed the maidens to an unhallowed area of the sacred ground, they asked how they were to be protected there from their cousins. Pelasgus, advising them to pray to the Argive gods, returned to Argos to consult with his people.

Left alone, the maidens resumed their earnest prayers and invocations to Zeus. They again recalled Zeus' love for their ancestress and appealed to him who, after all, was responsible for their being, to save them from the lust of Aegyptus' sons.

Danaus returned to report that to a man the Argives would defend any refugees from seizure. Pelasgus, too, had reminded the Argives that if they failed to assist and to offer sanctuary to suppliants, Zeus would send before the city a man-eating monster. The maidens then sang their gratitude to the people of Argos and invoked the gods to look ever auspiciously upon the land.

Danaus, standing on an elevated place in the sacred ground, saw the sons of Aegyptus approaching the shore in their ships. He calmed his frightened daughters by reminding them of the Argives' promise, but when he wished to leave them to summon help, they begged him to stay with them. He pointed out that since it would take Aegyptus' sons some time to make proper anchorage, there would be plenty of time for him to seek aid.

After Danaus had gone, the maidens, overcome with apprehension at the approach of their cousins, spoke of the death they preferred to the enforced love which appeared to be imminent. As they cried in anguish to Zeus, a messenger from the ships came to them and, brutally handling them, ordered the maidens to the ships. While he sneered at their frantic appeals to the Greek gods, Pelasgus came upon the scene of violence and demanded of the messenger his business. The Egyptian answered that he had come to take what belonged to him and that only force, not any fear of the Greek gods, could prevent his taking the maidens back to Egypt. Pelasgus declared that the sons of Aegyptus would have to fight to claim their captives. When the messenger asked his name, Pelasgus retorted that his name did not matter; what did matter was that the sisters would never be taken by force from Argos.

The messenger, having been repulsed by the king's words, returned to the ships. Pelasgus then invited the maidens to take shelter among the friendly people of Argos. The maidens first sought the approval of their father. Danaus, advising them to treasure their chastity before their lives, gave them permission to go.

Rejoicing, the daughters of Danaus sang reverently and thankfully to Artemis, goddess of chastity. They also invoked Aphrodite, goddess of love, who they were sure would help in guiding them to marriages blessed by true love.

THE SUPPLIANTS

Type of work: Drama
Author: Euripides (c. 485-c. 406 B.C.)
Type of plot: Classical tragedy
Time of plot: Immediately after the War of the Seven against Thebes
Locale: Eleusis, not far from Athens
First presented: c. 424 B.C.

Principal characters:
THESEUS, King of Athens
AETHRA, his mother
ADRASTUS, King of Argos
EVADNE, Capaneus' wife
IPHIS, her father
CHILDREN OF THE SLAIN CHIEFTAINS
THE GODDESS ATHENA
HERALD OF CREON
CHORUS OF ARGIVE MOTHERS

Critique:

Though *The Suppliants* is not a well-constructed play, it has as much tragic feeling, eloquence, and imagination as any other of the ancient Greek tragedies. The Peloponnesian War so dominated the thought of Euripides that every one of his plays set in Athens is easily seen as a lesson to his fellow citizens and a warning against the follies of war. But even though *The Suppliants,* like *Andromache* and the *Herakleidae,* is marred by this didactic urgency, it profoundly embodies a universal theme: the criminal folly of men who kill men and the desperate need for religion, law, and human compassion.

The Story:

Adrastus, the Argive king who had led the disastrous war of the Seven against Thebes and had alone escaped with his life, brought the mothers and the children of the slain chieftains to Athens, the most democratic and hospitable city of Greece. There they gathered at the temple of Demeter at Eleusis, and when Aethra, the mother of Theseus, came to pray they formed a ring of supplication about her, begging for help in recovering the dead bodies of their sons for burial according to the prescribed rites. The anguish of the mothers so moved Aethra that she sent at once for her own son.

The powerful young king closely cross-examined the defeated old ruler and, after discovering that Adrastus had foolishly married off his daughters to quarrelsome exiles, Tydeus and Polynices, and had even more foolishly engaged in war against Thebes despite the advice of the prophet Amphiaraus, refused to help. But Aethra discreetly reminded her son that although his logic was sound as far as it went, he was nevertheless obligated by honor and the religious customs of Attica to go to the aid of all who sought proper burial and funeral rites for the dead. Theseus, recognizing the wisdom and humanity of her counsel, departed to seek a vote of the Athenian assembly on the matter.

Upon his return, Theseus announced that with the support of the assembly he was ready to send two messages to Creon, King of Thebes: the first a polite request for permission to bury the dead, to be followed in case of refusal with a warning that his armies were on their way. But he was interrupted by the arrival of an insolent herald from Creon who demanded in the name of his despot that Adrastus be driven from Athens. The herald added that courageous wisdom called for peace. Theseus, although he detested war, felt obligated by the ancient laws of the gods to bury the dead, by force of arms if necessary. After a heated exchange of words the Theban herald withdrew and Theseus prepared for battle. He rejected Adrastus' offer of aid, for he was unwilling to blend his fortunes with those of a king who had brought upon himself the wrath of the gods. As Theseus marched off with his troops, the chorus chanted fear of the fickleness of heaven and prayed for deliverance.

Soon a messenger, bringing news of Theseus' victory, described how the Athenians arrived at the Theban gates, expressed a desire to avoid war provided they were permitted to bury the Argive chieftains, but finally found it necessary to slaughter the Thebans. But Theseus, refusing to enter the gates and sack the city, had personally gathered together the dead bodies and washed their wounds. Adrastus, deeply moved, lamented that the Thebans had not learned the lesson of compromise from his own experience and wished that he, too, had died with his fellow warriors.

When the bodies were brought to Athens, Adrastus delivered a eulogy over each (Capaneus, Eteocles, Hippomedon, Parthenopaeus, Tydeus, and Polynices) before they were prepared for cremation on the funeral pyre. Suddenly Evadne, widow of Capaneus, appeared on a rock overhanging the burning pyre, determined to marry him in death as she had in life. Her aged father, Iphis, pleaded with her in vain. Dressed in festive garments, she leaped into the fire. As the children of the cremated warriors carried away the ashes in funeral urns, the grief-stricken Iphis withdrew to the dark interior of his house to die.

Marching in funeral procession, the children (thereafter known as the Epigoni) chanted with the chorus an oath to avenge their fathers. Theseus extracted from them a promise, too, that they and all their children would always remember the kindness they had received from Athens and honor the city of democracy. But before the children could carry off the ashes of their fathers, the goddess Athena appeared in mid-air and called upon Theseus not to permit the ashes to be returned to Argos. Instead, after appropriate animal sacrifices, they must be delivered to the safekeeping of the oracle at Delphi. Then, turning to the children, Athena prophesied that when they reached manhood they would successfully sack the city of Thebes and avenge the slaughter of their fathers.

I SUPPOSITI

Type of work: Drama
Author: Ludovico Ariosto (1474-1533)
Type of plot: Farce
Time of plot: c. 1500
Locale: Ferrara, Italy
First presented: 1509

Principal characters:

DULIPPO, the true Erostrato, posing as a servant
EROSTRATO, the true Dulippo, posing as a student
POLYNESTA, a young lady of Ferrara
DAMON, a wealthy merchant, her father
CLEANDER, an ancient doctor of law, her suitor
A SIENESE, posing as Erostrato's father
PHILOGANO, a wealthy Sicilian merchant, true father of the true Eros-
    trato
PASIPHILO, a meddlesome parasite
BALIA, Polynesta's nurse

Critique:

Ariosto wrote two versions of his famous *I Suppositi* (*The Substitutes*) the first in prose, the second in poetry; the action, however, is essentially the same in each. The play stands as an excellent example of the classical influence on Italian Renaissance drama. It follows to the letter the rules for a five-act structure laid down by Landino; it adheres strictly to the unities of time, place, and action; it follows a Terentian plot line and employs the favorite Plautinian theme of mistaken identity. The play is also important in the history of English drama. Translated by George Gascoigne (under the title *Supposes*) for production at Gray's Inn in 1566, the work had a strong influence on the development of Elizabethan comic form, as may be seen from Shakespeare's early *The Comedy of Errors*. Aside from these historical considerations, *I Suppositi* is good comedy in its own right—a fast-moving, ribald, and extremely playable piece.

The Story:

Balia, nurse to beautiful young Polynesta, was concerned over her mistress' practice of sleeping with her father's servant, Dulippo. Polynesta reproved Balia, reminding her that it was she who had first given Dulippo access to her bedroom but reassuring her by giving the following situation.

Dulippo was, in reality, not a servant, but Erostrato, the son of a wealthy Sicilian merchant. Having come to Ferrara to pursue his studies, he had fallen in love with Polynesta upon his arrival. Consequently, he had taken the name of his servant Dulippo and secured employment in the house of his beloved's father. Meanwhile, the true Dulippo had assumed the identity of Erostrato and occupied the house next door.

This affair had been going on for two years; but now, Polynesta observed, it was being complicated by the fact that the doddering old doctor of law, Cleander, had become a suitor for her hand, tempting her father with an offer of two thousand ducats. Dulippo was attempting to forestall him by having the false Erostrato ask for her, too, and by having him meet Cleander's offer.

The old doctor arrived in the company of his ever-hungry parasite, Pasiphilo, and the two ladies retired. Cleander's eyesight was so bad that he could not tell who they were. Under Pasiphilo's prodding, Cleander boasted that he would go to any price to secure Polynesta. He had, he claimed, amassed a fortune of ten thousand ducats during the time he had lived in Ferrara, and he boasted that this was the second fortune he had made. The

3666

first he had lost at the fall of Otranto twenty years before. That loss, he recalled sadly, was nothing to the loss of his five-year-old son, captured by the Turks during the battle.

After Cleander had gone, Dulippo appeared to invite Pasiphilo to dinner. The false Erostrato confronted Dulippo with bad news: Damon, Polynesta's father, doubted Erostrato's ability to match Cleander's offer for his daughter. The two connivers agreed that they must devise some ruse to convince the grasping merchant of their ability to pay.

Dulippo, to alienate Cleander and Pasiphilo, told the old doctor that Pasiphilo had insulted him, illustrating the insults in an extremely comic way. After Cleander had left enraged, the false Erostrato arrived, this time with good news. He had met a foolish Sienese gentleman whom he had frightened with the claim that all visitors from Siena would be persecuted in Ferrara. The Sienese had sought protection by agreeing to pose as Erostrato's father. He would meet any sum that Cleander could offer.

But the trick was never played. Damon had overheard Balia quarreling with a servant over the propriety of Polynesta's conduct and had learned of his daughter's two-year-old affair. Dulippo and Balia were thrown into Damon's private dungeon. Damon, aware of the extralegal nature of this procedure, swore the servant to secrecy, but, unknown to him, Pasiphilo, who had been sleeping off an attack of indigestion in the stables nearby, had awakened in time to overhear everything.

Meanwhile, to complicate matters further, Philogano, Erostrato's true father, had arrived from Sicily. He had written asking Erostrato to return home but his pleas had been ignored, and he had decided to come in person for his son. He was conducted to Erostrato's house by a local innkeeper. The false Erostrato saw him in time, however, and attempted to hide.

A hilarious bit of byplay followed in which the Sienese, aided by Erostrato's

servants, on the one hand, and Philogano, assisted by his servants, on the other, both claimed to be Erostrato's father. Finally Philogano espied the false Erostrato, whom he knew as his servant Dulippo, and called on him to substantiate his claim. He was confounded when the real Dulippo declared that he was Erostrato, that the Sienese was Philogano of Sicily, and that the old man was an impostor or mad. Certain that Dulippo had done away with his son, Philogano went off to seek aid from the authorities.

Pasiphilo arrived to cadge a dinner from Erostrato. Concerned over the affair with Philogano, for he really loved the old man who had been a father to him, the false Erostrato asked Pasiphilo if he had seen Dulippo, and Pasiphilo told him the whole story of the discovery and imprisonment. Afraid that the ruse had gone too far, the servant rushed off to confess all to Philogano, leaving Pasiphilo, to the latter's delight, in charge of the dinner.

Philogano returned with the lawyer he had retained—old Cleander. He explained how his trusted servant whom he had saved from the Turks twenty years before had betrayed him. On hearing his story, Cleander closely questioned Philogano about the boy. To Cleander's delight, the real Dulippo turned out to be the old man's long-lost son.

Next came Damon. Polynesta had revealed the whole truth of her affair, and he had rushed out to check up on her claim that his servant was actually the wealthy and highborn Erostrato.

Finally the false Erostrato returned to make his confession, and all the entanglements were straightened out. The true Erostrato was released and united with his mistress, whom his father promised to procure as his bride—thereby pacifying Damon. Cleander renounced his claim on Polynesta; he had wanted a wife only to produce an heir and now he had one in the true Dulippo. Even Cleander and Pasiphilo were reconciled, and Pasiphilo was given a permanent invitation to dine at Cleander's house.

SURRY OF EAGLE'S-NEST

Type of work: Novel
Author: John Esten Cooke (1830-1886)
Type of plot: Historical romance
Time of plot: 1861-1863
Locale: Virginia
First published: 1866

Principal characters:
LIEUTENANT COLONEL SURRY, the narrator
MAY BEVERLEY, later his wife
COLONEL MORDAUNT, an embittered, melancholy planter
FENWICK, his enemy
MRS. PARKINS, Fenwick's confederate
HARRY SALTOUN, a young officer, Mordaunt's son
VIOLET GRAFTON, an orphan
ACHMED, Mordaunt's Arab companion
GENERAL STONEWALL JACKSON
GENERAL J. E. B. STUART
GENERAL TURNER ASHBY
MAJOR JOHN PELHAM
CAPTAIN WILLIAM D. FARLEY, a Confederate scout

Critique:

Surry of Eagle's-Nest, a romantic, historical novel of 132 brief chapters by Captain John Esten Cooke of the Confederate army, purports to be "the memoirs of a staff-officer serving in Virginia." It blends many facts and much fiction; and, even if its flavor is extremely melodramatic, in keeping with the literary style of its author's generation, it has continued to fascinate readers for nearly a hundred years. For the reader who might want to follow Surry's fortunes to the end of the war Cooke composed a sequel, which he completed three years after General Lee's surrender. Written in the same vein as *Surry of Eagle's-Nest,* but somehow not so well known, is *Mohun,* "the last days of Lee and his paladins."

The Story:

Cavalier Philip Surry, who rode and fought under Prince Rupert in the English Civil War, escaped to Virginia when King Charles I was beheaded. Establishing a home, which he named Eagle's-Nest, on the Rappahannock River below Port Royal, he enjoined in his will that the oldest son of the family in each generation should sign himself "Surry of Eagle's-Nest."

The present Surry, who had attended the Virginia Military Institute for one session and had studied law at the University of Virginia, was in Richmond in April, 1861, when the State Convention passed its ordinance of secession. One evening at the Capitol Square he saw with rapture a beautiful girl, whose dropped handkerchief contained the initials, M.B. On another day, in Hollywood Cemetery, he witnessed by chance a duel between a tall, bronzed stranger named Mordaunt and one Fenwick, the encounter ending when Mordaunt put a pistol bullet through Fenwick's lungs. Surry left Richmond the proud recipient of a captain's commission in the Provisional Army of Virginia, and in his new gray uniform he rode toward Harper's Ferry for duty under Colonel Jackson.

Losing his way in the Wilderness, which bordered the Rapidan River, he spent a night in a house where dwelt an insane woman in white, still possessing traces of youthful beauty, who was attended by her lovely young cousin, Violet Grafton, and by a harridan, Mrs. Parkins. Surprisingly there appeared at this house Fenwick, whose duel wound

had not been fatal. In the night "the White Lady," tiptoeing into Surry's room, slipped into his coat pocket a package bearing the words, "Read these when I am dead—and remember
Your own Frances."

Further, while en route to Harper's Ferry, Surry was overtaken by a hurricane in a forest and was knocked from his horse by a large limb. He was stunned and his arm was broken. A female equestrian, whom the flying branches had spared, ordered her servant to take the injured man to her father's home, "The Oaks." There he convalesced under the eyes of Colonel Beverley and his daughter May, his rescuer and the owner of the handkerchief which he had picked up in Richmond. Surry's heart was fully captivated, but May was already bound by a between-fathers contract and a young-girl engagement to Frederick Baskerville. The fact that her new lover knew Baskerville to be a scoundrel made Surry's plight doubly bitter.

Fairly near "The Oaks" was the home of Mordaunt, which Surry visited. Its owner, who lived hermit-like with Achmed, a faithful Arab, was destined to become one of Surry's best friends. Mordaunt's air of melancholy indicated the gentleman's deeply tragic past.

After long delays, Captain Surry finally reported for duty to Colonel Thomas J. Jackson, who made him an aide-de-camp. Shortly afterward the young staff officer met Colonel J. E. B. Stuart. The two colonels, soon to become generals, would be Surry's idols to the end of his days.

Before their first battle Surry and Mordaunt, now a Confederate colonel, saw an eerie night burial in the garden of a stone house at Manassas. They observed on the scene Fenwick, the Parkins woman, and Violet Grafton. The dead person was the insane "White Lady" of the Wilderness. Again Mordaunt tried to kill Fenwick, but without success. Soon afterward Surry delivered to Violet Grafton the package which her cousin had put in his pocket.

Wounded in the Battle of First Manassas, Surry was taken to the Fitzhugh home, "Elm Cottage," where he was well nursed. Mrs. Fitzhugh, charmed by Violet Grafton, gave the orphan girl a home.

In 1862, having recovered from his wound, Surry was with Jackson throughout his spectacular Valley Campaign and held General Turner Ashby in his arms when that "Knight of the Valley" expired on the battlefield. Briefly a prisoner, he met Sir Percy Wyndham, an Englishman wearing Federal blue. Also he met and admired Captain Farley of Stuart's staff, a scout extraordinary. When Jackson joined General Lee near Richmond to defeat McClellan, Surry shared in that campaign; then he was back near Fredericksburg, in the Wilderness area.

There one night, peering through a window shutter at the house where he had first seen "the White Lady" and Violet Grafton, Surry heard Fenwick, while intoxicated, acknowledge himself to be a Yankee spy. Moreover, Fenwick reviewed to Mrs. Parkins the story of his and Mordaunt's enmity. Years before, Mordaunt and Fenwick, youthful friends, had become rivals for the love of Frances Carleton. When she married Mordaunt, Fenwick planned revenge. Still posing as a devoted friend, he utilized a trip of Mordaunt's to London to forge a letter which made Frances believe that her husband had landed in New York and was requesting her to let Fenwick escort her there to meet him. Aided by the easily bribed Mrs. Parkins, Fenwick abducted his friend's wife to Maryland, where she gave birth to a son, who was afterwards reported dead, and where she contracted a fever which permanently affected her brain. Imitating Frances Carleton Mordaunt's handwriting, Fenwick perpetrated another forgery which duped Mordaunt into believing that his wife had forsaken him. Embittered, the young husband left Virginia for a long sojourn in Arabian lands. After drunken Fenwick's remarkable disclosure Surry captured him, but the prisoner escaped after bribing a guard. At a later date, however, in a face-to-face combat, Mordaunt pinned his enemy to a tree with a thrust of his sword.

Surry, who, as the war continued, rose to be major and later lieutenant colonel, saw old Stonewall Jackson, Longstreet, and Lee defeat Pope at Second Manassas. In the Maryland campaign which followed he was captured, interviewed by McClellan, and placed aboard a prison train headed for Baltimore; but he escaped by jumping through a window while the train was in motion. In December, 1862, he was present when Lee's two corps under Longstreet and Jackson repulsed Burnside at Fredericksburg. There he saw the youthful artillery genius, Major John Pelham, master-maneuver his guns. An ardent friendship between Surry and Pelham continued until the gallant young Alabaman was killed in battle.

The spring of 1863 brought Surry abundant joy. When Colonel Beverley's wealth at "The Oaks" was destroyed by invading armies, Frederick Baskerville lost interest in May so completely that he released her from her engagement. Consequently she married Surry, with her father's sanction.

Among Surry's friends was Harry Saltoun, a young Confederate lieutenant from Maryland. Fenwick, who repeatedly recovered from seemingly mortal wounds, by means of a lying anonymous letter provoked Saltoun to challenge Colonel Mordaunt to a duel. Tragedy was averted, however, when Violet Grafton sent Mordaunt the paper in which "the White Lady," Mrs. Frances Carleton Mordaunt, had recorded the whole truth about Fenwick and his evil deceptions. Also, through an affidavit of a Maryland woman, Harry Saltoun was proved to be Mordaunt's own son.

Fenwick's ultimate villainy was the abduction of Violet Grafton, but Mordaunt's devoted Arab companion, Achmed, trailed the knave to his hiding place. There Mordaunt and Fenwick had their final fight, but it was Achmed, not Mordaunt, who killed Fenwick with a gleaming dagger. Sadly, however, a ball from the dying villain's pistol wounded Achmed, who expired in the presence of the two persons whom he loved, Mordaunt and Violet Grafton.

"Fighting Joe" Hooker, who had succeeded Burnside as commander of the Federal army of invasion, thrust at Lee in the Wilderness, on the south side of the Rapidan and Rappahannock rivers. In a brilliantly conceived surprise movement Stonewall Jackson struck Hooker's right flank at Chancellorsville, to win a thrilling victory. This Southern triumph was dearly bought, for in the woods, on the night of May 2, 1863, Jackson was wounded by his own men, and on Sunday, May 10, that irreplaceable hero breathed his last.

Surry of Eagle's-Nest survived to tell his story and that of the war years. For him, only the ghosts of the past remained.

SWALLOW BARN

Type of work: Novel
Author: John P. Kennedy (1795-1870)
Type of plot: Comedy of manners
Time of plot: Early nineteenth century
Locale: Virginia
First published: 1832

Principal characters:
MARK LITTLETON, the narrator
NED HAZARD, his cousin
FRANK MERIWETHER, Ned's brother-in-law
MR. ISAAC TRACY, a gentleman farmer
BEL TRACY, his daughter
HARVEY RIGGS, a Tracy kinsman

Critique:

Although the author of *Swallow Barn* states definitely that the story is not a novel, it is usually listed as such because of the continuous thread or theme running through it. In reality the book is a series of sketches or dramatic episodes concerned with plantation life and manners in Virginia during the early eighteenth century, sketches held together by a continuity of characters and events. *Swallow Barn*, the first work of popular fiction to be set in Virginia, was the forerunner of a large number of novels dealing with the historic background of that state.

The Story:

After receiving many invitations from his cousin Ned Hazard, Mark Littleton at last felt that he could no longer put off a visit to Virginia. He left his mother and sisters in New York and began his journey south. At Swallow Barn, his cousin's home, Mark met or renewed acquaintance with a great many relatives and friends. Ned Hazard's sister had married Frank Meriwether, who was now the head of the family. The estate had been left to Ned. It had been heavily encumbered and Frank had paid off the heaviest debts and put the plantation on a paying basis. The house was filled with Meriwether and Hazard relatives, all permanent guests. Some performed small functions as a pretense of paying their own way, but their tasks were no more than token duties kindly thought up for them so that they would feel useful.

Mark found life in Virginia restful and pleasant, for there was an unhurried rhythm about Swallow Barn that appealed to him. The plantation was filled with slaves and freed Negroes who were fiercely loyal to Frank, a good master. Indeed, everyone loved Frank for his thoughtfulness and generosity. Mark's special favorite, however, was his cousin Ned Hazard. The two young men were inseparable companions. Ned was a man of excellent spirits, always indulging in pranks and jokes. Swallow Barn would one day revert to him, but he was content to let Frank use it as his own, wanting only to have a good time without the need of responsibilities. Ned took Mark on several excursions around the countryside and introduced him to local beauties of nature.

While Ned and Mark walked through the woods one day, they indulged in one of their favorite pastimes by singing their loudest, each trying to outdo the other. In one verse Ned called out the name of Bel Tracy. He was deeply chagrined when that lady, having ridden up unnoticed, answered him. Bel Tracy was the daughter of old Isaac Tracy, master of the neighboring estate, The Brakes. Ned's confusion at being discovered by Bel made Mark think that his cousin felt more than friendship for her. She teased him gently about his boisterous use of her name, leaving Ned stammering in confusion. Bel was accompanied by her sister and Harvey Riggs, a Tracy kinsman. Harvey joined in the teasing, but Mark saw at once that it was good-natured teasing and that Harvey felt great friendship for Ned.

The two parties went back to Swallow Barn, where Harvey delivered a letter from Mr. Tracy to Frank Meriwether. The subject matter was of long standing and it afforded Frank some amusement. For many years Mr. Tracy had imagined himself in possession of one hundred acres of marshland separating The Brakes from Swallow Barn. Every court in Virginia had denied his claim, but the old gentleman was adamant. Frank would long since have given him the land, for it was worthless, but he knew the old gentleman would be lost without the affair, which provided him with mental activity as he plotted ways to get possession of the land. In his letter Mr. Tracy suggested that he and Frank let their lawyers go over the matter again, the two disputants to abide by the legal decision. Frank planned to ask his lawyer to arrange matters so that Mr. Tracy would win the suit after what looked like a difficult legal maneuver.

Old Mr. Tracy was a detriment to Ned, even though Ned loved the old gentleman. He was a gentleman of the old school, dignified and sober; Ned, on the other hand, could not repress his merry spirits. But Bel had absorbed some of her father's dignity and was usually not very receptive to Ned's foolishness. The poor young man tried hard to change, but his disposition was almost as firm as Mr. Tracy's.

After Ned had admitted to Mark that he loved Bel, the two friends mapped out a campaign to win her heart to Ned's cause. Their plans were temporarily postponed, however, by the arrival of the lawyers who would decide the disputed land claim.

The legal gentlemen afforded the young men much entertainment, one being a dandy known throughout Virginia.

He was pursued by two of the maiden relatives, each of whom pretended to be pursued by him. When the dandy learned of their intentions, he finished his business and departed as quickly as possible. The settling of the suit gave everyone but old Mr. Tracy a lot of amusement. Because he was serious about the whole matter, Ned lost more ground in his suit when he unwittingly made light of the affair. It took a great deal of clever legal terminology to fool the old man, but at last he was awarded the land and convinced that justice had been done.

Sometimes Ned, Mark, and the others found entertainment in listening to the tales of goblins and ghosts told by old slaves on the plantation. The two families frequently gave large dinner parties, when the whole community would be invited to come and spend the day. Mark, thinking he would find it hard ever to return to New York and his own family, hoped to stay long enough to help Ned in his courtship of Bel. At one of the parties Ned had a little wine and became more boisterous than ever, causing Bel to lose the esteem she had gradually been developing for him. He gained her good will once more by finding her pet falcon which had flown away, but later he lost her affection by engaging in a fist fight with a town bully. Harvey Riggs, joining Mark in attempts to help Ned with his suit, told Bel that Ned had fought the bully because the ruffian had cast slurs on her father. Pity at last entered Bel's heart, and she treated her suitor with more favor.

Mark at last left Virginia and went home to New York. Some months later he learned that Ned had been successful; Bel had married him on New Year's Day. Ned wrote too that it was as Frank had feared. Old Mr. Tracy was sorry the land suit was settled and wished to open it again. Without the pending suit, he felt like a man who had lost an old and faithful friend.

THE SWISS FAMILY ROBINSON

Type of work: Novel
Author: Johann Rudolf Wyss (1781-1830)
Type of plot: Adventure romance
Time of plot: Late eighteenth century
Locale: An island near New Guinea
First published: 1813

Principal characters:

MR. ROBINSON, a shipwrecked Swiss gentleman
MRS. ROBINSON, his wife
FRITZ,
ERNEST,
JACK, and
FRANCIS, their sons
EMILY MONTROSE, an English girl, also shipwrecked

Critique:

The adventures of the Robinson family are familiar to most school children, for the account of their life on an uninhabited island has long been a favorite. For adults the story moves rather slowly; the events are related in such detail that they become tiring at times. All ages, however, can admire the perfect harmony in which the Robinsons lived. Obedience to parental wishes and love for one's family are points the author apparently wished to stress in the story.

The Story:

Of all the passengers and crew on board the ship, only the Robinson family was saved when the vessel broke apart on a reef and the crew and other passengers jumped into lifeboats without waiting for the little family to join them. As the ship tossed about, the father prayed that God would spare them. There was plenty of food on board, and after they had eaten the boys went to sleep, leaving the father and the mother to guard them.

In the morning their first concern was to get to the island they could see beyond the reef. With much effort, they constructed a vessel out of tubs. After they had filled the tubs with food and ammunition and all other articles of value they could safely carry, they rowed toward the island. Two dogs from the ship swam beside them, and the boys were glad they would have pets when they reached their new home.

Their first task on reaching the island was to erect a tent of sailcloth they had brought from the ship. They gathered moss and dried it, so that they would have some protection from the ground when they slept. They were able to find a lobster and to shoot some game, and thus to add fresh food to their supplies. Since they had no utensils for eating, they used shells for spoons, all dipping out of the iron kettle which they had brought from the ship. They had released some geese and pigeons while they were still on the ship and had brought two hens and two cocks with them. The father knew that they must prepare for a long time on the island, and his thoughts were as much on provisions for the future as for their immediate wants.

The father and Fritz, the oldest son, spent the next day exploring the island. They found gourds from which they would make dishes and spoons, and many edible fruits and roots. Coconuts, growing in abundance, provided a treat for the mother and the younger boys. Fritz captured a small monkey which he took back for a pet. The younger boys were enchanted with the mischievous little animal.

The Robinsons spent the next few days securing themselves against hunger and danger from wild animals. The father and Fritz made several trips to the ship in their efforts to bring ashore everything that they could possibly use. The domesticated animals on the ship were towed back to the island. There was also a great store of firearms and ammunition, hammocks for sleeping, carpenter's tools, lumber, cooking utensils, silverware, and dishes.

While the father and Fritz were salvaging these supplies, the mother and the younger boys were working on the shore, sowing seeds, examining the contents of the kegs which floated to shore, and in every way possible making the tent home more livable. The mother and boys also explored the island to find a spot for a more permanent home. When the father and Fritz could join them, the whole family helped to construct a tree house which would give them protection from wild animals which they feared might dwell on the island.

Through the following weeks each day brought a new adventure of some kind. There were encounters with wild birds and terrifying animals. Ernest, the second son, had studied nature with great interest before their ill-fated voyage, and it was he who identified many of the animals and birds. They found some food which they considered luxuries, sugarcane, honey, potatoes, and spices. They fenced in a secluded area for their cattle, so that they might have a constant supply of milk and fresh meat. Several new dwellings were constructed to provide homes on all sides of the island. The father found a tree which contained long threads, and after he had constructed a loom the mother was able to weave cloth for new clothing. Jack and Francis, the younger boys, contributed to the welfare of the family by helping their mother to care for the animals and thresh the grain grown from seeds brought from the ship.

Many times the little band found their labor destroyed by forces they could not control. Goats ate the bark off young fruit trees they had planted. Monkeys robbed their food stores frequently, and jackals and serpents killed some of their pets. But the family would not be too discouraged, for they knew that they had been very fortunate to be saved on an island which provided food and shelter in such abundance.

About a year later they discovered a cave which became a home and a storage place for their supplies. In it they were protected from the rains and their supplies were safe from intruders. They spent many enjoyable evenings reading books they salvaged from the ship. The father and mother had found a way to make candles from the sap of a native tree. Altogether, their lives were agreeable and happy, and each morning and evening they thanked God for His goodness.

Ten years passed. The boys had become young men, and Fritz often sailed long distances in the canoe he had constructed. One day he captured a wounded albatross and found attached to it a note, written in English, asking someone to help an English girl who was in a cave near a volcano. The father and Fritz decided that Fritz must try to find her without telling the rest of the family of the note or the proposed search. Fritz, successful in his search, found a young girl, Emily Montrose, who had also been shipwrecked as she was sailing from India to her home in England. The members of the Robinson family accepted Emily as a daughter and a sister who was able to help the mother in her duties and give the boys much joy with her stories of life in India. Her own mother was dead. Emily had lived in India with her father, an army officer, who had sailed back to England on a different ship. She knew he would be worried about her, but there was no way for her to communicate with him.

One morning, a few months later, the castaways were astonished to hear the sound of three cannon shots. Not knowing whether the sound came from a friendly ship or from a pirate vessel, they loaded their small boat with firearms and sailed out to investigate the noise. There they found an English ship which had been driven off her course by a storm. It was impossible for this ship to take Emily back to England, but the captain promised to notify her father and to send a ship back for her. A captain, his wife and two children, who were on board, were so enchanted with the island that they asked to be allowed to stay. It seemed as if a little colony would grow there.

Six months later the ship sent by Emily's father arrived. Fritz and Jack had a great longing to see their homeland again, and since they were now mature young men, their mother and father allowed them to return with Emily. Before he left Fritz told his father that he loved Emily and intended to ask her father's permission to propose marriage to her.

The Robinsons, who loved Emily dearly, gave their blessing to their son.

The father, who had prepared a manuscript relating their adventures, gave it to Fritz before the boy sailed, in the hope that their story might be of interest to the rest of the world. The father and mother wanted to spend their remaining days on the island. Now that their island was known, commerce would begin and a colony could grow there. The father prayed that the little colony would increase in prosperity and piety, and continue to deserve and receive the blessings of the merciful God who had cared for them all so tenderly in the past.

THE TALE OF GENJI

Type of work: Novel
Author: Lady Murasaki Shikibu (978?-1031?)
Type of plot: Courtly romance
Time of plot: Early medieval period
Locale: Japan
First transcribed: 1001-1015

Principal characters:
  PRINCE GENJI, the talented illegitimate son of the Emperor
  THE EMPEROR, Genji's father
  KIRITSUBO, Genji's mother, the Emperor's concubine
  LADY KOKIDEN, the Emperor's consort
  PRINCESS AOI, Genji's first wife
  UTSUSEMI, one of Genji's paramours
  YŪGAO, another noblewoman in love with Genji
  MURASAKI, a young girl reared by Genji, his second wife

Critique:

The Tale of Genji is the first and title volume of an extremely long court romance written by Lady Murasaki Shikibu, daughter of a famous provincial governor and widow of a lieutenant in the Imperial Guard. As a lady in waiting to the Empress Akiko, she was completely familiar with Nipponese court ritual and ceremony, and her knowledge of palace life is everywhere apparent in the adventures of her nobly-born hero, Prince Genji. The novel is undoubtedly the finest example of medieval Japanese storytelling, and in it one can trace the very growth of Japanese literature about the year 1000. In the beginning Lady Murasaki's romance is an adolescent affair, very much in the fairy-tale tradition of the old Japanese Chronicles. As it progresses, it reaches the full-blown stage of the prose romance, and it can be compared satisfactorily with the medieval prose romances of western Europe. In both, the love affairs of the heroes are dominant. The Tale of Genji, however, imparts the qualities of Japanese culture —similar to and yet quite different from the medieval culture of Europe. Here are people whose main occupation, far from the arts of war and chivalry, was living well: enjoying nature and art in all its forms. Also, in place of idealized woman we have the idealized man, with woman in a distinctly subordinate role.

The Story:

When the Emperor of Japan took a beautiful gentlewoman of the bedchamber as his concubine, he greatly displeased his consort, the Lady Kokiden. The lot of the concubine, whose name was Kiritsubo, was not easy, despite the protection and love of the Emperor, for the influence of Kokiden was very great. Consequently, Kiritsubo had little happiness in the birth of a son, although the child was beautiful and sturdy. Kiritsubo's son made Kokiden even more antagonistic toward the concubine, for Kokiden feared that her own son might lose favor in the Emperor's eyes and not be elevated to the position of heir apparent. Because of her hard life among the women, Kiritsubo languished away until she died.

After his mother's death the young child she had had by the Emperor was put under the protection of the clan of Gen by the Emperor, who gave the child the title of Prince Genji. The boy, spirited and handsome, was a popular figure at the court. Even Kokiden could not bear him a great deal of ill will, jealous as she was on behalf of her son. Prince Genji won for himself a secure place in the Emperor's eyes, and when twelve years old he was not only elevated to a man's estate, but was also given in marriage to Princess Aoi, the daughter of the Minister of the Left, a powerful figure at court. Genji, because of his age, was not impressed with his bride. Nor was she entirely happy with her bridegroom, for she was four years older than he.

Genji was soon appointed a captain of the guard and as such spent much of his time at the Emperor's palace. Indeed, he really spent little time with his bride in their apartment in her father's home. He found that his good looks, his accomplishments, and his position made it very easy for him to have any woman he was disposed to love. His wife, not liking this state of things, became very cool to him. Genji cared little what Princes Aoi said or did.

One of Genji's first amours was with a young gentlewoman named Fujitsubo, who, like his bride, was a few years older than he. His second adventure was at the home of a young courtier, Ki no Kami. At the home of Ki no Kami, who was honored to have the person of Prince Genji at his home, Genji went into the room of a pretty young matron, Utsusemi, and stole her away to his own quarters. The woman, because of Genji's rank and pleasing self, refused to be angered by his actions. In an effort to keep in touch with her, Genji asked that her brother be made a member of his train, a request that was readily granted. Utsusemi soon realized that such an affair could not long continue and broke it off; Genji named her his broom-tree, after a Japanese shrub that at a distance promises shade but is really only a scrawny bush.

Once, a short time later, Genji made another attempt to renew the affair with Utsusemi. But she was not asleep when he entered her room and was able to run out ahead of him. With her was another very charming young woman who had failed to awaken when Utsusemi left and Genji came in. Genji, refusing to be irritated by Utsusemi, gently awakened the other girl and soon was on the most intimate of terms with her.

One day, while visiting his foster mother, Genji made the acquaintance of a young woman named Yūgao. She was living a rather poor existence, in spite of the fact that she came from a good family. After paying her several masked visits, Genji became tired of such clandestine meetings. He proceeded to make arrangements for them to stay for a time in a deserted palace within the imperial domains. The affair ended in tragedy, for during their stay Yūgao was strangely afflicted and died. Only through the good offices of his retainers and friends was Genji able to avoid a disastrous scandal.

Shortly after the tragic death of Yūgao, Genji fell ill of an ague. In order to be cured, he went to a hermit in the mountains. While staying with the hermit, he found a beautiful little girl, an orphan of a good family. Seeing something of himself in little Murasaki, who was pretty and talented, Genji resolved to take her into his care. At first Murasaki's guardians refused to listen to Genji's plans, until he was able to convince them that he had only the girl's best interests at heart and did not plan to make her a concubine at too early an age. Finally they agreed to let him shape the little girl's future, and he took her to his own palace to rear. Lest people misunderstand his motives, and for the sake of secrecy, Genji failed to disclose the identity of the girl and her age, even though his various paramours and his wife became exceedingly jealous of the mysterious stranger who was known to dwell with Genji.

Soon after his return to the Emperor's court with Murasaki, Genji was requested to dance the "Waves of the Blue Sea" at the annual festival in the Emperor's court. So well did he impress the Emperor with his dancing and with his poetry that he was raised to higher rank. Had the emperor dared to do so, Genji would have been named as the heir apparent.

During this time, when Genji's star seemed to be in the ascendant, he was very worried, for he had made Fujitsubo, the Emperor's concubine, pregnant. After the baby's birth everyone noticed how like Genji the baby looked, but the likeness was, to Genji's relief, credited to the fact that they were both sons of the Emperor himself. So pleased was the Emperor that he made Fujitsubo his official consort after the unexpected death of Lady Kokiden.

Meanwhile Genji's marriage proceeded very badly, and he and his wife drifted farther and farther apart. Finally, however, she became pregnant, but far from making her happy her condition seemed to make her sadder. During her pregnancy Princess Aoi declined, filled with hallucinations that her rivals for Genji's affections were stealing her life from her by hatred and jealousy. So deep was her affliction that Princess Aoi died in childbirth, much mourned by Genji, who finally had come to appreciate and love her. A year after her death, however, when Murasaki, the girl he had reared, was of suitable age to marry, Genji took her for his wife and resolved to settle down.

A TALE OF TWO CITIES

Type of work: Novel
Author: Charles Dickens (1812-1870)
Type of plot: Historical romance
Time of plot: French Revolution
Locale: France and England
First published: 1859

Principal characters

DR. MANETTE, a former prisoner in the Bastille
LUCIE MANETTE, his daughter
MR. LORRY, an agent of Tellson & Co.
CHARLES DARNAY, Marquis St. Evrémonde
SYDNEY CARTON, a lawyer's clerk
MISS PROSS, a servant
MADAME DEFARGE, a French revolutionary
M. DEFARGE, her husband

Critique:

Dickens is a remarkable story-teller. Although one may complain of the many characters in his stories, each character is necessary to complete the pattern of the Dickens plot. In this novel of the French Revolution, Dickens' treatment of his complicated plot, every event of which draws toward one great climax against the greater drama of history, is both delightful and fascinating to experience.

The Story:

The early rumbling of the French Revolution was echoing across the English Channel. In Paris a lonely old man waited in an attic for his first meeting with a daughter whom he had not seen since she was a baby. With the aid of Mr. Jarvis Lorry, an agent for the Franco-British banking house of Tellson & Co., the lovely Lucie Manette had been brought to Paris to find her father, imprisoned for eighteen years in the Bastille. Above the wine shop of Madame and M. Defarge, Dr. Manette was kept secretly until his rescuers could take him safely back to England. Day after day Madame Defarge sat outside her wine shop, knitting into a long scarf strange symbols which would later spell out a death list of hated aristocrats.

Five years later Lucie Manette sat beside her father in the courtroom of the Old Bailey, where Charles Darnay, a teacher of languages, was on trial for treasonable activities which involved his passing between France and England on secret business. A man named John Barsad had brought charges against him. Lucie and her father had testified they had met Darnay on the boat when they had traveled from France five years earlier. But an unusual circumstance saved the prisoner. Mr. Stryver, the prisoner's counsel, pointed across the courtroom to another man who so resembled the prisoner that legal identification of Darnay was shaken. The other man was Sydney Carton, and because of the likeness between the two Mr. Stryver secured an acquittal for the prisoner. Carton's relationship to Stryver was that of the jackal to the lion, for the alcoholic, aimless Carton wrote the cases which Stryver pleaded in court.

Lucie and her father lived in a small tenement under the care of their maid, Miss Pross, and their kindly friend, Mr. Lorry. Jerry Cruncher, porter at Tellson & Co., and a secret resurrectionist, was often helpful. Darnay and Carton became frequent callers in the Manette household, after the trial which had brought them together.

In France the fury of the people grew. Monseigneur the Marquis St. Evrémonde, was driving in his carriage through the countryside when he carelessly killed a child of a peasant named Gaspard. The nobleman returned to his castle to meet his nephew, who was visiting from England. Charles Darnay's views differed from those of his uncle. Darnay knew that his family had committed grave injustices, for which he begged his uncle to make amends. Monseigneur the marquis haughtily refused. That night the marquis was murdered in his bed.

Darnay returned to England to seek Dr. Manette's permission to court Lucie. In order to construct a bond of complete honesty, Darnay attempted to tell the doctor his true French name, but Manette fearfully asked him to wait until the morning of his marriage before revealing it. Carton also approached Lucie with a proposal of marriage. When Lucie refused, Carton asked her always to remember that there was a man who would give his own life to keep a life she loved beside her.

Meanwhile in France Madame Defarge knitted into her scarf the story of the hated St. Evrémondes. Gaspard had been hanged for the assassination of the marquis; monseigneur's house must be destroyed. John Barsad, the spy, brought news that Lucie Manette would marry Charles Darnay, nephew of the marquis. This news disturbed Defarge, for Dr. Manette, a former prisoner of the Bastille, held a special honor in the eyes of the Revolutionists.

Lucie and Darnay were married. Sydney Carton became a loyal friend of the family. Time passed, and tiny Lucie arrived. When the child was six years old, in the year 1789, the French people stormed the Bastille. At the Bastille Defarge went to the cell where Dr. Manette had been a prisoner and extracted some papers hidden behind a stone in the wall.

One day, while Darnay was talking to Mr. Lorry at Tellson & Co., a letter addressed to the Marquis St. Evrémonde was placed on Mr. Lorry's desk. Darnay offered to deliver it to the proper person. When he was alone, he read the letter. It was from an old family servant who had been imprisoned by the Revolutionists. He begged the Marquis St. Evrémonde to save his life. Darnay realized

that he must go to Paris. Only Dr. Manette knew of Darnay's family name, and the doctor had been sworn to secrecy.

Darnay and Mr. Lorry went to Paris, the latter to look after the French branch of Tellson & Co. Shortly after his arrival Darnay was seized as an undesirable immigrant after Defarge had ordered his arrest. Mr. Lorry was considerably upset when Lucie and Dr. Manette suddenly arrived in Paris. Some of the doctor's friends had informed him of Darnay's arrest. The old man felt that his own imprisonment in the Bastille would win the sympathy of the Revolutionists and enable him to save his son-in-law.

After fifteen months of waiting, Darnay was brought to trial. Able to prove his innocence of harming the French people, he was freed, but forbidden to leave France. A short time later he was again arrested, denounced by Defarge and one other person whose name the officer refused to disclose.

While shopping one day in the Paris market, Miss Pross and Jerry Cruncher, who were in Paris with Lucie and Mr. Lorry, met a man who caused Miss Pross to scream in amazement and Jerry to stare in silent astonishment. The man was Solomon, Miss Pross' lost brother. Jerry remembered him as John Barsad, the man who had been a spy-witness at the Old Bailey. Carton arrived on the scene at that moment, and he was able to force Barsad to come with him to the office of Tellson & Co. for a private conference. Barsad feared detection of his duplicity for he was now an employee of the Republican French Government. Carton and Jerry threatened to expose him as a former spy for the English government, the enemy of France. Carton made a deal with Barsad.

When Darnay was once more brought before the tribunal, Defarge testified against him and named Dr. Manette as the other accuser. Defarge produced the papers which he had found in Dr. Manette's cell in the Bastille. Therein the doctor had written the story of his arrest and imprisonment because he had learned of a secret crime committed by a St. Evrémonde against a woman of humble birth and her young brother. His account was enough to convict Darnay. Sentenced for the crimes of his ancestors, Darnay, the young St. Evrémonde, was condemned by the tribunal to the guillotine.

Now Sydney Carton began to act. He visited the Defarge wine shop, where he learned that Madame Defarge was the sister of the woman ruined by St. Evrémonde years before. Then with the help of the false Barsad, he gained admittance to the prison where Darnay had been taken. There he drugged the prisoner and, still aided by the cowed Barsad, had him carried from the cell. Carton remained. The resemblance between the two would allow him to pass as Darnay and prevent discovery of the aristocrat's escape.

Madame Defarge went to the lodgings of Lucie and Dr. Manette to denounce them. Only Miss Pross was there; the others, including Darnay, were already on their way to safety. To keep Madame Defarge from learning of their escape, Miss Pross struggled with the furious woman demanding admittance to Lucie's apartment. Madame Defarge was killed when her pistol went off. Miss Pross was deaf for the rest of her life.

Lucy and Darnay returned safely to England. Sydney Carton died at the guillotine, giving his own life for the happiness of his dear friends.

TALES OF ISE

Type of work: Stories and poems
Author: Arihara no Narihira (825-880)
Time: Ninth century
Locale: Japan
First transcribed: Ninth century

Both the work commonly known as the *Ise Monogatari* (*Tales of Ise*) and the identity of its author have been long disputed. However, it is generally conceded that the principal author was Narihira and that, as the collection of tales and poems now stands, later hands made additions after Narihira's death.

There are slight differences in text and sequence among the various hand-copied versions that have survived, but in general the work consists of 125 episodes, most of which open with the phrase, "Once upon a time there was a man. . . ." These episodes, put together with no particular order, chronologically or otherwise, vary in length and contain poems, sometimes only one, sometimes two or more, mostly by Narihira. Almost all of these episodes deal with amorous dalliances, and in time cover the hero's life from the time of his maturity rite to his death. That many of the tales are autobiographical in nature, based on real people and events, is undeniable.

This work, although slight, has a position in Japanese literature out of proportion to its length. Its strong influence may easily be seen, for instance, in Lady Murasaki's *Tale of Genji* (*Genji Monogatari*). The hundreds of later commentaries and studies dealing with the *Ise Monogatari* attest to its importance. Because of its episodic and disordered nature, no synopsis is possible, but through the 125 episodes there runs the central theme of the loves of the principal author who never clearly identifies himself, but who expresses the many aspects and manifestations of love: its joys, its despair, its pain, its triumphs, its comedy. A summary of some of the episodes follows:

Not too many years after the capital has been moved from Nara to Kyoto

(A.D. 794), there lived a man who loved love. Shortly after his maturity rite, which at that time was usually at the age of eleven and when the boy had grown four and a half feet tall, the youth went falcon hunting at Kasuga in the former capital. There he happened to see two beautiful sisters and sent them a poem. The poem begins the description of the love life of this "man."

The later Imperial Consort Takako was the daughter of Middle Counselor Nagayoshi; in A.D. 859 she served as one of the performers at a court ceremony. About that same time the hero of the *Tales of Ise* met and began to visit her. When their love affair began to be bruited about, the girl was made unavailable by the simple expediency of placing her in service at court where, in 866, she became the consort of the Emperor Seiwa.

Tiring of life in the capital, the man went on a trip to eastern Japan, but he has gone no further than the border of Ise and Owari Provinces when he became homesick and composed poems to express his nostalgia. He met an itinerant priest, saw Mount Fuji for the first time, and composed a poem. Entering the province of Musashi, at the Sumida River which runs through present Tokyo, he composed a celebrated poem of nostalgia concerning the oyster-catcher birds. In Musashi he also met and was attracted to various women. Later he wandered through the region to the northeast, where he made love to the local country women.

A check with the Imperial Anthology, the *Kokin-shû* (*Poems, Old and New,* A.D. 905)—for of the 209 poems in the *Ise Monogatari,* sixty-two also appear in the *Kokin-shû*—reveals that the woman in Episode 19 is in all likelihood the daughter of Ki no Aritsune, who is mentioned in Episode 16. Aritsune was a close friend of Narihira, and at least one of Aritsune's daughters married Narihira, perhaps the one presented in Episode 19. It has also been thought that one of the girls in the first episode is the same girl as well. Aritsune had an unfortunate life, according to the standards of the court nobility of the time. His younger sister was the mother of Emperor Montoku's first born son, Prince Koretaka. But in 850, the year Montoku succeeded to the throne, another son, Prince Korehito, was born to Akirakei-ko, a daughter of Fujiwara no Yoshifusa, just at the time when the Fujiwara clan under Yoshifusa was about to achieve its hegemony at the court—a power which they achieved largely by intermingling with the imperial family through their daughters' marriages to future emperors, or through becoming the mothers of future emperors. No doubt Montoku was inclined to make his older son his successor, but because of pressure brought upon him, the Fujiwara-mothered Korehito succeeded him. This accession left Aritsune on the outer fringe of power, and his subsequent career as a courtier was not a happy one. Yoshifusa went on to become prime minister during Montoku's reign.

Friends since early childhood, this daughter of Aritsune eventually married Narihira, but Narihira did not long remain faithful to her. However, scattered through the earlier episodes are hints which cause the reader to believe that she managed to draw him back to her after each infidelity.

There is also the eternal triangle involving two men and one woman, with the usual tragic results. The woman in this case had been waiting three years for the return of a man who had left to make his way in the capital. Meanwhile, she was courted by a second man, who finally won her promise of marriage. The first man, returning on the wedding night, learned what had happened during his absence and left the woman with his blessing. Following him, she lost her life.

There are passages of young love between a weakling son of good family and a household maid; or the love of a young girl, too shy to make her feelings known, who dies with her love unrequited as a result; of an affair between two faithless people who send each other poems charging the other with faithlessness; of a beloved wife whose husband is so busy with his duties at court that she feels neglected, and goes off with another man to the country. Eventually the husband is appointed an imperial emissary to an important shrine and there meets the woman, who is now the wife of a country official. She realizes her mistake, and becomes a nun. There is the story of an elderly woman, the mother of three sons, who is amorously starved but too diffident to say so openly, so she tells her sons of her craving as something she had dreamed. The third son alone is sympathetic to his mother's plight, and he arranges for her relief through the kind offices of the handsome Narihira.

From the earliest times it had been the custom for the emperor to appoint through divination an unmarried imperial princess to serve as the head priestess at important shrines. In Narihira's time the head priestess of the great shrine of Ise was Princess Yasuko, second daughter of Emperor Montoku. Her appointment, made in 859, lasted until 876. Sometime after her appointment, there appeared in Ise a handsome inspector in the guise of a falcon hunter. The priestess, having received word of his arrival on official matters, greeted him with special kindness; the meeting led to their falling in love with each other. For the sake of discretion she waited until night before paying him a visit, and she left long before dawn. That same morning a messenger arrived from her with a poem, the gist of which said, "Did you come to see me last night, or was it I who went to see you? I do not remember. Nor do I know whether it was all a dream, or was real."

Narihira replied with another poem making a tryst for that evening, but the governor of the province gave an all-night banquet; thus Narihira's plans were thwarted because on the following day it was necessary for him to continue his tour of inspection. The lovers parted, promising each other in poems to meet again, somewhere, sometime.

So the episodes go, to end with the poem which might be roughly translated:

Long have I known
That this last journey must be made,
But little did I know
That it might be so soon.

TALES OF SOLDIERS AND CIVILIANS

Type of work: Short stories
Author: Ambrose Bierce (1842-1914?)
First published: 1891

Ambrose Bierce wrote volumes of acid, satirical prose in his long career as a journalist, and even managed to get a somewhat pretentious twelve-volume edition of his collected works published. Most of it, because of its time-bound nature, was doomed to oblivion by the time the edition appeared. The work that continues and promises to survive is the collection of short stories titled *Tales of Soldiers and Civilians*. Bierce's literary reputation rests essentially on this book.

The bland title of this collection stands in ironic contrast to the vision of life which informs the stories themselves. Indeed, Bierce seems to have striven for bland, noncommittal titles to most of his stories. Titles like "Chickamauga," "An Occurrence at Owl Creek Bridge," and "The Mocking-Bird" tell little of the macabre nature of these tales. Bierce seems to have chosen his mild titles with deliberate irony.

When this volume was reprinted in 1898, it was given a more meaningful title, *In the Midst of Life*. The irony is more obvious and more indicative of the true content of the book: in the midst of life is death.

Death is the sole absolute of this book, the common denominator of each story, and the final proposition in a logic of ruthless necessity. Each protagonist is part of a greater logic; each is subordinate to the plot, and each is cursed. Death is separated from life, is raised up as a separate principle antagonistic to life, and becomes an entity in its own right. Death is seen as a hostile specter, rather than a normal process of life. As such, Death seeks to conquer life rather than aid it. Death then becomes an inevitable victor which "has all seasons for his own," as Bierce was fond of remarking.

Against such a powerful antagonist the heroes become victims in a web of cruel necessity, shadow figures drawn into the Valley of the Shadow; and as such they are depicted with sharp, relentless strokes. Bierce's heroes are essentially lonely men who derive their reality from the fear they experience. These men are cursed and driven by the logic of their curse. Their strongest motivation is fear, an all-pervasive anxiety that frequently annihilates them. The success of each story depends on its ability to arouse this same fear in the reader.

In consequence, Bierce places a great value on courage, fearlessness in the face of death. However, he is acute enough to see that courage is not so much fearlessness as it is a greater fear overcoming a lesser fear, in most cases a fear of dishonor overcoming a fear of death. Courage, then, is the faith that one's honor is more important than one's life. Frequently the heroes Bierce admires court death with an awesome recklessness. His heroes are inevitably damned. There is no escape, no transcendence, and no salvation from the macabre situations into which they are drawn. Their dooms are inescapable facts. But the measure of their manhood is how they meet death.

Bierce's vision of life is fatalistic, but there is more to it than that. Avenging Furies hover about his stories, but they are not the same Furies that haunted Orestes. Bierce is nihilistic, but inevitably there is a macabre humor in his nihilism. The acid, satirical touch that colors the rest of Bierce's work is present here as well. Bierce's Furies are diabolical jesters, who love irony more than they love the wretched human spirit. His Furies are divine practical jokers, who drum "Dixie" and "John Brown's Body" on the human skull for laughs. One can scarcely tell whether the shriek one senses in Bierce's prose is that of humor or horror.

Bierce's grotesque wit serves as a relief from the horror of his situations. A related technique that serves the same purpose is his ironic stance, one which removes him from the petty human scene and separates him from the terror of his heroes. Bierce assumes a godlike attitude that determines the objective nature of his prose. He uses a naturalistic style that is precise in diction, spare in depiction, ironic in narration.

In effect, Bierce takes on the cruel role of the Furies in narrating his stories, and the tone of his prose is frigid, caustic, and inhuman. Yet it is precisely this emotional sterility, this godlike irony, that makes his stories so powerfully chilling. If, for example, Bierce were to sympathize with his heroes, we would have pathos rather than terror. The very lack of an appropriate emotional response in the narration stimulates to an excessive degree the proper emotional response in the reader. The fact that Bierce himself was caustic, cruel, and sharp, demanding perfection of his fellow human beings, admirably served his limited artistic abilities and enabled him to focus his talent on evoking both terror and humor.

Tales of Soldiers and Civilians is divided into two parts, as the title suggests. There are the war stories and the mystery stories, and each type develops Bierce's vision of life in a different literary direction. The war tales anticipate Hemingway, while the civilian stories anticipate modern horror-tale writers like H. P. Lovecraft.

Beyond a doubt, Bierce reached his artistic peak in the soldier tales. War stories provided the perfect medium for someone of his character and experience. First of all, Bierce had served in the Civil War and undoubtedly his stories draw much of their vigor and reality from firsthand experience. His depiction of various battles and their effects have an unmistakable aura of reality. His description of war is hauntingly vivid and stands in marked contrast to the maudlin accounts given in the vast bulk of Civil War writings.

Secondly, war tales provided an acceptable outlet for his obsessions with fear, courage, and death. These leitmotifs could be presented naturally in tales of soldiers. Since war abounds in abnormal situations, Bierce could write naturally about a twin killing his twin, about a son killing his father, and about an artillery man killing his wife. In the context of their stories these plots become necessary accidents, part of some divine causality.

Thirdly, Bierce's naturalistic style was admirably suited to describing the limited vision of the soldier in war, a vision which is not permitted the luxury of feeling pity and which must avoid all contemplation. It is a vision, moreover, that must concentrate on immediate objectives and on carrying out specific orders.

Finally, the army subjugates individuals to the mass. Deeds of fear and courage are the only acts by which a soldier is individualized and judged. Bierce's characters draw their reality from the way they face death. Each hero undergoes an ordeal which means death either for him or for someone close to him, and that test determines his character. Apart from that ordeal Bierce's characters are lifeless puppets dancing to a meretricious plot.

Bierce's war stories are his best. Nowhere else did he achieve such a perfect fusion of form and content, except perhaps in his aphorisms. In quality the tales are superior to about ninety-nine percent of the short fiction that was being written during the nineteenth century in America. In many instances they anticipate or rival Hemingway's stories. Actually, many points of comparison can be drawn between Bierce and Hemingway. Both show obsession with fear, courage, and death. Both use a crisp, ironic prose to communicate their vision. Both were to find happy expression in stories of war. Both present character tested through some ordeal. And both possess a cruel, evocative power at times giving their fiction a haunting quality as vivid as a nightmare.

Bierce's war tales, particularly "Chickamauga," "An Occurrence at Owl Creek Bridge," "One Kind of Officer," and "Killed at Resaca," are first-rate for what they attempt to do. His civilian stories, however, fall somewhat short of the high standards he achieved in his war tales.

The reason for this diminished quality is that Bierce attempted to impose on his stories of civilians the same vision of life that pervades his soldier tales, and the grafting was not always successful. Pictures of war provided the perfect literary vehicle for his outlook, since war abounds in pathological situations. When he tried to impose this vision on civilian reality, however, the imperfections of plot, the implausibilities, and the grotesqueness showed up much more glaringly. The trick endings came off much worse. The characters and plots never matched those of the war stories. To inject a pathological fear into stories about civilians requires great skill.

What Bierce succeeded in doing in these stories was to extend a relatively new prose genre, the short mystery tale. In this lesser genre Bierce came off rather well when compared with writers who today create in this vein. His stories continue to hold their own in the anthologies.

That Bierce was neurotic is beside the point. Successful in turning his neuroses into fine artistic stories, he has few equals in suspense, evocative power, clarity, and irony.

TALES OF UNCLE REMUS

Type of work: Tales
Author: Joel Chandler Harris (1848-1908)
First published: 1880-1910

An old Negro sits talking to a little boy in his cabin on a cotton plantation not far from Atlanta, Georgia. The Civil War has not yet been fought, and the old man, a slave, belongs to the family that owns the cabin, the big house a few yards away, and the fine plantation. His loyalty is boundless to the parents of the little boy, the lady he calls "Miss Sally" and her husband "Mars John." He has known them a long time and he shares their memories of earlier times. Occasionally he speaks of those old days, but it is more usual for him to tell of times far more distant, when "my great-grandaddy's great-grandaddy live nex' door ter whar ol' Grandaddy Cricket live at" or of "one time, way back yander, 'fo' you wuz borned, honey, en 'fo' Mars John er Miss Sally wuz borned—way back yander 'fo' enny un us wuz borned." When he talks to the little boy who sits beside him (and years later to the son of the first little boy), both he and his listener move in imagination into legendary eras which have no calendar dates and need none. For the stories which Uncle Remus tells are drawn from the legends of many lands and ancient times.

Though Joel Chandler Harris wrote the tales of Uncle Remus, he laid no claim to having invented them. He looked upon himself as a mere recorder. A shy, modest, and somewhat diffident author who once described himself as a "cornfield journalist," Harris admitted, in the introduction to *Uncle Remus: His Songs and His Sayings* (1880), his indebtedness to the Negroes from whom he heard the tales. In a later volume, *Nights with Uncle Remus* (1883), he gave credit not only to the Georgia Negroes but also to the many correspondents who, having enjoyed his first Uncle Remus book, had supplied him with material which he embodied in later stories.

Harris was uncertain as to where the Uncle Remus tales originated. Readers curious about possible origins may consult the introductions to the two volumes cited above and a number of articles listed in Lewis Leary's *Articles on American Literature, 1900-1950* (1954). Old tales like those told by Uncle Remus in the middle Georgia Negro dialect and by his less-known friend Daddy Jake in the Gullah dialect of the coastal areas of South Carolina and Georgia have been found in Africa, Europe, South America, and the Orient.

Questions of origin are for specialists, however, not for lovers of the tales themselves. There are clear resemblances between the characters and the simple plots of many of the Uncle Remus tales and those in folk tales from many nations. What gives these stories their special appeal is not their content but the manner in which they are told. (Mark Twain once wrote Harris: "In reality the stories are only alligator pears—one eats them merely for the sake of the dressing.") In addition, Uncle Remus himself is one of the most lovable characters in American literature. The sly humor of the old man, his pretended gruffness followed quickly by tender concern when he sees he has hurt the little boy's feelings, his ingenious parrying of the little boy's searching questions, his moralizing on the behavior of both children and adults, and his citing of ancient authority for the particular form of the tales ("de tale I give you like hit wer' gun to me")—all make him seem a very real person. Children see in him a kindly old man who loves to entertain children; to adults he is, in addition, a philosopher of life whose thoughts are based on close observation of people over many years. As to the origin of Uncle Remus, Harris replied when he was asked about it:

He was not an invention of my own, but a human syndicate, I might say, of three or four old darkies whom I had known. I just walloped them together into one person and called him "Uncle Remus."

Though Brer Rabbit does not appear in all of the Uncle Remus tales, he is the hero of many of them. The reason was given by Harris in his first volume, when he said that ". . . it needs no scientific investigation to show why he [the Negro] selects as his hero the weakest and most harmless of all animals, and brings him out victorious in contests with the bear, the wolf, and the fox. It is not virtue that triumphs, but helplessness; it is not malice, but mischievousness." Moralists may complain that the mischievousness sometimes becomes cruelty and that Brer Rabbit is a remarkably accomplished liar, but to most adult readers these would seem carping criticisms. Perhaps some of the children who have known the tales through three generations may have objected to a code of conduct in the tales which is very different from what they have been taught in Sunday School or at home. Most have probably thought that the world of Uncle Remus's animals and birds is simply a story world anyway, one in which many things seem all right that would not be so elsewhere. Even Uncle Remus suggests, now and then, that he does not entirely approve of what has been done in a certain tale, as when several terrapins have been used to make it seem that Brer Rabbit has lost his race with Brer Tarrypin, and the little boy objects, "But, Uncle Remus, that was cheating." The old man answers:

"Co'se, honey. De creeturs 'gun ter cheat, en den folks tuck it up, en hit keep on spreadin'. Hit mighty ketchin', en you min' yo' eye, honey, dat somebody don't cheat you 'fo' yo' ha'r git gray. . . ."

The Negro dialect of Uncle Remus presents a greater hindrance to readers today than it did when the tales first appeared. Even Southern Negro children

have been known to ask in public libraries for a version of several of the tales simplified and "modernized" a few years ago. They complained that they could not understand the original tales. As the educational level rises for both whites and Negroes in the Southern states and as Southern speech becomes more like that in other parts of the nation, the dialect of Uncle Remus may come to seem as foreign to Americans as the Scottish dialect of Burns, and perhaps not much more comprehensible than Chaucer's English. Uncle Remus's tales are essentially oral ones, and they are best when read aloud. But if future readers come upon the stories without ever having heard anyone talk like Uncle Remus, they will find it difficult to imagine the sounds, the inflections, and the easy flow of the old man's words in such a passage as the following:

"You kin put yo' 'pennunce in ole Brer Rabbit. . . . He wuz dere, but he shuffle up kinder late, kaze w'en Miss Meadows en de balance un um done gone down ter de place, Brer Rabbit, he crope 'roun' ter de ash-hopper, en fill Brer Coon slippers full er ashes, en den he tuck'n put um on en march off. He got dar atter w'ile, en soon's Miss Meadows en de gals seed 'im, dey up'n giggle, en make a great 'miration kaze Brer Rabbit got on slippers. Brer Fox, he so smart, he holler out, he did, en say he lay Brer Rabbit got de groun'-eatch. . . ."

Another barrier to comprehension of the Uncle Remus tales by future readers has been pointed out by Jay B. Hubbell in *The South in American Literature, 1607-1900* (1954). American life has become increasingly urban in the last half century, and many children now grow up with scarcely any knowledge of the ways of animals like the rabbit, the fox, and the wolf, or of what life is like on a farm. It is true that Uncle Remus does make some allowance, in several tales in *Told by Uncle Remus* (1905), for the ignorance of the second little boy, who has lived in Atlanta and whose ac-

3689

tions Uncle Remus frequently contrasts with those of the first little boy a generation earlier. But most of the tales were told to the first little boy, and Uncle Remus makes no explanation, for example, of the "spring-'ouse" that Brer Fox and Brer Rabbit put some butter in, or of what the "go'd er water" is that Brer Rabbit gives Brer B'ar to keep him from "stranklin'" after he has bit all the hair off Brer Possum's tail.

It is to be hoped, however, that the reading handicaps of dialectal spelling and strange words, or of the frequent use of terms from Southern farm life before it was transformed by mechanization and electrification, will not be strong enough to prevent future generations of American children and adults from relishing the story of Brer Rabbit's escape in "How Mr. Rabbit Was Too Sharp for Mr. Fox," from secretly rejoicing at "The Awful Fate of Mr. Wolf," or from joining in the merriment at "Brother Rabbit's Laughing Place."

THE TALISMAN

Type of work: Novel
Author: Sir Walter Scott (1771-1832)
Type of plot: Historical romance
Time of plot: Twelfth century
Locale: The Holy Land
First published: 1825

Principal characters:
RICHARD THE LION-HEARTED, King of England
SIR KENNETH, Knight of the Couchant Leopard
EL HAKIM, a Moslem physician
THEODORICK OF ENGADDI, a hermit
QUEEN BERENGARIA, Richard's wife
LADY EDITH PLANTAGENET, Richard's kinswoman
CONRADE, the Marquis of Montserrat
THE GRAND MASTER OF THE KNIGHTS TEMPLARS

Critique:

The Talisman has been read by almost every high school student for generations, because it contains all the ingredients for a romantic adventure: far-away lands, love, mystery, and chivalric courage and daring. Sir Walter Scott has woven these ingredients together with his usual skill, bringing the several subplots together in the final scenes. As is usual with him also, he makes history serve his own purposes by inventing characters and situations and blending them with real people and historical events. The result is so interesting, however, that we join the author in ignoring the facts, and enjoy the story—an excellent tale, well told.

The Story:

Sir Kenneth, the Knight of the Couchant Leopard, was one of the knights who followed King Richard the Lion-Hearted to the Holy Land during the Third Crusade. At the time Richard was ill of a fever, and the Council of Kings and Princes had sent Kenneth on a mission to Theodorick of Engaddi, a religious hermit who acted as a go-between for both Christians and Moslems. Richard did not know of the mission, for the other leaders in the crusade were jealous of him and his power, and they resented his high-handed methods and his conceit. On the desert, Kenneth met and fought with a Saracen, an infidel who did not at first know that Kenneth carried a pass from Saladin, the leader of the Moslems. Neither warrior was injured in the fight, and since at that time there was a truce between the Christians and the Moslems, they continued their journey together, the Saracen having promised to conduct Kenneth to Theodorick's retreat.

Theodorick showed Kenneth a crypt containing a piece of the Cross. As the knight knelt by the holy relic a group of nuns, novices, and others living at the convent came into the holy place singing and strewing flowers. Each time one of the robed ladies passed him at his devotions, she dropped a single rose by his side. She was the Lady Edith Plantagenet, King Richard's kinswoman. Although she and Kenneth had never spoken, they loved each other. Marriage was impossible, however, for she was related to the English king and he was only a poor Scottish knight. Both his birth and his nationality formed a bar between them, for England and Scotland were constantly at war. Edith was at the convent because she was one of the ladies attending Richard's wife, Queen Berengaria, who was on a pilgrimage to pray for the king's recovery.

Forcing himself to put Lady Edith out of his mind, Kenneth delivered his message to Theodorick, who promised to carry it to Saladin. When Kenneth returned to Richard's camp, he took with him a Moslem physician called El Hakim. This learned man had been sent by Saladin to cure Richard's fever, for though the two rulers were enemies, they respected each other's valor and honor. El Hakim used a talisman to cure the king; the potion he made with it took the fever from Richard. Still weak but restored to health, Richard was grateful to Kenneth for bringing the physician but furious with him for acting as a messenger for the Council of Kings and Princes without the king's knowledge. He felt certain the other leaders would soon withdraw from the crusade, for the Christians were greatly outnumbered by the infidels. It would be impossible for Richard to continue the war with his small band of followers.

In the meantime the other leaders grew more restless and dissatisfied. Two of them, in particular, wished to see Richard disgraced. Conrade, Marquis of Montserrat, wanted to gain for himself a principality in Palestine, and the Grand Master of the Knights Templars wanted Richard killed and out of the way for good. The other leaders merely wanted to give up the crusade and return to their homes. Conrade's sly hints and slurs moved the Archduke of Austria to place his flag next to Richard's standard on the highest elevation in the camp. Richard, learning of this act, arose from his bed, for he was still weak, tore down the flag and stamped on it. Then he ordered Kenneth to guard the English flag and to see that no one again placed another near it.

Queen Berengaria, growing bored with life in the camp, sent Kenneth a false message saying that Edith wanted him to come to her tent. He was bewildered by the message, and torn between love for Edith and duty to King Richard. At last love became stronger than duty. Leaving his trusted dog on guard, he walked to Edith's tent. There he overheard the plotters giggling over their joke. When Edith heard of the plot, she disclaimed any part in the trick and sent him at once back to his post.

There he found the royal standard of England gone and his dog apparently dying. El Hakim, appearing suddenly, said that he could cure the animal with his talisman. He offered also to take Kenneth to the Moslem camp to escape the king's wrath, but Kenneth refused to run away. Instead, he confessed his desertion to Richard and was instantly condemned to death. Everyone tried to save him, the queen even confessing the trick played upon him, but Richard could not be moved. Kenneth, refusing to plead his own cause, believed he deserved to die for deserting his post. He asked for a priest and made his confession. Then El Hakim asked the king for a boon in return for saving the royal life with his talisman. He was granted the favor he requested, the privilege of taking Kenneth with him. So Kenneth became an outcast from the Christian camp.

The other leaders continued their scheming to rob Richard of his power. At last the Grand Master persuaded Conrade to join him in a plot to kill the king. They captured a dervish, a rabid Moslem member of a wild tribe of desert nomads, disguised him, and sent him, pretending to be drunk, to Richard's tent. The king's guards were lax, but he had been sent, as a gift from Saladin, a mute Nubian slave who was extremely loyal to him. As the assassin raised his poniard to strike the king, the slave dashed him to the ground. In the scuffle the Nubian received an arm wound from the dagger. Knowing that the knife was probably poisoned, Richard himself sucked the slave's wound.

Grateful, the slave wrote a note promising that if Richard would have all the leaders pass in review he, the slave, could identify the one who had stolen the royal flag. The slave was, in reality, Kenneth in disguise. El Hakim, after curing his dog, had told him that the animal undoubtedly could identify his assailant. Richard agreed to the plan, and as the suspected plotters passed by, the dog attacked Conrade of Montserrat. Conrade denied his guilt, but Richard declared that his innocence could be decided only by trial of arms. The king asked Saladin to choose a neutral ground for the match, and in courtesy invited Saladin to be present at the combat to test Conrade's innocence or guilt.

At the place of combat, when Richard and Saladin met for the first time other than in battle armor, Saladin revealed himself as El Hakim. Richard in turn confessed that he knew the slave was Kenneth, whom he also named as the king's champion. In the fight Conrade was seriously wounded and hastily carried away by the Grand Master of the Knights Templars, who feared that Conrade would reveal the whole plot against the king. At the same time Richard revealed to the queen and Edith that Kenneth was in reality David, Earl of Huntingdon, Prince Royal of Scotland. The king had learned his true identity from one of Kenneth's retainers. That noble knight, having vowed not to reveal himself until the Holy City had been taken, would not break his oath even to save his life after he had deserted his post.

The king then promised to give the knight Edith's hand in marriage, even though their betrothal belied Theodorick's earlier prophecy that Edith would marry Saladin. Abashed, the old hermit confessed that he had interpreted the signs incorrectly. His vision was that a kinswoman of the king would marry Richard's enemy in a Christian marriage. Theodorick had thought his vision meant that Saladin would be converted and marry Edith. The true prophecy was that Kenneth, a Scot and thus an enemy of the English king, would marry the king's kinswoman and that they, both Christians, would have a Christian wedding.

At a noontime repast given by Saladin in honor of his friends, Saladin killed the Grand Master of the Knights Templars because the Moslem leader learned that the Grand Master, while bending over Conrade to hear his confession, had stabbed him with a dagger so that he could not confess the plot against Richard.

Richard and Saladin both realized that the crusade had failed, for the Christian forces could never hope to overcome the Saracens. The two men parted friends, each honoring the other's skill and valor. A short time later Edith and Kenneth were married, Kenneth receiving the lucky talisman as a wedding gift from Saladin. Although the magic token effected some cures in Europe, it did not again have the power given it by the famous infidel.

TAMAR

Type of work: Poem
Author: Robinson Jeffers (1887-1962)
Type of plot: Psychological melodrama
Time of plot: World War I
Locale: Carmel Coast Range, California
First published: 1924

Principal characters:
TAMAR CAULDWELL, a neurotic girl
LEE CAULDWELL, her brother
DAVID CAULDWELL, her father
JINNY CAULDWELL, David's idiot sister
STELLA MORELAND, sister of David's dead wife
WILL ANDREWS, Tamar's suitor

Critique:

Tamar is one of the greatest of Jeffers' long narrative poems. In powerful and rugged language he outlines the turbulent lives of the Cauldwell family and their terrible but inevitable destruction. The symbol which he employs to indicate humanity's absorption in itself is incest and its resulting miseries. Tamar is a violent and powerful story told against the harshly magnificent background of the Carmel coastline range. It is at once thrilling and moving.

The Story:

Injured when his horse stumbled and fell over a sea cliff, young Lee Cauldwell was nursed back to health by his sister Tamar. Lee, who had lived a wild and dissolute life, vowed to give up his drinking and debauchery. He and Tamar became devoted to each other during his convalescence, so much so that Lee jealously warned a former suitor of his sister to stay away from her. Old David Cauldwell feared what might result from the isolation of his family. His fears were confirmed when the brother and sister, after swimming in the river, were drawn to each other against their wills.

The Cauldwell family was a peculiar group. Besides the father and the two children, it contained two old women. Aunt Jinny, an idiot sister of David Cauldwell, was cared for by Aunt Stella, the sister of David's dead wife. Through the confused mumblings of Jinny, Tamar realized that an incestuous relationship had occurred between David and his own sister Helen.

A short time later, Tamar discovered that she was pregnant. Rather than admit that Lee was the father of her child, she deliberately sought out and seduced her former suitor, Will Andrews. Disgust and revulsion grew in her until she hated her two lovers and, most of all, herself. She felt that she would lose her mind unless she talked to someone.

Aunt Stella was a medium through whom the voices of the dead sometimes spoke. In desperation, Tamar appealed to her to let her speak to Helen. That evening she and Stella, with the imbecile Jinny between them, stole down to the seashore, so that they would not be discovered by the men. Stella gradually fell into a trance, and through her lips Tamar heard the voice of a man who told her that the coastline country had been the land of the Indians, where their gods used to come to them. He ordered Tamar to strip and dance so that the gods would come again. Against her will, Tamar danced to strange guttural chants from the lips of the tranced woman. After a while the chanting ceased and Tamar returned slowly to her senses. Then through the lips of Stella she heard the voice of Helen taunting her for the shameful orgy. The voice, after warning Tamar that she would lose her child, told her that a fire Tamar had earlier set in the cabin would be quenched before it fulfilled its purpose of destroying the corruption of the Cauldwell family. Then in a mournful voice Helen told Tamar of the horror of death, of her longing for life, and of her need to haunt Tamar as long as she lived, because she possessed life. On the shore, unassisted by anyone and in great agony, Tamar lost her baby.

Back in the cabin once more, Tamar could scarcely restrain the hatred she felt for her family. All pity had left her, and all love. In order to revenge herself on Helen, she tempted her old father with her beauty. Through the medium of Stella, Helen cursed Tamar and pleaded with her not to commit that ultimate folly.

Lee, who had returned to his drinking, enlisted in the army, but Tamar was determined not to let him go. She told him that the child had not been his but the child of Will Andrews, who had visited her late at night after she had set a lighted lamp in her window as a signal. Tamar taunted Lee until he lashed her with a whip.

When Will Andrews came to the cabin that night, Tamar told him that Lee would leave the following day for the army and would like to say goodbye to him. The meeting between the two men was cool but amiable. But while Lee was out of the room, Tamar showed Will her whip-lash wounds and told him that she had lost his child through outrages which both her father and Lee had perpetrated upon her. When Lee returned with his father, Will accused him of those atrocities. In turn, Lee accused Will of having attempted to set fire to their home. Tamar, who herself had been responsible, said nothing but goaded on the fight with her smiles and wordless encouragement to Will. Lee stabbed Will horribly and fatally.

Helen, through the person of Stella, tried to save old David Cauldwell from the destroying forces of hate and evil, but he refused to heed her warnings. Downstairs the idiot Jinny, alone and disturbed, was attracted by the light of a candle. She carried it to the window, where the flame set fire to the blowing curtains. Her dying shrieks attracted the attention of those upstairs.

Lee tried to run to her, but Tamar clung to him and would not let him go. Will, dying, dragged himself as far as the window. Stella rushed out into the flaming hall and perished. The old man prayed brokenly, groveling on the floor. Lee made one last effort to escape, but Tamar, glorying in the destruction of her three lovers, embraced him until the flames consumed them all.

TAMBURLAINE THE GREAT

Type of work: Drama
Author: Christopher Marlowe (1564-1593)
Type of plot: Romantic tragedy
Time of plot: Fourteenth century
Locale: Asia
First presented· 1587

Principal characters:
TAMBURLAINE, the Scythian conqueror
ZENOCRATE, his wife
BAJAZETH, Emperor of the Turks
CALLAPINE, his son
MYCETES, King of Persia
COSROE, his brother
THERIDAMAS,
TECHELLES, and
USUMCASANE, followers of Tamburlaine
ORCANES, King of Natolia

Critique:

A study of driving ambition, *Tamburlaine the Great* is also notable for the dignity and beauty of Marlowe's lines. The poetry of the play is all the more remarkable in view of the fact that it was among the first written in English blank verse. Marlowe wrote so well, with so much original invention, that for a time many scholars believed him the author of some plays now attributed to Shakespeare. It is safe to say that Marlowe is the best of pre-Shakespearean playwrights.

The Story:

When Mycetes became king of Persia, his brother, Cosroe, blatantly told the new king that he was not fit for the office. Among Mycetes' greatest concerns were the raids of Tamburlaine, the Scythian bandit, upon the Persian people. Because it was rumored that this robber chief aspired to rule the East, Mycetes sent Theridamas with a thousand troops to capture Tamburlaine, and ordered another lord named Menaphon to follow Theridamas. Cosroe sarcastically pointed out to the king that Menaphon was needed in Babylon, where the province was about to revolt against such an inferior sovereign as Mycetes. At this insult Mycetes vowed to revenge himself against his brother.

Menaphon asked Cosroe if he were not afraid of the king's threat, but Cosroe assured the Persian lord that there was a plot afoot to make Cosroe emperor of Asia, explaining that it hurt him to witness the scorn now being directed toward the Persian monarchy, which had formerly awed the entire world. Shortly afterward there was a revolt, and the rebellious lords offered Cosroe the crown. Cosroe set out to annex the thousand troops of Theridamas in order to conquer his brother Mycetes.

Meanwhile, on a Scythian hill, Tamburlaine held Zenocrate, the daughter of the sultan of Egypt. To her the former shepherd spoke grandly of kingdoms he would conquer. Techelles and Usumcasane echoed his boasts, vowing to follow Tamburlaine to the death. To Zenocrate the ambitious leader promised all the wealth and power in his kingdom; he was in love. Suddenly the thousand horse troops of Mycetes attacked the five hundred foot soldiers of Tamburlaine. When Theridamas accosted the Scythian, he was so impressed by the appearance of the former shepherd that Tamburlaine was able to persuade Theridamas to become an ally. Visions of mighty kingdoms and power had persuaded Theridamas.

Cosroe, smugly discussing Tambur-

3696

laine's personality and latest conquest, was preparing to send troops to join Tamburlaine and Theridamas by the river Araris, there to engage the forces of Mycetes, who was fuming with rage at the revolt. Meander, a follower of Mycetes, conceived the idea that he who could conquer Tamburlaine would be offered the province of Albania, and whoever took Theridamas could have Media, but Mycetes asked that Cosroe be captured alive. Mycetes was convinced that the followers of the bandit Tamburlaine could be bribed to desert their leader, who had purchased them by bribes in the first place.

When Cosroe met Tamburlaine, the Scythian boasted of his great future; Theridamas indicated to Cosroe that he believed in Tamburlaine's ability. Certain of victory, Cosroe promised Techelles and Usumcasane rewards for their deeds.

Mycetes was defeated. After the victory, Tamburlaine bribed Theridamas, Techelles, and Usumcasane with a promise of kingdoms of their own if they would attack Cosroe. Marveling at Tamburlaine's arrogant daring, Cosroe prepared for battle. Cosroe was wounded in battle, and Tamburlaine, gloating over his easy conquest, proclaimed himself king of Persia.

At the court in Algiers, the kings of Fez, Morocco, and Algiers fumed at the bandit who had taken Persia and who now was forcing them to raise their siege of Greek Constantinople. Bajazeth, king of the Turks, dispatched a message to Tamburlaine and offered threats if the Scythian conqueror dared set foot in Africa. Meanwhile the kings planned to take Greece by siege.

Zenocrate had grown slowly to admire Tamburlaine, who was now plotting the conquest of the Turkish kings. Zabina, wife of Bajazeth, sneered at Zenocrate and called her a concubine. When he had subdued Bajazeth, Tamburlaine made Zabina Zenocrate's attendant slave.

The next victim of the Scythian's lust for power was the sultan of Egypt, Zeno-crate's father. To show his might, Tamburlaine had put Bajazeth in a cage and subjected him to base ridicule by using his prisoner as a footstool. Still Bajazeth and Zabina courageously insulted their master by hurling disdainful remarks and threats at him.

As Tamburlaine's armies prepared to take Damascus, Zenocrate gently asked her paramour to deal kindly with the city of her father, but he refused. Zenocrate grieved until Tamburlaine promised not to harm her father when Damascus fell. By now the Scythian conqueror loved Zenocrate dearly, and while he ordered three emissaries from Damascus to be killed, he thought of his beloved's beauty and tenderness. Zenocrate herself was torn between her conscience, which revolted against her lord's cruelty, and her love for him.

When Tamburlaine brought the sultan alive to Zenocrate, the conqueror promised to give the sultan's kingdom back to him if Zenocrate would accept the title of Queen of Egypt. She readily accepted this condition and Tamburlaine planned his wedding with Zenocrate.

Bajazeth and Zabina had killed themselves by dashing their heads against the bars of the cage in which Tamburlaine had imprisoned the Turkish monarch.

Orcanes, king of Natolia, preparing for a battle with Sigismund, king of Hungary, learned that Tamburlaine was mustering for an attack. He sent for all the Christian rulers of Europe to form an alliance against an invasion by the Scythian. The former enemies, Sigismund and Orcanes the Mohammedan, entered into a pact of friendship with the rulers of Buda and Bohemia.

Callapine, son of Bajazeth and a prisoner of Tamburlaine, was guarded by Almeda, whom the young prince bribed with offers of wealth and power if he would help Callapine to escape. Tamburlaine by now had three sons, Calyphas, Amyras, and Celebjnus. Calyphas expressed a desire to lead a peaceful life with his mother Zenocrate.

The treaty of the monarchs against Tamburlaine did not hold. When the Mohammedan Orcanes withdrew his troops from his campaign against the Christians, Sigismund was urged by his allies to attack Orcanes. Orcanes was trapped, for he was at the same time preparing to attack Tamburlaine. The betrayed monarch, crying for his enemies' Christ to help him defeat the traitors, prepared to defend himself. Sigismund was killed in the fighting, and Orcanes was the victor in the battle.

Zenocrate had become ill, and when she died, Tamburlaine was overcome with such grief that he would not have her buried until after his own death.

Escaping with the aid of Almeda, Callapine returned to his father's kingdom and marshaled the allies to defeat Tamburlaine and revenge Bajazeth's death. Inconsolable in his grief for Zenocrate, Tamburlaine prepared to fight the forces of Callapine. The Scythian's sons, Amyras and Celebinus, were eager for battle, but Calyphas, disliking his father's career of bloodshed, refused to join the fighting.

After he had vanquished his Turkish enemies, Tamburlaine returned to his camp and wrathfully stabbed Calyphas, who had remained in his tent all the while. The Turkish monarchs were bridled like horses, and under Tamburlaine's whip, forced to pull his carriage. The conqueror then planned to take Babylon. After this city was taken, terrible plunder, rape, and murder followed. Tamburlaine was now mad with lust and power. Only Callapine was still free to oppose him.

Tamburlaine fell ill with some mysterious malady, and his physician declared that he was dying. After the dying conqueror had crowned his son Amyras monarch of his empires, he sent for Zenocrate's hearse. Bidding his son to reign with power, Tamburlaine, the scourge of God, died leaning over his beloved Zenocrate's coffin.

THE TAMING OF THE SHREW

Type of work: Drama
Author: William Shakespeare (1564-1616)
Type of plot: Farce
Time of plot: Sixteenth century
Locale: Padua, Italy
First presented: c. 1593

Principal characters:
BAPTISTA, a rich gentleman of Padua
KATHARINA, his shrewish daughter
BIANCA, another daughter
PETRUCHIO, Katharina's suitor
LUCENTIO, a student in love with Bianca
TRANIO, his servant
VINCENTIO, Lucentio's father
GREMIO, and
HORTENSIO, Lucentio's rivals
A PEDANT

Critique:

Often called rough and bawdy, *The Taming of the Shrew* has none of the lyrical poetry or the gentle humor that characterizes most of Shakespeare's plays. This dramatic work is filled with wordy puns and coarse illusions; however, the vividness of language and rapid action sustain with excellent effect the demands of the plot. The play has long been one of the most popular of Shakespeare's works, and its main characters have become models for a shrewish woman and a strong woman-tamer. Some literary authorities think that Shakespeare did not write the whole play, that the subplot was written by another. This scholarly dispute is not likely to concern the reader who enjoys a lusty, witty play.

The Story:

As a joke, a beggar was carried, while asleep, to the house of a noble lord and there dressed in fine clothes and waited on by many servants. The beggar was told that he was a rich man who in a demented state had imagined himself to be a beggar, but who was now restored to his senses. The lord and his court had great sport with the poor fellow, to the extent of dressing a page as the beggar's rich and beautiful wife and presenting the supposed woman to him as his dutiful and obedient spouse. The beggar, in his stupidity, assumed his new role as though it were his own, and he and his lady settled down to watch a play prepared for their enjoyment.

Lucentio and Tranio, his serving-man, had journeyed to Padua so that Lucentio could study in that ancient city. But Tranio persuaded his master that life was not all study and work and that he should find pleasures also in his new residence. On their arrival in the city Lucentio and Tranio encountered Baptista and his daughters, Katharina and Bianca. These three were accompanied by Gremio and Hortensio, young gentlemen both in love with gentle Bianca. But Baptista would not permit his younger daughter to marry until someone should take Katharina off his hands. Although Katharina was wealthy and beautiful, she was such a shrew that no suitor would have her. Baptista, not knowing how to control his sharp-tongued daughter, announced that Gremio or Hortensio must find a husband for Katharina before either could woo Bianca. He charged them also to find tutors for the two girls, that they might be skilled in music and poetry.

Unobserved, Lucentio and Tranio witnessed this scene. At first sight Lucentio also fell in love with Bianca and determined to have her for himself. His first act was to change clothes with Tranio, so that the servant appeared to be the master. Lucentio then disguised himself as a tutor in order to woo Bianca without her father's knowledge.

About the same time Petruchio came to Padua. He was a rich and noble man of Verona, come to Padua to visit his friend Hortensio and to find for himself a rich wife. Hortensio told Petruchio of his love for Bianca and of her father's decree that she could not marry until a husband had been found for Katharina. Petruchio declared the stories told about spirited Katharina were to his liking, particularly the account of her great wealth, and he expressed a desire to meet her. Hortensio proposed that Petruchio seek Katharina's father and present his family's name and history. Hortensio, meanwhile, planned to disguise himself as a tutor and thus plead his own cause with Bianca.

The situation grew confused. Lucentio was disguised as a tutor and his servant Tranio was dressed as Lucentio. Hortensio was also disguised as a tutor. Petruchio was to ask for Katharina's hand. Also, unknown to anyone but Katharina, Bianca loved neither Gremio nor Hortensio and swore that she would never marry rather than accept one or the other as her husband.

Petruchio easily secured Baptista's permission to marry his daughter Katharina, for the poor man was only too glad to have his older daughter off his hands. Petruchio's courtship was a strange one indeed, a battle of wits, words, and wills. Petruchio was determined to bend Katharina to his will, but Katharina scorned and berated him with a vicious tongue. Nevertheless she must obey her father's wish and marry him, and the nuptial day was set. Then Gremio and Tranio, the latter still believed to be Lucentio, vied with each other for Baptista's permission to marry Bianca. Tranio won because he claimed more gold and vaster lands than Gremio could declare. In the meantime Hortensio and Lucentio, both disguised as tutors, wooed Bianca.

As part of the taming process, Petruchio arrived late for his wedding, and when he did appear he wore old and tattered clothes. Even during the wedding ceremony Petruchio acted like a madman, stamping, swearing, cuffing the priest. Immediately afterward he dragged Katharina away from the wedding feast and took her to his country home, there to continue his scheme to break her to his will. He gave her no food and no time for sleep, while always pretending that nothing was good enough for her. In fact, he all but killed her with kindness. Before he was through Katharina agreed that the moon was the sun, that an old man was a woman.

Bianca fell in love with Lucentio, whom she thought to be her tutor. In chagrin, Hortensio threw off his disguise and he and Gremio forswore their love for any girl so fickle. Tranio, still hoping to win her for himself, found an old pedant to act the part of Vincentio, Lucentio's father. The pretended father argued his son's cause with Baptista until that lover of gold promised his daughter's hand to Lucentio as he thought, but in reality to Tranio. When Lucentio's true father appeared on the scene, he was considered an impostor and almost put in jail for his deceit. The real Lucentio and Bianca, meanwhile, had been secretly married. Returning from the church with his bride, he revealed the whole plot to Baptista and the others. At first Baptista was angry at the way in which he had been duped, but Vincentio spoke soothingly and soon cooled his rage.

Hortensio, in the meantime, had married a rich widow. To celebrate these weddings, Lucentio gave a feast for all the couples and the fathers. After the ladies had retired, the three newly married men wagered one hundred pounds each that his own wife would most quickly obey his commands. Lucentio sent first for Bianca, but she sent word she would not come. Then Hortensio sent for his wife, but she too refused to obey his summons. Petruchio then ordered Katharina to appear, and she came instantly to do his bidding. At his request she also forced Bianca and Hortensio's wife to go to their husbands. Baptista was so delighted with his daughter's meekness and willing submission that he added another twenty thousand crowns to her dowry. Katharina told them all that a wife should live only to serve her husband and that a woman's heart and tongue ought to be as soft as her body. Petruchio's work had been well done. He had tamed the shrew forever.

TAPS FOR PRIVATE TUSSIE

Type of work: Novel
Author: Jesse Stuart (1907-   )
Type of plot: Regional romance
Time of plot: Twentieth century
Locale: Kentucky
First published: 1943

Principal characters:
GRANDPA TUSSIE, head of the Tussie clan
GRANDMA TUSSIE, his wife
GEORGE TUSSIE, his brother
UNCLE MOTT TUSSIE, his son
UNCLE KIM TUSSIE, his deceased son
AUNT VITTIE TUSSIE, Kim's wife
SID SEAGRAVES TUSSIE, a grandson

Critique:

Jesse Stuart, who came into sudden fame with his book of Kentucky poems, *Man With a Bull-Tongue Plow*, has continued to use this familiar background in the series of novels and short stories which have followed. Stuart displays a great understanding for the people about whom he writes in *Taps for Private Tussie*. In this novel of the Kentucky mountain people the plot is unimportant; the characters are the story. Stuart's treatment of this region grows out of his deep familiarity with the place and its people. He himself has lived the life about which he writes.

The Story:

There was trouble at Grandpa Tussie's. In the coal shed behind the schoolhouse where the Tussies lived, Uncle Kim's body was beginning to smell. Kim Tussie had been killed in the war. The government had sent his body home, and now the Tussie clan had gathered for the funeral. Kim's folks, Grandpa and Grandma Tussie, comforted Aunt Vittie, Kim's wife, who was screaming and wailing. Uncle Mott, Kim's brother, was telling how he had identified the body. Sid, Kim's young nephew, was just excited. There had not been so much going on since he could remember. The noise the Tussie kin made as they carried

the coffin up the mountainside could not soon be forgotten by a young boy.

Uncle Kim had left Aunt Vittie ten thousand dollars in government insurance, and the day after the funeral she rented the Rayburn mansion and filled it with new furniture, all ready for Grandpa and Grandma, Uncle Mott, and Sid to move in. It was the biggest and best house any of the Tussies had ever seen. Uncle Mott flicked the electric lights off and on all day. Sid used the bathroom over and over. Aunt Vittie bought them all new clothes to go with the house. To Sid it was all wonderful, but his happiness was spoiled a little when he realized Uncle Kim had to die in order for the rest of them to have that splendor.

The next few weeks were really a miracle in the lives of the Tussies. Grandpa continued to get his relief groceries and Aunt Vittie bought more groceries at the store. Grandpa began to look for more of the Tussies to come when they heard about the money. Grandpa thought his brother George would be the first. Brother George had been married five times. He could play a fiddle till it made a man cry.

Grandpa was right. When George heard about the money, he decided to come home to die. Uncle Mott hoped that that time would come soon, but Aunt Vittie looked at George and smiled. George played his fiddle far into the night, playing tunes Aunt Vittie asked for, and Grandpa knew George had come to stay. Aunt Vittie bought George new clothes, too, and Uncle Mott began to look mean.

Then more Tussies came, first Uncle Ben, then Dee, then Young Uncle Ben, then Starkie, then Watt, then Sabie, then Abe, all with their wives and young ones. The mansion was ready to burst. Only Grandpa knew them all. When Grandma counted forty-six of them, she would stand for no more.

The money began to go fast. Sid knew now why Grandpa and Grandma had not cried at Kim's funeral. They had known Aunt Vittie would get the money and all the Tussies would live high. Brother George's fiddle playing had Aunt Vittie looking as she had never looked before. Uncle Mott was losing out and he looked dangerous.

Grandpa knew things were bound to change. He was right. First the government man came and stopped their relief. It hurt Grandpa to lose his relief. He had had it for years and had expected it to go on forever. Then George Rayburn came to inspect his house. When he saw the floor full of nail holes, the broken windowpanes, the charcoal and pencil marks on the walls, he threatened to bring suit if the Tussies did not leave at once. But the uncles and the brothers and the cousins twice removed refused to leave. It was not until Sheriff White-apple came with the law papers that they knew they were whipped. That night there was the grandest dance of all. Aunt Vittie kissed Brother George and then she kissed Uncle Mott, but not very hard. It looked as if George were winning.

The next day the Tussies began to leave. Grandpa and Grandma, Aunt Vit-rie, Brother George, Uncle Mott, and Sid were the last to go. Aunt Vittie had bought fifty acres of land and an old shack with the last of her money, and

she put the farm in Grandpa's name. They had no furniture, no sheets, no dishes, since Rayburn had attached everything to pay for damages to his house. There was only Grandpa's old-age pension check to look forward to. But Uncle Mott and Brother George made a table and sapling beds and Sid found their old dishes in the gully by the old schoolhouse, and the Tussies began living as they had always lived.

Then came the worst blow of all. Someone had reported that Grandpa now owned land, and his old-age pension was stopped. Sometimes there was not enough to eat. Uncle Mott and George began to look dangerous. Sid knew bad trouble was coming. After Brother George and Vittie were married, Uncle Mott stayed in town most of the time, drinking bootleg and getting mean drunk.

Grandpa knew his time on earth was about up, but he felt something was going to happen that he did not want to miss. And he was right again. Uncle Mott came home from town one day and told them that he had found Young Uncle Ben and Dee and had shot them for reporting Grandpa to the relief agency. As Uncle Mott talked, Brother George began to stroke his fiddle, and he played a note of death. Uncle Mott, cursing the fiddle for being the cause of all his trouble, shot the fiddle from George's hands. George drew his gun and shot Uncle Mott through the head.

Aunt Vittie had been to town, too, begging food for Grandpa and the rest, and now they saw her coming, walking close beside a strange man. That is, he was a stranger until he came nearer, and then they saw that it was Uncle Kim, who was supposed to be buried on the mountainside. When George saw the ghost, he went through the windowpane. But it was simple for Sheriff Whiteapple, when he came a little later, to follow his footprints in the snow.

After Kim had explained that he had not been killed after all, they began to understand what had happened. Uncle Mott had always wanted Aunt Vittie, and it had been easy for him to identify a body as Kim's. And Kim told more. He told Sid that he was Aunt Vittie's son, that she had been wronged by a rich man who paid Kim to marry her, and that now Sid would be their son.

That night it was as if nothing had happened, except for Uncle Mott's body in the shack. To Sid it was like a dream, but a dream with life in it. For the first time he began to feel really good. Peace had come to the Tussies.

TARAS BULBA

Type of work: Novel
Author: Nikolai V. Gogol (1809-1852)
Type of plot: Historical romance
Time of plot: Fifteenth century
Locale: Russia
First published: 1835

Principal characters:
TARAS BULBA, a Cossack warrior
OSTAP, Taras' older son
ANDRÍI, Taras' younger son
YANKEL, a Jewish merchant
DAUGHTER OF THE POLISH WAIWODE, Andrii's sweetheart

Critique:

Taras Bulba is a prose poem in praise of the Cossack warrior, celebrating, as it does, the brave deeds of those hardy fighters. Presenting the life of the Cossack band on the march and in battle, Gogol uses a theme which is truly epic. Certainly Gogol intended this heroic tale as a romantic commentary of the dullness of life in his own day. Its application for our own time is just as apt.

The Story:

When the two sons of Taras Bulba returned home after finishing their studies at the Royal Seminary in Kiev, their father ridiculed their monastic garb. Ostap, the older of the two, insisted that any insult must be avenged, and father and son began to exchange blows. Taras, learning in this manner that Ostap was a stout contender, embraced him heartily. The father would have liked also to try the mettle of his younger son, Andrii, but his wife intervened, preventing any more fisticuffs.

In honor of his sons' arrival Taras entertained all the local officers of the Zaporozhian Cossacks. Under the stimulus of corn brandy, Taras resolved to take his sons the next day to the Setch, the permanent camp of the fighting Cossacks. The mother was heartbroken to hear that she must part with her sons, but Taras was firm. Before the party left for the encampment, all sat down, even the servants, while the mother blessed her sons and gave them holy pictures to wear around their necks.

Taras Bulba and his sons rode off together across the steppes, each concerned with his own thoughts. Taras was a Cossack leader imbued with the old-fashioned ideas that the only good life was that of the soldier. Ostap, when first enrolled at the seminary, had found life there unbearable; but he gradually grew accustomed to scholastic life and became a good student. Though not a leader at the seminary, he was willing to follow other boys whose main interests, like his own, were war and revelry. Andrii was of a different sort. He was a willing student, a better leader, but was also passionately fond of women, who came in his dreams to trouble his sleep. He remembered a beautiful girl who one day had laughed from her window. Learning that she was the daughter of the Polish Waiwode of Koven, Andrii daringly visited the girl in her bedroom the following night. To his regret she left the city with her father soon afterward.

Three days later Taras and his sons reached the suburb of the Setch, where the workmen and merchants for the great encampment were located. Finally they came to the Setch itself, and the Cossacks uproariously greeted Taras, their old comrade-in-arms. The only requirements for admission to the Setch were belief in Christ, the Holy Trinity, and the Church. If the members lacked money, they simply plundered the merchants in the suburb. Andrii and Ostap fitted well into this wild life and soon they gained recognition among the Cossacks for their bravery and daring.

Not wanting his sons to be idle, Taras

consulted the Cossack leader about the possibility of stirring up some bold enterprise. Taras suggested attacking the Turks, but he was told that a treaty of peace had been signed with the sultan. Sly Taras then arranged for a meeting of the whole encampment, at which Kirdyaga, a close friend, was chosen as the new leader. The next day Kirdyaga called the group together and harangued them into voting for a raid on the coasts of Anatolia.

Immediately the Setch became active with preparations for the march. Before arrangements were completed, however, a group of Cossacks appeared in a barge and reported persecution and defeat at the hands of the Poles. The Jews were also accused, and so the enraged Cossacks threw the Jewish merchants into the Dnieper River. Only one escaped, a trader named Yankel, who was saved by the intercession of Taras Bulba.

The Zaporozhti began their trek of pillage and plunder throughout southeast Poland. Arriving at the city of Dubno, they found it heavily garrisoned and walled. The Zaporozhti then surrounded Dubno, cutting off all food supplies from the surrounding district, and gave themselves up to pillage and drunken revelry.

Both of Taras' sons were bored with this inactivity. One night Andrii was awakened by a Tatar serving-woman. She told him that her mistress was the beautiful daughter of the waiwode, the girl whom he had encountered at Kiev. Having seen him from the walls, the girl had sent her servant through a secret gate to ask Andrii to visit her in the city and to bring food for her starving family. Andrii stole a sack of bread and accompanied the Tatar into Dubno. When he met the waiwode's daughter, she seemed more beautiful to his sight than ever; in her embrace he forgot home, honor, country, loyalty, and Church.

A short time later Taras learned of his son's treachery from Yankel, who had been inside the city walls. The old Cossack was furious at Andrii, but proud of Ostap, who had been raised in rank and put in command of a large unit. Then

news came that the Setch had been invaded by the Tatars. Half of the Cossacks departed to pursue the Tatars, while the others remained at the siege of Dubno, Taras and Ostap among them. Taras, to bolster the courage of his warriors, gave the Cossacks a large supply of wine he had brought along for just such a purpose.

One day there was a great battle, a fight in which most of the Cossacks were killed or captured. Toward the end of the fray Andrii appeared, richly attired, to fight against his own people. Taras, who saw him come into the battle, maneuvered his men so that he and his son met alone. Taras shot Andrii, who died with the name of the waiwode's daughter on his lips. The victorious Poles captured Ostap, who had distinguished himself in the battle. After receiving a serious wound, Taras was rescued by a faithful servant. He regained consciousness on the way back to the Setch, where he learned that not another man who had been on the expedition had returned.

Unable to forget Ostap, now a prisoner of the Poles, Taras set out for the city of Ouman. There he found Yankel, who for a large sum was persuaded to conduct Taras to the hostile city of Warsaw in search of Ostap. Hidden under a load of bricks, Taras entered the city, but he was unable to see Ostap before the day the Cossack prisoners were led out for torture and death. When Ostap called out for his father, Taras was unable to endure the sight of his son's torture in silence. Taras answered him so that Ostap knew his father was close by at his death.

Thus discovered, Taras was pursued but escaped to the Ukraine, where he became the leader of a Cossack band. When the Zaporozhian chiefs made peace with the Poles, Taras broke away with a band of his followers and raided towns and cities through all Poland. Finally, pursued by five regiments, he was taken prisoner. Crucified to a burning tree, Taras Bulba died calling to his comrades to carry on their fight for freedom.

TARR

Type of work: Novel
Author: Wyndham Lewis (1886-1957)
Type of plot: Psychological realism
Time of plot: About 1910
Locale: Paris
First published: 1918

Principal characters:

FREDERICK TARR, an English artist
BERTHA LUNKEN, Tarr's fiancée, a German art student
OTTO KREISLER, a German artist
ANASTASYA VASEK, a Russian
LOUIS SOLTYK, a Pole

Critique:

In this novel, Lewis presents a psychological study of a group of artists in the Paris of the days before the First World War. In the main, it is concerned with the emotional effects that these characters have upon each other as they are juxtaposed in various combinations. Lewis was also concerned with the national psychologies involved—in particular, English vs. German. He detested the Germans, and on Nietzsche he placed the blame for the over-inflated egos of the many nonentities who infested the artistic world of this period. The novel is largely a satire on certain German characteristics: sentimentality, solemnity, and various aspects of Prussianism. The story is grotesque, farcical, and yet tragic; it is also a warning that the famous English "grin" can be a mask for a sentimentality as bad as that of the Germans. By making Tarr, the main character, his mouthpiece, Lewis foreshadowed some of the famous novels of the 1920's, in which the discussion of ideas was the main point of the book.

The Story:

Frederick Tarr, an English artist living in Paris, was engaged to a young German woman, Bertha Lunken, a student in the Parisian art schools. Tarr rather disliked Germans, although he knew a great many of them in Paris. It was his theory that their only use was to be very

intimate with, and that the real problem was how to put up with them when one was not intimate. Not wishing to have it known that he was engaged to Fräulein Lunken, he was on the point of breaking with her, for he considered her a dolt. He justified his strange attitude on the grounds that all his finer feelings had gone into his art and had left nothing over for sex. He admitted that his taste in women was deplorable.

After a conversation with a friend, during which he explained his theory, Tarr went to his fiancée's apartment. He felt some remorse for his treatment of Bertha, but he had been attracted by her bourgeois-bohemian absurdities and her Germanic floridity and had unwittingly become too involved. Now, he felt, a break had to be made. But he had underestimated the intensity of feeling that Bertha had developed for him. The scene in the apartment, carefully decorated with sham art that Tarr loathed, was comic yet tragic. Tarr could not help feeling that he was treating Bertha shabbily, yet he was passionately convinced that marriage was not for him. Nor had he expected such floods of tears. But somehow the break was accomplished, and Tarr departed with the promise to see Bertha again after a few days.

Otto Kreisler, an impecunious German artist, lived on a small allowance grudgingly doled out by his father. Just returned from a trip to Italy, he was more than usually hard up. Four years before Otto had made the mistake of marrying off an old sweetheart to his father. Since he refused his father's urgings that he give up art, return to Germany, and settle down into business, the monthly check, in revenge, was sent at irregular intervals. At this point, he was concerned with pawning his portmanteau as the result of failure to borrow money from an affluent compatriot, Ernst Volker. On his return from Italy, Kreisler had discovered, to his horror, that his position as the recipient of Volker's bounty had been taken by a Pole, one Louis Soltyk, and that no more money could be expected. He already owed Volker fifteen hundred marks. It was the psychological effect of lack of money that, by indirect means, propelled Kreisler toward his final tragedy

In a mood of discouragement—the check from home was late again—he went to the Café Vallet for lunch. By chance, he found himself at the same small table with an extraordinarily beautiful young woman who, after some preliminary conversation, explained that she was Anastasya Vasek and that she had escaped to Paris from her parents' bourgeois home. Kreisler was strongly attracted to her because to him women had always been a kind of emotional pawnshop where he could dump his sorrows. With German sentimentality, he thought of love as sorrowful. Determined to follow up that chance meeting, and in spite of the fact that his evening clothes were in pawn, he accepted an invitation from a member of the German colony, Fräulein Lipmann, to join her group at a dance at a club in the neighborhood.

On the afternoon before the dance he came upon Anastasya sitting with Soltyk in a café. Again, he decided, the Pole was interfering in his affairs.

Driven by a kind of persecution mania, Kreisler deliberately made a fiasco of the evening. On the way to the dance, he found himself walking with Bertha and somewhat behind the other members of the party. Again, their peculiar German

psychologies inter-reacted; he wished to avenge himself through her on the more affluent guests; she felt that he was suffering and that she should make a sacrifice to console him. So Kreisler kissed her roughly and she permitted the kiss. They were seen by the other Germans, who were walking ahead. Arrived at the dance, Kreisler, dressed in rumpled morning clothes and still under the spell of his mania, behaved abominably. He insulted nearly every woman present and was almost thrown out. Worse, Anastasya laughed at him, turning his admiration to hate. The next morning, when the long-awaited allowance arrived accompanied by a command to return to Germany, Kreisler replied to his father that he would kill himself in exactly one month.

Shortly afterward Bertha received a letter from Tarr, informing her that he had heard of the episode with Kreisler and that he was leaving for London. Further, the "Kreisler affair" had rather embroiled Bertha with her German friends. In a dreary mood, she went out to buy lunch and met Kreisler; after some conversation, she accepted his invitation to visit a café the following evening. This curious act was a defense against her friends; it was part of her theory that he was in distress and it would contradict the story, now current, that his outrageous behavior had been the result of Anastasya's snub. Also, her meeting with Kreisler would be a kind of revenge on Tarr. So she succeeded in convincing herself that she was being driven into this strange friendship. Eight days later, in Kreisler's studio, he possessed her by force, and the situation that she had created became suddenly tragic. Kreisler came to her apartment, offered to shoot himself, and finally departed after swearing to be her eternal servant. With her usual sentimentality, Bertha felt uplifted, as if together they had done something noble.

Meanwhile, Tarr had merely moved to the Montmartre district, where he felt that he could work in peace. He continued to frequent his old section with its German colony so that he could keep an eye on Bertha. Inevitably, he met Anastasya, and just as inevitably he encountered Bertha and Kreisler together. He could not resist joining this pair; their "Germanness" gave him an ironic pleasure. Kreisler was baffled by the Englishman's sudden friendship that led Tarr to join him at a café evening after evening, and he found his Teutonic solemnity not equal to the situation. Fearful of being driven mad, he threatened the Englishman with a whip when Tarr went to his room and then pushed him out the door.

During this time Tarr and Anastasya, attracted to each other, had long café conversations about life and art. But a storm was gathering. One evening Tarr, who had joined Kreisler and a Russian at a café, saw the German jump from his seat, rush across the room to a group of Russians and Poles, and slap Soltyk's face. That afternoon Kreisler had met Anastasya and Soltyk and, in a cold fury, had struck Soltyk. Now he was challenging the Pole to a duel; after much excited conversation the challenge was accepted.

The duel next morning was another mixture of comedy and tragedy. The seconds were trying to effect an honorable compromise when Kreisler's mood suddenly changed: he offered to forgive Soltyk if the latter would kiss him! As he leaned forward the enraged Pole leaped upon him; they fell to the ground, and the seconds began fighting among themselves. When the dust had settled, Soltyk's friends tried to lead him away, but they were stopped by Kreisler, who still held his pistol. A Pole struck at him; Kreisler fired and killed Soltyk. Kreisler fled. Five days later, penniless and hungry, he reached a village near the border and was put in jail. In a last display of his disordered temperament, he hanged himself in his cell. His father paid the exact sum demanded by the town for the burial.

In Paris, meanwhile, Tarr and Anastasya had rapidly become involved in an affair, and Tarr continued to see Bertha in decreasing "doses," as though he were taking medicine. As he was about to give her up, she told him that she was pregnant and that the child was Kreisler's. Out of pity, Tarr married her. But he lived with Anastasya. Two years later, Bertha divorced him to marry an eye doctor. Tarr never married Anastasya. He had three children by another woman.

TARTARIN OF TARASCON

Type of work: Novel
Author: Alphonse Daudet (1840-1897)
Type of plot: Satiric romance
Time of plot: Nineteenth century
Locale: France and North Africa
First published: 1872

Principal characters:
TARTARIN, a huntsman
BAÏA, a Moorish beauty
PRINCE GREGORY OF MONTENEGRO
BARBASSOU, captain of the Zouave

Critique:

The saying is that words fly so quickly in southern France because the air is so light and buoyant. Indeed the Midi is renowned for its braggarts. Tartarin was a real braggart, but in this story he made good his boasts — to a certain extent. Tartarin of Tarascon was written with the sure touch of a humorist combined with the fantastic imagination of the Provençal poet. In his understanding of people and in his method of character portrayal, Daudet is often compared with Dickens.

The Story:

In the little town of Tarascon in the Midi, Tartarin enjoyed an enviable reputation which was based first of all on his garden. But Tartarin grew no plants of France. He had banana trees, palm trees, cacti, and all the most exotic plants he could find.

To understand the second reason for Tartarin's fame one must know the town of Tarascon. The Tarasconese were mighty hunters and all the men had ample arsenals. Tartarin's study contained a complete collection of deadly weapons. He had rifles, carbines, blunderbusses, Malayan krishes, and Indian tomahawks. It was too bad that there was no game at all for many leagues around the town, for in order to indulge their passion for the chase, the Tarasconese had to hunt their own caps. A man would throw his cap in the air and fire while it was still in flight. Tartarin had the distinction of ruining more caps than

all his rivals put together.

The third reason for his fame came from the custom of each Tarasconese to sing his own particular song at all social events. Tartarin had no particular song, for he could sing them all. It was a brave thing to hear Tartarin sing "NO. NO, NO" in a duet with Mme. Bezuquet. True, all Tartarin could sing was "No," but this he sang with enviable gusto.

Fourth, Tartarin had once been offered a job as clerk in the Shanghai office of a French importing firm. Although he had not taken the job, it was almost the same to him in later years, when he talked in a knowing way of the mysterious customs of the Far East. Even if he had never stayed overnight outside of Tarascon, he was a true cosmopolite.

Often he would roam the poorer streets of Tarascon looking for those stealthy people who carry on international intrigue and thuggery. He would arm himself with knuckle dusters, his bowie knife, his trusty forty-five, and then fearlessly seek adventure. Every one he met, unfortunately, was a harmless citizen who greeted him by name. However, one never knew when something unusual might happen.

One night a member of the club came running to announce that a carnival had brought a lion to Tarascon. Tartarin bravely affixed a bayonet to his elephant gun and went to the carnival. It was an inspiring sight to see Tartarin swagger in front of the lion's cage, and he never flinched no matter how the lion roared.

3710

This experience, coupled with his own ability at telling tales, soon gave Tartarin a reputation as a great lion hunter, and in some way the impression grew that Tartarin was actually going to Africa to hunt lions. It must be admitted that Tartarin enjoyed the story and actually talked about his coming trip. But as the months went by he showed no signs of leaving. He could not bring himself to give up his regular hot chocolate.

Finally even the Tarasconese could no longer stand the suspense. When Commander Bravida told Tartarin that he must go, Tartarin, with uneasy heart, put on his costume of full white linen trousers, a cummerbund two feet wide, and a gigantic red fez. On each shoulder he carried a heavy gun, in his belt a hunting knife, and on his hip a revolver. In his two copper-lined chests were his reserve weapons. Other boxes contained drugs, pemmican for emergency rations, and a shelter tent. Thus attired and supplied, he put on his spectacles and left, amid the hurrahs of the town.

On the trip across the sea the good ship *Zouave* was unsteady, and Tartarin's great fez was often inclined over the rail. But in Algeria he still had strength to go on deck, where to his horror, he saw the ship invaded by hordes of natives he mistook for Algerian pirates. Taking out his sheath knife, he courageously rushed upon the invaders. Luckily Captain Barbassou caught him around the middle before he could harm the startled porters.

The first morning in Algiers Tartarin arose at daybreak and prepared to hunt lions. Dashing out into the road, he met hunters with game bags filled with rabbits. Tartarin pushed on over the desert country. By nightfall he was in a thicket. Uttering cries to imitate a stray kid, he settled down to wait. Before long he saw a lion bearing down upon him. Up went his trusty gun. Two shots rang out, and the wounded lion thrashed away. Not daring to move for fear the female would come to the aid of her mate, Tartarin sat uneasily until dawn. Then to his dismay he found himself

sitting in a garden among rows of beets. He had killed no lion, but there in a ditch lay a donkey with two bullet holes in him.

Tartarin decided to go back to Algiers, get his equipment, and head south. On the bus he was stricken by the bold glance of a Moorish lady. Losing his head, he started on a conquest of love.

After weeks of fruitless searching, Prince Gregory of Montenegro, whom he had met aboard the *Zouave*, helped Tartarin find the beautiful Moor. She was Baïa, a widow of twenty and sister of a pipe seller in the bazaar. Prince Gregory kindly offered to placate the brother by buying his pipes. The smitten Tartarin gave his friend enough money over several weeks to buy gross after gross of pipes before the matter was arranged to the satisfaction of all.

Tartarin took a house in the native quarter with his Baïa. At first glance Baïa seemed much fatter than the lady in the bus, but Tartarin put down such base suspicions. Now he was known as Sidi Tart'ri ben Tart'ri. All day he puffed his narghilé and ate sweetmeats flavored with musk. Baïa entertained her lord by singing monotonous airs through her nose or dancing the stomach dance. The only flaw in the household was that Baïa spoke no French and Tartarin no Arabic.

One day Tartarin met Barbassou by chance. The cynical captain warned Tartarin against all Montenegrin princes and expressed doubt that Baïa knew no French. Although Tartarin disdained the suspicions of Barbassou, the sight of a fellow Tarasconese again recalled lion hunting to his mind. He stoutly resolved to leave his bliss and go south to hunt the terrible lion.

After two days of rough jolting in an obsolete coach, Tartarin entered the city of Milianah, where on a street corner he saw a degrading sight. A lion had been trained to hold a bowl in his mouth and beg for alms. Incensed at this debasement of the most noble of beasts, Tartarin seized the bowl from the lion's jaws and dashed it on the ground. Thinking him a robber, the two Negro attendants set on him with clubs. A riot was averted by the arrival of suave Prince Gregory, who had hurried south after his friend.

Now with a proper caravan made up of the prince, Tartarin, and one camel, Tartarin wandered for nearly a month. Each time they entered a town, the prince would visit the military post, the commander would extend full hospitality to Tartarin, and Tartarin would pay the bill. But he found no lions anywhere.

Finally, on a notable night, Tartarin was hiding in a copse of oleanders when he heard a lion cough. Giving his purse to the prince to hold, he lay in wait. No lion appeared. The prince vanished. Without lion or money, Tartarin sat in despair on the steps of a saint's tomb. To his great astonishment, a noble lion advanced down the path. Tartarin fired twice, and bagged his lion at last.

But the lion was a holy, blind lion belonging to a Mohammedan convent, and Tartarin had to pay a fine of twenty-five hundred francs. He was forced to sell all his fine weapons to pay the sum, but he skinned the lion and sent the skin to Tarascon.

In disgust Tartarin walked back to Algeria, followed by his faithful camel, which had formed a liking for him. Tartarin could not shake off the beast. The camel swam the Mediterranean behind the *Zouave* and trotted behind the train from Marseille to Tarascon.

So the great hero of Tarascon came home. The story of how he killed twenty lions was told over and over again.

TARTUFFE

Type of work: Drama
Author: Molière (Jean Baptiste Poquelin, 1622-1673)
Type of plot: Comedy
Time of plot: Seventeenth century
Locale: Paris
First presented: 1664

Principal characters:
ORGON, a wealthy ex-officer of the King's Guard
MADAME PERNELLE, his mother
ELMIRE, his wife
DAMIS, his son
MARIANE, his daughter
VALÈRE, Mariane's lover
DORINE, Mariane's maid
CLÉANTE, Orgon's brother-in-law
TARTUFFE, a hypocrite

Critique:

It is almost impossible for a modern reader to realize the disturbance *Tartuffe, or the Hypocrite* caused when it was originally produced. Molière was attacked for undermining the very basis of religion in his portrait of the hypocrite. For moderns, the comedy is valuable mainly as the ancestor of similar satiric portraits, ranging from Dickens' Mr. Pecksniff to Sinclair Lewis' Elmer Gantry. Molière's Tartuffe is hardly convincing to us, however, because we do not know why or how he became what he was.

The Story:

Orgon's home was a happy one. He himself was married to Elmire, a woman much younger than he, who adored him. His two children by a former marriage were fond of their stepmother, and she of them. Mariane, the daughter, was engaged to be married to Valère, a very eligible young man, and Damis, the son, was in love with Valère's sister.

Then Tartuffe came to live in the household. Tartuffe was a penniless scoundrel whom the trusting Orgon had found praying in church. Taken in by his cant and his pose of fervent religiousness, Orgon had invited the hypocrite into his home. As a consequence, the family was soon demoralized. Once established, Tartuffe proceeded to change their normal, happy mode of life to a strictly moral one. He set up a rigid

puritan regimen for the family, and persuaded Orgon to force his daughter to break her engagement to Valère in order to marry Tartuffe. He said she needed a pious man to lead her in a righteous life.

Valère was determined that Mariane would marry no one but himself, but unfortunately Mariane was too spineless to resist Tartuffe and her father. Confronted by her father's orders, she remained silent and remonstrated only weakly. As a result, Tartuffe was cordially hated by every member of the family, including Dorine, the saucy, outspoken servant, who did everything in her power to break the hold that the hypocrite had secured over her master. Dorine hated not only Tartuffe but also his valet, Laurent, for the servant imitated the master in everything. In fact, the only person besides Orgon who liked and approved of Tartuffe was Orgon's mother, Madame Pernelle, who was the type of puritan who wished to withhold from others pleasures she herself could not enjoy. Madame Pernelle highly disapproved of Elmire, maintaining that in her love for clothes and amusements she was setting her family a bad example which Tartuffe was trying to correct. Actually, Elmire was merely full of the joy of living, a fact that her mother-in-law was unable to perceive. Orgon himself was little better. When Elmire fell ill, and he was informed of this fact, his sole concern was for the health of Tartuffe. Tartuffe, however, was in fine fettle, stout and ruddy-cheeked. For his evening meal, he consumed two partridges, half a leg of mutton, and four flasks of wine. He then retired to his warm and comfortable bed and slept soundly until morning.

Tartuffe's designs were not really for the daughter, Mariane, but for Elmire herself. One day, after Orgon's wife had recovered from her illness, Tartuffe appeared before her. He complimented Elmire on her beauty, and even went so far as to lay his fat hand on her knee. Damis, Orgon's son, observed all that went on from the cabinet where he was hidden. Furious, he determined to reveal to his father all that he had seen. Orgon refused to believe him. Wily Tartuffe had so completely captivated Orgon that he ordered Damis to apologize to Tartuffe. When his son refused, Orgon, violently angry, drove him from the house and disowned him. Then to show his confidence in Tartuffe's honesty and piety, Orgon signed a deed of trust turning his estate over to Tartuffe's management, and announced his daughter's betrothal to Tartuffe.

Elmire, embittered by the behavior of this impostor in her house, resolved to unmask him. She persuaded Orgon to hide under a cloth-covered table and see and hear for himself the real Tartuffe. Then she enticed Tartuffe to make love to her, disarming him with the assurance that her foolish husband would suspect nothing. Emboldened, Tartuffe poured out his heart to her, leaving no doubt as to his intention of making her his mistress. Disillusioned and outraged when Tartuffe asserted that Orgon was a complete dupe, the husband emerged from

his hiding place, denounced the hypocrite, and ordered him from the house. Tartuffe defied him, reminding him that the house was now his according to Orgon's deed of trust.

Another matter made Orgon even more uneasy than the possible loss of his property. This was a casket given him by a friend, Argas, a political criminal now in exile. It contained important state secrets, the revelation of which would mean a charge of treason against Orgon and certain death for his friend. Orgon had foolishly entrusted the casket to Tartuffe, and he feared the use that villain might make of it. He informed his brother-in-law, Cléante, that he would have nothing further to do with pious men; that in the future he would shun them like the plague. But Cléante pointed out that such rushing to extremes was the sign of an unbalanced mind. Because a treacherous vagabond was masquerading as a religious man was no good reason to suspect religion.

The next day Tartuffe made good this threat, using his legal right to force Orgon and his family from their house. Madame Pernelle could not believe Tartuffe guilty of such villainy, and she reminded her son that in this world virtue is often misjudged and persecuted. But when the sheriff's officer arrived with the notice for evacuation, even she believed that Tartuffe was a villain.

The crowning indignity came when Tartuffe took to the king the casket containing the state secrets. Orders were issued for Orgon's immediate arrest. But fortunately the king recognized Tartuffe as an impostor who had committed crimes in another city. Therefore, because of Orgon's loyal service in the army, the king annulled the deed Orgon had made covering his property and returned the casket unopened.

THE TASK

Type of work: Poem
Author: William Cowper (1731-1800)
First published: 1785

The first popular poetic success of William Cowper was *The Task,* which was also his first major venture in blank verse. For the fifty-four-year-old recluse the reception of his poem must have had a salutary effect, for he went on to become, according to his greatest champion, Robert Southey, "The most popular poet of his generation. . . ."

Cowper's place in literary history is often in dispute. Coming as he did exactly one hundred years after Dryden, he completed his best work in the year of Dr. Johnson's death. He neither aspired to become poet laureate nor did he wish to be the critical arbiter of his day. Yet in many ways he was the successor of both men. His blank verse is perhaps the best between Milton and Wordsworth, while his criticism expresses dissatisfaction with the extreme formalism of his age and anticipates in some measure the nineteenth-century revolt against neoclassicism. He is usually said to be a writer of this transition toward romanticism and realism.

His first work of any magnitude, *Olney Hymns* (1779), he undertook with his evangelical friend, the Reverend John Newton, while living at Olney with the Unwin family. "Oh! for a closer walk with God" is the most beautiful of his hymns, rivaling the best of both Newton and Wesley, and perhaps superior in poetical form and sentiment.

Although Cowper's writing of the then fashionable couplet was not successful, his early verse was at least simple. (He objected strenuously to Pope's influence, which resulted in the highly ornamented versification of that age.) Several long poems in this genre, published in 1782, serve as a kind of prelude to *The Task.* "Table Talk," written in rather abstract couplets, is a dialogue concerning the political, social, moral, and literary topics of the day. Here Cowper's dislike for the

artifice of the eighteenth century is quite clear, and he damns most of the literary cults with faint praise, at the same time urging a return to God and nature for inspiration. "The Progress of Error" outlines the follies of high life and living as these affect the social structure: in this work he suggests a return to Christianity for the solutions to vexing problems. "Truth" extends Cowper's religious beliefs almost as if his distant relationship, through his mother's line, with the cleric John Donne were making itself felt. His thesis here is that pride is truth's greatest foe, while humility will uplift mankind. In "Expostulation" he particularly decries anti-Semitism and urges England to remove this mote from the public eye. "Hope" and "Charity" celebrate God's nature (not the human nature of the Age of Reason) as the proper study, or at least reflection, of mankind. Satirically, he contrasts man's ways with God's. Another poem of this early group is "Retirement," an apology for his life as a recluse, his justification for giving up a life of action for the contemplative life of the poet.

By happy chance, in 1783 one of Cowper's intimate friends, Lady Austen, urged him to abandon the restrictive couplet form for blank verse. Cowper tells of this happening in the "Advertisement" of *The Task:*

A lady, fond of blank verse, demanded a poem of that kind from the author, and gave him the SOFA for a subject. He obeyed; and, having much leisure, connected another subject with it; and, pursuing the train of thought to which his situation and turn of mind led him, brought forth at length, instead of the trifle he at first intended, a serious affair—a Volume!

This volume of five thousand lines is divided into six parts: "The Sofa," "The

Time-Piece," "The Garden," "The Winter Evening," "The Winter Morning Walk," and "The Winter Walk at Noon." The poem's success was immediate, launching for the middle-aged poet a career and a reputation.

The sofa Cowper describes in the opening lines is the effete summation of man's efforts to indulge in slovenly comforts, a human failing the poet presents with evident good humor. He leaves the sofa, as he says, "for I have lov'd the rural walk . . ." with a good companion at his side. It is immediately apparent that the poet's work is to justify man's ways to God: "The task of new discov'ries falls on me," he suggests as he goes abroad. The next lines indicate that he will not countenance romantic illusions of the peasant's hard life or such poetic effusion of his age that tend to overlook the sordid, cruel, or ungodly. In comparing country and town he sets up a dichotomy which persists throughout the poem: God creates and man destroys.

In "The Time-Piece"—really time-serving or expediency—Cowper takes a long look at institutions, especially political. After a close examination of events now forgotten, he remarks in a memorable line, "England, with all thy faults. I love thee still." But the England he loves is the nation of an earlier, more virtuous, simpler time. He examines public figures, especially ministers, and finds them wanting. He suggests that God must be in every heart, Christ in every act. The river Ouse he describes as a symbol of immortality and ease. "The Garden" brings the poet to the eternal verities of nature and causes him to celebrate family life, domestic happiness. Within this poem is the parable of Cowper ("I was a stricken deer, that left the herd . . .") who, wounded by society, retired to a life of religious contemplation. From this vantage point he asks men to be humane and Christian, to eschew wars, to learn wisdom. "Who loves a garden loves a greenhouse too" is his plea to men to cultivate simple pleasures in a rural setting: "Health, leisure, means t' improve it, friendship, peace . . ." are what he thinks worth while. He concludes with a harsh renunciation of the city.

Continuing his statement of conflicting interests, in "The Winter Evening" Cowper compares the tragic news of the world with the simple man who delivers the post, unmoved. So should man live, he says, interested and sympathetic but apart; nothing is pleasanter than a winter night spent with good friends in good talk, and before a good fire. Again the town appears as the corrupter, its poison filtering down in the form of fashions spoiling the simple folk and altering the landscape. While there are consolations in poetry, especially Milton's, rural life brings more compensations and inspiration.

"The Winter Morning Walk," a bracing though aesthetic experience, restores the poet's good humor as he observes beast and man under winter's thrall. Cowper sees in winter a hope for immortality, for as the seeds and hibernating creatures wait out the ice, so man is bound in history. He next shames the great men of history as tyrants of oppression and great countries as slave holders:

'Tis liberty alone that gives the flow'r
Of fleeting life its lustre and perfume

. . . .

He is a freeman whom the truth makes
free, and all are slaves besides. . . .

This is the substance of his argument. He concludes with an apostrophe to godly graces and offers thanks to God.

Finally, in "The Winter Walk at Noon," William Cowper in sonorous polysyllables celebrates village bells as symbols of harmonious living—and offers also a backward glance at his own life. Here he describes the winter landscape in an ode to the cold, crisp season. In memorable passages he anticipates the spring. Finally, he justifies the life of the rambler, the contemplative life of the poet who sounds the note of God's truth, whether of castigation or exaltation.

THE TEMPEST

Type of work: Drama
Author: William Shakespeare (1564-1616)
Type of plot: Romantic fantasy
Time of plot: Fifteenth century
Locale: An island in the sea
First presented: 1611

Principal characters:
PROSPERO, the rightful Duke of Milan
MIRANDA, his daughter
FERDINAND, son of the King of Naples
ARIEL, a spirit, Prospero's servant
CALIBAN, Prospero's slave
ALONSO, King of Naples
SEBASTIAN, Alonso's brother
ANTONIO, Duke of Milan, Prospero's brother
GONZALO, a philosopher who saved the lives of Prospero and Miranda

Critique:

The Tempest, written toward the close of Shakespeare's career, is a work of fantasy and courtly romance. The story of a wise old magician, his beautiful, unworldly daughter, a gallant young prince, and a cruel, scheming brother, it contains all the elements of a fairy tale in which ancient wrongs are righted and true lovers live happily ever after. The play is also one of poetic atmosphere and allegory. Beginning with a storm and peril at sea, it ends on a note of serenity and joy. No other of Shakespeare's dramas holds so much of the author's mature reflection on life itself.

The Story:

When Alonso, King of Naples, was returning from the wedding of his daughter to a foreign prince, his ship was overtaken by a terrible storm. In his company were Duke Antonio of Milan and other gentlemen of the court. As the gale rose in fury, and it seemed certain the vessel would split and sink, the noble travelers were forced to abandon ship and trust to fortune in the open sea.

The tempest was no chance disturbance of wind and wave. It had been raised by a wise magician, Prospero, as the ship sailed close to an enchanted island on which he and his lovely daughter Miranda were the only human inhabitants. Theirs had been a sad and curious history. Prospero was

rightful Duke of Milan. Being devoted more to the study of philosophy and magic than to affairs of state, he had given much power to ambitious Antonio, his brother, who twelve years before had seized the dukedom with the aid of the crafty Neapolitan king. The conspirators set Prospero and his small daughter adrift in a boat, and they would have perished miserably had not Gonzalo, an honest counsellor, secretly stocked the frail craft with food, clothing, and the books Prospero valued most.

The helpless exiles drifted at last to an island which had been the refuge of Sycorax, an evil sorceress. There Prospero found Caliban, her son, a strange, misshapen creature of brute intelligence, able only to hew wood and draw water. Also obedient to Prospero's will were many good spirits of air and water, whom he had freed from torments to which the sorceress Sycorax had condemned them earlier. Ariel, a lively sprite, was chief of these.

Prospero, having used his magic arts to draw the ship bearing King Alonso and Duke Antonio close to his enchanted island, ordered Ariel to bring the whole party safely ashore, singly or in scattered groups. Ferdinand, King Alonso's son, was moved by Ariel's singing to follow the sprite to Prospero's rocky cell. Miranda, who remembered seeing no human face

3717

but her father's bearded one, at first sight fell deeply in love with the handsome young prince, and he with her. Prospero was pleased to see the young people so attracted to each other, but he concealed his pleasure, spoke harshly to them, and to test Ferdinand's mettle commanded him to perform menial tasks.

Meanwhile Alonso, Sebastian, Antonio, and Gonzalo wandered sadly along the beach, the king in despair because he believed his son drowned. Ariel, invisible in air, played solemn music, lulling to sleep all except Sebastian and Antonio. Drawing apart, they planned to kill the king and his counsellor and make Sebastian tyrant of Naples. Watchful Ariel awakened the sleepers before the plotters could act.

On another part of the island Caliban, carrying a load of wood, met Trinculo, the king's jester, and Stephano, the royal butler, both drunk. In rude sport they offered drink to Caliban. Tipsy, the loutish monster declared he would be their slave forever.

Like master, like servant. Just as Sebastian and Antonio had plotted to murder Alonso, so Caliban, Trinculo, and Stephano schemed to kill Prospero and become rulers of the island. Stephano was to be king, Miranda his consort; Trinculo and Caliban would be viceroys. Unseen, Ariel listened to their evil designs and reported the plan to Prospero.

Meanwhile Miranda had disobeyed her father to interrupt Ferdinand's task of rolling logs and, the hidden magician's commands forgotten, the two exchanged lovers' vows. Satisfied by the prince's declarations of devotion and constancy, Prospero left them to their own happy company. He, with Ariel, went to mock Alonso and his followers by showing them a banquet which vanished before the hungry castaways could taste the rich dishes. Then Ariel, disguised as a harpy, reproached them for their conspiracy against Prospero. Convinced that Ferdinand's death was punishment for his own crime, Alonso was moved to repentance

for his cruel deed.

Returning to his cave, Prospero released Ferdinand from his hard toil. While spirits dressed as Ceres, Iris, Juno, nymphs, and reapers entertained Miranda and the prince with a pastoral masque, Prospero suddenly remembered the schemes which had been devised by Caliban and the drunken servants. Told to punish the plotters, Ariel first tempted them with a display of kingly garments; then, urging on his fellow spirits in the shapes of fierce hunting dogs, he drove them howling with pain and rage through bogs and brier patches.

Convinced at last that the King of Naples and his false brother Antonio had repented the evil deed they had done him years before, Prospero commanded Ariel to bring them into the enchanted circle before the magician's cell. Ariel soon returned, luring by strange, beautiful music the king, Antonio, Sebastian, and Gonzalo. At first they were astonished to see Prospero in the appearance and dress of the wronged Duke of Milan. Prospero confirmed his identity, ordered Antonio to restore his dukedom, and severely warned Sebastian not to plot further against the king. Finally he took the repentant Alonso into the cave, where Ferdinand and Miranda sat playing chess. There was a joyful reunion between father and son at this unexpected meeting, and the king was completely captivated by the beauty and grace of Miranda. During this scene of reconciliation and rejoicing, Ariel appeared with the master and boatswain of the wrecked ship; they reported the vessel safe and ready to continue the voyage. The three grotesque conspirators were driven in by Ariel, and Prospero released them from their spell. Caliban was ordered to prepare food and set it before the guests. Prospero invited his brother and the King of Naples and his train to spend the night in his cave.

Before he left the island, Prospero dismissed Ariel from his service, leaving that sprite free to wander as he wished. Ariel promised calm seas and auspicious winds for the voyage back to Naples and Milan, where Prospero would journey to take possession of his lost dukedom and to witness the marriage of his daughter and Prince Ferdinand.

THE TEMPLE

Type of work: Poetry
Author: George Herbert (1593-1633)
First published: 1633

Sir Richard Herbert, an aristocrat of Norman descent, died when his son George was three years old. His ten children were reared by their mother, who is known to have been a wise, witty, generous, and religious woman. John Donne said: "Her house was a court in the conversation of the best." Too frail for the family profession of soldiering, George Herbert was early guided toward the priesthood by his mother. He was not, however, ordained until 1630. Nevertheless, Magdalen Herbert seemingly influenced the course of his life as much as Donne influenced his poetry. The first sonnets he wrote were addressed to her and in them he vowed to devote himself to religious poetry.

The Latin verses that Herbert wrote at Cambridge are full of classical allusion. In *The Temple,* which consists of the main body of his English verse, he eschewed all archaic references and poetic rhetoric as studiously as Donne himself. From Donne he also learned to transmute thought into feeling so that the intellectual concept becomes the emotional experience of the poem. Like Donne's, his rhythms are colloquial and his imagery, although not often as dramatic as that of Donne, is similarly practical, concrete, and arresting.

Herbert's range was narrower than Donne's; he wrote only religious poetry and it is not turbulent or exacerbated. One should beware of calling Herbert "simple"; or it can be said that he is simple rather than tortuous or complicated, and he does have a moral simplicity. His thought is varied, but evidences one central preoccupation. In his last letter to Nicholas Ferrar, to whom he sent the manuscript of *The Temple,* he described his poems as "A picture of the many spiritual conflicts that have passed betwixt God and my soul, before I could subject mine to the will of Jesus my master, in whose service I have now found perfect freedom." His anguish was lest he should not be a good and worthy servant to God, and not that he had lost faith or was threatened with damnation. His main temptation was worldly ambition.

At Cambridge, Herbert's main relaxation was music; he played the lute and wrote accompaniments to his Latin poems. This interest is evident in the vocabulary and also in the rhythm of many of his poems. Some, like his version of the Twenty-third Psalm, were written to be sung. In "Easter" the lute is an image for the body of Christ on the cross:

> The cross taught all wood to resound his name,
>   Who bore the same.
> His stretched sinews taught all strings, what key
> Is best to celebrate this most high day.

This equation, in the second stanza, of the crucifixion and the lute communicates the glory and pathos of Easter. The eager invocations to the poet's own heart and lute in the first stanza are found also in the third, which carries the full implications of the previous image and reinforces it:

> Consort both heart and lute, and twist a song
>   Pleasant and long:
> Or since all musick is but three parts vied,
>   And multiplied;
> O let thy blessed Spirit bear a part,
> And make up our defects with his sweet art.

Ambition for worldly acclaim is as recurrent in Herbert's poetry as music. In *The Temple* he often analyzes the delights of success, and the rejection of these delights is as meaningful poetically as it was in his life. In "The Pearl" Herbert speaks of his knowledge of

3720

learning, honor, and pleasure, and concludes each stanza with the refrain, "Yet I love thee." In the last stanza the value of such knowledge is justified and explained: it renders his love of God significant and reasoned. "Therefore not sealed but with open eyes/I flie to thee." This quality of quietness, certitude, and moral simplicity at the end of many of Herbert's poems gives them peculiar power. A controlled and intense late poem of rebellion contemplated, "The Collar," reflects at its close Herbert's complete humility and devotion in spite of all ambition and restlessness. The poem describes all that was lost:

> Sure there was wine,
> Before my sighs did drie it: there was corn,
> Before my tears did drown it.
> Is the yeare onely lost to me?
> Have I no bayes to crown it?
> No flowers, no garlands gay? all blasted?
> All wasted?
> Not so, my heart: but there is fruit,
> And thou hast hands.
> Recover all thy sight-bloom age
> On double pleasures: leave thy cold dispute
> Of what is fit, and not forsake thy cage. . . .

The poem is forceful, quick and argumentative; at the height of its fierceness the poet interrupts himself:

> Methought I heard one calling, *Childe:*
> And I reply'd, *My Lord*

Herbert's devotion to God is usually expressed with this humility and with a sensitive awareness of personal unworthiness. The ability to love is itself a gift of God. The search for a way of service is complemented by Herbert's intense consciousness of the sacrificial nature of Christ's life. In the sonnet "Redemption," the poet records a search for Christ first in heaven, then in earth's palaces, cities, and courts. Finally He was found in a rabble of thieves and murderers:

> . . . there I him espied,
> Who straight, *Your suit is granted,* said, and died.

The common meeting grounds of people and mundane activities and possessions are a great source of imagery to Herbert. His lyrics are probably his greatest poetry, and their structure, imagery, vocabulary, and rhythm all encompass one dominant idea, which, after the thought that inspired the lyric has been thoroughly explored, is finally, exactly, and directly communicated. These poems have total unity, and the impression of ease (in craftsmanship, not of feeling) is obtained by the logical and perceptive argument. Technically, this effect is most often achieved in the development of the images. In "Vertue," the clear and sensuous expression of the death of the day and a rose and of the spring which is composed of days and roses, "A box where sweets compacted lie," leads to an image of natural strength, where the virtuous soul "Like season'd timber; never gives"; and the penultimate line, following logically from the timber image, uses a most commonplace object, coal, as a continuation of it, and reverberates with the conviction of the immortality of the soul:

> But though the whole world turn to coal,
> Then chiefly lives.

In "Affliction (1)" Herbert's feeling of unworthiness is clearly related to his ill health. There is a carefully balanced argument: at first loving God was a joyous experience and Herbert uses the metaphor of a furnished house to express his contentment: "Thy glorious household stuff did me entwine." After the first rapture in which there was no room for fear, sorrow and sickness overcame him. This situation was partly improved when he turned from "the way that takes the town" and won "Academic praise." Then, lest he should "too happie be" in his unhappiness, God sent him further sickness. "Thus does thy power cross-bias me." A note of rebellion sounds at the seemingly contradictory demands of God, but the poem concludes:

Ah my deare God! though I am clean
forgot,
Let me not love me, if I love thee not.

Herbert's poetry is a constant commun-
ing with God, and it presents a great variety of moods. The firm tone of "Affliction (1)" can be contras·ed with the delicacy and gentleness of "Love (111)," in
which the alternating long and short
lines illus·ra·e the hesitancy of a soul
yearning for God's love and yet not able
to grasp it because of its own inadequa-
cies. The tenderness of love is implicit in
the vocabulary: "welcome," "sweetly,"
"smiling," and "quick-eyed love." Flat
monosyllables convey the soul's guilt:
"sinne," "slacke," "marr'd," and "shame."
But love made the eyes that call themselves unworthy, and love bore the blame
for the sin; love encourages the soul until
it can accept these things and the gift of
love itself:

You must sit down, sayes Love, and
taste my meat:
    So I did sit and eat.

Another poem in which the length of
line echoes the feeling is "Easter Wings."
The affected device of writing a poem in
the shape of "wings"—and it was in the
early editions printed vertically on the
page—is effective in this instance. The
first and last lines of both verses are
long and each verse has middle lines of
only two words each. This arrangement
conveys in reading the rise and fall of the
lark's song which is the image for the fall
of man and his resurrection in Christ.
"Easter Wings" is the best of the poems
in which Herbert uses some trick to illustrate his meaning. Other examples are
"The Altar" and "Paradise."

Donne's influence on Herbert's poetry
can thus be seen in the variety of his
lyrical forms, the directness of his language, and his less learned but equally
arresting imagery. In contrast to Donne's
poetry, Herbert's is essentially peaceful.
His poems never end on a note of desperation. His way of thinking and his
sensibility, by which he perceives the
nuances in an idea and the connections
between varied images and then fuses
these to communicate feeling, is essentially metaphysical. The quiet tone of
Herbert's poetry with its power of persuasion by gentle argument is entirely
original and something for which, as the
"Jordan" poem tell us, he consciously
strove and beautifully achieved:

As flames do work and winde, when
they ascend;
So did I weave myself into the sense.
But while I bustled, I might hear a
friend
Whisper, How wide is all this long pre-
tence!
There is in love a sweetness readie
penn'd:
Copie out only that, and save expense.

Herbert had great influence on other
seventeenth-century poets: Vaughan borrowed from him extensively, and Cra-
shaw called his own first volume The
Steps to the Temple. He was, together
with the other metaphysical poets, criticized in the eighteenth century. Pope,
although disliking his poetic method, in
his Essay on Man appears to have been
influenced by Herbert's philosophy. Cole-
ridge restored critical favor to Herbert,
and he profoundly influenced Gerard
Manley Hopkins. The delighted response
of twentieth-century poets to the metaphysical poets is well known.

THE TEMPLE BEAU

Type of work: Drama
Author: Henry Fielding (1707-1754)
Type of plot: Comedy of manners
Time of plot: Eighteenth century
Locale: London
First presented: 1730

Principal characters:
WILDING, a wild young man supposed to be a law student
SIR HARRY WILDING, his father
BELLARIA, a young woman supposed to marry Wilding
SIR AVARICE PEDANT, Bellaria's miserly uncle
PEDANT, Sir Avarice's son
LADY LUCY, Sir Avarice's coquettish second wife
LADY GRAVELY, Sir Avarice's prudish sister
VEROMIL, Bellaria's lover
VALENTINE, Veromil's rakish friend

Critique:

Because of his fame as a novelist, relatively few modern readers are aware of Fielding as a playwright. Certainly his abilities as a dramatist have been overshadowed by his fame as the author of such novels as *Tom Jones* and *Joseph Andrews*. He was also the last of the great eighteenth-century playwrights of the comedy of manners, and this particular drama is one of his best. Yet even his work in comedy cannot compare with the polish of his later farces, in which he found his best dramatic medium. Very apparent in *The Temple Beau* is Fielding's attitude that high life in the eighteenth century was of the dullest and that the people, both men and women, who made up the highest circles were entirely without shame. Though he pictured high life amusingly in his plays, in private life Fielding could see little that was comic in it.

The Story:

Sir Avarice Pedant, who had lost a great deal of money in the South Sea Bubble, decided to marry his son to Bellaria, his rich niece. An opportunity presented itself when her father, sending Bellaria to London in order to get her away from a fortuneless young man, asked her uncle to see that she married the son of Sir Harry Wilding. Sir Avarice, who saw a chance to make ten

thousand pounds, had no intention of furthering the request.

Young Pedant was too deep in his studies of philosophy, however, to wish to marry Bellaria. Only after Sir Avarice threatened to disinherit him did he agree to follow his father's wishes.

In the meantime Sir Harry Wilding came down to London to arrange the marriage between his son and Bellaria. He found that his son, young Wilding, was not a lawyer, but had been spending his time as a gay man about town. In fact, young Wilding had been flirting with Sir Avarice's young second wife, who was a coquette of the worst kind. She also was flirting with Valentine, one of the most licentious young men in town. For her coquetry, Lady Avarice was constantly badgered by her older sister-in-law, Lady Gravely, who seemed on the surface to be a prude. Actually, Lady Gravely was merely jealous of her reputation and, when opportunity presented itself, discreetly had affairs of her own.

Also in London was Veromil, a friend of Valentine's who had been cheated of his inheritance by his brother. Veromil, the young man with whom Bellaria was really in love, had come to London to solicit his friend's aid in marrying Bellaria before she could be married off to someone else. Valentine, not knowing that Bellaria was the object of Veromil's affections, agreed to help him. Valentine had just thrown over his own fiancée in hopes of winning Bellaria for himself.

While Valentine and Veromil went to see Bellaria, Sir Harry Wilding went to call on his son. In young Wilding's rooms, instead of books, he found packets of love letters and a crowd of tradesmen who were about to send him to debtors' prison. Sir Harry went about the rooms in a fury, breaking open closets and chests to learn what the young man had been doing. From there he went immediately to Sir Avarice's house in hopes of finding his son. He and Sir Avarice discovered Wilding in the garden embracing young and pretty Lady Avarice. Both men were furious, the father because he found his son a rakish fop and the husband because he suspected that he had been made a fool and a cuckold. Lady Avarice saved the day by telling a lie; she said that young Wilding had merely been importuning her to help him win Bellaria. The husband and father were satisfied with the answer.

Young Wilding still had to answer for the lack of law books and the presence of love letters and duns at his rooms; to do so he told his father that he had gone into the wrong apartment. The father, believing the lie, was immediately fearful lest he be arrested as a housebreaker. Through a servant young Wilding played upon his father's gullibility and persuaded Sir Harry to offer an annuity to the army officer whose rooms he had supposedly broken into. Sir Harry, rather than be hanged for what he thought was a felony, was glad to comply.

Meanwhile Valentine had discovered that the object of Veromil's affections was Bellaria and became so angry that he offered to kill his friend. Finally friendship overcame his passion, and he once more agreed to help Veromil win the girl. He was partly persuaded by the discovery that his own fiancée loved him so much that she would take him back, even after his rudeness in breaking their engagement.

Valentine persuaded Sir Avarice to give him seven thousand pounds for help in marrying off Bellaria. Sir Avarice thought Valentine had reference to the marriage of Bellaria to his son, but Valentine, leaving the agreement vague, planned to marry Bellaria to his friend Veromil and still have the money. He told Sir Avarice to bring the young people to young Pedant's apartment at the Inns of Court at a certain time. Young Pedant, not knowing of the scheme, had lent his apartment to young Wilding, who intended to pass it off to his father as his own. Hoping to embarrass them both into letting him alone thereafter, Wilding had also made assignations with both Lady Avarice and Lady Gravely for the same time. He too had fallen in love with Bellaria and hoped to marry her according to his father's wishes.

The two women, arriving first at the apartment, were utterly confused to find themselves dupes. They agreed to stick together, however, and try to save their reputations. A short time afterward Valentine, his fiancée, Veromil, and Bellaria, arrived. Within a few minutes the clergyman appeared to officiate at the marriage of Veromil and Bellaria. But at the last minute Valentine could not bear to see Bellaria married to Veromil. He tried to interrupt the ceremony, but his fiancée, with the help of Lady Avarice and Lady Gravely, held him back. Just then Sir Harry Wilding appeared with his son and young Wilding's servant. Veromil, drawing his sword, threatened them unless they let him pass with Bellaria. He was disarmed by young Wilding before any mischief was done. Veromil was beside himself until Bellaria told him that nothing could force her marriage to anyone else.

Just then Sir Avarice and his son arrived, expecting to find no one but a clergyman, Bellaria, and Valentine, for they had come to marry Bellaria, according to Valentine's agreement, to young Pedant. When Sir Harry Wilding demanded to know why all these people were in his son's apartment, young Wilding's ruse was disclosed. Sir Harry, furious at the trick played upon him, swore he would disinherit his son. Then young Wilding revealed that the annuity his father had signed was actually made out to him. Sir Harry left in a rage.

Veromil picked up a letter which Sir Harry had torn from the pocket of his son's servant. It was a letter from Veromil's brother and it related how Veromil had been cheated of his inheritance. The servant, after confessing to his part in the crime, promised to admit his perjury in court, thereby permitting the restoration of Veromil's rightful property. Sir Avarice was only too glad to give his blessing to the match between Bellaria and Veromil; under the circumstances he would not be forced to pay the seven thousand pounds to Valentine for arranging a marriage between Bellaria and his own son. Valentine, however, pointed out to the miser that the contract had only called for an arrangement of a marriage for Bellaria and did not name anyone as the husband in the affair, and so Sir Avarice, much to his dismay, was still liable for the payment. Young Pedant was only too happy to learn that he could continue his studies instead of taking up the burdens of a husband.

THE TEMPTATION OF SAINT ANTHONY

Type of work: Novel
Author: Gustave Flaubert (1821-1880)
Type of plot: Historical romance
Time of plot: The fourth century
Locale: Egypt
First published: 1874

Principal characters:
SAINT ANTHONY
HILARION, his disciple
THE DEVIL
THE QUEEN OF SHEBA
TERTULLIAN
MONTANUS
APOLLONIUS

Critique:

In this novel we find many indications of Flaubert's religious thought: not only the conclusions of his later life but also his attempts to find in the past some hope for his day; his realization of the attractions of the heresies of history; his knowledge of the struggle for faith. It is a novel which combines vast knowledge with a romantic imagination. We see also, even in translation, the results of Flaubert's careful and laborious method of writing.

The Story:

Having lived the life of a hermit for over thirty years, Anthony had come almost to the point of despair. He was extremely weary of life and with the world as he saw it from the limited point of view of his cell high in the mountains. At one time people had made pilgrimages to see him and be advised by him. These same people had furnished him with whatever money and clothing he needed. But everyone had stopped coming years before and Anthony had begun to fear that his life was worthless. He then began to long for the money, women, and goods of this world through which he might regain some sort of recognition and pleasure.

One night his solitude became too much for Anthony. He remembered his early life as a monk with its adventures and successes, and he thought of the things he might have done if he had not become a hermit. At last he decided that it was merely his own stubbornness that kept him alone in the mountains. Rather than allow himself to be guilty of such a sin, he prepared to depart. But he got no farther than the cleared area before his cell. Realizing that he had almost yielded to temptation, he threw himself upon the ground. Then, in order to regain his strength and courage, he read from the Acts of the Apostles and tried to think. His mind, however, kept coming back to worldly matters that still tempted him.

Anthony then began to review in his mind the things that were a credit to him in this world, the good works of his life. He praised himself for hardships he had suffered and for the things which he had denied himself. Again he began to feel sorry for himself; the desire for the money, goods, and women that had earlier been denied became too much for him. He fell into a trance.

While Anthony lay on the ground the Devil appeared, his wings spread like those of a giant bat to reveal beneath them the Seven Deadly Sins. Anthony awoke hungry and thirsty. Taking up a scrap of bread, which was all that he could find to eat in his cave, he threw it on the ground in anger. Then there appeared before him a table laden with all manner of meat and fruit from which he might satisfy himself. As he watched, the table grew and things which he had

3726

never seen before appeared on it. Anthony almost indulged himself, but he realized, in time, that this also was the work of the Devil. When he kicked the table, it disappeared.

Soon afterward Anthony found on the ground a silver cup which had a gold coin at the bottom of it. When he picked up the coin another appeared, and then another, until the cup filled and began to overflow. As Anthony watched, he began to dream of the power that could be his because of so much wealth. He soon saw himself as second in power only to the emperor and at the same time he thought of the revenge he could take on all his enemies. He even imagined himself as the emperor, taking precedence in Church affairs over the fathers of the Council of Nicaea. During this time, however, his bodily form had become more and more degraded until at last he saw himself as a beast. At this point he awoke.

Anthony flogged himself furiously for indulging in such sinful dreams, but as he was doing so he became aware of the arrival of a caravan. Soon the Queen of Sheba presented herself before him with many promises of love and luxury, the only condition being that Anthony had to give up his solitary life and live with her. Although she used all of her feminine charms to lure him away, Anthony firmly resisted the temptation she offered.

After she had disappeared, Anthony noticed that a child, whom he supposed had been left behind by the caravan, was standing in the door of his cell. The child was Hilarion, a former disciple. As Anthony watched, the child grew to the height of a man and began accusing the saint of leading a sinful life. He charged that Anthony's abnegation was merely a subtle form of corruption, that his solitude simply freed him from the outbreak of his lusts, and that he only thought he held all the wisdom of the world because he was too lazy to learn anything new. When Anthony defended himself by saying that the Scriptures held all the wisdom necessary for mankind,

Hilarion pointed out various minor contradictions in the New Testament. He then tempted Anthony by offering to lead him to a knowledge of the Unknown, the sources and secrets of life. At that point Anthony fell into another trance.

When he again became aware of his surroundings he found himself in a large congregation which included all the great heretics of history, each propounding his own theories of God and the universe. Some suggested that God was feminine. Others were devoutly following one aspect of Christianity, such as drinking the blood of Christ while completely ignoring all other aspects. Some were warming their naked bodies by an open fire in order to show the purity of Adam in paradise. Soon a man dressed as a Carthaginian monk leaped into the middle of the crowd, named them all for the impostors they were, and drove them away. Anthony, recognizing Tertullian, rushed forward to meet him but he found, instead, a woman seated alone on a bench.

The woman began to talk about Montanus, whom she believed to be the incarnation of the Holy Ghost. When Anthony suggested that he was dead, Montanus appeared before them in the form of a Negro. Then followed another succession of people, each propounding a different heresy, until a woman called Marcellina suggested that she could cause Christ himself to appear if she invoked him with the aid of a silver image. When she was put to the test, however, only a python appeared. It quickly wrapped itself around Anthony, and the people began to proclaim him the Christ. At that point Anthony swooned in horror.

When he awoke, he found himself in prison with the early Christians who had been thrown to the lions, and he found himself wishing that he too could give his life to God in such a way. Then Simon appeared before him with a woman who he claimed was the embodiment of all the infamous women of history, but who had now been cleansed through him. He offered Anthony the secret of his magic but disappeared at the men-tion of holy water. Apollonius and his disciple then appeared before Anthony and offered to describe the long road to salvation and immortality. Anthony was about to yield to their eloquence, but he drew back in horror when Apollonius began to describe his visions and his power of curing the sick and predicting the future. Because these proved the hardest of the temptations offered thus far, it was not until Anthony clung to the cross and prayed that Apollonius and his disciple disappeared.

But Apollonius' taunts that Anthony's fear of the gods kept him from knowing them awakened in him a desire to see them. Hilarion then caused to appear before him the gods of men in all ages. When Anthony laughed at them, Hilarion pointed out that there was an element of Truth in each one, which fact caused Anthony to grieve that these false religions could so easily lead man astray. He himself almost succumbed to the beauty of Olympus and the Greek gods, but he was able to repel their images by repeating the Apostles' Creed. Although Anthony had seen and learned enough of the false gods, the vision continued until he confessed to a desire to see the Devil. He hoped that his horror of Satan would rid him forever of such an evil. When the Devil appeared, Anthony was immediately filled with regret, but it was too late to recall his wish.

The Devil carried Anthony into space in order to show him that man and the world were not the center of the universe. that there were no limits to space and no purpose in its being. While the two engaged in a discussion on the nature of God, the Devil attempted to dispel all Anthony's beliefs in divine goodness, love, and infinite power. He tried to show that before understanding a God that had no limitations whatsoever, we must first understand the infinite. By spreading his wings to cover all space, he showed himself to be infinite and called upon Anthony to believe in him and curse God. Only by raising his eyes in a last desperate movement of hope was the saint able to rid himself of this evil.

When Anthony next awoke, the figures of Death and Lust confronted him, each begging him to come and escape the ugliness of this world. Refusing to yield, Anthony was no longer disturbed by what had seemed the disparateness of all things. As dawn began to break he no longer felt afraid; he enjoyed life once more. When the clouds rolled back, and he saw the face of Jesus Christ in the middle of the sun, he made the sign of the Cross and resumed his prayers.

THE TENANT OF WILDFELL HALL

Type of work: Novel
Author: Anne Brontë (1820-1849)
Type of plot: Domestic romance
Time of plot: Early nineteenth century
Locale: England
First published: 1848

Principal characters:
HELEN GRAHAM, in reality Helen Huntingdon, the tenant
FREDERICK LAWRENCE, her landlord
ARTHUR HUNTINGDON, her first husband
GILBERT MARKHAM, her second husband

Critique:

The story of *The Tenant of Wildfell Hall* is told in a series of letters written by Gilbert Markham to his brother-in law, Mr. Halford. This epistolary device, so common to fiction writers of the eighteenth and nineteenth centuries, gives a certain psychological value to Anne Brontë's study of marital difficulties. There is keen irony here, as well, for Arthur Huntingdon's male superiority and brutal dominance is offset in large measure by the inherent priggishness and short-sightedness of the woman whom he should never have married. Huntingdon, the attractive but drunken profligate, is generally identified with Bramwell Brontë, brother of the writer.

The Story:

Gilbert Markham, a young man of good family, was mildly interested when the strange tenant came to Wildfell Hall. Mrs. Graham, as her neighbors knew her, was young and beautiful, and her demand for seclusion stimulated the interest of the gentry of the neighborhood. She was particularly criticized for the way in which she was caring for her small son, Arthur, whom she would not allow out of her sight. Gilbert's mother declared the child would become the worst of milksops.

On his first visit to Wildfell Hall, Gilbert learned that Mrs. Graham was a landscape painter of considerable ability and that she was concealing her whereabouts from her former friends. Her air of secrecy aroused both his curiosity and sympathy.

Hoping to avoid the attentions of a local girl for whom he had at one time shown a preference, Gilbert spent much of his time in the company of the young widow. He accompanied her and young Arthur on long walks to find scenes for Mrs. Graham to paint. His friends, however, attempted to discourage his attentions to the tenant of Wildfell Hall. Rumor spread that she was having an affair with Frederick Lawrence, her landlord, and Lawrence assured Gilbert that he would fail in his attentions to Mrs. Graham. When he tried to tell her of his growing affection, Mrs. Graham herself insisted that Gilbert regard her simply as a friend.

After the vicar of the parish had accused the widow of improper conduct, Gilbert overheard Mrs. Graham deep in a mysterious discussion with her landlord. Suspecting that the rumors about them were true, Gilbert resolved to have no more to do with her. On his next encounter with Lawrence, Gilbert struck his rival and wounded him severely.

A short time later Gilbert met Mrs. Graham and she gave him a copy of her journal to read. The journal, beginning in 1821, told the story of Helen Graham's life for the past six years. It opened with an account of her meeting with Arthur Huntingdon, whom she loved in spite of her aunt's claim that the young man was wild and wayward. Her aunt, with whom she made her home, had taken her away so that she might see no more of the objectionable Huntingdon. But by a miscalculation

3729

her unwelcome suitor was invited to their summer home for partridge hunting. That autumn the two were married, and shortly afterward the young wife discovered that her husband's true character was exactly that which her aunt had described. He was a drunkard, a man incapable of high principle or moral responsibility. She began to be contemptuous of him, and he responded by growing indifferent to her. More and more frequently he began to absent himself from his home, and during his absences she had no way of knowing where he was.

Several years passed. When Helen bore a child, a boy, she hoped that her husband's conduct would improve. But Huntingdon absented himself again and again. Each time she welcomed him back because she still loved him.

When Helen's father died, she was greatly disturbed by her husband's callous attitude toward her grief. Then a reconciliation took place, and for a time Huntingdon seemed to reform. One day, however, she discovered her husband making love to Lady Lowborough, a visitor in their house. When she demanded a separation for herself and her child, Huntingdon refused. To keep the affair from becoming known to others, Helen decided at last to stay on with her husband.

Lord Lowborough also learned of the affair Helen's husband was having with Lady Lowborough. Indifferent to public scandal, Huntingdon kept up his wild hunting parties and filled his house with drunken, riotous men. Helen began to make her plans for escape. All that time she had to fight off a would-be lover of her own, a Mr. Hargrave, who was determined to win her. She hoped to find refuge in a place where her husband could not find her and legally take her child from her. Her pride kept her from appealing to her brother or her uncle and aunt.

Helen's husband learned of her plan when he read her journal. From that time on he had her closely watched. He refused to let her have any money in her possession.

Her position became unendurable, however, when Huntingdon brought his mistress into the house on the pretext of providing a governess for young Arthur. Helen determined to make her escape without money or resources. The diary ended with the arrival of Helen at Wildfell Hall.

Reading the journal, Gilbert realized that Frederick Lawrence was the brother mentioned several times in the diary. He at once sought out Helen to renew his suit, but in spite of his entreaties she insisted that they should not see each other again. Gilbert then went to see her brother, whom he had treated so roughly at their last meeting. The reconciliation between the two men was prompt and sincere.

A short time later the whole community learned the secret of the tenant of Wildfell Hall. Huntingdon had a fall from his horse and his wife, learning of his serious condition, went to his house at Grassdale to look after him. Frederick Lawrence told Gilbert that Huntingdon had received her ungraciously, but that she was determined to stay with him out of a sense of duty.

In spite of her care, however, Huntingdon secured a bottle of wine and drank it in defiance of his doctor's orders. His indiscretion brought on a relapse which ended in his death.

Several months later Gilbert heard that Helen's uncle had died and that she had gone to live with her aunt at Staningley. More than a year passed before he dared to go to her. He found her at Staningley, and the welcome of young Arthur was as joyous as Helen's was warm and gracious. She and Gilbert were married a short time later.

TENDER IS THE NIGHT

Type of work: Novel
Author: F. Scott Fitzgerald (1896-1940)
Type of plot: Social criticism
Time of plot: The 1920's
Locale: Europe
First published: 1934

Principal characters:
DICK DIVER, a psychologist
NICOLE, his wife
ROSEMARY HOYT, an actress
TOMMY BARBAN, a professional soldier

Critique:

Fitzgerald's reputation rests mostly on *The Great Gatsby,* but in many ways *Tender is the Night* is a more penetrating work. The characters, expatriate Americans wandering from one fashionable place to another in Europe, seem to bear superficially a great resemblance to a common type written about in literature of the twenties, but there is a difference in treatment and significance. Dick and Nicole are well portrayed, Nicole being an especially sympathetic creation. The result is an artistic portrayal of believable people whose experiences add up to a keen analysis of the spiritual disintegration and bankruptcy of an expatriate generation.

The Story:

Rosemary Hoyt was just eighteen, dewy fresh and giving promise of beautiful maturity. In spite of her youth, she was already a famous actress, and her movie, *Daddy's Girl,* was all the rage. She had come to the south of France with her mother for a rest. Rosemary needed relaxation, for she had been very ill after diving repeatedly into a Venetian canal during the shooting of her picture.

At the beach she met Dick Diver, and suddenly she realized that she was in love. After she became well acquainted with the Divers, she liked Diver's wife Nicole, too. Nicole was strikingly beautiful and her two children complemented her nicely. Rosemary's mother also approved of Dick. When Rosemary attended one of the Divers' famous parties, she told Dick outright that she loved him, but he made light of her declaration.

During the party a Mrs. McKisco saw Nicole behaving hysterically in the bathroom, and on the way home she tried to tell about it. Tommy Barban, a war hero, made her keep silence. Resenting Tommy's interference, Mr. McKisco provoked a quarrel with him. The quarrel ended in a duel in which several shots were exchanged but no one was hurt. Rosemary was greatly moved by the occurrence.

Rosemary traveled to Paris with the Divers and went on a round of parties and tours with them. Often she made advances to Dick. He refused, apathetically, until one day a young college boy told of an escapade in which Rosemary had been involved, and then Dick began to desire the young girl. Although their brief love affair was confined to furtive kisses in hallways, Nicole became suspicious.

Abe North, a brawling composer, offended two Negroes and involved a third. While Dick was in Rosemary's hotel room, Abe brought one of the Negroes to ask Dick's help in straightening up the mess. When Dick took Abe to his own room, the Negro stayed in the corridor. The two other Negroes killed him and laid the body on Rosemary's bed. When the body was found, Dick carried it into the hall and took Rosemary's spread into his bathtub to wash it out. Seeing the bloody spread, Nicole broke down and in an attack of hysteria accused Dick of many infidelities. Her breakdown was like the one Mrs. McKisco had previously seen in the bathroom at the party.

Some years before Dick had been doing research in advanced psychology in Zurich. One day in the clinic he had met a pathetic patient, beautiful young Nicole Warren. Attracted to her professionally at first, he later learned the cause of her long residence in the clinic.

Nicole came from a wealthy Chicago family. When she was eleven her mother died, and her father became very close to her. After an incestuous relationship with him, she suffered a breakdown. Her father, too cowardly to kill himself as he had planned, had put her in the clinic at Zurich. For many reasons Dick became Nicole's tower of strength; with him she was almost normal. Finally, motivated by pity and love, Dick married her. For a time he was able to keep her from periodic schizophrenic attacks and the marriage seemed to be a success, aided by the fact that Nicole's family was rich, so rich that Nicole's older sister was able to buy Dick a partnership in the clinic where Dick had first met Nicole.

For some time after the episode involving Rosemary, Nicole was quite calm, but too withdrawn. Then a neurotic woman wrote her a letter accusing Dick of misdeeds with his women patients. The letter was the working of a diseased mind, but Nicole believed what the writer said and had another relapse. She left her family at a country fair and became hysterical while riding on the ferris wheel.

At one time Dick had shown great promise as a writer and as a psychologist. His books had become standard and among his colleagues he was accounted a genius. It seemed, however, that after Nicole's hysterical fit on the ferris wheel he could do little more real work. For one thing, Nicole was growing wealthier all the time; her husband did not have to work. At thirty-eight, he was still a handsome and engaging man, but he began to drink heavily.

On several occasions Nicole was shamed by her husband's drunken behavior. She did her best to make him stop, and in so doing she began to gain a little moral strength of her own. For the first time since the long stay at the clinic she gradually came to have an independent life outside of Dick's influence.

Dissatisfied with the life he was leading, Dick decided to go away by himself for a while. He ran into Tommy Barban, still a reckless, strong, professional soldier. Tommy had just had a romantic escape from Russia. While still absent from his wife, Dick received word that his father had died.

Going back to America was for him a nostalgic experience. His father had been a gentle clergyman, living a narrow life; but his life had had roots, and he was buried among his ancestors. Dick had been away so long, had lived for so many years a footless, unfettered life, that he almost determined to remain in America.

On the way back to meet his family Dick stopped in Naples. In his hotel he met Rosemary again. She was making another picture, but she managed to find time to see him. Not so innocent now, she proved an easy conquest. Dick also met Nicole's older sister in Naples.

One night Dick drank far too much and became embroiled with a chiseling taxi driver. When he refused to pay an exorbitant fee, a fight broke out and Dick was arrested. The police captain unfairly upheld the taxi driver. Blind with rage, Dick struck a policeman and in return was severely beaten by the Fascist carabinieri. Thinking his eye had been gouged out, Dick got word to Nicole's sister, who brought all her influence to bear upon the consul to have her brother-in-law released.

Back in Zurich, Dick was busy for a time at the clinic. On a professional visit to Lausanne, he learned to his surprise that Nicole's father was there, very near death. When the dying man expressed a wish to see his daughter again, Dick sent for Nicole. Strangely enough, the weakened father still could not face his daughter. In a despairing frenzy he escaped from the hospital and disappeared.

Dick continued to go downhill. He always drank too much. A patient, objecting to the liquor on his breath, created a scene. At last Dick was forced to surrender his partnership in the clinic.

With no job, Dick wandered about restlessly. He and his wife, he realized, had less and less in common. At last, after Dick had disgraced his family many times in drunken scenes, Nicole began to welcome the attentions of Tommy Barban. She confidently looked forward to an independent life with Tommy. She no longer needed Dick.

After the divorce Dick moved to America. Nicole heard of him occasionally. He moved several times to successively smaller towns, an unsuccessful general practitioner.

TESS OF THE D'URBERVILLES

Type of work: Novel
Author: Thomas Hardy (1840-1928)
Type of plot: Philosophical realism
Time of plot: Late nineteenth century
Locale: England
First published: 1891

Principal characters:
JACK DURBEYFIELD, a poor worker
TESS, his daughter
ALEC D'URBERVILLE, her betrayer
ANGEL CLARE, her husband

Critique:

Thomas Hardy's *Tess of the d'Urbervilles* has become a modern classic. In it Hardy concerned himself with the question of fate and its influence upon the lives of most people. If Tess's father had not learned that he was a d'Urberville, if Angel had found the letter Tess slipped under the door, her life would have been much different. But fate ruled that these things were to happen, and so determined the course of Tess's life. Hardy called Tess a pure girl, and so she was. He believed that she was not responsible for her actions, and he forces us to agree with him.

The Story:

It was a proud day when Jack Durbeyfield learned that he was descended from the famous d'Urberville family. Durbeyfield had never done more work than was necessary to keep his family supplied with meager food and himself with beer, but from that day on he ceased doing even that small amount of work. His wife joined him in thinking that such a high family should live better with less effort, and she persuaded their oldest daughter, Tess, to visit the Stoke-d'Urbervilles, a wealthy family who had assumed the d'Urberville name because no one else claimed it. It was her mother's hope that Tess would make a good impression on the rich d'Urbervilles and perhaps a good marriage with one of the sons.

When Tess met her supposed relatives, however, she found only a blind mother and a dapper son who made Tess un-comfortable by his improper remarks to her. The son, Alec, tricked the innocent young Tess into working as a poultry maid, not letting her know that his mother was unaware of Tess's identity. After a short time Tess decided to look for work elsewhere to support her parents and her numerous brothers and sisters. She was innocent, but she knew that Alec meant her no good. Alec, more clever than she, at last managed to get her alone and then possessed her.

When Tess returned to her home and told her mother of her terrible experience, her mother's only worry was that Alec was not going to marry Tess. The poor girl worked in the fields, facing the slander of her associates bravely. Her trouble was made worse by the fact that Alec followed her from place to place, trying to possess her again. By going about to different farms during the harvest season, Tess managed to elude Alec long enough to give birth to her baby without his knowledge. The baby did not live long, however, and a few months after its death, Tess went to a dairy farm far to the south to be dairymaid.

At the dairy farm Tess was liked and well treated. Also at the farm was Angel Clare, a pastor's son who had rejected the ministry to study farming. It was his wish to own a farm some day, and he was working on different kinds of farms, so that he could learn something of the many kinds of work required of a general farmer. Although all the dairymaids were attracted to Angel, Tess interested him the most. He thought her a beautiful and innocent young maiden, as she was, for it was her innocence which had caused her trouble with Alec.

Tess felt that she was wicked, however, and rejected the attentions Angel paid to her. She urged him to turn to one of the other girls for companionship. It was unthinkable that the son of a minister would marry a dairymaid, but Angel did not care much about family tradition. In spite of her pleas, he continued to pay court to Tess. At last, against the wishes of his parents, Angel asked Tess to be his wife. Not only did he love her, but also he realized that a farm girl would be a help to him on his own land. Although Tess was in love with Angel by this time, the memory of her night with Alec caused her to refuse Angel again and again. At last his insistence, coupled with the written pleas of her parents to marry someone who could help the family financially, won her over, and she agreed to marry him.

On the night before the wedding, which Tess had postponed many times because she felt unworthy, she wrote Angel a letter, telling everything about herself and Alec. She slipped the letter under his door, sure that when he read it he would renounce her forever. But in the morning Angel acted as tenderly as before and Tess loved him more than ever for his forgiving nature. When she realized that Angel had not found the letter, she attempted to tell him about her past. Angel only teased her about wanting to confess, thinking that such a pure girl could have no black sins in her history. They were married without Angel's learning about Alec and her dead baby.

On their wedding night Angel told Tess about an evening of debauchery in his own past. Tess forgave him and then told about her affair with Alec, thinking that he would forgive her as she had him. But such was not the case. Angel was at first stunned, and then so hurt he could not even speak to Tess. Finally he told her that she was not the woman he loved, the one he had married, but a stranger with whom he could not live, at least for the present. He took her to her home and left her there. Then he went to his home and on to Brazil, where he planned to buy a farm. At first neither Tess nor Angel told their parents the reason for their separation. When Tess finally told her mother, that ignorant woman blamed Tess for losing her husband by confessing something he need never have known.

Angel had left Tess some money and some jewels which had been given to him by his godmother. The jewels Tess put in a bank; the money she spent on her parents. When it was gone, her family went hungry once more, for her father still thought himself too high-born to work for a living. Tess again went from farm to farm, doing hard labor in the fields in order to get enough food to keep herself and her family alive.

While she was working in the fields, she met Alec again. He had met Angel's minister father and, repenting his evil ways, had become an itinerant preacher. The sight of Tess, for whom he had always lusted, caused a lapse in his new religious fervor, and he began to pursue her once more. Frightened, Tess wrote to Angel, sending the letter to his parents to forward to him. She told Angel that she loved him and needed him, that an enemy was pursuing her. She begged him to forgive her and to return to her.

The letter took several months to reach Angel. Meanwhile Alec was so kind to Tess and so generous to her family that she began to relent in her feelings toward him. At last, when she did not receive an answer from Angel, she wrote him a note saying that he was cruel not to forgive her and that now she would not forgive his treatment of her. Then she went to Alec again, living with him as his wife.

It was thus that Angel found her. He had come to tell her that he had forgiven her and that he still loved her. But when he found her with Alec, he turned away, more hurt than before.

Tess, too, was bitterly unhappy. She now hated Alec because once again he had been the cause of her husband's repudiation of her. Feeling that she could find happiness only if Alec were dead, she stabbed him as he slept. Then she ran out of the house and followed Angel, who was aimlessly walking down a road leading out of the town. When they met and Tess told him what she had done, Angel forgave her everything, even the murder of Alec, and they went on together. They were happy with one another for a few days, even though Angel knew that the authorities would soon find Tess.

When the officers finally found them, Tess was asleep. Angel asked the officers to wait until she awoke. As soon as she opened her eyes, Tess saw the strangers and knew that they had come for her and that she would be hanged, but she was not unhappy. She had had a few days with the husband she truly loved, and now she was ready for her punishment. She stood up bravely and faced her captors. She was not afraid.

THADDEUS OF WARSAW

Type of work: Novel
Author: Jane Porter (1776-1850)
Type of plot: Historical romance
Time of plot: Late eighteenth century
Locale: Poland and England
First published: 1803

Principal characters:
THADDEUS SOBIESKI, a patriotic young Pole
COUNT SOBIESKI, his grandfather
GENERAL KOSCIUSKO, a Polish leader
PEMBROKE SOMERSET, Thaddeus' English friend
GENERAL BUTZOU, another Polish patriot
MARY BEAUFORT, Somerset's cousin, whom Thaddeus married

Critique:

This novel combines factual history with considerable imaginative invention. The Englishman of the early nineteenth century was already familiar with the spectacle of the political refugee. Pity for the plight of the exile who must adapt himself to a different land and strange customs is one of the chief themes of Miss Porter's novel.

The Story:

Thaddeus Sobieski was educated in the palace of Count Sobieski, his grandfather, an enlightened nobleman of Warsaw. On the evening of Thaddeus' eighteenth birthday, his mother gave him a letter in which she revealed that his father. an Englishman, had deserted his mother in Italy before Thaddeus was born. The man's name was Sackville. Thaddeus' mother had returned to Poland and her father maintained the fiction that she had married and had been widowed within two months. None knew of the deception save the king. At the end of the letter Thaddeus' mother begged him to be honorable always for the sake of his grandfather and the illustrious Sobieski name.

In 1792 the Poles began a war of independence against Russia. Before Thaddeus and his grandfather set off to the war, Thaddeus heard the story of how Count Sobieski and General Butzou had long ago saved the life of King Stanislaus of Poland. Both the knowledge of his own past and the story of his grandfather's bravery helped to shape Thaddeus' character into heroic mold.

Later, Thaddeus met General Kosciusko and was filled with hope for Poland. In one of the skirmishes with the enemy Thaddeus displayed both bravery and intelligence. With dismay he learned that the Poles were immediately to retreat, for they were outnumbered by the Russians. His grandfather was injured during the retreat but refused to let Thaddeus attend him. He ordered him to stay with the troops. . .

Thaddeus took a prisoner, an Englishman named Pembroke Somerset, who had joined the Russian army for the sake of adventure. Somerset and Thaddeus became close friends. Thaddeus gained Somerset's freedom, and when Thaddeus returned to his mother's home Somerset accompanied him.

The tremendous patriotism and the sense of honor existing in Thaddeus now transferred themselves to Somerset, who in his letters home wrote of his great admiration of the Poles. Somerset soon returned home to England, at the insistence of his family.

Count Sobieski had greater cares, for Poland was falling under the Russian attack. When the Germans broke their treaties of assistance, the king decided that organized resistance was useless. He surrendered for his people. In Warsaw the sons of the nobles vowed eternal resistance to the enemy, and Thaddeus was among those taking the sacred oath.

Poland in November, 1793, was shorn of her best lands and her nobles were humbled. In the meantime Thaddeus led troops into the south, where resistance continued. He managed to join with General Kosciusko and so brought a measure of hope to the Poles.

Thaddeus managed to free his grandfather from a Russian prison. Later Thaddeus led the other nobles in the surrender of all his personal property for the continuation of the war. In a battle fought soon afterward, Thaddeus' grandfather was killed. With his last breath he made Thaddeus promise never to take any name other than Sobieski.

Devastation spread over Poland as the fighting continued. In one of the last campaigns of the war Thaddeus found a moment to talk to his mother, who said she would not survive the destruction of Poland. She made him promise to go to England if Poland should fall. The Sobieski palace was burned to the ground. Thaddeus, along with General Butzou, watched as the towers of Villanow crumbled. Inside lay the dead body of his mother, who had died during the battle. Taking his farewell of the defeated king, Thaddeus left Poland forever.

True to his promise, he went to England. In London he took lodgings under the name of Mr. Constantine and then became ill with a slow and disastrous fever which threatened his life. His landlady, Mrs. Robson, had become quite attached to him because of his gentle manners and deep courtesy and she watched over him during his illness. When he recovered he sold his jewelry in order to pay his bills. He tried also to sell some original drawings but was insulted by the merchant to whom he showed them, and he refused to do business with the man.

Mrs. Robson's sick grandson died in spite of the care that Thaddeus gave the child. Dr. Vincent, suspecting that Thaddeus had a large fortune, sent a huge bill for his services. Thaddeus promised to raise the money for the medicine and for the burial, but he had not a shilling in his pocket. He was forced to sell more of his possessions.

Thaddeus tried to contact Somerset, but without success. About the same time he found General Butzou in the greatest distress of poverty and took him to his lodgings with Mrs. Robson. Thaddeus now began to earn enough for the expenses of himself and the penniless general by means of his drawings. Once he saw Pembroke Somerset on the street, but Somerset passed without noticing him.

One day Thaddeus saved a woman, Lady Tinemouth, from ruffians in Hyde Park. Out of gratitude, Lady Tinemouth took Thaddeus in hand and found employment for him as a tutor in German. At the same time her friend, Lady Sara Ross, attempted to involve him in a love affair, but she found him indifferent.

The old general was going mad. The doctor whom Thaddeus called in was Dr. Cavendish, a good man who would not take the payment when he heard the cause of the old general's illness.

Thaddeus went to the home of Lady Dundas, where he was to serve as a tutor. Lady Dundas proved to be a bore and her daughters ill-favored and ill-mannered. Attracted by Thaddeus' noble appearance, the two girls, Diana and Euphemia, determined to study hard. Euphemia Dundas and Lady Sara Ross pursued him.

A visitor in the Dundas household was Miss Mary Beaufort, a gentle girl who saw at once the noble nature of Thaddeus and tried to ease the slights and rebuffs he received from the rich and vulgar Lady Dundas on the one hand and the embarrassing attentions of Euphemia Dundas on the other. In the meantime Mary Beaufort occupied herself with trying to discover the true name of Mr. Constantine.

One day some of Lady Tinemouth's friends were discussing the tutor. One laughed at Euphemia for her interest in a man no better than a mere schoolmaster. But Mary Beaufort defended him. Lady Tinemouth remained silent, for to her alone Thaddeus had confessed his true identity. Shortly afterward gossip caused Lady Tinemouth to receive unpleasant notice from her relatives that her attentions to Mr. Constantine were intolerable. Lady Tinemouth planned to leave London. In her letter announcing her departure she told Thaddeus that Mary Beaufort was deeply interested in him.

When old General Butzou died, Thaddeus realized that one of Poland's bravest sons was dead. In order to meet the death expenses, Thaddeus, who still had not received any payment from Lady Dundas, was forced to sell his last tokens. The same pawnbroker took them, but the amount gained was not enough to pay his debts and Thaddeus was put in Newgate prison.

Hearing of his misfortune, Mary Beaufort searched out his apartment and learned from Mrs. Robson the story of his imprisonment. Mary's plan to aid Thaddeus was interrupted by the arrival of Pembroke Somerset, her cousin, and by the betrayal of Euphemia. Euphemia declared that Thaddeus had made passionate love to her. Euphemia's mother screamed for revenge and announced her intention of sending her daughter to Scotland.

Somerset, not knowing that Mr. Constantine was really his old friend Thaddeus, paid the debt of the tutor at Mary's request, but he did not so much as look at Thaddeus.

When Thaddeus returned to his room, he discovered a note in which Lady Dundas called him a rogue. Before he could demand an explanation for the note, the whole group had left London. He then took a stage to the place where Lady Tinemouth had found refuge.

At Lady Tinemouth's home Thaddeus and Somerset met again and Somerset revealed that he actually had not seen Thaddeus on the occasion of their meeting on a London street.

This meeting also brought about a reunion between Thaddeus and Mary Beaufort. A more surprising revelation was the discovery that Somerset's father was the same Sackville who was the father of Thaddeus. To right the old wrong, Thaddeus was given a large inheritance from the Somerset estate. With this fortune he married Mary Beaufort and spent the rest of his days happily with his wife and the half-brother whom he had found after many strange adventures.

THE THEBAIS

Type of work: Poem
Author: Publius Papinius Statius (c. 45-c. 96)
Time: Remote antiquity
Locale: Argos, Nemea, Thebes
First transcribed: Last quarter of first century

Principal characters:
OEDIPUS, deposed King of Thebes
JOCASTA, his wife and mother
ETEOCLES,
POLYNICES,
ANTIGONE, and
ISMENE, their children
CREON, Jocasta's brother
MENOECEUS, his son
ADRASTUS, King of Argos
ARGIA, his daughter, Polynices' wife
TYDEUS,
CAPANEUS,
AMPHIARAUS,
HIPPOMEDON, and
PARTHENOPAEUS, Argive heroes of the march against Thebes
HYPSIPYLE, the former Queen of Lemnos, now a slave

The *Thebais* of Statius, a retelling in epic form of the *Seven Against Thebes*, by Aeschylus, draws extensively on the general body of material dealing with the ill-fated family of Oedipus. Statius' version of the tale of the contending brothers, Eteocles and Polynices, extends to twelve books. Written over a period of twelve years, this narrative of bloody and tragic conflict is a product of the so-called Silver Age of Latin literature. Statius' epic, produced during the reign of the Emperor Domitian, represents a falling off from a great work like Vergil's *Aeneid*, the model for this lesser and more melodramatic poem.

Statius himself was a native of Naples, and legend tells us that he used to visit Vergil's tomb there. His father, a rhetorician, held up to his son for admiration the great works of Latin poetry in the time of Augustus and encouraged him to make his career by continuing the tradition of measured utterance in which he had been reared.

Students of Latin poetry find, however, that a considerable gap separates Statius from the Golden Age writers whom he desired to imitate. In this epic the machinery of the gods who intervene and often direct the course of fratricidal strife are dead gods indeed, pale figures beside the lusty deities who battle and love in Homer's great works or in Vergil's national epic. The narrative line of the poem is gratifyingly simple, and the inclusive proportion is well-considered; but these matters often drop from sight, hidden beneath the deliberate rhetorical effect of the parts. Angry lions, ramping bulls, ships fighting their way through a storm to a safe harbor, and rivers in full spate are used again and again as figurative devices, sometimes with such facility and in such detail that the object of comparison is lost sight of. Some of the moralizing in the *Thebais* is telling and sincere, but much of it is quite as perfunctory as the figures of speech. The most striking defect in the *Thebais* is the taste for blood: both the battlefields around Thebes and the verses that describe them are gorily presented. The aesthetics of slaughter in the contemporary Roman arena, difficult for the modern mind to grasp, are amply illustrated in

3740

the epic, in which mingle a welter of carnage and lamentation for the dead.

The story, following the general line of the Greek play, pits Eteocles and Polynices, the two sons of Oedipus and Jocasta, against each other when, after the fall of Oedipus, it was arranged that the sons would alternate as rulers. The plan was doomed to failure because Oedipus had called down the wrath of the Furies upon his unnatural sons. The first year of the kingship falling to Eteocles, Polynices went into temporary exile in Argos. There he quarreled with Tydeus, a great warrior and hero, but King Adrastus, obeying the prompting of an oracle, settled the dispute by betrothing one of his daughters to each of the young men.

At the end of a year, however, Eteocles refused to step aside in favor of Polynices, according to the agreement between them. Argia, the wife of Polynices, then persuaded her father to aid the prince in asserting his right to the Theban throne. Tydeus was first dispatched as an envoy to the city. Jealous of the fame of the young warrior, Eteocles set an ambush for Tydeus, who killed all his attackers except one. The survivor, Maeon, returned to tell Eteocles what had happened and then killed himself.

The march against Thebes began. At Nemea the army was halted by a great drought, but the Argives were saved from their distress when Hypsipyle, the one-time Queen of Lemnos before the great massacre there, and now a slave entrusted with the care of King Lycurgus' small son, guided them to a stream that still flowed. When a snake bit her infant charge, the Argives protected her from the king's anger and in observance of the boy's funeral instituted the Nemean games. On the arrival of the army before the walls of Thebes, Jocasta and her daughters appeared to plead with Polynices in an effort to prevent bloodshed. The battle was joined, however, when two tigers attacked the driver of Amphiaraus' chariot; Amphiaraus himself dis-

appeared into the underworld when the earth suddenly opened and swallowed him alive. In an engagement with the Thebans, Tydeus fell mortally wounded; he died while gnawing the skull of his foeman. The Argive heroes were killed one by one, fighting valiantly but powerless against the might of the gods. Capaneus, who had rested from battle to challenge the justice of the gods, was struck by one of Jove's own thunderbolts as he attempted to scale the wall of the city. In a hand to hand combat, Eteocles and Polynices killed each other. Only King Adrastus survived. The war ended with the intervention of King Theseus of Athens, who had been moved by the prayers of the Argive women. Creon died at the hands of King Theseus; his son, Menoeceus, had previously listened to the words of the oracle and had thrown himself from the city wall.

The materials used in the *Thebais* served their purpose admirably in Greek tragedy; their use by Statius in his epic suggests, however, that the convention which barred slaughter from the stage was a wise one. But in spite of its obvious defects and the author's exploitation of melodrama for its own sake, Statius' work is not without its power to move, especially when the unhappy mother of warring sons pleads with them to end their strife, when Oedipus laments his banishment from the city, or when Antigone attends the body of Polynices after it has been abandoned in death. In moments like these tenderness and psychological insight are never sacrificed to sentiment or contrived excitement.

Statius was a popular poet in his own day and throughout the medieval period. Chaucer, who ranked him with Homer and Vergil, paid him the compliment of imitation in *Troilus and Criseyde*. Dante, who apparently thought of the Roman writer as a Christian, told in his *Purgatorio* of his encounter with the author of the *Thebais*.

THERE ARE CRIMES AND CRIMES

Type of work: Drama
Author: August Strindberg (1849-1912)
Type of plot: Symbolic realism
Time of plot: Late nineteenth century
Locale: Paris
First presented: 1899

Principal characters:

MAURICE, a young Parisian playwright
JEANNE, his mistress
MARION, their five-year-old daughter
ADOLPHE, a young Parisian painter
HENRIETTE, his mistress, a sculptress
EMILE, Jeanne's brother, a workman
MADAME CATHERINE, the proprietress of the crêmerie
THE ABBÉ

Critique:

There Are Crimes and Crimes was written soon after August Strindberg himself had passed through a period of profound depression and was entering into the final phase of his prolific career. Thus the play is a combination of the realism that he had mastered so well in his earlier works and the symbolism that was to mark his later triumphs. The setting is definite and the characters are actual personalities, but woven into the action is the foreboding presence of a greater meaning and a motivation that is more than human. There are crimes punishable by law, Strindberg is saying, but there are others, undetected by human eyes, that are punished by a higher power.

The Story:

Early in the day that was to mark his first theatrical triumph, Maurice met Jeanne, his mistress, and Marion, their young daughter, in the Montparnasse Cemetery. He promised them that the success of his play was assured and that with the money he would make he would finally be able to marry Jeanne. Unable to leave Marion to attend the performance of the play, Jeanne presented Maurice with a tie and a pair of gloves to wear in her honor in his hour of victory.

That afternoon Maurice went to the headquarters of his set, the crêmerie of Madame Catherine. There he saw for the first time the beautiful Henriette, the mistress of his painter-friend, Adolphe. Immediately attracted to her, he felt, at the same time, a strange premonition of evil. Madame Catherine, also sensing the evil, and thinking of Jeanne and her child, pleaded with him to leave. He started to go out but, ironically, collided with Emile, Jeanne's brother, as he walked toward the door. While Emile was apologizing, Henriette came up to him. Once in her presence, he found it impossible to retreat. When Adolphe finally arrived, he realized at once that he had lost his mistress to his friend.

Maurice's play was as great a success as he had hoped. Although his friends arranged a victory celebration for him at the crêmerie, he never appeared; he and Henriette had gone to an inn, ostensibly to wait for Adolphe. Adolphe, having misunderstood the meeting place, failed to appear, and Maurice and Henriette openly declared their passion for each other. Henriette, even though she admitted her propensity for evil and acknowledged that she had once committed a crime, easily convinced Maurice that she was more worthy of sharing his triumph than the dull, uneducated Jeanne. To stress her point she threw Jeanne's present, the tie and gloves, into the fire and placed her own laurel wreath on Maurice's brow.

When Adolphe finally met the pair the next morning, he realized the situation that now existed. After he had discreetly retired, Henriette attempted to persuade Maurice to run away with her. Maurice admitted that it was not Jeanne who held him, but the child Marion. Henriette replied that she wished the child were dead. Maurice agreed that things would be simpler if she were, and that he would go away with Henriette if she would consent to his seeing the child once before he left. Henriette reluctantly granted this favor, and Maurice went off for his last visit with his daughter.

Later that morning the customers of the crêmerie, smarting from the slight Maurice had paid them by not attending their party in his honor, were astounded by the news, brought by the Abbé, that Maurice's daughter was dead. Apparently she had been murdered by someone who had visited her in her mother's absence, for there was no sign of illness. A commissaire of police arrived to question the patrons as to Maurice's whereabouts. At first they protested that Maurice was incapable of such a crime as the murder of his own daughter; but as the evidence against him and Henriette began to accumulate—waiters had overheard all their remarks, the tie and gloves had been recovered from the fire, Maurice was known to have visited the little girl—even Madame Catherine and the Abbé began to waver, the Abbé maintaining, however, that the whole business was the work of a higher power.

When Maurice and Henriette arrived to bid their friends adieu, the evidence against them was so strong that they were taken into custody. Presently it was decided that there was as yet no proof that the child had actually been murdered,

and so they were released. But public opinion was against them. Maurice's play was taken from the stage and that of a rival put in its place. Worse still, his payments were suspended. The hero of the night before was now shunned and penniless. He and his new mistress were haunted by men they imagined detectives, who were waiting for them to convict themselves with a chance word or gesture.

The situation was too much for their love. Held together only by fear, they began to hate each other, to suspect each other of the murder. Maurice was convinced of Henriette's guilt when she confessed the details of her earlier crime: she had assisted in an abortion performed on a friend, and the friend had died. She lived in terror, fearing that her dead friend's lover would, in a moment of contrition, confess his guilt and thereby reveal hers. Her wanton existence had been the result of this constant dread. Maurice suggested that since they were bound by hate and fear they should be married. Henriette would not agree.

Finally Henriette left Maurice outside the closed Luxembourg gardens near the statues of Adam and Eve and returned to the crêmerie where she made her accusations to Adolphe. The previously despised Adolphe, seeing the effect of success on Maurice, had just refused a coveted painting prize. From the newspaper he had learned the verdict that Marion had died of some rare disease and that Maurice and Henriette were exonerated. Obsessed by guilt and her hatred of Maurice, however, Henriette at first rejected the news. At last, however, Adolphe persuaded her to give up her Bohemian existence and return to her mother.

After the departure Maurice returned and made his accusation to Adolphe. Adolphe informed him of his exoneration and the consequent restaging of his play. Even the news that his payments would be resumed gave him little pleasure, for he was too strongly aware of his crime of intention. He began to have some hope of atonement when Emile arrived to present him once again with the tie and gloves from Jeanne. The Abbé offered him an even stronger hope. He agreed to meet the Abbé at the church that night instead of attending the re-opening of his play.

THÉRÈSE

Type of work: Novel
Author: François Mauriac (1885-   )
Type of plot: Psychological realism
Time of plot: Twentieth century
Locale: France
First published: 1927

Principal characters:
BERNARD DESQUEYROUX, a petty landowner
THÉRÈSE DESQUEYROUX, his wife
MARIE DESQUEYROUX, their daughter
GEORGES FILHOT, a law student and Marie's lover
ANNE DE LA TRAVE, Bernard's half-sister
JEAN AZÉVÉDO, a young intellectual

Critique:

The story and meaning of the life of Thérèse Desqueyroux preoccupied Mauriac's mind over a long period of time. The book is not a novel in the conventional sense, being a series of four stories tied together by the mind of the major character rather than by incident. But it is a powerful and dramatic revelation of the human condition and its relation to sin as seen through the eyes of one of the most interesting and influential of Catholic authors. In Thérèse, his central character, Mauriac has caught the complex movement of guilt as it exists in everyone.

The Story:

In the little French town of Argelouse where she spent the first part of her life, Thérèse Desqueyroux was known not so much for her beauty as for her charm. Her wit and independence of mind made her conspicuous in the stifling and inbred atmosphere of her native province, and she inspired in her friends and relatives as much disapproval as admiration. Left to her own devices by a father more intent on his political career than the problems of fatherhood, Thérèse had spent her girlhood in isolated brooding. Her one friend was Anne de la Trave, the half-sister of Bernard Desqueyroux, whom Thérèse was later to marry.

Of her youth and the days leading to

her marriage, Thérèse could remember little. For the most part her memories were clouded over by the confusion in her own mind: an intense love of life and a desire for experience joined to provincial willingness to sacrifice self to tradition. Her marriage to Bernard Desqueyroux she saw as only the natural culmination of a social cycle.

Before the honeymoon was over Thérèse felt acutely the loss involved in her marriage. In Bernard she discovered all that was worst in provincial life: a fanatical pride of family and material possessions. To a fatal degree, he lacked the insight and imagination to understand his wife. For her own part, Thérèse found herself disgusted by the marriage.

During the honeymoon a letter came to Bernard from his family informing him that his half-sister Anne had fallen in love with a penniless young man, Jean Azévédo. To preserve the family name and honor, Bernard prevailed on Thérèse to help stop the affair. Returning to Argelouse, Thérèse persuaded Anne to go off on a trip. After Anne had gone Thérèse met Azévédo and discovered in him that intensity and individualism she missed in her own life. Azévédo told her that he was not really in love with Anne, and he readily agreed to write to the girl confessing his true feelings. In the meantime he and Thérèse met from

THÉRÈSE by François Mauriac. Translated by Gerard Hopkins. By permission of the publishers, Farrar, Straus and Cudahy, Inc. Copyright, 1947, by Henry Holt & Co., Inc.

time to time and the two were drawn to each other. When Azévédo left Argelouse, it was with the promise that they would be reunited in a year.

After Azévédo had gone, Thérèse settled into the normal routine of a farmer's wife. Even the birth of a child, Marie, failed to give her life meaning, for motherhood only further intensified her frustration. Almost involuntarily she decided to poison Bernard.

The attempted murder was quickly discovered and Thérèse was brought to trial. At the last moment, however, a trumped up explanation by Bernard saved her from conviction. Thérèse returned home to learn that Bernard had lied only to save the family from scandal. After telling her that divorce was impossible, he forced her, under threat of revealing her true actions, to live a life of semi-imprisonment in her bedroom.

Thérèse regained her freedom, however, when Bernard reconsidered and allowed her to go to Paris to begin a new but distant life.

Alone in Paris, Thérèse tried to make a new life for herself, but without success. The sense of sin she carried within her perverted all attempts to find happiness. As the years passed she retreated more and more into herself.

Fifteen years after her banishment from Argelouse, Thérèse was found by her daughter, Marie, now a young girl of seventeen, living in retirement in an apartment in Paris. Marie, who explained that she had followed to Paris a young law student from her native province, was shocked to find Thérèse broken in health and old before her time. Thérèse, hoping to extirpate the sense of her own sinfulness, decided to help Marie win the love of the student, Georges Filhot. To persuade Filhot to marry Marie and to modify his parents' disapproval, Thérèse told her daughter that she would turn over to her all her own landholdings in Argelouse. The next day Thérèse visited Filhot and invited him to dinner. At the conclusion of the evening Marie returned to Argelouse with the promise of a final reunion with Filhot in three months.

In the next few days it became painfully and thrillingly evident to Thérèse that Filhot was not in love with Marie but with herself; and in a violently emotional scene she confessed to the student not only her past crime but a whole series of crimes for which she believed herself guilty but which were not recognized as criminal by the law. Then she sent Filhot away. Rather than insist that he sacrifice himself to her daughter, however, she urged him to write to Marie saying that he did not love her.

A short time later Marie returned to Paris to face her mother, who by that time was living in a confused and paranoid world in which she believed all her acquaintances were engaged in a plot to bring her to justice for her sins, both real and imaginary. Marie's anger was softened, and when she returned to Argelouse she took the sick Thérèse with her.

Returned to her birthplace, Thérèse slowly regained her sanity; the doctor predicted, however, that she would soon die. Nursed during her last days by her daughter and Bernard—for whom, by this time, she felt neither pity nor disgust—Thérèse tried to put her mind in order. She awaited death hopefully, seeing it as the final deliverance from self.

THE THESMOPHORIAZUSAE

Type of work: Drama
Author: Aristophanes (c. 448-c. 385 B.C.)
Type of plot: Satiric comedy
Time of plot: Fifth Century B.C.
Locale: Athens
First presented: 411 B.C.

> Principal characters:
> EURIPIDES, the playwright
> MNESILOCHUS, his father-in-law
> AGATHON
> CHORUS OF THESMOPHORIAZUSAE, fertility celebrants
> LEADER OF THE CHORUS
> A SCYTHIAN POLICEMAN

Critique:

The *Thesmophoriazusae*, one of the liveliest and wittiest of Aristophanes' eleven extant plays, is a satiric comedy with two targets, both squarely hit: Euripides, the notorious misogynist, and the loose morals of the women of Athens. It is a lusty drama, fully appreciated only by the most sophisticated of audiences. The Thesmophoria referred to in the title was a fertility festival, celebrated only by women, at which the seed corn was mixed with the putrid remains of dead pigs. The time of the plot is the third day of that festival, when the Senate and the tribunals are not in session.

The Story:

En route to the house of Agathon, Euripides, the celebrated dramatist, explained to his aged but lusty father-in-law, Mnesilochus, that he was in great danger of his life. The Thesmophoriazusae were gathered at the temple of Demeter to decide on an appropriate punishment for the playwright—Euripides—who had so consistently and so bitterly insulted their sex in his plays. Agathon would surely be able to help him. At the door of Agathon's house a servant appeared and ordered the people and the winds to be quiet because his master was seized with poetical inspiration. Mnesilochus knew at once that no real help could come from such a man. When Agathon appeared, reposing on

a bed, dressed in a saffron tunic, and surrounded by feminine toilet articles, Mnesilochus insulted him roundly for his lack of manhood. As expected, Agathon refused to aid Euripides by dressing as a woman in order to mix with the fertility celebrants and plead Euripides' cause; the plan was simply too risky. Mnesilochus then offered himself and was promptly and painfully shaved, undressed, and depilated. Disguised as a woman, the old man was suddenly very reluctant to go to the temple until Euripides swore by all the gods to come to his aid if anything went wrong.

Striving to act as womanly as possible and giving his voice a feminine lilt, the old man entered the temple with a prayer to Demeter and Persephone that he would not be recognized. After certain preliminaries the women within began their deliberations concerning Euripides' fate. The First Woman, after spitting as orators do, opened with the charge that Euripides presented women in his plays as adulterous, lecherous, bibulous, treacherous, and garrulous; he caused husbands, especially old ones, to be suspicious of their wives; and he provoked them into keeping the keys to the storerooms and sealing doors upon their wives. She declared that the playwright deserved any form of death, but preferably by poison. The Second Woman explained that she, a widow with five children, had supported herself by selling religious chaplets until Euripides convinced spectators of his plays that there were no gods. Mnesilochus, unable to restrain himself upon hearing his son-in-law so defamed, agreed that Euripides had indeed committed two or three such indiscretions, but he urged the women to consider all their horrendous faults that Euripides had not attacked. Mnesilochus then proceeded to present a detailed catalogue of feminine failings.

The outraged women turned upon Mnesilochus in furious wrath, but before the face-slapping could lead to hairpulling Clisthenes arrived with the warning that a man disguised as a woman was in their midst. Unmasked, the desperate Mnesilochus seized what he thought was a woman's child and threatened to slit its throat if he were not allowed to go free. But the "child" turned out to be a wineskin and the enraged women began to gather faggots in order to roast Mnesilochus alive.

Euripides, summoned by messages scratched on wooden idols that Mnesilochus had thrown out of the temple, entered declaiming Menelaus' lines from his play *Helen*. Mnesilochus responded with Helen's lines, but before a rescue could be effected a Magistrate accompanied by a Scythian Policeman arrived and Euripides fled. The Magistrate, after ordering Mnesilochus to be lashed to a post, left him under the guard of the Scythian. As the women began their ceremonies, Euripides, playing Echo of his drama on Perseus and Andromeda, began to echo Mnesilochus' laments as he entered the temple in the dress of Perseus. But the illiterate Scythian refused to believe that old Mnesilochus was really Andromeda, as Euripides insisted.

During the ceremonies the guard fell asleep. Euripides proceeded to disguise himself as a procuress. He then offered the women a proposal of peace: if they would release his father-in-law, he would no longer insult them in his plays. The women agreed, but there remained the Scythian to be outwitted. Still disguised as a procuress, Euripides offered the Scythian a good time with the little flute girl whom the barbarian eagerly purchased. While the two were away, Euripides released his father-in-law and they both escaped. His lust satisfied, the Scythian returned to find his prisoner gone and the obliging Thesmophoriazusae sent him off in hot pursuit—in the wrong direction.

THE THIN MAN

Type of work: Novel
Author: Dashiell Hammett (1894- 1961)
Type of plot: Mystery romance
Time of plot: 1930's
Locale: New York
First published: 1934

Principal characters:
MIMI JORGENSEN, Clyde Wynant's ex-wife
DOROTHY WYNANT, her daughter
GILBERT WYNANT, her son
CHRISTIAN JORGENSEN, her present husband, Wynant's former associate
NICK CHARLES, a detective
NORA CHARLES, his wife
HERBERT MACAULAY, Wynant's attorney
MORELLI, a gangster
ARTHUR NUNHEIM, an ex-convict

Critique:

As detective fiction, this novel presents a picture of sophisticated New York life at the end of the prohibition era. The plot itself follows the pattern set by Poe in *The Murders of the Rue Morgue* in 1841 and by Arthur Conan Doyle in his Sherlock Holmes stories. Here are the astute detective, the somewhat obtuse and distrustful police, the questioning companion, the dropping of clues to give the reader a chance to solve the mystery, and the final explanation by the detective.

The Story:

Nick Charles, one-time detective and now a California lumberman, arrived in New York with his wife Nora for the Christmas holidays. He was drawn into investigation of a murder case because the dead woman, Julia Wolf, was the secretary of Nick's old client, a lunatic-fringe inventor whose wife had divorced him in order to marry a man named Christian Jorgensen. Clyde Wynant, the inventor, was reported to be out of town, working on some new project. Herbert Macaulay, attorney for Wynant, had told police that he had not seen Wynant since October, when Wynant had given the lawyer power of attorney. Suspicion fell on Mimi Jorgensen, just returned from Europe, for she had gone to see Julia on the afternoon of the murder, had arrived, in fact, in time for Julia to die in her arms. She had wanted, she said, to get her husband's address, for she needed more money to support his two children, twenty-year-old Dorothy and eighteen-year-old Gilbert, since Jorgensen had run through the large settlement Wynant had made on Mimi at the time of their divorce.

Suspicion fell on Jorgensen, who turned out to be a man formerly known as Kelterman, with whom Wynant had worked several years before. He thought that Wynant had not treated him fairly. Then it was discovered that Jorgensen had a wife living in Boston and that he had married Mimi only to get Wynant's money.

Suspicion fell on Morelli, a gangster who had been fond of Julia. When he learned that Nick was on the case, Morelli went to Nick's apartment and, as the police arrived, shot Nick in the chest, a glancing shot that did not produce a serious wound. Nick told the police he would not press charges, for the man was apparently in enough trouble. Although the police beat up Morelli, they could find no reason for holding him. He was released the same day.

Suspicion fell on Gil Wynant, for the

THE THIN MAN by Dashiell Hammett. By permission of the publishers, Alfred A. Knopf, Inc. Copyright, 1934, by Alfred A. Knopf, Inc.

3749

members of the Wynant family did not have much love for one another. Gil was an odd young man who asked Nick about bizarre subjects such as incest and cannibalism. He was frequently found at keyholes listening to private conversations.

Suspicion fell on Arthur Nunheim, who identified Julia Wolf's body. When Nick went with Guild, a detective, to see Nunheim, they found him living in an extremely untidy apartment with a big, frowzy blonde. In the presence of their callers, Nunheim and the blonde insulted each other until the woman left him. Nunheim escaped from Nick through a back window. He was reported murdered a little while later.

Suspicion fell on Wynant himself, for Macaulay reported that Wynant had made an appointment with him on the day the murder was committed, but had failed to appear. During the course of the investigation several people received from Wynant communications which seemed to throw suspicion on Mimi and Jorgensen. One day Wynant was reported to have tried to commit suicide in Allentown, Pennsylvania. The report was false, however, for the man was not Wynant.

On First Avenue Wynant had maintained a shop which the police had given a cursory examination. Nick insisted that they return and tear it apart if necessary, for he felt sure that some clue was to be found there. The police discovered a section of the cement floor newer than the rest. When they tore it up, they found the bones of a dead man, with a cane, some clothes apparently for a larger man than Wynant and a key chain bearing the initials D.W.Q.

At last Nick accused Macaulay of murdering Wynant, Julia, and Nunheim. He believed that Macaulay and Julia had joined forces to get Wynant's money, that Wynant had gone to Macaulay's house in Scarsdale to accuse Macaulay of the plot, and that Macaulay had killed his client there. Then, Nick reasoned, Macaulay had dismembered the

body and brought it back to the workshop, where he discharged the two mechanics and buried the body under new cement. The cane, the large-size clothes, and the key chain were intended to prevent identification of the body.

Macaulay, according to Nick, had renewed the lease on the shop and kept it vacant while with a forged power of attorney and Julia's help he began to transfer Wynant's fortune to his own accounts. Then Mimi had come back from Europe with her children and had asked for Wynant. When Nick had arrived for his Christmas holiday and had agreed to help Mimi find the missing inventor, Macaulay felt he would be safer with Julia dead. Later he sent letters to members of Wynant's family, and even to himself, supposedly from Wynant. Nick thought Macaulay had killed Nunheim because the ex-convict had been near Julia's apartment and had probably heard the shots that killed her. When Nunheim had demanded hush money from Macaulay, the lawyer had murdered him also to keep him permanently quiet.

So Nick outlined his case. But on the day he made the accusation, Gilbert Wynant received a letter, supposedly from his father, telling him to use the enclosed key, go to Julia's apartment, and look for an important paper between the pages of a certain book. Following the instruction in the letter, Gilbert entered the apartment, where a plainclothesman struck him, fettered him, and took him to police headquarters. The boy showed the officials and Nick the letter that he had received. The book and paper had been invented. When Nick took Gilbert home, he learned from Mimi that Wynant had just been there to leave with Mimi ten thousand dollars in bonds.

As it turned out, Macaulay, knowing that the police would be in Julia's apartment, had sent the letter to Gilbert in an attempt to shift the suspicion back to Wynant once more. Also, Macaulay himself had brought Wynant's bonds to Mimi, making her promise to say that

3750

Wynant had brought them and thus give credence to his own story that Wynant was in town. Nick forced Mimi to admit the truth by explaining that Macaulay now had possession of Wynant's fortune and that if she played his game she would have to be satisfied with comparatively small sums occasionally, whereas if she were to stop shielding Macaulay — however innocent of Wynant's death—she would, through her children, have control of her ex-husband's entire fortune. Jorgensen, meanwhile, had gone back to his legal wife in Boston.

After Nick had explained the whole case to Nora, she could not help feeling that the business of a detective, based as it is on so much probability, is at best unsatisfactory.

THE THIRTY-NINE STEPS

Type of work: Novel
Author: John Buchan (1875-1940)
Type of plot: Adventure romance
Time of plot: 1914
Locale: England and Scotland
First published: 1915

Principal characters:
RICHARD HANNAY, a retired mining engineer
FRANKLIN SCUDDER, a private investigator
SIR WALTER, a government official
THE BLACK STONE, espionage agents

Critique:

Well-told spy stories are always exciting, and The Thirty-Nine Steps is no exception to the rule. Both as fiction and in motion picture versions, the novel has survived with remarkable popularity the time for which it was written. Buchan's style was always crisp and lively, a fact which helps to explain the widespread appeal of his novels during the first three decades of this century.

The Story:

Richard Hannay was a mining engineer who had made a modest fortune in South Africa and returned to England to retire. Before long he found himself bored beyond belief with the conversations and actions of the Englishmen he met. He had just about decided to return to South Africa when a strange series of events provided him with ample excitement.

As he was unlocking the door of his flat, he was startled by the sudden appearance of Franklin Scudder, another tenant in the building. Scudder, obviously a badly frightened man, begged Hannay to give him refuge in his flat. After the two men were settled comfortably, Scudder told Hannay a fantastic tale. He said that a plot to start a war between England and Germany was being hatched. A Greek diplomat, Karolides, the only really strong man in Europe, was to visit London on June

fifteenth. At that time his assassination would create an excuse for a declaration of war.

Scudder told Hannay that a group called The Black Stone were the agents arranging for the assassination. This group of men knew that Scudder had learned of their plot, and they had tried several times to kill him. He had now planted a body in his flat, hoping that the murderers would think the body his. He asked Hannay to let him stay with him until plans could be made to prevent the assassination.

Impressed by the sincerity of Scudder's story, Hannay gave him sanctuary. One day he returned to his flat to find Scudder with a knife through his heart. Hannay knew then that The Black Stone had found Scudder and that his own life was in danger. The police, too, would want Hannay for questioning.

When he saw two men strolling in front of his flat, he decided that they were part of the enemy group. By a ruse he exchanged clothes with the milkman and left his flat, taking with him a little black book in which he had seen Scudder making notes. He was afraid to go to any government office with his fantastic story. His plan was to disappear for the three weeks remaining before June fifteenth, and at the last minute to try to get to someone in authority to listen to him.

He went to Scotland, thinking that he could hide more easily there. But the London papers carried the story of the murder of Scudder and Hannay's description. He had several narrow escapes from local Scottish police. The Black Stone had also traced him. When an airplane flew low over his refuge, obviously on the lookout for him, he took shelter in an inn until The Black Stone found him there and he was forced to flee again. In every spare moment he studied Scudder's little black book. Deciphering the code, he learned that Scudder had told him only part of the truth. The murder of Karolides was only a small part of the plot. The main threat of the plan was an invasion of England without warning. Airfields were already laid out and mines had been placed to line the shores at a given signal. The time for invasion was to be determined after The Black Stone intercepted a French envoy who was coming to London to secure the plans which showed the arrangement of the British fleet. When the enemy learned where the ships were, they could lay mines in strategic positions and destroy a great portion of the fleet. The only clue Hannay could find about the time and place of the enemy operation was a reference to thirty-nine steps and a high tide at 10:17 P. M.

By luck, Hannay met a man who had an uncle in an influential position in the government. This man believed the story and promised to write his uncle and ask him to talk to Hannay and to help in thwarting the plot. Hannay traveled carefully, for the police and The Black Stone were still after him. Once he was captured by a member of The Black Stone, but he blew up the building in which he was held and escaped. At last he reached Sir Walter, the uncle of his friend, and Sir Walter listened carefully to Hannay's report. At first he dismissed Scudder's story as that of a loyal but overly anxious young man. But when he received a call informing him that Karolides had been killed, he knew that Scudder's information had been right, and he promised to take Hannay's information to the proper authorities.

Although Hannay was not to be allowed to attend the secret conference of government officials, he had the uneasy feeling that his presence there was of utmost importance, that only he could find out how the highly confidential information about the French envoy's visit had leaked out to the enemy. Against Sir Walter's orders, he went to the house where the officials were meeting. As he sat in the hall waiting to be admitted, one of the officials came out of the meeting room. Realizing that the man had recognized him and that he had seen the official elsewhere, he burst into the room and told the astonished officials that the man who had just left was an impostor.

They thought him mad, for the man was the First Lord of the Admiralty and they knew him well. But at Hannay's insistence they called the official's home and learned that he was there. Then they remembered that the impostor had scanned the drawings and figures carefully and could have memorized them. If he left the country, the whole plan of defense would be in the hands of the enemy. The only hope was to capture him. But there were hundreds of small ports where a little boat could leave English shores; not all could be watched.

By checking isolated spots along the coast, Hannay finally found a small cove where the tide was high at 10:17 P. M. and nearby a house with thirty-nine steps leading down to the cove. Accompanied by police, he went to the house. There he found three Englishmen on a vacation. Their actions were so natural that he doubted that they could be spies. Only the presence of a fast yacht in the water close to the cove supported his suspicions. But an unconscious finger tapping by one of the vacationers identified him as the enemy agent who had once captured Hannay. Hannay and the police were able to capture two of the men. The third escaped to the ship, but as it had already been boarded by English police, he too was taken.

The murder charge against Hannay had been dropped, and he was safe for the first time in many weeks. Three weeks later war was declared between England and Germany. But the war was not fought on English soil and there was no surprise invasion. Hannay enlisted in the army, but he knew that he had done his greatest service for his country before he put on a uniform. The Black Stone was no more and Scudder's murder was avenged.

THIS ABOVE ALL

Type of work: Novel
Author: Eric Knight (1897-1943)
Type of plot: Sentimental romance
Time of plot: Summer, 1940
Locale: England
First published: 1941

Principal characters:
CLIVE BRIGGS, a soldier
PRUE CATHAWAY, in love with Clive
MONTY, Clive's friend
DR. CATHAWAY, Prue's father

Critique:

This Above All is a story of great emotional conflict between a girl who knew and loved the England of hunting, cricket, and afternoon tea, and a man who knew and hated the England of slums, mines, starvation, and disease. The author attempted to show what war can mean to a civilian as well as to a front-line soldier.

The Story:

Home on rest leave, after the disaster of Dunkirk, Clive Briggs went first to Leaford and then to Gosley, both resort towns on the coast of England. At a band concert in Gosley he met Prudence Cathaway, who was stationed nearby with the women's army corps. Prue was of an upper middle-class family and Clive was from the slums, but they were attracted to each other and became lovers the second time they were together.

Prue told him of her family. Her grandfather had been a general in the last war and felt unwanted and useless in this one; her father was a doctor, a famous brain specialist. She told him of her Aunt Iris, who wanted only to get to America and who pretended that she wanted her children to be safe when it was really for herself she feared. Iris' brother was in America, buying steel for the British government. Prue also told Clive that she had broken her engagement to a conscientious objector, and because she was ashamed for him she had joined the W. A. A. F.

Clive seemed reluctant to talk about himself, other than to say he had been born in the slums. In fact, it was many days before Prue knew he was in the army and had been in the rear-guard action at Dunkirk.

When they found that Prue could get a leave which would give them ten days together, they went to Leaford. Most of the time they were quite happy but each time Prue mentioned the War Clive became angry and sullen and seemed to get pleasure from taunting her about her family. Sometimes they quarreled without knowing the reason and were reconciled only because of their desire for each other.

During the last five days of their stay, Clive's friend Monty joined them. Monty was also slum-born. It was Monty who told Prue of Clive's heroism at Dunkirk. Monty's story puzzled Prue more than ever. She could understand even less why Clive was so bitter.

While they were at Leaford, air raids became frequent. One night during a heavy raid Clive told Prue why he would not go back to the army, why he intended to desert. He told her of his childhood, of his illegitimate birth and of his sordid remembrances of childhood in the slums. He asked her if a country that ignored its poor were worth fighting for. England was still fighting a gentleman's war, he said, and the leaders were asking the slum boys to win the war and then go back to the mines and the factories and the mills from which they had come. He was through. Prue tried to tell him that he must go back to save himself. She said it was his pride that had brought him up from the filth, and his pride and that of the others like him would change all the conditions of which he had told her. He would not listen to her.

At the end of the leave Prue returned to her camp. Clive, true to his word, did not go back to the army at the end of his furlough. He wandered along the coast while trying to decide what he really wanted to do. Once he went into a church and talked with the pastor, but he scoffed when the minister told him that we fight because we have faith in our ability to build a better life than we have had. He accused the minister and all the churches of betraying Christ and His teachings because the rich who support the church must not be told of their sin in neglecting their fellow men. Before he left the church the minister told him that realism and reasoning like his had brought war and hunger and cruelty, and that only faith could restore human dignity and freedom throughout the world.

At last Clive tired of running away; there was no place for him to go. Finally he decided to give himself up, to let the army decide for him whether he was wrong, for he was too exhausted to decide his problem for himself. Perhaps Prue and the minister had been right; perhaps faith in himself meant faith in his country and the willingness to die for it.

On the train to London, Clive suddenly remembered something Prue had said, a remark which had no meaning at the time. Now he knew she was going to have a baby. He felt that he could not give himself up before he saw Prue and asked her to marry him. He managed to evade the military police in London and call Prue. They arranged to meet at the station in London and to marry as soon as possible. Clive knew at last that he loved Prue, and he was determined that his child would never know the hurt an illegitimate child must always feel.

While he was waiting for Prue's train, a bomb fell on a nearby building. As he tried to help rescue a woman trapped in the basement of the building, the wall collapsed on him. He regained consciousness with Prue sitting beside him in a hospital room. Monty and her father had helped her find him. Prue's father was honest with her. He had tried to save Clive's life with an emergency operation, but part of the brain tissue was gone and there was no hope that Clive would live. During one of his periods of consciousness Clive told Prue that he had risked his life to save a strange woman, because he knew at last that he did have faith in himself and his country.

Clive died in the night during a heavy bombing raid. Afterward Prue walked along the streets of London and saw the volunteer firemen and the Cockney policemen performing their duties among the wreckage, and she knew why Clive had died. Feeling the child stir within her, she hoped that by sacrifices like Clive's his child and all children might have the chance to live in a good and free world.

THE THREE BLACK PENNYS

Type of work: Novel
Author: Joseph Hergesheimer (1880-1954)
Type of plot: Period chronicle
Time of plot: c. 1750-1910
Locale: Pennsylvania
First published: 1917

Principal characters:
HOWAT PENNY, son of the owner of Myrtle Forge
LUDOWIKA WINSCOMBE, in love with Howat Penny
JASPER PENNY, Howat Penny's great-grandson
SUSAN BRUNDON, Jasper's sweetheart
HOWAT PENNY, Jasper's and Susan's grandson
MARIANA JANNAN, Howat's cousin
JAMES POLDER, Mariana's lover

Critique:

The Three Black Pennys is, in an unusual way, the history of American culture, the first of the Pennys representing the beginning of a culture, the second representing the essential crudeness of the early nineteenth century, and the last Penny representing the effete qualities of a Victorian generation which passed away without ever understanding the modern society supplanting it. The author aptly named the three sections of his book The Furnace, The Forge, and The Metal, in keeping with a story dealing with a family engaged in the steel industry in Pennsylvania. The symbolism is obvious. The characterization is excellent, as is the description. Two of the highlights of the book are the descriptions of an all-night raccoon hunt in the eighteenth century and the tapping of an open-hearth converter in a twentieth-century steel mill.

The Story:

The Penny family was English, except for a Welsh ancestor whose blood cropped out from time to time among his descendants. Those who showed the Welsh strain were called black Pennys by their relatives in an attempt to describe the mental make-up of individuals to whom it was applied. Howat was the first black Penny in over a hundred years; the last one had been burned to death as a heretic by Queen Elizabeth, long before the family had emigrated to the Colonies.

Living at Myrtle Forge, on the edge of the Pennsylvania Wilderness, Howat Penny was far more interested in the deep woods than he was in becoming an ironmaster. Nor did the appearance of Ludowika Winscombe make him any more satisfied or contented with his life.

Ludowika Winscombe, the young Polish wife of an elderly British envoy, had been left at the Penny home while her husband traveled through the Colonies on the king's business. Before long Howat Penny fell in love with her. Ludowika warned him, however, that she was a practical person who felt it was best for her to remain married to her husband rather than to run away with a young frontiersman. Howat stubbornly told her that she would have to marry him, for he would permit nothing to stand in the way of their happiness.

Winscombe returned ill to Myrtle Forge and Howat Penny found himself acting as Winscombe's nurse. It was an ironic situation filled with tension. Howat Penny waited for the old man to die. Ludowika was torn between two desires. She wanted Howat Penny, but she hated to face a life with him in the wilderness. The climax came late one night while Howat and Ludowika sat by the sick man's bed while Winscombe made a gallant effort to remain alive. Howat and Ludowika dared not even look at each other for fear of what they might see behind each other's eyes. Early in the morning the old man died. As they faced each other in the gray dawn Howat and Ludowika realized that she was destined to remain with him in Pennsylvania and never to see London again.

Three generations later the Welsh Penny blood again appeared in the person of Howat's great-grandson, Jasper. By that time the forge, which had been the beginning of the Penny fortune, had been replaced by a great foundry with many furnaces. Jasper Penny was a rich man, steadily growing richer by supplying the tremendous amounts of iron needed for the new railroads in the United States.

Jasper Penny had never married. Like his great-grandfather Howat, he was a man of great passions whose energies were spent in building up his foundry and fortune. He was still painfully reminded, however, of his earlier indiscretions with a woman who had borne him an illegitimate daughter. The woman hounded Jasper for money and he found it easier to give her money than it was to refuse her demands.

He saw very little of Eunice, his daughter, for he assumed that she would be cared for by her mother as long as he paid all expenses. One day in Philadelphia Jasper decided, on impulse, to visit Eunice. He discovered her, ill-clothed and underfed, in the home of a poor family, and, horrified, he took her away with him. Not knowing what to do with her, he finally placed her in a school in New York.

In Philadelphia Jasper had also met Susan Brundon, mistress of a girls' school and friend of a distant branch of Jasper's family Jasper fell in love with her and in his abrupt fashion proposed marriage. Being honest, he told her that he had an illegitimate child. Susan refused to marry Jasper because she felt that his first duty was to Eunice's mother.

Shortly after his proposal Jasper was involved in a murder. Eunice's mother had killed another lover and suspicion fell on Jasper Penny. He hated to involve Susan Brundon in the sordid affair, but he found that the only way he could clear himself was through her testimony that he had been with her when the crime was committed.

After the trial Susan told Jasper that she could not marry him until Eunice's mother was dead, that she could not have the past intruding itself upon her love for him after they were married. Almost a decade passed before they were finally able to marry.

The last of the black Pennys was also the last of the family name, for the family died out with the second Howat Penny, the grandson of Jasper Penny and Susan Brundon. Howat was a bachelor who lived alone in the country near the site of the original Penny forge. Interested in music and art, he had never married, and the management of the Penny foundries had gone out of his hands. Possessed of a comfortable fortune, he had in the closing years of his life the companionship of Mariana Jannan, a cousin. She was a young woman in her twenties and little understood by old-fashioned Howat.

He did not understand Mariana because he could not understand her generation. Because Jasper's son and grandson had never had anything to do with that branch of the family descended from Jasper's illegitimate daughter, Howat was horrified when Mariana told him that she was in love with James Polder, a distant cousin.

Howat thought Mariana mad to fall in love with James Polder, who had begun working in the Penny foundries as a boy. The fact that he had worked his way up to a position of importance failed to redeem him in old Howat's eyes.

Polder finally ran away with an actress. Three years after his marriage,

Mariana and Howat Penny called on him and his wife. Polder, unhappy with his slatternly wife, had begun drinking heavily. Howat, at Marianna's insistence, invited Polder to visit his home in the country. Polder accepted. Shortly afterward he learned that his wife had deserted him and returned to the stage. He no longer cared; in love once more, he and Mariana realized they should never have permitted family differences to come between them.

Mariana's relatives, shocked by the affair, protested to Howat. Howat himself said nothing, for he now felt that he was too old and understood too little of modern life to intrude in the affairs of Mariana and Polder. Although he was as much Mariana's friend as ever, he could not understand how she was able to live with Polder as his mistress while they waited for his wife to divorce him. Howat believed until the end of his life that women should be protected from reality. Even when he knew he was dying, he said nothing to Mariana, who sat reading by his side. The delicacy of his sensibilities prevented him from shocking her with the fact of his approaching death and kept him from saying goodbye to her when he died, the last of the three black Pennys.

THE THREE-CORNERED HAT

Type of work: Novel
Author: Pedro Antonio de Alarcón (1833-1891)
Type of plot: Comedy of intrigue
Time of plot: Early nineteenth century
Locale: Spain
First published: 1874

Principal characters:
LUCAS, a miller
FRASQUITA, his wife
DON EUGENIO, the corregidor
DOÑA MERCEDES, the corregidor's wife

Critique:

This novel is based on a famous folk tale that could belong to every age and almost every people. The plot is simple yet satisfying; the characters lack complexity but are delightful and real. Although the story is set in a particular place and time, it is basically universal, for the cuckold is an invariable subject for humor in all nations. This story is among the most delightful on the subject ever written.

The Story:

The early years of the nineteenth century were calm ones for Spain. Life there still followed the old pattern, and an almost medieval attitude toward government existed. The Church was a great power, and government officers treated their commands like petty kingdoms. Corregidor Don Eugenio was a fine example. He ruled one of the Andalusian cities like a little Caesar.

Near the city was a famous old flour mill. Lucas was its owner. There the military and the gentry visited every day to eat the miller's good food and to talk with the miller's beautiful wife, Frasquita.

These daily visits the miller shrewdly put to good use. He did not give his food without recompense, although he was never so blunt as to demand anything for his hospitality. If he needed some wood, a word to the bishop would secure him the right to cut some on the bishop's grounds, or if he needed to have his taxes lowered, a word to Don Eugenio, the corregidor, would suffice. Life for him was pleasant and fruitful. His wife Frasquita was a beautiful woman who loved him deeply and sincerely despite the miller's ugly face and the slight hump on his back. They joked together, and tried to outdo one another in kindness. Only children were lacking to make their love complete.

To those who met every day under the shady grape arbor outside the mill, it became obvious that Don Eugenio had fallen in love with Frasquita. There was nothing unusual in this, for everyone who knew her was in love with her. Fortunately, the miller was not jealous of his wife; she had never given him any reason to be so. Yet where so important a person as Don Eugenio was concerned, suspicion was certain to arise.

Don Eugenio was a sight to see. He wore a huge black three-cornered hat, a scarlet cape, white stockings, and black shoes with gold buckles. His face was deeply wrinkled, for he had no teeth. On his back was a hump much larger than the miller's, and in his breast a heart much smaller. But he was the corregidor, and everyone bowed to him when he passed, with his bailiff, Weasel, following always at his heels.

One day Don Eugenio came to the mill much earlier than usual, and the miller, spying him at a distance, plotted to surprise him. Knowing that Don Eugenio would try to make love to Frasquita, the miller hid in the grape arbor above the spot where the corregidor would sit. He told his wife to act as if she knew nothing of his presence there.

Don Eugenio began to talk of love, but when he tried to take one of Frasquita's hands in his own she knocked over his chair in pretended confusion. At that moment the miller fell from the arbor. Don Eugenio was furious. The couple pretended that the miller, asleep in the arbor, had not overheard the silly love scene. Although the affair seemed to pass off easily, Don Eugenio planned revenge.

That night, as the miller and his wife were preparing for bed, they heard a knock at the door. It was a messenger from the mayor, demanding that the miller go at once to testify in an important case. The miller, guessing correctly that this request was part of Don Eugenio's plot, told Frasquita to bolt the door and not to let anyone in after he had gone.

When the miller arrived at the mayor's home, he found that his testimony was not needed. The mayor insisted, however, that he go up to the loft and spend the night, to be on hand for the trial the next morning. The miller pretended to go to bed, but shortly afterward he let himself down from the window, got his mule, and started back to the mill. On his way he passed another rider whose mule neighed at his and received an answer. Alarmed, the miller turned aside from the road. When he arrived at the mill, he found the doors all open. Furious, he got a gun and crept up to the bedroom. Peeking through the key-hole, he saw Don Eugenio in his bed. The miller did not know what to do. He wanted to kill his wife and Don Eugenio, but he knew he would be hanged for the crime. He went down-stairs, where Don Eugenio's clothes were scattered about on chairs in front of the fire. An idea came to the miller. Turn about is fair play. He dressed in Don Eugenio's clothes and set out for town. What had actually happened was different from what the miller suspected.

Don Eugenio had come to the house, but Frasquita had let him in only after he had fallen into the millpond. When he had tried to make love to her, she threatened him with a gun. Then she had called the bailiff, who was waiting outside, and told him to put his master to bed. Saying that she was going for a doctor, she had started out to get her husband. It had been her mule that had alarmed the miller on his way to the house. Don Eugenio had sent the bailiff away at the moment the miller arrived home and judged the circumstances so falsely.

Arriving at the mayor's house, Frasquita learned that her husband had fled. Together she and the mayor set out for the mill. They arrived in time to meet Don Eugenio leaving in the miller's clothes. The bailiff had returned, noticed that his master's clothes were gone, and guessed that the miller had taken them. The whole group, for different reasons, started out for Don Eugenio's house.

On their arrival the maid, insisting that Don Eugenio had returned home some time before, refused to admit them. Don Eugenio angrily demanded entrance, and at last his wife told the maid to admit the party. They all went upstairs.

Doña Mercedes refused to recognize Don Eugenio until she had learned what he had been doing. Frasquita would not speak to the miller. Doña Mercedes ordered her husband to leave the room. Then she told Frasquita that she had found the miller hiding under her bed. At first she had been furious, but after she heard his story she had become angry at her husband. Frasquita, reconciled with the miller, proved her own inno-cence by telling him about the neighing mules, and he apologized for doubting her honor.

When Don Eugenio returned to the room, Doña Mercedes refused to tell him anything about what had happened that night and ordered him never to come to her room again. There was noth-ing his guilty conscience would allow him to say. The miller and his wife went home.

The next day the bishop and the other officials came to the mill as usual, for they did not want anyone to feel that the night's happenings had anything to do with the miller's reputation. But Don Eugenio never came to the mill again. The miller and his wife both lived to a happy and prosperous old age.

THREE MEN IN A BOAT

Type of work: Novel
Author: Jerome K. Jerome (1859-1927)
Type of plot: Comic romance
Time of plot: Nineteenth century
Locale: England
First published: 1889

> *Principal characters:*
> J., the narrator
> HARRIS, his friend
> GEORGE, another friend
> MONTMORENCY, a dog

Critique:

Three Men in a Boat, which has always been popular with many readers, is a slight tale with only a thin thread of plot. The humor lies in the digressions, which make up the bulk of the book, and in some of the incidents. Jerome had a light and sure touch which only occasionally betrayed him into sentimentality, as when he dealt with a moral fable or attempted a profound look into the meaning of history. In this novel he captured much of the charm of boating on the Thames. The characters are delightfully human.

The Story:

J., Harris, and George were feeling seedy. They sat around idly in J.'s room discussing their ailments. J., especially, was prone to ailments. Once he had gone through a medical book and discovered that he had all the symptoms of typhoid, cholera, and zymosis; in fact, he had all the ills described except housemaid's knee.

He visited a doctor, intent on giving him practice in diagnosis. After the examination the doctor gave him a prescription for a pound of beefsteak and a pint of bitter beer every six hours. The prescription must have been efficacious; J. was still alive.

The three friends decided they needed a complete change and rest. Various possibilities were suggested, including a sea voyage. J. knew from experience that nearly everyone became sick on sea voyages. He had a friend who paid two pounds and a half in advance for his board during a week's trip. By the end of the week he had eaten so little that the steward had at least two pounds clear. A sea voyage was out. As a compromise, they decided on a boat trip up the Thames to Oxford. Montmorency was opposed to the idea but was outvoted.

They were to start from Kingston. George, who had to work until two on Saturdays, would join them at Chertsey. They discussed sleeping and eating arrangements. Although Harris was doubtful, they agreed to sleep in the boat and cook their own meals. Harris had no poetry in his soul; life in the raw had no appeal for him, for he was the type who always knew the best pub in every town in England.

In making their grocery list, J. remembered the time he was in Liverpool. A friend asked him if he would take two cheeses back with him on the train to London. J. willingly agreed. The train was crowded and he found a seat in a full compartment. One by one the others left, overpowered by the odor, and J. had the compartment to himself all the way to London. After he delivered the cheeses to his friend's wife, she promptly moved into a hotel until her husband could get home. He had to bury them on a deserted beach. That experience showed how careful one should be in selecting provisions.

Although Harris and J. were to get an early start, they overslept. It was well after nine before they got all their rugs and hampers together. Then they could not get a cab. They stood on the sidewalk, attracting a curious crowd of hangers-on who made unkind remarks about their many bundles. At Waterloo no one could tell them the platform from which their train would leave. Even the district superintendent was vague. They solved the problem by bribing the engineer of a waiting train to take them to Kingston. The engineer agreed because he had no idea where his train was supposed to go anyway. At last the Exeter mail train took them to Kingston.

Harris had had an experience once in finding his way. He bought a map of Hampton Court maze. It looked simple on the map to visit the place and get out again. A number of innocent bystanders trusted him and his map to their sorrow. The worst of it was that the keeper on duty was new and had little idea how to get out. They all waited hours for the old keeper to come back on duty.

The travelers set out upriver from Kingston. Dividing the work evenly, according to J.'s suggestion, Harris sculled, J. steered, and Montmorency was the passenger. All was going well as J. dreamed along. Suddenly Harris threw away his sculls, left his seat, and threw his legs into the air. J. had daydreamed too long; they had run head-on into the tow path. Shortly afterward they picked up George, and the three men in a boat were fairly off.

Their boat had a series of hoops and a canvas roof over them so that they could sleep on board at night. The first time they tried to set up the apparatus, the hoops became tangled. The canvas was even worse. George and Harris stood at the bow to unroll the canvas and stationed J. at the stern to receive the end. Somehow both George and Harris got rolled up in the canvas. J. noticed that they were struggling for a long time, but he faithfully stuck by the stern to receive the end and fasten it. Finally George got his head out and shouted for help. Harris' face was black by the time they got him unwound.

They made tea on a spirit stove. Their method was to put the kettle on and then make sure not to look at it or show any signs of impatience. Usually the method worked and the kettle boiled. Sometimes they had to make loud remarks about not wanting any tea that meal before the water would get hot enough. Montmorency was hostile toward the kettle. The first time it boiled he took the noise for a challenge and bit the spout. After that he was content merely to growl at the bubbling steam.

They had trouble at times getting water. An old lock tender told them he always used river water. Thinking that boiling the water would make it safe, they tried it once for tea. Just as they were sitting down to tea, a dead dog came floating down the stream.

None of them could cook very well, but George proposed an Irish stew one night. They put potatoes, a peck of peas, two heads of cabbage, some bacon, and whatever else they could find in the pot. George, rummaging for ingredients, expounded the theory that an Irish stew was a handy dish because it got rid of all the leftovers. Montmorency watched the proceedings with interest. When he understood the theory, he trotted off on his own foraging trip. He proudly brought back a dead rat as his contribution.

At Streatley they hired a washerwoman to do their laundry. The original idea had been to do their own washing in the Thames, but that idea had not been successful; the clothes caught all the silt in the river. The woman charged them a triple rate for what was scarcely an ordinary washing job. It was more in the nature of excavating.

Near Wallingford, George and J. stopped at an inn which displayed an enormous trout in a glass case. One by one each of the local hangers-on told them how he had caught the big fish. When the landlord came in, he laughed at the wild claims; he himself had caught it when he was a boy. George, excited, climbed up on a chair for a closer look.

The chair slipped, George clutched, and the glass case came down. Amid the broken glass on the floor lay the broken trout. It was not stuffed; it was made of plaster of Paris.

On the way downstream from Oxford the weather was bad. To while away a rainy evening they played cards, but they had to quit because George won fourpence. They finally grew so bored that Harris and J. asked George to play his banjo and sing.

They finally gave up their trip. Leaving the boat at Pangbourne, they took a train to London. At a select French restaurant they had a light dinner and left an order for a late supper. Then, boating clothes and all, they went to the Alhambra. There was some difficulty getting in because of their wet flannels, but they persevered. Then, after a hearty supper, they watched in comfort the rain outside. Harris thought they were three men well out of a boat.

THE THREE MUSKETEERS

Type of work: Novel
Author: Alexandre Dumas, father (1802-1870)
Type of plot: Historical romance
Time of plot: 1626
Locale: France
First published: 1844

Principal characters:
D'ARTAGNAN, a Gascon adventurer
ATHOS,
PORTHOS, and
ARAMIS, the three musketeers
CONSTANCE BONACIEUX, the queen's seamstress
LADY DE WINTER, Cardinal Richelieu's agent
CARDINAL RICHELIEU, minister of state

Critique:

Of all the stories by Dumas, this is probably the best. It is true that today we may find it too melodramatic, but once we accept the fact that the novel is a romance, we can read it as such and enjoy it. For it is a highly interesting story, full of adventure and intrigue, considered a classic of its type by all who admire historical romances of love and intrigue.

The Story:

In the spring of 1625 a young Gascon named D'Artagnan, on his way to Paris to join the musketeers, proudly rode up to an inn in Meung. He was mounted on an old Béarn pony given him by his father, along with some good advise and a letter of introduction to the captain of the musketeers. In Meung he showed his fighting spirit by fiercely challenging to a duel a stranger who seemed to be laughing at his orange horse. Before continuing his journey to Paris he had another encounter with the stranger, identified by a scar on his face, and the stranger's companion, a young and beautiful woman.

Athos, Porthos, and Aramis were the three best blades in the ranks of the Musketeers of the Guard, in the service of Louis XIII. D'Artagnan became a fourth member of the group within three months of his arrival in Paris. He had made himself loved and respected by the others when he challenged each in turn to a duel and then helped them drive off Cardinal Richelieu's guards, who wished to arrest them for brawling.

D'Artagnan was not made a musketeer at once; he had to serve an apprenticeship as a cadet in a lesser company of guards before being admitted to the musketeer ranks. Athos, Porthos, and Aramis looked forward to the day he would become their true comrade in arms and each took turns accompanying him when he was on guard duty. D'Artagnan was curious about his friends, but could learn nothing about them. Athos looked like a nobleman. He was reserved, never mentioned women, and it was said that a great treachery had poisoned his life. Porthos was a squire of dames, bragging incessantly of his loves. Aramis, who always dressed in black, insisted that he was a musketeer only temporarily, that he was a churchman at heart and soon would enter a monastery and exchange his plumed hat for a monk's cowl.

The three musketeers had been rewarded in gold by the timid king for their bravery against the cardinal's guards, but had since spent all their money. They were trying to figure a way out of their difficulties when Bonacieux, D'Artagnan's landlord, came to D'Artagnan because he had heard that his tenant was a brave man. He said that his wife Constance, who was a seamstress to the queen and whose devotion to the queen was well-known, had been abducted. He suggested that D'Artagnan find and rescue Constance in payment for long-overdue rent and for financial compensation.

When Bonacieux described the abductor, D'Artagnan recognized him as the man he had challenged at Meung. On these two scores, the Gascon was willing to help the stricken husband. But he was even more eager when he discovered that the purpose of the abduction was to force Constance to tell what she knew of a rumored romance between the queen and the Duke of Buckingham.

Constance escaped her abductors and returned to her home, where the cardinal's men again tried to seize her, only to be attacked and scattered by D'Artagnan who had overheard the struggle. Later that evening D'Artagnan met Constance who was hurrying along alone on the streets at a late hour. He questioned her, but she would not say where she was going. He told her that he loved her, but she gave him no encouragement. Still later that evening he encountered her again as she was leading the Duke of Buckingham, in disguise, to the queen.

The queen had sent for Buckingham to beg him to leave the city where his life was in danger. As they talked she confessed her love for him, and gave him as a memento a rosewood casket containing twelve diamond studs that the king had given her.

Richelieu, through his spies, learned of the gift and suggested to the king that he should give a fête and ask the queen to wear her diamond studs. The cardinal then ordered Lady de Winter who was in London, to snip off two of the studs from Buckingham's clothing. This deed gave him a chance to strike at the king, the queen, and also Buckingham. Learning of this scheme, Constance went to D'Artagnan. Because he loved Constance and because he wanted to serve his queen, he undertook to recover the jewels. With his three comrades he

started out for London. Only D'Artagnan arrived there, for when the cardinal's agents ambushed the comrades the three musketeers were wounded and left behind. D'Artagnan reached the duke in time to recover the studs and return to Paris with them. Richelieu's plot was foiled.

After D'Artagnan had received the thanks of the queen he was to meet Constance that evening, but Constance was again seized and imprisoned by the cardinal's spies, one of whom was identified as the man from Meung. D'Artagnan decided he needed the help of his three friends and, accompanied by his servant Planchet, he went to find them. First he called at the inn where he had left Porthos and found him still there, recovering from his wounds. Later he found Aramis talking with some doctors of theology and about to renounce the world. Athos had barricaded himself in a wine-cellar. Drunk, he related a story about a friend of his, a count, who, when he was young, had married a beautiful girl and had made her the first lady in his province. However, he had later discovered that she was branded on the shoulder with the fleur-de-lis, the brand for a convicted criminal, and he had hanged her on a tree, leaving her for dead.

Once again the four friends were together. Then D'Artagnan, who had followed Porthos into a church, saw a beautiful woman whom he recognized as the companion of the man he had met at Meung. He followed her out of church and saw her get into her coach. Later he and his friends took the same road her coach had taken and encountered the coach by the side of the road. The lady was talking to a young man who, D'Artagnan discovered, was her brother-in-law, Lord de Winter. D'Artagnan became a friend of Lord de Winter after sparing his life in a duel; the lord introduced him to his sister-in-law. D'Artagnan fell in love with Lady de Winter. But she loved another, a M. de Wardes, who, unknown to her, had been killed.

D'Artagnan deceived her one night into believing she had an assignation with de Wardes. D'Artagnan presented himself to her as de Wardes that night and she gave him a magnificent sapphire ring. When D'Artagnan showed the ring to Athos, he recognized it as the one which had belonged to his mother and which he had given to his wife. Athos began to suspect that his wife was not dead, but was Lady de Winter.

D'Artagnan overheard Lady de Winter make slurring remarks about him because he had spared the life of her brother-in-law. She was Lord de Winter's heir. D'Artagnan also realized that Lady de Winter was the cardinal's spy. At his next meeting with her, D'Artagnan, as himself, confessed his duplicity to her and she angrily struck a blow which caused him to step on her dress. The dress pulled from her shoulder, exposing the brand of the fleur-de-lis. As D'Artagnan realized the truth, Lady de Winter attacked him with a knife and screamed that she would get revenge. D'Artagnan fled to Athos.

The war between England and France was reaching a climax, and the siege of La Rochelle was of particular political importance. The four friends prepared to go to La Rochelle. Before they left, D'Artagnan was called for an interview with the cardinal. Richelieu tried to bribe D'Artagnan to enter his own guards, but D'Artagnan refused and left with the knowledge that his refusal might mean his death. In La Rochelle two young soldiers tried to kill D'Artagnan. From them he learned that they had been hired by Lady de Winter to kill him, and he also learned that she was responsible for the imprisonment of Constance.

The musketeers did not have much to do with the siege and led a carefree life. One evening they encountered two horsemen on a lonely road. One was the cardinal on his way to a nearby inn. The cardinal ordered the musketeers to go with him. Lady de Winter was at the

inn and the musketeers overheard the cardinal instruct her to go to London, where she was to tell Buckingham that unless he ended the war his affair with the queen would be exposed. If he refused, Lady de Winter was to poison him. As her reward Lady de Winter asked to have two of her enemies killed. These two were Constance, who had been conveyed to a convent by an order the king had obtained from the king, and D'Artagnan. Richelieu then wrote out a safe-conduct for Lady de Winter.

A few minutes later, Athos, who had recognized her voice, was in Lady de Winter's room. There he revealed himself as the Count de la Fère, her husband. She was terrified, for she had thought him dead as well. Athos took from her the cardinal's letter of safe-conduct and ordered her to leave France at once under threats of exposure.

The four friends returned to the siege of La Rochelle, where they conducted themselves with such bravery that they again drew notice from the cardinal. When the cardinal spoke of them to him, their captain said that D'Artagnan was not in the service of the musketeers. The cardinal then gave orders that D'Artagnan was to be made a musketeer, and this news, when relayed to D'Artagnan, made him very happy. The friends now wrote out a message to warn Lord de Winter against his sister-in-law and sent Planchet to deliver it. They also sent a message to a cousin of Aramis, and learned from her the name of the convent in which Constance had been confined.

When Lady de Winter arrived in England, she was held a prisoner by Lord de Winter. But her pretense of religious fervor and her beauty convinced her young Puritan jailer of her innocence. After she had told him a fantastic tale to the effect that her downfall had been caused by Buckingham, he helped her to escape. To avenge her he then went to Buckingham and stabbed him. De Winter, who discovered her escape also hurried to Buckingham, but arrived too late to save his life. Before he died, a messenger from Paris brought Buckingham word from the queen of her faithful love.

Lady de Winter escaped to France, to the convent where Constance was staying. There she managed to poison Constance and flee again before the four companions arrived to rescue the queen's faithful servant. Lord de Winter, also in pursuit of Lady de Winter, arrived a few minutes after they had discovered Constance. Continuing their pursuit of Lady de Winter, they overtook her and held a trial. They condemned her to die. She was executed by the public executioner of Lille, who had branded her for her crimes, many years before.

On his return to La Rochelle, D'Artagnan was arrested and taken to the cardinal. The man who took him prisoner was the stranger D'Artagnan had met at Meung, identified now as the Chevalier de Rochefort. The cardinal charged D'Artagnan with treason, but D'Artagnan interrupted and named the long list of crimes of the woman who had charged him. Then he informed the cardinal of her death and produced the safe-conduct pass, signed by the cardinal, which Athos had taken from the woman. D'Artagnan told Richelieu that as bearer of the pass he should be allowed to go free. The cardinal was so pleased by the Gascon's cleverness that he could not be angry. Instead, he offered D'Artagnan a commission in the musketeers. D'Artagnan offered it to his friends, but each refused it, insisting that he deserved the rank, an honor great nobles often sought in vain.

La Rochelle surrendered to the French and the faithful four disbanded. Athos returned to his estate, Porthos married a rich widow, and Aramis became a monk. D'Artagnan became a famous soldier. He and de Rochefort, his old enemy at Meung, fought three times, but finally became good friends.

THE THREE SISTERS

Type of work: Drama
Author: Anton Chekhov (1860-1904)
Type of plot: Impressionistic realism
Time of plot: Nineteenth century
Locale: Russia
First presented: 1901

Principal characters:
ANDREY PROZÒROV, a student
NATASHA, his fiancée, afterwards his wife
OLGA,
MASHA, and
IRINA, his three sisters
FYODOR KULIGIN, husband of Masha
ALEXANDR VERSHININ, a battery commander
BARON TUSENBACH, a lieutenant
VASSILY SOLYONY, a captain
IVAN TCHEBUTYKIN, an army doctor

Critique:

The Three Sisters is a good example of Chekhov's feeling for people. His male characters are inclined to be weak-willed, incapable of acting, much as Tchebutykin, the old army doctor, and Andrey are throughout the play. On the other hand, his women are likely to be stronger, if only because they live on dreams or hopes, like the three sisters, or Natasha. Yet Chekhov never makes fun of these people; he feels for them with a deep tolerance for human frailty and a hatred of ugly conditions. While the over-all effect of the situation in which the three sisters find themselves is pessimistic, Vershinin provides the leavening that Chekhov always uses to show that, though this world is sad, there is usually someone who thinks that it will be brighter sometime; perhaps not while we live, but sometime.

The Story:

On Irina's name-day, her friends and family called to wish her happiness. It was exactly one year after the death of their father, who had been sent from Moscow eleven years before to this provincial town at the head of a brigade. Irina and Olga longed to go back to Moscow, and Masha would have liked to go too, except that she had married Kuligin, whom she once thought the cleverest of men. They all pinned their hopes on their brother Andrey, who was studying to become a professor.

An old army doctor, Tchebutykin, brought Irina a samovar because he had loved her mother. Masha's husband gave her a copy of the history of the high school in which he taught; he said he wrote it because he had nothing better to do. When Irina told him that he had given her a copy for Easter, he merrily handed it over to one of the army men who was calling. Tusenbach and Solyony quarreled half-heartedly because Tusenbach and Irina had decided that what they needed for happiness was work. Tusenbach had never done anything but go to cadet school, and Irina's father had prepared his children only in languages. Both had a desire to labor hard at something.

Vershinin, the new battery commander, came to call, reminding the girls that he had lived on the same street with them in Moscow. When he praised their town, they said they wanted to go to Moscow. They believed that they had been oppressed with an education which was useless in a dull provincial town. Vershinin thought that for every intelligent person then living, many more would appear later on, and that the whole earth would be unimaginably beautiful two or three hundred years hence. He thought it might be interesting to relive one's life to see if one could improve on the first version.

Natasha came in while they were still sitting at the dinner table. Olga criticized her dress and the men began to tease her about an engagement. Andrey, who could not stand having her teased, followed her out of the room and begged her to marry him. She accepted.

After their marriage Andrey lost any ambition he ever had to become a professor and spent much of his time gambling in order to forget how ill-bred, rude, and selfish Natasha really was. Irina, meanwhile, had taken a job in the telegraph office and Olga was teaching in the high school. Tired when they came home at night, they let Natasha run the house as she pleased, even to moving Irina out of her own bedroom so that Natasha and Andrey's baby could have it.

Vershinin had fallen in love with Masha, though he felt bound to his neurotic wife because of his two daughters. Kuligin realized what was going on but cheerfully hoped Masha still loved him.

Tusenbach, afraid that life would always be difficult, decided to give up his commission and seek happiness in a workingman's life. Vershinin was convinced that by living, working, and struggling we create a better life all the time. Since his wife periodically tried to commit suicide, he did not look for happiness for himself but for his descendants.

Andrey asked Tchebutykin to prescribe for his shortness of breath, but the old doctor swore he had forgotten all the medical knowledge he had ever known.

Solyony fell in love with Irina, who would have nothing to do with him. He declared that he would have no happy rivals.

One night all gathered to have a party with some mummers who were to come in. Natasha, however, decided that the baby was not well and called off the party at the last minute. Then Protopopov, the Chairman of the Rural Board, came by with his carriage to take Natasha riding while Andrey sat reading in his room.

A short time later fire destroyed part of the town. Olga gave most of her clothes to those whose homes had been burned and, after the fire, invited the army people to sleep at the house. Natasha berated Olga for letting her old servant sit in her presence and finally suggested that Olga herself move out of the house. The old doctor became drunk because he had prescribed incorrectly for a woman who had died. After the fire people wanted him to help them, but he could not. In disgust, he picked up a clock and smashed it.

Masha, more bored than before, gave up playing the piano. She was disgusted, too, because Andrey had mortgaged the house in order to give money to Natasha. Everyone but he knew that Natasha was having an affair with Protopopov, to whose Rural Board Andrey had recently been elected.

Irina, at twenty-four, could not find work to suit her, and she believed she was forgetting everything she had ever known. Olga persuaded her to consider marrying Tusenbach, even if he was ugly; with him Irina might get to Moscow.

Masha confessed that she was in love with Vershinin and that he loved her, though he was unable to leave his children.

Andrey berated his sisters for treating his wife so badly and then confessed that he had mortgaged the house which belonged to all four of them. He had so hoped they could all be happy together.

Irina heard a report that the brigade would move out of town. If that happened, they would have to go to Moscow because no one worth speaking to would be left.

On the day the first battery was to

leave, the officers came to say their farewells to the sisters. Irina had heard of an incident the day before which the old doctor dismissed as not worth talking about. Kuligin, however, told her that Tusenbach and Solyony had had words because both of them were in love with her and she had promised to marry Tusenbach. Kuligin eagerly anticipated the departure of the brigade because he hoped Masha would then again turn to him. Masha was bored and spiteful. She felt that she was losing, bit by bit, the small happiness she had.

Andrey wondered how he could love Natasha when he knew she was so vulgar. The old doctor claimed that he was tired of their troubles, and he advised Andrey to walk off and never look back. But the doctor, who was to be retired from the army in a year, planned to come back to live with them because he really loved them all.

Irina hoped to go off with Tusenbach. Olga intended to live at the school of which she was now headmistress. Natasha, expecting to be left in sole charge of the house, planned all sorts of changes to wipe away the memory of the sisters' having been there. Andrey wondered how his children could possibly overcome the deadening influence of their mother's vulgarity.

After Tusenbach had fought a duel with Solyony, Tchebutykin returned to tell them that Tusenbach had been killed. So the sisters were left alone with their misery, each thinking that she must go on with her life merely to find out why people suffer so much in a world that could be beautiful.

THREE SOLDIERS

Type of work: Novel
Author: John Dos Passos (1896-   )
Type of plot: Social criticism
Time of plot: 1917-1919
Locale: France
First published: 1921

Principal characters:
DAN FUSELLI, an American soldier from San Francisco
CHRISFIELD, an American soldier from Indiana
JOHN ANDREWS (ANDY), an American soldier from Virginia
GENEVIÈVE ROD, Andrews' friend

Critique:

This novel attempts to do for World War I what Stephen Crane's *The Red Badge of Courage* did for the Civil War; that is, to destroy the myth of glamour and glory and to expose the brutal reality of war. Unlike the hero of *The Red Badge of Courage*, who deserts in fright and returns proudly to battle, John Andrews of *Three Soldiers* can only take a self-respecting step by deserting after months of ignominious conformity. The novel succeeds best in its presentation of the tedium, de-humanizing regimentation, and the physical horrors of war. As such, it is a vividly realized social document.

The Story:

Private Dan Fuselli was anxious to become Corporal Dan Fuselli. He had seen movies of Huns spitting Belgian babies on their bayonets and then being chased like rabbits by heroic Yankee soldiers who were later rewarded with embraces by the pretty and picturesque Belgian milkmaids. He looked forward to the time when his girl, Mabe, writing from San Francisco, his home town, would address her letters to Corporal Dan Fuselli.

Private First Class Fuselli of the Medical Corps hated the Army and everything about it, but he knew that to become a corporal he must keep clean, keep his mouth shut, obey the brass, and continually cajole the sergeant. He was infuriated one night when he went to town to see Yvonne and learned that the sergeant had taken her over. Then, when he returned to camp, he heard that the consumptive corporal was back, the one in whose absence Fuselli had been made acting corporal. But Private Fuselli kept his mouth shut. Someday he would be a corporal, perhaps even a sergeant; but now he kept his mouth shut.

Finally, after a setback doing endless K. P. and following his recovery from a venereal disease, after the Armistice, he did become Corporal Dan Fuselli. But by that time his girl had married a naval officer.

Matters worked out differently for Chrisfield. The Army was not as easy-going as life in the Indiana farm country had been. The officers shouted at you, made you do things you hated. You had to take it. One night Chrisfield was so furious he pulled a knife on a sergeant named Anderson, but his friends held him back and nothing happened. In Europe, things were not much better. Occasionally he had a talk about the stars and the fields with his educated buddy, John Andrews. Mostly, however, the war was awful.

The marches were endless, and his shoulders ached from his heavy pack. When bombardments came, the marchers scattered face down in a field. Once Chrisfield asked Andrews to speak French for him to a French girl at an inn, but nothing came of it.

One day, walking alone through a wood near the front, Chrisfield found a dead German lying prone. When he kicked the body over, he saw that it had no face, only a multicolored, pulpy mass with green flies hovering around it. In the man's hand was a revolver—he was a suicide. Chrisfield ran off panting.

Chrisfield was high-strung. When he was sitting thinking, a soldier prodded him and asked him what he was dreaming about. Chrisfield punched the fellow in the nose. He and Andy hated the Y. M. C. A. men who were always telling the men at the front what brutes the Huns were and urging them in the name of Old Glory to kill Germans. Chrisfield was court-martialed when he announced that he intended to kill Sergeant Anderson after the war was over.

One day he went wandering and made his way silently into the kitchen of a house near the front. Looking into the next room, he saw a man in a German uniform. He reached into his pocket, pressed the spring on the grenade he had, withdrew it, and tossed it into the room. Not long afterward he came across Anderson, now a lieutenant, seated wounded in a deserted section of the wood. Chrisfield had two more grenades in his pocket, and he threw them at the man he hated.

After the Armistice, the rumor that he had killed Anderson somehow leaked out. Afraid, Chrisfield went A. W. O. L. and became a refugee in France, eternally on the move.

John Andrews was a Harvard graduate and a would-be composer. The Queen of Sheba section of Flaubert's *Temptation of Saint Anthony* kept recurring to his mind as he washed the barracks windows, and he thought how fine the subject would be for a musical composition. He cursed the Army for slowly stamping him into its iron mold. Overseas, he saw action and was more convinced than ever that war was needless butchery. He felt happiest away from the regiment. One day he walked away from his company in order to be alone.

He was looking at little frogs in a pool when a shell burst near him. He awoke on a stretcher.

For a while the hospital was a relief from the endless orders and general mechanization of Army routine. Lying in his bed, he began to realize that he had respect for himself only when he thought of rebelling against the system, of going A. W. O. L. Soon the tedium of the hospital began to gall him. After his leg healed, he rejoined his company reluctantly and full of rebellion. The Armistice had been signed. When he heard that he could go to a French University through a school detachment being set up, he lied, secured some recommendations, and found himself in Paris.

In Paris he met Geneviève Rod, a young Frenchwoman who admired his piano playing and his artistic tastes. She thought of artists as men who, because of their special sensitivity, should be exempt from the horrors of war. Andrews disagreed; one worker was like another; it was the whole of humanity that should be exempt. One day he left Paris without official leave for a country trip with Geneviève. An MP picked him up and took him to a local office where he was beaten by several MP's. He was sent to a labor battalion loading concrete for a stadium being presented by the Americans to the French. It was crushing work. Convinced that Army life was a menace to human freedom, Andrews decided to desert, for one man less in the system made it weaker by that much. One night he leaped from a plank and swam out to a barge in the Seine.

The barge family cared for him for a few days. They sank his uniform in the river, bought him new clothes, and as anarchists proclaimed their solidarity with him. He went back to Paris to find Geneviève, and stayed for a while with Chrisfield and a group of other concealed deserters. Then, hearing that Geneviève was at her country place, he joined her there.

At first he did not tell her of his desertion. He lived in an inn nearby and

3774

began composing, not about the Queen of Sheba, but about John Brown, liberator of slaves. When he finally confessed his plight to Geneviève, a noticeable reserve crept into her attitude toward him. Perhaps, she suggested, he should give himself up. She could not comprehend the social motive in his rebellion.

One day he heard an American officer's voice at the door of the inn below his window. He thought of the prison sentence he must face. Too late he discovered that the landlady, experienced in the ways of impecunious Americans who were possible deserters, had stolen his revolver. As the MP's took him away, the wind blew in through the window of his room and the music papers on which he had been working fluttered one by one to the floor.

THROUGH THE LOOKING GLASS

Type of work: Imaginative tale
Author: Lewis Carroll (Charles Lutwidge Dodgson, 1832-1898)
Type of plot: Fantasy
Time of plot: Nineteenth century
Locale: The dream world of an imaginative child
First published: 1871

Principal characters:
ALICE, a fanciful child
DINAH, a cat
THE BLACK KITTEN
THE WHITE KITTEN
THE WHITE KING AND QUEEN
THE RED KING AND QUEEN
GNAT
TWEEDLEDUM AND TWEEDLEDEE
HUMPTY DUMPTY
THE LION AND THE UNICORN
THE WHITE KNIGHT AND THE RED KNIGHT

Critique:

A continuation of the adventures of Alice in the marvelous country of Wonderland, this story takes her into Looking-Glass Land, filled with talking insects and live chessmen. Although the story may perhaps be a gentle satire on mid-Victorian life and customs, it is primarily a children's fantasy and the reader need not look for nor concern himself with deeper meanings. Alice undoubtedly led a lonely and sometimes confusing life, and we delight with her in her new, though peculiar, friends. Indeed, we must envy the real Alice, a little girl who could inspire such wonderful stories.

The Story:

Alice was sure the whole thing was not the white kitten's fault. It must surely have been the fault of the black kitten. For Dinah, the mother cat, had been washing the white kitten's face when it happened; she certainly had had nothing to do with it. But the mischievous black kitten had been unwinding Alice's yarn and in all ways acting naughty enough to cause the whole strange affair.

While the black kitten curled up in Alice's lap to play with the yarn, Alice told it to pretend that the two of them could go right through the mirror and into Looking-Glass House. As she talked,

the glass grew all misty and soft, and in a moment Alice was through the mirror and in the Looking-Glass room. The place was very strange, for although the room looked just the same as the real room she had seen in the mirror, the clock and the fire and the other things in the room seemed to be alive. Even the chessmen, for Alice loved to play chess, were alive.

When Alice picked up the White Queen and set her on the table, the White Queen screamed in terror, thinking that a volcano had shaken her about. The White King had the same fear, but he was too astonished to cry out. They seemed not to see or hear Alice, and even though she wanted to stay and watch them and read the king's rather funny poetry, she felt she must look at the garden before she had to go back through the Looking Glass. When she started down the stairs, she seemed to float, not even once touching the steps.

In the garden every path Alice took led her straight back to the house. She asked Tiger Lily and Rose and Violet whether there were any other people in the garden; she hoped they might help her find the right path. The flowers told her there was only one, and Alice found her to be the Red Queen—but a very strange chess figure, for the Red

Queen was taller than Alice herself. As Alice walked toward the Red Queen, she once more found herself back at the door of the house. Then Alice figured out that in order to get *to* any place in this queer land one must walk in the *opposite* direction. Doing so, she came face to face with the Red Queen.

The queen took Alice to the top of a hill. There, spread out below them, was a countryside that looked like a large chessboard. Alice, delighted, said that she would love to play on this board. Then the Red Queen told her that they would play and that Alice could be the White Queen's Pawn. They would start on the Second Square and—but at that moment the Red Queen grabbed Alice's hand and they started to run. Alice had never run so fast in her life, but even though she was breathless from such fast running the things around them never changed a tiny bit. When they finally stopped running, the queen told Alice that in this land one had to run as fast as she could to stay in the same place and twice as fast as she could to get somewhere else. Then the queen showed Alice the pegs in the Second Square and told her how to move. At the last peg the Red Queen disappeared, leaving Alice alone to continue the game.

Alice started to run down the hill. The next thing she knew she was on a train filled with insects and having quite an unpleasant time because she did not have a ticket. All of the insects talked unkindly to her, and to add to her discomfort the train jumped over the brook and took them all straight up in the air. When she came down, she was sitting under a tree, talking to a Gnat. Gnat was as big as a chicken but very pleasant. He told her about the other insects that lived in the woods; then he too melted away and Alice had to go on alone.

Turning a corner, she bumped into two fat little men, called Tweedledum and Tweedledee, the funniest little creatures she had ever seen. Everything they said seemed to have two meanings. It was fun to listen to the merry little men as they recited a long poem about a Walrus and a Carpenter and some Oysters. While they were explaining the poem to Alice, she heard a puffing noise, like the sound of a steam engine. Tweedledee told her it was the Red King snoring. Sure enough, they found him asleep. Tweedledee told Alice that the Red King was dreaming about her and that if he stopped dreaming Alice would be gone for good. Alice cried when they told her she was not real but only a part of the Red King's dream.

As she brushed her tears away, she saw Tweedledum staring in terror at something on the ground. It was an old broken rattle, over which the two foolish men got into a terrible fight. That is, they *talked* a terrible fight, but neither seemed very anxious to have a real battle. The Crow flew over and frightened them so that the funny men ran away into the wood. Alice ran too, and as she ran she saw a shawl blowing about.

Alice, looking for the owner of the shawl, saw the White Queen running toward her. The White Queen was a very queer person; she lived backward and remembered things *before* they happened. For example, she hurt *before* she pricked her finger. While the queen was telling these strange things to Alice, the queen turned into a Sheep and was in a shop with Alice. It was a very curious shop, the shelves full of things that disappeared when Alice looked at them. Sometimes the boxes went right through the ceiling. Then Sheep gave Alice some needles and told her to knit.

As she started to knit, the needles became oars and she found herself and Sheep in a little boat rowing in a stream. The oars kept sticking in the water. Sheep explained that the crabs were catching them. Alice picked some beautiful, fragrant rushes that melted away as soon as she picked them. Soon, to her surprise, the river and boat vanished, and Alice and Sheep were back in the shop. She bought an egg, even though in this shop two were cheaper than one, but when she started to get the egg, as Sheep would not reach it for her, the egg began to grow larger and larger and more and more real, with eyes, a nose, and a mouth. Then Alice could tell as plain as day that the egg was Humpty Dumpty.

She had a queer conversation with Humpty Dumpty, a conversation all filled with riddles. They took turns at choosing the topic to talk about, but most of the subjects turned into arguments, even though Alice tried hard to be polite. Humpty Dumpty explained to Alice what the "Jabberwocky" poem meant, the one she had seen in the White King's book. Then, while reciting another poem, he stopped right in the middle, saying that was all. Alice thought it very queer but did not tell Humpty Dumpty so. She thought it time for her to leave, but as she walked away there was a terrible crash that shook the whole forest.

Thousands of soldiers and horses came rushing toward her, the riders constantly falling off their horses. Frightened, she escaped from the wood into the open. There she found the White King, who told her that he had sent the soldiers and horses and that the loud crash she had heard was the noise of the Lion and Unicorn fighting for the crown. She went with the king to watch the fight, which was indeed a terrible one. It was really silly of them to fight for the crown, since it belonged to the White King and he had no notion of giving it away. After the fight Alice met the Unicorn and the Lion. At the king's order she served them cake, a very strange cake which cut itself when she carried the dish around.

A great noise interrupted the party. When it stopped Alice thought she must have dreamed the whole thing until the Red Knight came along, followed soon by a White Knight. Each claimed her as a prisoner. Alice thought the whole business silly, since neither of them could do

anything except fall off his horse and climb back on again, over and over and over. At last the Red Knight galloped off and the White Knight told her that she would be a queen as soon as she crossed the next brook. He was supposed to lead her to the end of the wood, but she spent the whole journey helping him back on his horse each time he fell off. The trip was filled with more queer conversation. By that time Alice was used to strange talk from her Looking-Glass friends. At last they reached the brook. The knight rode away and Alice jumped over the brook and into the last square of the chess board. To her delight, when she reached that square she felt something tight on her head—a crown! She was a queen.

Soon she found the Red Queen and the White Queen confronting her, very cross because she also thought she was a queen. They gave her a test for queens which she must have passed, for before long they were calling her "Your Majesty," and inviting people to a party which she was to give. The Red and the White Queens went to sleep after a time. Alice watched them until they disappeared. Then she found herself before a doorway marked "Queen Alice." All of her new friends were there, including the queens who had just vanished. The party was the most amazing experience of all. Puddings talked, guests poured wine over their heads, and the White Queen turned into a leg of mutton. Alice was exasperated, so much so that she seized the tablecloth and jerked it and everything on it to the floor. Then she grabbed the Red Queen and shook her as she would a kitten. But what was this? It was a kitten she was shaking, the black kitten.

Alice talked to Dinah and both the kittens about the adventure they had all had, but the silly kittens did nothing but purr.

3778

THUS SPAKE ZARATHUSTRA

Type of work: Philosophical comments as parable and prophecy
Author: Friedrich Wilhelm Nietzsche (1844-1900)
First published: Parts I-III, 1883-1884; Part IV, 1891

Only a philosopher with a great ego (resulting from a fear of failure) and a great passion would have conceived the idea of putting his most radical thoughts into the mouth of a Persian mystic dead over five hundred years before the birth of Jesus. Zarathustra, or Zoroaster, was a Persian religious leader whose revolutionary religious activity stimulated the growth of the religion that bears his name: Zoroastrianism. Nietzsche fancied that he found similarities between his ideas and passions and those of Zarathustra, but whether he was justified in using the name of the Persian in order to give his paradoxical and poetic work a certain mystical quality is a problem that can be left to those who moralize about art. The important word to remember is "art": *Thus Spake Zarathustra* is a work of art in which a radical inversion of traditional values is expressed in the guise of poetic prophetic writings.

Nietzsche's prologue, entitled "Zarathustra's Prologue," tells us that Zarathustra went up into the mountains when he was thirty and stayed there ten years. When he came down he went to the market place of the nearest town and said, "I teach you the Superman. Man is something that is to be surpassed. What have you done to surpass man?"

The book is Nietzsche's attempt to help man surpass himself, to become Superman. Of course, Superman is the author's conception, and the qualities which make Superman distinctive can most readily be understood as the opposite to whatever is enervating and spiritless in traditional Christianity. It is easy to read Nietzsche as one who condemns whatever is generally regarded as worth-while and virtuous; he condemns Christianity as fostering a "slave morality." But what he says makes some sense, whatever its excesses, if considered as having been stimulated by Christianity at its sentimental and dogmatic worst.

Nietzsche's basic idea is that the most important feature of all existence is will, an idea he received from Schopenhauer. But, unlike the pessimistic Schopenhauer, he did not believe that man's objective should be to abolish the will and, consequently, to be nothing; on the contrary, Nietzsche thought that man should seek to surpass himself, to strengthen his will, to rise above ordinary men, and to achieve greatness of will and being. For him, pride is a great virtue and so is contempt of everything that ordinary men believe and worship.

Zarathustra speaks to the spectators of a rope-dancing performance and tells them to "remain true to the earth" and not to believe "those who speak unto you of superearthly hopes!" He tells them that the greatest thing they can experience is "the hour of great contempt" in which they look with loathing upon their happiness, their reason, and their virtue. When the rope-dancer falls and is fatally injured, Zarathustra tells him not to worry about being dragged to hell; he assures the dying man that his soul will be dead before his body is. When the rope-dancer replies that if this is so, he is nothing more than an animal, Zarathustra objects by pointing out that the rope-dancer had made danger his calling, and he adds that ". . . therein there is nothing contemptible."

Nietzsche's ideas have sometimes been compared to those of the Nazis, but it is probably more accurate to suppose that the virtues Nietzsche endorses are those which Hemingway extols in his novels. Both writers ask men to surpass themselves, to be courageous and proud, to face danger, to love action and to act, and to respect those who can kill and be killed; both writers regard love as important only when it is biologically compelling, and even then it is regarded as something of a nuisance.

Nietzsche is famous not only for his denunciation of Christianity but also for his attacks on women. In Section 18 of the First Part, Zarathustra gives his views on women: "Everything in woman is a riddle, and everything in woman hath one solution—it is called pregnancy. . . . Two different things wanteth the true man: danger and diversion. Therefore wanteth he woman, as the most dangerous plaything. Man shall be trained for war, and woman for the recreation of the warrior: all else is folly." Zarathustra concludes with a "little truth" which the old woman to whom he expressed his ideas gave him: "Thou goest to women? Do not forget thy whip!"

Although it is possible for the critic so to consider *Thus Spake Zarathustra* that it becomes sensible to speak of its philosophic content, it is more helpful to take the book as a prose poem, a passionate and sometimes incoherent injunction to men to become more than they have been and to go beyond the petty limits prescribed for them by conventional moralities.

Nevertheless, when the effort is made to extract from this curious book its philosophic claims, it soon becomes clear that for Nietzsche values make sense only if they are relative to the individual, not only in the respect that whatever is good or bad is so *to* a person, but also in the respect that whatever is good or bad (according to Nietzsche) is so *for* a person. There would be no point in telling the author that some men value the welfare of other persons; such sentimental attachment to others is what keeps a man from surpassing himself, Nietzsche believes. To be great, to surpass himself, a man must consider his own power and know how he can best use that power to extend himself and to satisfy himself. "One must learn to love oneself . . . with a wholesome and healthy love." he writes, "that one may endure to be with oneself, and not go roving about." To be more than man, to discover oneself, involves giving up the moral habits and injunctions we learned "almost in the cradle." Nietzsche claims that with the words "brotherly love" there has been "the best lying and dissembling, and especially by those who have been burdensome to every one." And he argues that "He, however, hath discovered himself who saith: This is *my* good and evil: therewith hath he silenced the mole and the dwarf who say: 'Good for all, evil for all.'" The conclusive statement of the relativity of values comes at the end of the section titled "The Spirit of Gravity," from which the quotations of this paragraph come: "'This—is now *my* way,—where is yours?' Thus did I answer those who asked me 'the way.' For *the* way—it doth not exist!"

In "Old and New Tables" Nietzsche reaches the extreme point of demanding the destruction of old laws and commandments. Nietzsche venerates the creator of new values and, consequently, the destroyer of old ones. The creation of new values is important, not because it rights wrongs and liberates men, but because the creative process itself is an exercise of the will's power; it is the way to Superman. Nietzsche argues that the greatest danger to any man and to mankind comes from the good and the just: that is, from the defenders of the old morality. He writes that "The good *must* crucify him who deviseth his own virtue!"

Again, when one considers Nietzsche philosophically, it is possible to find in *Thus Spake Zarathustra* many ideas which connect Nietzsche with modern Existentialism. He argues that God is dead, the old God that preached brotherly love; man faces an abyss and before the response of petty men the higher man feels nothing but disgust. The proper response to the abyss is the creative act of a man who loves himself and takes pride in his power to create new values through his acts. "Doth not—man's *future* strive and struggle in you?" he asks.

These ideas are presented to the reader in the midst of strange accounts of Zarathustra's wanderings and encounters with the mass of the market place and with a few eccentric persons who in one way or another suggest the Superman ideal.

To suppose that Nietzsche created the ideal of the Superman as the destroyer of old values and the creator of the new, the teacher of the virtue of pride, in order to justify a totalitarian state, is to misread him. Because of the superficial resemblance of Nazi propaganda to Nietzschean utterances, it is easy to fall into the error of taking Nietzsche as an apologist for a state controlled by self-styled "supermen." Early in *Thus Spake Zarathustra*, Nietzsche condemns the state for its pretension to be identified with the people. Not only is it a lie to identify the state with the people, but it is destructive of men to believe the lie. Only where the state falls does man rise and make Superman possible.

Many persons dismiss Nietzsche contemptuously, knowing only that he contemptuously dismissed Christianity. But throughout *Thus Spake Zarathustra* and *Beyond Good and Evil* (q.v.), Nietzsche reveals a constant and impassioned concern for that part of each man which is lost, in his opinion, because of slavish obedience to a conventional, effeminate morality. His scorn of the "rabble"—"Life is a well of delight; but where the rabble also drink, there all fountains are poisoned."—is not so much a scorn of men and virtue as it is of those who pervert themselves and others in the name of virtue. He writes, "And many a one who cannot see man's loftiness, calleth it virtue to see their baseness far too well. . . ." Nietzsche creates Zarathustra as a liberator, as one who brings the new word that all men might be free—not to march onward in any regimented way, but to stream outwards as individually creative beings. Much of what Emerson endorsed as "self-reliance" Nietzsche endorses as "the will of power."

If Nietzsche is to be criticized for his shortcomings, it would be better to call attention to the absence of development and order in his work. However one may sympathize with his love for the creative man, certain problems remain: How does one come to choose or to create the new law? Is it possible for a man desiring to be Superman—to surpass himself—to be free and creative in the wrong way, and thus to destroy himself?

Nietzsche's failure to clarify the procedure of value-creation is his greatest fault. His work remains a paean of praise for an art he never elucidates.

THYESTES

Type of work: Drama
Author: Lucius Annaeus Seneca (c. 4 B.C.-A.D. 65)
Type of plot: Tragedy of revenge
Time of plot: The Heroic Age
Locale: Greece
First presented: c. A.D. 60

Principal characters:
ATREUS, King of Argos
THYESTES, his brother
THYESTES' THREE SONS

Critique:

The most fiendish revenge play in the history of drama is this Senecan tragedy, the gruesome story of a banquet at which the father partakes of his own children. The play is also a landmark in dramatic history, for it was the model of many revenge plays appearing in the sixteenth and seventeenth centuries in English drama. As such, it was the forerunner of Thomas Kyd's *The Spanish Tragedy,* Shakespeare's *Hamlet,* Chapman's *Revenge of Bussy D'Ambois,* and Webster's *The Duchess of Malfi.* Seneca was not the first ancient author to make use of the Thyestes legend. It had been used by Sophocles, Euripides, Ennius, and Accius. None of the versions by those authors have, however, survived the years, and we do not even have enough information about them to compare the treatment by those authors with that of Seneca.

The Story:

Megaera, one of the Furies, summoned the ghost of Tantalus to return from Hades to Argos, where Tantalus in life had been king, to watch revenge, hate, and havoc spread across that kingdom. Tantalus was hesitant because of the part he had played in the story of his royal house, but Megaera forced him to witness the fate of his descendants.

The grandsons of Tantalus, the sons of Pelops, whom Tantalus had sacrificed to the gods, were at war with one another. The oldest of Pelops' sons, Atreus, was the rightful ruler of Argos, but his brother, Thyestes, had seduced Atreus' wife and carried her away. With them they took the golden ram, the symbol of power held by the ruler of the kingdom. Civil war broke out, and Thyestes was defeated. After his defeat he was exiled by Atreus.

But exile was not sufficient punishment for Thyestes. The fierce hatred of Atreus, burning over his brother's crimes and his own misfortune in the loss of his wife, demanded greater revenge. A tyrant who believed that death was a comfort to his subjects, Atreus brooded over fierce and final vengeance upon his younger brother. He felt that no act of revenge could be a crime when committed against a man who had worked against him as his brother had. Moreover, he felt that he, as a king, could do as he wished; private virtues were not for rulers.

When an attendant suggested that Atreus put Thyestes to the sword, Atreus said that death was only an end. He wanted Thyestes to suffer even greater torture. The punishment Atreus finally hit upon was a scheme to feed Thyestes' own children to him at a banquet.

Atreus took the first step toward accomplishing his revenge. He sent his own sons, Agamemnon and Menelaus, as emissaries of good will to Thyestes and asked the exile, through them, to return to a place of honor at his brother's side. Fearing that his sons, forewarned, might lack the discretion needed to act as friendly ambassadors, he did not tell them the part they were playing in his scheme of revenge.

Thyestes, trusting the king, returned to Argos with his three sons, including one named Tantalus, after his great-grandfather of famous memory. But when he looked again at familiar landscapes, Thyestes felt a sense of foreboding. His footsteps faltered, and his sons noted his apparent unwillingness to return. The offer of peace and half the kingdom seemed to Thyestes unlike his brother's earlier hatred and fury. He felt that there had been too much hate and bloodshed between them for real peace. But his sons, silencing his doubts, led him on to the court of Atreus.

Atreus, overjoyed to see his brother and nephews in his power and apparently unmindful of the revenge plotted against them, concealed his hatred and welcomed them to the kingdom once again.

Atreus announced a great feast to celebrate his brother's homecoming. Then, taking the three sons of Thyestes aside, he led them to a grove behind the palace and there slew them with all the ceremony of a sacrifice to the gods. The first he stabbed in the neck, the second he decapitated, and the third he killed by a thrust through the body. The boys, knowing that appeals were useless, suffered death in silence. Atreus drew off their blood and prepared the carcasses like so much beef. The limbs he quartered and placed upon spits to roast; the bodies he hacked into small pieces and placed in pots to boil.

The fire seemed reluctant to burn as an accomplice to his deed, but Atreus stood by and acted as cook until the ghastly banquet was ready. As he cooked, the sky grew dark and an unnatural night settled across the face of the earth. The banquet prepared, Atreus felt that he was the equal of the gods themselves.

The feast began. After the banquet had progressed to the point that the guests were glutted by all they had eaten, Atreus prepared for Thyestes a drink of wine and blood drained from the bodies of Thyestes' sons.

All the while a premonition of evil hung like a cloud in the back of Thyestes' mind. Try as he would, he could not be gay and enjoy the feast, for vague terrors struck at his heart. When Atreus gave him the cup of blood and wine, he could not lift it to drink at first, and when he did try to drink the wine seemed to roll around the brim of the cup rather than pass through his lips. Filled with sudden fears, Thyestes demanded that Atreus produce his sons.

Atreus left and returned with the heads of the three sons on a platter. Thyestes, chilled with horror at the sight, asked where the bodies were. He feared that Atreus had refused them honorable burial and had left them for the dogs to eat. Atreus told Thyestes that he had eaten his own children. Then Thyestes realized why unnatural night had darkened the skies.

Still Atreus was not satisfied. He felt disappointed that he had not planned to force Thyestes to drink some of his children's blood while they were yet alive. The king bragged of what he had done and described how he himself had committed the murders and spitted the meat before the fires.

Atreus, enjoying his revenge, could never believe that the greatest weight upon Thyestes' mind was regret that he had not thought of such revenge and caused Atreus to eat of his own children.

THE TIME MACHINE

Type of work: Novel
Author: H. G. Wells (1866-1946)
Type of plot: Fantasy
Time of plot: Late nineteenth century
Locale: England
First published: 1895

Principal characters:
THE TIME TRAVELER
WEENA, a woman the Time Traveler meets in the future

Critique:

The Time Traveler's description of the people of the future, the weak Eloi and the predatory Morlocks, has its roots in some interesting scientific hypotheses. This speculative chronicle of a space-time concept and a picture of life in the world of the future is so exciting, however, that it may be read merely as an adventure story. The book is a mixture of fantasy and pseudo-scientific romance.

The Story:

After dinner, one evening, the Time Traveler led the discussion to the subject of the relationship of time and space. It was his theory that time was a fourth dimension, and that his concept could be proved. To the astonishment of his guests, he exhibited a model of his Time Machine, which, he declared, could travel backward or forward in time. One of the guests was invited to touch a lever. To the amazement of all, the machine disappeared. The Time Traveler explained that the instrument was no longer visible because it was traveling into the past at such great speed that it was below the threshold of visibility.

The following week the Time Traveler was not at home to greet his dinner guests when they arrived, but he had left word that they were to proceed without him. Everyone was at the table when their host came in, dirty from head to toe, limping, and with a cut on his chin. After he had changed his clothes and dined, he told his friends the story of the day's adventures.

That morning he had taken off on his Time Machine. As he reeled through space, the days shot past him like minutes, the rapid alternation of light and darkness hurting the Time Traveler's eyes. Landing and falling from his machine when he braked too suddenly, he found himself on the side of a hill. In the misty light he could see the figure of a winged sphinx on a bronze pedestal. As the sun came out, the Time Traveler saw enormous buildings on the slope. Some figures were coming toward him. One was a little man about four feet tall. Regaining his confidence, the Time Traveler waited to meet this citizen of the future.

Soon a group of these creatures gathered around the voyager. Without a common language, he and his new acquaintances had to communicate with signs. After they had examined the Time Machine, from which he had the presence of mind to remove the levers, one of them asked him if he had come from the sun.

The Time Traveler was led to one of the large buildings, where he was seated upon a cushion and given fruit to eat. Everyone was a vegetarian, animals having become extinct. When he had eaten, he tried to learn his new friends' language, but without much success. These people, who called themselves the Eloi, were not able to concentrate and tired quickly.

Free to wander about, the Time Traveler climbed a hill and from the crest saw the ruins of an enormous granite structure. Looking at some of the creatures who were following him, he realized that all wore similar garb and had the same soft, rounded figures. Children could be distinguished only by their size.

The Time Traveler realized that he was seeing the sunset of humanity. In the society of the future there was no need for strength. The world was at peace and secure. The strong of body or mind would only have felt frustrated.

As he looked about to find a place to sleep, he saw that his Time Machine had disappeared. He tried to wake the people in the building in which he had dined, but he succeeded only in frightening them. At last he went back to the lawn and there, greatly worried over his plight, fell asleep.

The next morning he managed to trace the path the Time Machine made to the base of the sphinx, but the bronze doors in the pedestal were closed. The Time Traveler tried to intimate to some of the Eloi that he wished to open the doors, but they answered him with looks of insult and reproach. He attempted to hammer in the doors with a stone, but he soon stopped from weariness.

Weena, a young girl he rescued from drowning, became the Time Traveler's friend and guide. On the fourth morning, while he explored one of the ruins, he saw eyes staring at him from the dark. Curious, he followed a small, apelike figure to a well-like opening, down which it retreated. He was convinced that this creature was also a descendant of man, a subterranean species that worked below ground to support the dwellers in the upper world.

Convinced that the Morlocks, as the subterranean dwellers were called, were responsible for the disappearance of his Time Machine and hoping to learn more about them, he climbed down into one of the wells. At its bottom he discovered a tunnel which led into a cavern in which he saw a table set with a joint of meat. The Morlocks were carnivorous. He was able to distinguish, too, some enormous machinery.

The next day the Time Traveler and Weena visited a green porcelain museum containing animal skeletons, books, and machinery. Since they had walked a long distance, he planned to sleep in the woods that night with Weena and to build a fire to keep the dark-loving Morlocks away. When he saw three crouching figures in the brush, however, he changed his mind and decided he and Weena would be safer on a hill beyond the forest. He started a fire to keep their enemies at a distance.

When he awoke the fire had gone out, his matches were missing, and Weena had vanished. A fire he had started earlier was still burning, and while he slept it had set the forest on fire. Between thirty and forty Morlocks perished in the blaze while the Time Traveler watched.

When daylight returned, the Time Traveler retraced his steps to the sphinx. He slept all day and in the evening prepared to ram open the doors in the pedestal with the lever he had found in the porcelain palace. He found the doors open, his machine in plain view. As a group of Morlocks sprang at him, he took off through space.

The Time Traveler had his encounter with the Morlocks and the Eloi in the year 802,701. On his next journey he moved through millions of years, toward that time when the earth will cease rotating. He landed on a deserted beach, empty except for a flying animal, which looked like a huge white butterfly, and some crab-like monsters. On he traveled, finally halting thirty million years after the time he had left his laboratory. In that distant age the sun was setting. It was bitter cold and it began to snow. All around was deathly stillness. Horrified, the Time Traveler started back toward his present.

That evening, as he told his story, his guests grew skeptical. In fact, the Time Traveler himself had to visit his laboratory to make sure his machine existed. The next day, however, all doubts ceased, for one of his friends watched him depart on his vehicle. It was this friend who wrote the story of the Time Traveler's experiences three years later. The Time Traveler had not reappeared during that time, and his friends speculated on the mishap which had made him a lost wanderer in space and time.

THE TIME OF MAN

Type of work: Novel
Author: Elizabeth Madox Roberts (1886-1941)
Type of plot: Regional romance
Time of plot: Early twentieth century
Locale: Kentucky
First published: 1926

Principal characters:
ELLEN CHESSER, a farm girl
NELLIE, her mother
HENRY, her father
JASPER KENT, her husband
JONAS, her fiancé

Critique:

The Time of Man is a farm story that strikes a nice balance between the sordid and the romantic. Here we have the life of the migrant Kentucky farmer as it is, unvarnished and plain. But deeper, we see the springs from which these people draw their strength. They lived in poverty, with little hope of security. But in their love for the soil and in their fierce independence they find meaning for their lives. To call this novel a story of local color would be true but inadequate. The regionalism of The Time of Man is but a convenient frame for the depiction of human and enduring values.

The Story:

Henry and Nellie Chesser had been on the road a long time. People sometimes called the Chessers and their friends gipsies, and they did tell fortunes and swap horses and mules. But Henry liked the earth, and he worked as a tenant for different farmers from time to time. Only his restless spirit kept him from settling somewhere permanently.

One day Henry's wagon broke down. The others could not wait for the Chessers, and Henry haunted the smithy, hoping to speed repairs. But when Hep Bodine offered him twenty dollars a month, a tenant house, and a garden spot, he accepted. The house had only one room and a loft, but it was better than sleeping outside.

Henry's daughter, Ellen, was greatly disappointed. She hated to leave Tessie, her great friend, the fortune-teller. Ellen knew no one on the Bodine farm, nor did she make friends easily. Mrs. Bodine even ordered her out of the berry patch. Only Joe Trent, home from college, noticed her.

Joe was elegant, always wearing shoes and clothes of different kinds of cloth. He would joke with Ellen as she got in the firewood. She was growing up, and Joe awakened some spark of longing in her thin body. Then one day Joe drove past her with Emphira Bodine. He pretended not to see Ellen in her skimpy skirt above her bare feet and legs. After that, Joe would stand behind a big bush where the men from the house could not see him and call to Ellen. Ellen was ashamed. She was glad when her father decided to move over to the Wakefield farm.

Their new house was better; even the loft had once been papered. Miss Tod Wakefield let Ellen look after the turkeys for money wages. So with setting out tobacco plants, getting in the firewood, and going regularly to the big barnyard, she settled into a pleasant routine. By fall Nellie was able to get Ellen a store dress and new shoes.

In an old abandoned barn where she went to look for turkey eggs she often noticed Amanda Cain waiting in the hay loft for Scott MacMurtrie, who was married to Miss Cassie. All the field workers knew of the affair, and they discussed eagerly how Miss Cassie would lay into Scott when she learned he was carrying on with her cousin Amanda, for Miss Cassie was strong and independent. One day Scott and Amanda disappeared. That night Ellen was awakened by the tolling bell on the MacMurtrie place. She hurried over, outdistancing her father, who thought the barn must be on fire. Ellen found the old Negress pulling the bell rope in a frenzy. Miss Cassie had hanged herself.

Dorine moved into one of the tenant houses. She was merry and gay and attracted others to her. She and Ellen became friends. At her house Ellen went to her first party. Shy, she hoped desperately that no one would notice her. But in her agony of timidity she sang a ballad her father had taught her, and she was accepted as one of the group. At their dances and games and on their Sunday walks she went sometimes with Jonas Prather but more often with Sebe Townley. Sebe was kind and gentle, but she liked Jonas better.

Jonas took little part in their gay dances. He would call the figures and then retire with the old folks. He seemed to withdraw from contact with girls; some even said he had got religion.

One night Jonas told Ellen he wanted her to marry him. When he went away to work for wages, he promised to come back during the summer to get married. Ellen had a letter from him and she wrote him a letter in return. But the summer wore on and Jonas did not come. At last she heard that Jonas had married Sallie Lou.

When Henry rented a patch of twenty-five acres called the Orkeys place, Ellen felt a sense of escaping from her troubles. Their new home had once been a toll house. It contained three rooms on one floor, and Ellen's bedroom was weather-tight.

The nearest neighbors were on the Wingate place. Old Mrs. Wingate, half mad, sat suspiciously in her house all day long and Jasper Kent worked her farm on half shares. Albert Wingate, the son, seldom came to the farm, and when he did appear he would often be roaring drunk. He would beg or steal money from his mother and sometimes he would turn the house upside down looking for more. When he began driving off cattle in which Jasper had a half interest, Jasper felt his anger mount.

Although Jasper prudently kept his own pigs in a corral far from the house, Albert discovered them. One morning Jasper found the corral empty; Albert had sold the pigs to a passing trader. That night Albert and Jasper fought in the barn. Jasper was stronger than his opponent. Then Albert drew a gun. Jasper wrested it away and threw it in the brush. But in the fighting Jasper forgot his lantern on the barn floor. When the building went up in flames, Jasper fled. He had been in jail before, and he was afraid.

He found work on the Phillips farm. Joe Phillips offered a house to Jasper. So Jasper and Ellen were married and set up housekeeping in their own place. Their house was tight, and Joe promised to add a room. Ellen was carrying her first child and was very content with her marriage.

The letter they had been dreading came, an indictment for arson drawn up against Jasper for the burning of the Wingate barn. Henry was Jasper's witness and Jasper was freed. At last Ellen and Jasper seemed to be free of all care; they had only to work the land and raise their family. Each year they had another child.

Following the custom of the migrant people, they left the Phillips farm. It became a matter of indifference to Ellen where she lived; a year on the Goodrich place, a year on the McKnight farm—it was all the same. Then they moved back to the Phillips farm. Joe Phillips, greatly attracted to Ellen, spoke sweet words to her. When Jasper began to go off for all-night carouses, Ellen accepted Joe's attentions. She did not tell Jasper right away about the new baby she was carrying. When she did, Jasper was bitter and swore it was Joe's. But when the sickly child was born, Jasper was very fond of it. The baby died in its third year.

When a nearby barn burned, suspicion unjustly fell on Jasper. One night masked raiders came to their home, seized Jasper while he slept, and bound him with ropes. They beat him savagely. Ellen brought him in and washed his bleeding welts. Jasper was greatly shamed.

The family loaded all their goods on the wagon and set out. They scarcely knew where they were going, but it would be far away. As they went they dreamed of a homeplace of land they could call their own. Perhaps they could even set out trees for an orchard, somewhere, someday.

TIMON OF ATHENS

Type of work: Drama
Author: William Shakespeare (1564-1616)
Type of plot: Tragedy of delusions
Time of plot: Fourth century B.C.
Locale: Athens and the nearby seacoast
First presented: c. 1605-1608

Principal characters:
TIMON, an Athenian lord
FLAVIUS, his faithful steward
APEMANTUS, Timon's candid friend
ALCIBIADES, an Athenian general

Critique:

Shakespeare did not finish *Timon of Athens.* Perhaps he was able to see that this bitter play, which was another of his dramatic commentaries on enormities brought about by ingratitude, was too stark in its contrasts and too obviously moralistic ever to be successful with the public. There is no neutral ground here to which one can retreat to draw his breath: the good are almost impossibly good, the bad are unbelievably bad. Shakespeare derived the plot from the life of Mark Antony in North's *Plutarch's Lives,* as well as from Lucian's dialogue, *Timon,* which was available to him in Latin and French.

The Story:

In Athens, the house of Timon, a wealthy lord of the city, was the scene of much coming and going. Poets, artists, artisans, merchants, politicians, and well wishers in general sought the friendship and favors of a man whose generosity knew no bounds. While waiting to speak to Timon, a poet disclosed his vision to an artist: Timon was depicted as the darling of Dame Fortune, and his friends and acquaintances spared no effort in admiring his favored position. But, so went the vision, Fortune turned and Timon tumbled into penury, his friends doing nothing to comfort him.

Timon joined the crowd of suitors in his reception chamber. When a messenger reported that Ventidius, his friend, had been jailed for a debt, Timon promised to pay the debt and to support Ventidius until he became solvent again. An old man complained that one of Timon's servants had stolen the heart of his only daughter. Timon promised to match the girl's dowry with an equal sum. Then he received the poet and the painter and the jeweler graciously, accepting their shameless flattery. Apemantus, a crudely candid friend, declared broadly that these flatterers and seekers of bounty were a pack of knaves. Alcibiades, a great military leader, came with a troop of followers to dine with Timon. As all prepared to feast at Timon's bounteous table, Apemantus cursed them roundly.

A great feast was served to the accompaniment of music. Ventidius, having been freed from jail, offered to repay the money spent in his behalf, but Timon declared that friendship would not allow him to accept Ventidius' money. When Apemantus warned Timon that men will readily slay the man whose food and drink they consume, Timon expressed his gratitude at having so many friends to share his generosity; he wished, however, that he might be poorer in order that these good friends might know the joy of sharing their largess with him. Timon's eyes filled with tears, so overcome was he by the sentiments of friendship, as a group of costumed Athenian ladies presented lavish gifts to him from men of wealth. Timon then presented rich gifts to his departing friends. Flavius, his steward, observed that his master's infinite generosity had almost emptied his coffers. Timon told Apemantus that he would give him gifts, too, if he would cease railing at these felicities of friendship.

Before long Timon was reduced to insolvency and near beggary. A senator to whom he owed a great sum of money sent his servant to collect. Other servants of Timon's creditors had gathered in front of his house. Timon, who had never given Flavius a chance to explain that there was no more money, asked the steward the reason for the crowd outside. When Flavius told him the truth, Timon ordered the sale of all his lands. Flavius disclosed that the lands had been sold or mortgaged. Timon, refusing to share Flavius' alarm, declared that he now had the chance to test his friends. He directed his servants to borrow money from his friends Lucius, Lucullus, and Sempronius. Then they were to go to the senators and borrow more. Flavius disclosed that he had already tried without success to borrow from these sources. Timon made excuses for them, however, and suggested that the servants try Ventidius, who had recently come into a large fortune.

The servant who went to Lucullus was told that times were difficult and that Timon's friendship was not sufficient security for a loan. When Lucullus offered the servant a bribe to say that he had been unable to see Lucullus, the servant, horrified, threw down the bribe money and departed in disgust. Lucius claimed that he, needing money, had hoped to borrow from Timon. A third servant went to Sempronius. Upon learning that Timon had been denied a loan by Lucullus, Lucius, and even by Ventidius, Sempronius, pretending to be hurt that Timon had not sent to him first, also refused.

As Timon continued to be importuned by his creditors' servants, he went out in a rage and bade them cut what he owed their masters out of his heart. Still enraged, he directed Flavius to invite all of his creditors to a feast.

Alcibiades, meanwhile, pleaded in the senate for the remission of the death sentence on a veteran soldier who had committed murder. The senators, deaf to his arguments that the man had killed in self-defense, persisted in their decision. When Alcibiades continued his plea, the senators sentenced him, on pain of death, to be banished from Athens.

At Timon's house, tables were arranged as though for a great banquet. Timon's guests, apologizing profusely for their inability to honor his requests for money, appeared in expectation of a lavish banquet. When Timon bade them eat, they discovered that the covered dishes were filled with warm water. Timon then cursed them for what they were, threw the water in their faces, and drove them out of his house.

A confirmed misanthrope, Timon left Athens. For the moment he focused all of his hatred on Athens and her citizens, but he predicted that his curses would eventually encompass all mankind. Flavius, meanwhile, announced to his fellow servants that their service in Timon's house had come to an end; what little money he had, Flavius shared with his fellows. He pocketed his remaining money and declared his intentions of seeking out his old master.

One day Timon, who was living in a cave near the seashore, dug for roots and discovered gold. As he was cursing the earth for producing this root of all evil, Alcibiades appeared, accompanied by his two mistresses. Timon cursed the three and told them to leave him. When Alcibiades disclosed that he was on his way to besiege Athens, Timon gave him gold and wished him every success. He also gave the two women gold, after exhorting them to infect the minds and bodies of all men with whom they came in contact. When Alcibiades and his troops marched away, Timon continued to dig roots for his dinner.

Apemantus appeared to rail at Timon for going to the opposite extreme from that which had caused his downfall. He declared that wild Nature was as cruel as men, that Timon, therefore, would do well to return to Athens and flatter men who were still favored by Fortune. After Apemantus had left, a band of cutthroats, having heard that Timon possessed a great store of gold, went to the cave. When they told Timon that they were destitute, he threw gold at them and ordered them to practice their malign art in Athens. So bitter were Timon's words that they left him, determined to abandon all violence.

Flavius, finding the cave, wept at the pitiful state to which his master had fallen. Timon, at first rude to his faithful steward, was almost overcome by Flavius' tears. He gave Flavius gold, wished him well, and admonished him to succor only dogs.

The reports of Timon's newly found wealth having reached Athens, the poet and the painter went to his cave. He greeted them sarcastically, praised them for their honesty, and gave them gold to use in destroying other sycophants and flatterers. Flavius returned, accompanied by two senators. The senators, apologizing for the great wrongs done Timon, offered to lend him any amount of money he might desire. They promised him, furthermore, command of the Athenian forces in the struggle against Alcibiades. Timon wished a plague on both Athens and Alcibiades. His prescription to the Athenians for ending their troubles was that they come to the shore and hang themselves on a tree near his cave. When he retreated into his cave, the senators, knowing their mission fruitless, returned to Athens.

In Athens, the senators begged Alcibiades to spare the city because its importance transcended the petty griefs of an Alcibiades or a Timon. Alcibiades agreed to spare Athens only on the condition that those who had offended him and Timon should be punished. As the city gates were opened to the besiegers, a messenger reported that Timon was dead. Alcibiades read Timon's epitaph, copied by the messenger. It reaffirmed Timon's hatred of mankind and expressed his desire, in death, that no one pause at his grave.

'TIS PITY SHE'S A WHORE

Type of work: Drama
Author: John Ford (1586-1640?)
Type of plot: Horror tragedy
Time of plot: Renaissance period
Locale: Parma, Italy
First presented: c. 1624

Principal characters:

FLORIO, a citizen of Parma
GIOVANNI, his son
ANNABELLA, his daughter
PUTANA, her duenna
DONADO, another citizen of Parma
BERGETTO, his foolish nephew
SORANZO, a nobleman
GRIMALDI, a Roman gentleman
VASQUES, Soranzo's servant
RICHARDETTO, a supposed physician
HIPPOLITA, his wife
FRIAR BONAVENTURA, Giovanni's tutor and confessor

Critique:

Poetically, John Ford followed closely the magnificent tradition established by Shakespeare and Webster, but the vehicles for his poetry were marked by Caroline decadence. Perhaps Burton's *Anatomy of Melancholy* (1621) led Ford to probe the more obscure aspects of human relationships. In *'Tis Pity She's a Whore*, the main plot is concerned with brother-sister incest. Surely Ford grew too expansive in plotting this play, for the several substantial subplots anticipated early in the drama fade out somewhat indecisively. The intensity of the main plot, while it may have drawn Ford away from his original intentions, compensates for the resulting inconclusiveness of structure.

The Story:

In Parma a brilliant young gentleman named Giovanni fell in love with his sister Annabella. Maddened by his passion, Giovanni went to his tutor, Friar Bonaventura, for advice and shocked the friar by his use of fallacious arguments to justify his unnatural love. The friar, deploring Giovanni's willingness to ignore religious and moral strictures on such a love, advised the youth to remain in his room for a week, at the end of which time he surely would realize the enormity of his passion.

When Grimaldi, a Roman gentleman, and Vasques, servant of Soranzo, met in front of Florio's house, Vasques thrashed Grimaldi. Florio, the father of Giovanni and Annabella, accompanied by Donado and Soranzo, came upon the fracas and separated the antagonists. Soranzo explained to Florio that Vasques was disturbed because Grimaldi, obviously an inferior man to the noble Soranzo, was competing with Soranzo for the hand of Annabella.

During the street disturbance Annabella and her duenna, Putana, appeared on the balcony. Putana pointed out to Annabella that she was being fought over, that she should be proud to have two such excellent suitors. Although Putana especially praised Soranzo, Annabella was plainly not interested. As they stood on the balcony Bergetto, the foolish nephew of Donado, passed by and declared his intention of winning the hand of Annabella.

Giovanni, returning from his talk with the friar, approached and entered the house. Annabella, not recognizing him at first, praised his manly beauty. Then, realizing who he was, she hastened into

3793

the house to join him and to comfort him in the melancholy from which he appeared to suffer.

Giovanni despaired. The more he strove to forget his love for Annabella, the more he seemed to love her. When Annabella joined him, no longer able to contain his maddening obsession, he confessed his love. Then he offered her his dagger and begged her to love him or to end his life. Annabella expressed dismay at Giovanni's revelation. He assured her that the Church had approved of his love for her. She then revealed that she loved him with equal passion.

Donado, in the meantime, advanced the cause of his nephew Bergetto. Florio, pleased by Donado's promise to leave the youth a fortune, said that the final choice must be left to Annabella herself.

After Giovanni and Annabella had consummated their love, he expressed the jealous fears of a lover. Annabella assured him that she found her suitors repulsive. When Giovanni had left her, Annabella was introduced to Richardetto, a supposed doctor, and his niece Philotis, who carried a lute. Florio had retained the doctor because Annabella appeared to him to be sickly.

Meanwhile Soranzo, distracted in his love for Annabella, was confronted by Hippolita, a woman he had wronged. She told him that her husband was dead and that he must fulfill his promise to marry her now that she was a widow. Soranzo, preoccupied with his love for Annabella, dismissed her. Vasques encouraged Hippolita, however, by telling her that perhaps Soranzo would be more amenable another day. Hippolita then tried to enlist Vasques' aid in a plot to avenge herself on Soranzo. Vasques pretended to become her accomplice.

Richardetto privately informed Philotis that during a journey away from home he had had his death reported so that he might return to Parma in disguise and discover the adulterous activities of his wife Hippolita. Grimaldi asked Richardetto for a love potion which

would win Annabella's love. Richardetto, after assuring Grimaldi that Soranzo was his only rival, promised to provide him with a poison for his rapier so that he might mortally wound Soranzo in a fight.

The foolish Bergetto, meanwhile, continued his silly courtship of Annabella. Donado, after reading an inane letter Bergetto had written to Annabella, advised his nephew to remain indoors lest his idiocy get him into trouble. After Donado left, Bergetto went with his servant Poggio to see a prodigious horse in a side show.

When Giovanni revealed the state of his affair with Annabella, the friar, shocked because the youth had refused to heed his warnings, decided to visit Annabella.

At Florio's house Donado presented an acceptable letter, allegedly written by Bergetto, to Annabella. She expressed no interest. When her father suggested that she send an heirloom ring to Bergetto, she had to admit that Giovanni had taken it to wear. Quite frankly, she told Donado that it would be impossible for her ever to love Bergetto. Bergetto arrived with word that he had allowed himself to be thrashed in the street and that a doctor newly arrived in Parma had ministered to his wounds. Bergetto also disclosed that he had been charmed by the doctor's niece, who had kissed him. Donado, accepting defeat, asked Annabella to keep as a marriage gift a jewel that he had given her as a courtship token from Bergetto. Later, encountering his sister alone, Giovanni jealously commanded her to return the jewel.

Florio next chose Soranzo as the suitor most acceptable to him. Annabella disclosed to Soranzo that she was determined to remain a maid, but that if she ever married it should be to Soranzo. Giovanni listened secretly to the conversation in order to convince himself of her fidelity to him. As Annabella and Soranzo talked, the girl was suddenly taken sick.

Later, when Putana told him that Annabella was with child, Giovanni directed Putana to admit no doctor to his sister and to tell Florio that Annabella had merely suffered from indigestion. In the meantime Florio, conferring with Richardetto about his daughter's health, learned that Annabella suffered nothing more than ills common to young womanhood and that she should be married. Florio, ignorant of Annabella's refusal of Soranzo, decided that Soranzo and his daughter should be married by Friar Bonaventura immediately. Giovanni, meanwhile, conducted the friar to the house, ostensibly to give spiritual comfort to his sister. Richardetto, having learned of Florio's plans for the marriage of Soranzo and Annabella, gave Grimaldi the promised poison.

Annabella, in her chamber, confessed to the friar and, fearful of eternal damnation, agreed to his suggestion that she marry Soranzo immediately. Soranzo was called and, in the friar's presence, the pair made their betrothal vows. The wedding ceremony was to take place in two days' time. Vasques, pretending to be Hippolita's ally, reported that Soranzo would marry Annabella.

Grimaldi waited outside the monastery for the arrival of Soranzo and Annabella. Bergetto and Philotis, sent by Richardetto, also went to the monastery to be married. In the dark Grimaldi mistook Bergetto for Soranzo and mortally wounded the silly youth.

Having murdered Bergetto, Grimaldi took refuge in the house of the cardinal, who, confronted by Donado, Florio, Richardetto, and police officers, disclosed that he already knew of Bergetto's death. Grimaldi, confessing to the murder, insisted that he had mistaken one man for another. The cardinal declared that Grimaldi, because of his noble Roman blood, would be protected by the Church. Donado and Florio, deploring what seemed to them a gross injustice, left the cardinal's house.

Two days later Soranzo and Annabella were married. Giovanni, racked by jealousy and grief, refused to drink a health

to the newlyweds. His slight was overlooked, however, when Hippolita, disguised, arrived with some masked maidens to present a masque in honor of Annabella. Hippolita, joining the hands of the couple, called for a cup of wine to drink their health. Vasques handed her a poisoned cup intended for Soranzo. After Hippolita had drunk the fatal potion, Vasques revealed his trickery. Hippolita died cursing the marriage. The friar expressed to Giovanni his fear of that omen of blood at the marriage feast.

When Soranzo, having discovered his wife's pregnancy, berated her viciously, Annabella tortured him with words of praise for the father of her unborn child. Soranzo, threatening to kill her if she did not disclose the identity of her lover, drew his sword. Vasques entered and calmed his master; he advised Soranzo to be gentle with Annabella and to let his servant seek out the lover. Soranzo then turned to Annabella and apologized for his brutality, declaring that one must have compassion for weaknesses of the flesh.

Vasques tricked Putana into telling him about Annabella's love for her brother. When Putana had declared that Giovanni was the father of Annabella's child, Vasques called in a band of ruffians and at his command they gagged Putana and carried her away to put out her eyes. Meeting Giovanni, Vasques told him that Annabella was alone in her chamber and suggested that he go to her.

Annabella, filled with remorse for her sins, stood at her window and declared her repentance. The friar, passing below, was amazed at her change of heart. She threw down to him a letter in which she urged her brother also to repent. The friar delivered the letter to Giovanni, who read that their incestuous love had been discovered. As he expressed his disbelief, Vasques brought Giovanni an invitation from Soranzo to attend his birthday feast. Giovanni, in spite of the friar's warning, promised to be present. The friar, convinced that matters were coming to a dreadful conclusion, left Parma.

While Soranzo was greeting his guests, Giovanni went to his sister in her chamber. When he chided her for her repentance, Annabella warned him that the feast had been arranged in order that Soranzo might destroy them both. Giovanni, determined to take a desperate course, told Annabella to pray and to forgive him; then he stabbed her. With Annabella's heart on the point of his dagger, he went to the banquet hall. There, to the amazement of his father, he confessed his incestuous love. Vasques, who had gone to Annabella's chamber, returned with word that she was dead. Florio collapsed and died. Soranzo and Giovanni drew and fought, and Soranzo fell, mortally wounded. Then, while Vasques and Giovanni fought, Vasques signaled his ruffians, who surrounded Giovanni and mortally wounded him. He died still unrepentant of his unnatural love.

Blind Putana, having confirmed the relationship between brother and sister, was condemned to be burned to death for her part in the affair. Vasques was banished from Italy.

THE TITAN

Type of work: Novel
Author: Theodore Dreiser (1871-1945)
Type of plot: Naturalism
Time of plot: 1890's
Locale: Chicago
First published: 1914

Principal characters:
FRANK ALGERNON COWPERWOOD, a multimillionaire and financial genius
AILEEN COWPERWOOD, his mistress and then his wife
PETER LAUGHLIN, his business partner
STEPHANIE PLATOW, Cowperwood's mistress
BERENICE FLEMING, Cowperwood's protégée and mistress

Critique:

Dreiser's full-length portrait of a great financial wizard is one of the triumphs of the naturalistic school of writers. Between 1890 and the publication of this book scores of novels dealing with the American financier were published, but none approached the thoroughness and the psychological insight of *The Titan*, which continues the psychological and sociological study of Cowperwood begun by Dreiser in *The Financier*. While the man Dreiser portrays is wholly without a conventional moral code, he is nevertheless a strong man with a purpose. The author makes no effort to judge his character, and the reader feels that it is best if he, too, refrains from passing judgment.

The Story:

Released from a Pennsylvania prison in the 1870's, Frank Algernon Cowperwood, still young and a millionaire, went to Chicago to begin a new life with Aileen Butler, his mistress. Within a short time Cowperwood made friends among influential businessmen there.

Divorced by his first wife, Cowperwood finally married Aileen. He prepared to increase his fortune, to become a power in the city, and to conquer its society. To this end, he sought an enterprise which would quickly yield him heavy returns on his investment. His first battle among the financial barons of Chicago was to gain control of the gas companies.

At the same time the Cowperwoods made their first attack on Chicago society, but with little success. Aileen Cowperwood was too high-spirited and lacking in the poise which would win her social success. Then Cowperwood became involved in several lawsuits and his earlier political-economic disgrace in Philadelphia was exposed in the Chicago newspapers. But after a long battle Cowperwood was able to force the rival gas companies to buy out his franchises at a profit to himself.

Unfortunately, the deal brought social defeat, at least temporarily, to the Cowperwoods, for his rivals in finance were the social powers of Chicago at that time. Cowperwood turned once again to a mistress, but the affair ended when Aileen attempted to kill her rival.

For several years a cable-car system of street railways claimed most of Cowperwood's time. He bought control of the horsecar company which served the north side of Chicago. Then the naturally promiscuous temperament of Cowperwood intruded itself when he met dark, lush Stephanie Platow. Ten years younger than his wife and interested in art, literature, and music, she was able to occupy a place in his life Aileen could never fill.

While involved in that affair, Cowperwood coerced the west side street railway company into giving its franchise to him. But the sweetness of his victory was partially lost by the exposure of Stephanie as another man's lover. Meanwhile financial forces were at work against Cowperwood. Through two city bosses, these forces hoped to play the city politicians against Cowperwood, for without the support of the city council to aid him with franchises and grants the financier would find himself helpless to merge all the street railways of the city under his control.

The first battle was fought in an election to gain possession of the Chicago city council. It was far more painful for Cowperwood to learn at this time that his wife had been unfaithful to him than to discover that he had arrayed the whole financial and social element of the city against himself. The loss of the election proved no permanent setback to Cowperwood, however, nor did his wife's infidelity. From the latter he recovered, and the first was soon undone by his opponents because they did not pave the way with favors and money when they tried to push bills through the new reform council. Even the new mayor was soon an ally of Cowperwood.

Soon afterward Cowperwood met Berenice Fleming, daughter of a procuress, who was being prepared in a fashionable boarding-school for a career in society. Taking her and her family under his wing, Cowperwood became her lover with some misgivings, for the girl was but seventeen and he was fifty-two at the time. By this time his enemies were trying to gain franchises for elevated lines powered by electricity.

This new effort by his financial rivals meant that his own street railways had to be converted to electricity, and he had to compete for at least a share of the elevated lines to prevent his ruin. The south side "L" was already a tremendous success because of the World's Fair of 1893, and the whole city was now clamoring for better transportation service. Cowperwood's opponents held control over the city banks, which prevented those institutions from lending him funds needed to begin his operations. When he attempted to secure funds in the East, Cowperwood discovered that his assets were in question. But by one master stroke the financier wiped out any question of his ability and his credit; he donated three hundred thousand dollars to the local university for a telescope and observatory.

Even with unlimited credit, the problem of gaining franchises was not easy. He was determined to keep control of the Chicago transportation system, but he began to realize that neither he nor his wife could ever become socially acceptable there. He decided to build a mansion in New York to hold his collection of art and be his card of entry into society.

Meanwhile, having obtained his franchises, he began work on Chicago elevated lines. Cowperwood's enemies planned to let him overreach himself, so that they could force him out of Chicago financially as well as socially. Then the collapse of the American Match Corporation, partially engineered by Cowperwood, began a series of runs on the Chicago banks controlled by his enemies. When their attempts to recall the enormous loans made to Cowperwood failed, he emerged from the affair stronger than ever.

The final battle, the climax of Cowperwood's financial career in Chicago, was the one he waged to secure fifty-year franchises for his growing transportation system. This project was made doubly difficult because of Cowperwood's latest property, the Union Loop, by which he controlled the elevated lines. This loop of elevated track, encircling the downtown business district, had to be used by all the lines in the city. The moneyed interests opposed Cowperwood because he was not with them; the newspapers, because they wanted to see

3798

better and cheaper facilities. In the face of the opposition, even the most reckless of the city's aldermen feared to grant the franchises Cowperwood wanted, regardless of the money and power he was prepared to give to them. Then his lawyers informed Cowperwood that the state constitution prevented the city from granting such long-term franchises, even if the city council could be coerced into approving them.

Cowperwood's next idea was to have a transportation commission set up by bribery in the state legislature. In the bill which set up the commission was a clause extending existing franchises for a period of fifty years. The bill, passed by the legislature, was vetoed by the governor.

Meanwhile the New York mansion had been completed, and Aileen Cowperwood moved in. She met with no social success, except among the Bohemian set. Berenice Fleming was settled at the same time with her family in a mansion on Park Avenue. The next step in Cowperwood's personal affairs was to be his second divorce. Then Aileen heard of his affair with Berenice Fleming. When he asked her for the divorce, she tried to commit suicide but failed.

Cowperwood again tried to force his bill through the Illinois Legislature, but the legislators returned it to the city council. There, as before, Cowperwood lost. The people and the newspapers frightened the aldermen so that they dared not grant what the financier wished, despite his fantastic bribes.

With his hope of controlling the Chicago transportation system gone, Cowperwood sold his interests. Admitting defeat, he and Berenice went to Europe. The Titan's empire had fallen.

TITUS ANDRONICUS

Type of work: Drama
Author: William Shakespeare (1564-1616)
Type of plot: Tragedy of revenge
Time of plot: Early Christian era
Locale: Rome and vicinity
First presented: 1594

> *Principal characters:*
> SATURNINUS, Emperor of Rome
> BASSIANUS, his brother
> TITUS ANDRONICUS, a Roman general
> LAVINIA, his only daughter
> MARCUS, his brother, a tribune
> TAMORA, Queen of the Goths
> AARON, her lover, a Moor
> ALARBUS,
> DEMETRIUS, and
> CHIRON, her sons

Critique:

Shakespeare idolaters have for centuries sought to dissociate the name of the bard from this brutal play. The unsavory episodes would suggest the work of an apprentice playwright following the tradition of Thomas Kyd, whose *The Spanish Tragedy*, a violent drama of revenge, was enormously popular in the last decade of the sixteenth century. Conclusive proof of authorship appears, however, in the virtues of this play. They adumbrate Shakespeare at the peak of his powers: flights of excellent poetry, tight construction, and a genuine sense of the dramatic. For his plot, Shakespeare had recourse to two classical revenge legends, the revenge of Atreus from Seneca's *Thyestes* and the rape of Philomela from Ovid's *Metamorphoses*.

The Story:

Early in the Christian era, Saturninus and Bassianus, sons of the late emperor, contended for the crown of the Roman Empire. Both men were leaders of strong factions. Another candidate, a popular one, was Titus Andronicus, a Roman famed for his victories over the barbarian Goths to the north.

Marcus Andronicus, brother of Titus, stated in the forum that Titus was the popular choice to succeed the late emperor. The sons, willing to abide by the desires of the populace, dismissed their factions.

As the prominent men of the city went into the senate house, Titus made his triumphant entry into Rome. He was accompanied by his surviving sons and by a casket containing the body of another son. In his train also were Tamora, Queen of the Goths; her sons, Alarbus, Demetrius, and Chiron, and her lover, Aaron, a Moor. Before the senate house, Lucius, one of Titus' sons, demanded that a Gothic prisoner be sacrificed to appease the spirit of his dead brother in the casket. When Titus offered as sacrifice the oldest son of Tamora, the queen pleaded for mercy, reminding Titus that her sons were as precious to her as his were to him. Titus paid her no heed. Alarbus was sacrificed and the casket then laid in the tomb of the Andronici. At that moment Lavinia, Titus' only daughter, appeared to greet her father and brothers and to pay her respects to her fallen brother.

Marcus came out of the senate house, greeted Titus, and informed him that he was the choice of the people for the emperorship. Titus, unwilling to take on that responsibility at his age, persuaded the people to name Saturninus emperor

3800

instead. Saturninus, in gratitude, asked for and received the hand of Lavinia to become his queen. But Bassianus, to whom Lavinia had given her heart, seized the maid with the help of Marcus and the sons of Titus and carried her away. Titus' son Mutius, who stayed behind to cover their flight, was killed by his father.

Saturninus, who begrudged Titus his popularity with the people, disavowed all allegiance and debt to the general and planned to take Tamora as his wife. Titus, deserted by his emperor, his brother, and his sons, was deeply shaken.

Marcus and Titus' sons returned and expressed the desire to bury Mutius in the family vault. Titus at first refused, saying that Mutius had been a traitor; then he relented after his brother and his sons argued effectively for proper burial.

When Bassianus appeared with Lavinia, Saturninus vowed that he would avenge the stealing of the maid who had been given him by her father. Bassianus spoke in Titus' behalf, but Titus declared that he could plead his own case before the emperor. Tamora openly advised Saturninus to be gracious to Titus, but secretly she advised him to curry Titus' friendship only because Titus was so popular in Rome. She assured Saturninus that she would destroy Titus and his family for their having sacrificed one of her own sons. Saturninus therefore pardoned the Andronici and declared his intention of marrying Tamora. Believing their differences reconciled, Titus invited Saturninus to hunt with him the next day.

Aaron, contemplating Tamora's good fortune and the imminent downfall of Saturninus and of Rome as well, came upon Chiron and Demetrius, disputing and about to draw their swords over their chances of winning the favors of Lavinia. Advising the youths to contain themselves, he told them that both could enjoy Lavinia by seizing her in the forest during the hunt, which would be attended by the lords and ladies of the court.

Later, while the hunt was under way, Aaron hid a sack of gold at the foot of a large tree in the forest. He had previously arranged to have a pit dug near the tree; this pit he covered over with undergrowth. There Tamora found him and learned that both Bassianus and Lavinia would come to grief that day. Before Aaron left Tamora, he gave her a letter with directions that the message reach the hands of Saturninus. Bassianus and Lavinia approached and, seeing that the Moor and Tamora had been together, chaffed Tamora and threatened to tell Saturninus of her dalliance in the forest. Chiron and Demetrius came upon the scene. Informed by Tamora that Bassianus and Lavinia had insulted her, they stabbed Bassianus to death. But when Tamora urged them to stab Lavinia they refused, saying that they would enjoy her first. Lavinia then appealed to Tamora to remember that Titus had spared her life. Tamora, recalling how Titus had ignored her pleas to spare her son from sacrifice, was determined that her sons should have their lustful pleasure. The brothers, after throwing the body of Bassianus into the pit, dragged Lavinia away to violate her.

Meanwhile, Aaron, on the pretext that he had trapped a panther, brought two of Titus' sons, Quintus and Martius, to the pit and left them there. Martius fell into the trap, where he recognized the murdered Bassianus by a ring he wore on his finger. When Quintus tried to pull Martius out of the pit, he lost his balance and tumbled in. Aaron, returning with Saturninus, claimed that Titus' sons had murdered Bassianus. Tamora then gave Saturninus the letter that Aaron had given her. The letter, written ostensibly by one of the Andronici, outlined a plot to assassinate Bassianus, to bury him in a pit, and then to collect payment, which was a bag of gold hidden near the pit. When the bag of gold was found where Aaron had placed it, Saturninus was convinced of the brothers' guilt. Despite Titus' offer of his own person as security for his sons, Saturninus sentenced them to be tortured. Tamora assured Titus that she would speak to Saturninus in his behalf.

In another part of the forest, Chiron and Demetrius, their evil deed accomplished, cut off Lavinia's hands and tongue so that she would be able neither to write nor to tell of what had befallen her. Alone in the forest, Lavinia was joined at last by her uncle, Marcus, who led her away to her father.

Later, in Rome, Titus recalled his years of faithful military service to the state and begged the tribunes to spare his sons, but they would not listen to him. Another son, Lucius, a great favorite with the people, attempted unsuccessfully to rescue his brothers. He was banished from the city. As Titus pleaded in vain, Marcus brought the ravished Lavinia to him. The sight of his daughter led Titus to wonder to what infinite depths of grief a man could come. Aaron announced to the grieving Andronici that Saturninus would release Martius and Quintus if one of the family would cut off his hand and send it to the court. Titus agreed to let Lucius and Marcus decide between them; when they went to get an ax, Titus directed Aaron to cut off his hand. Later, a messenger brought Titus his hand and the heads of Martius and Quintus as well. Having suffered as much as a man could suffer, Titus vowed revenge. He directed the banished Lucius to raise an invading force among the Goths.

At his home, Titus appeared to be demented. Even so, it was clear to him one day that Lavinia was trying desperately to tell him something. She indicated in Ovid's *Metamorphoses* that section in which the story of Tereus' brutal rape of Philomela was recounted. Suddenly, it occurred to Marcus that he could, by holding a staff in his teeth and between his knees, write in the sand on the floor. Lavinia took the staff thus and wrote in the sand that Chiron and Demetrius were her violators.

Titus now sent his grandson Lucius with a bundle of weapons to present to Tamora's sons. The youths did not understand the message that Titus had attached to the gift, but Aaron quickly saw that Titus knew Lavinia's ravishers. As the brothers admired their gift, a blast of trumpets announced the birth of a child to Tamora. A nurse entered with the newborn baby, who was black, and stated that Tamora, fearful lest Saturninus see it, had sent the child to Aaron to dispose of. Chiron and Demetrius, aware of their mother's shame, insisted that the infant be killed immediately. When they offered to do the murder, Aaron, the father, defied them. As a precaution, he killed the nurse, one of three women who knew the baby's color. Then he had a fair-skinned baby, newly born, taken to Tamora before he fled to the Goths.

Titus, now reputed to be utterly demented, wrote messages to the gods, attached them to arrows, and, with Marcus and his grandson, shot the arrows into the court. He persuaded a passing farmer to deliver a letter to Saturninus. The emperor was already disturbed because the messages carried by the arrows stated Titus' grievances against the state. When Saturninus threatened to execute justice on old Titus, Tamora, feeling her revenge complete, advised him to treat the distracted old soldier gently. The farmer, meanwhile, delivered Titus' letter. Enraged by its mocking message, Saturninus commanded that Titus be brought to him to be executed.

A messenger brought word that the Goths, led by Lucius, threatened to sack Rome. Knowing Lucius' popularity with the Romans, Saturninus was fearful. But Tamora, confident of her ability to save the city, directed the messenger to arrange a conference with Lucius at the house of Titus.

In the camp of the Goths, Aaron and his child were brought before Lucius. Aaron's captor disclosed that he had come upon the Moor in a ruined monastery and had heard him state aloud that the baby's mother was Tamora. At Lucius' promise to preserve the life of the child,

Aaron confessed to his crimes against the Andronici. Lucius decreed that the Moor must die a horrible death.

Tamora, meanwhile, believing that Titus was demented beyond all reason, disguised herself as Revenge and with her sons, also disguised, presented herself to Titus. Although Titus recognized her, she insisted that she was Revenge, his friend. Titus, for his own purposes, pretended to be taken in by the disguises; he told Rapine and Murder, Revenge's cohorts, to seek out two such as themselves and destroy them. At Tamora's bidding, Titus directed Marcus to invite Lucius to a banquet, to which Saturninus and Tamora and her sons would also come.

Titus persuaded Chiron and Demetrius to stay with him while their companion, Revenge, went to perform other duties. He then called in his kinsmen, who seized and bound the brothers. Titus told them that he intended to kill them and feed to their mother a paste made of their bones and blood. Lavinia held a bowl between the stumps of her arms to catch their blood as Titus cut their throats.

Lucius, accompanied by a guard of Goths, came to his father's house, where he put Aaron in the charge of Marcus. Saturninus and Tamora made their appearance and were ushered to a banquet served by Titus, dressed as a cook. Titus, hearing from Saturninus that Virginius, in the legend, had done well to kill his ravished daughter, stabbed Lavinia. The startled Saturninus asked if Lavinia had been ravished and by whom. When Titus disclosed that Tamora's sons had done the evil deed, Saturninus asked to see the youths at once. Titus, declaring that Tamora was eating their remains, stabbed her. Saturninus stabbed Titus, and Lucius, in turn, stabbed Saturninus. A general fight ensued. Lucius and Marcus, with their followers, retired to a balcony to tell the people of Rome of the manifold evils wrought by Tamora, her sons, and Aaron.

After the people had chosen him their new emperor, Lucius sentenced Aaron to be buried waistdeep and left to starve. He also decreed that Tamora's body be fed to wild beasts.

TO BE A PILGRIM

Type of work: Novel
Author: Joyce Cary (1888-1957)
Type of plot: Social realism
Time of plot: Late 1930's
Locale: Tolbrook, England
First published: 1942

Principal characters:

TOM WILCHER, an old lawyer, the narrator
SARA MONDAY, his former employee
ANN WILCHER, Tom's niece, a doctor
ROBERT BROWN, her husband, Tom's nephew, a farmer
EDWARD WILCHER, Tom's brother, a politician
LUCY WILCHER, Tom's wild sister
PUGGY BROWN, Lucy's husband, a Benjamite preacher
JULIE EELES, an actress, Edward's mistress, later Tom's mistress
BILL WILCHER, Tom's brother, a military man
AMY SPROTT, Bill's devoted wife
LOFTUS WILCHER, their son
JOHN WILCHER, another son, a car salesman
FRED, Sara's latest man

Critique:

To Be a Pilgrim, the second novel in Cary's most famous trilogy, depicts events from the point of view of Tom Wilcher, the last surviving member of his generation of an old West-Country liberal and religious family. He is about to die, as the novel opens, and he is concerned about the future of his family, his property, his convictions, and his country. In his reflections, he considers all the events of his life, attempting to shape them into some kind of meaningful pattern. Although liberal by conviction, he wishes to conserve the values of his past and his family, and he feels unhappy because the values of the past, along with its religious and political significance, seem lost to the younger members of his own family. Through the use of this narrator, Cary is able to develop the character of Tom Wilcher—a representative of a vanishing type of Englishman—with power, sympathy, and depth. In addition, the technique of the novel allows the author to explore many of the other characters fully. Ann comes to stand as the symbol for the modern, emancipated, scientific young woman. Robert represents the at-tempt of the new farmer to get back to the soil. The novel, told with a great deal of humor and insight, is an integral part of Cary's full, varied, complex, inter-related fictional world.

The Story:

When Tom Wilcher, a lawyer seventy-one years old and the owner of Tolbrook Manor, suffered a heart attack, his niece Ann, a doctor, came down to his home at Tolbrook to take care of him. Ann was the daughter of Edward, Tom's oldest brother and a liberal politician in the early years of the twentieth century. Ann was willing to take care of the old man because the family felt that Tom should be kept away from Sara Monday, his old housekeeper.

While working for Tom some time before, Sara had stolen some of his pos-sessions and the family had sent her to jail. But Tom, who had never regarded Sara's action as criminal, wanted her found when she was released. He re-alized that she never had stolen things actually in use, but only old relics stored in the attic; he was also aware that she really cared for old things. He revered Sara as an example of the past, as a lover of the old, humane, settled life rapidly giving way to the new society of text books and technology. He would have gone to Sara if Ann had not kept close watch over him.

Tom's nephew, Robert, visited him at Tolbrook and soon fell in love with Ann. Robert was the son of Tom's wild sister, Lucy, and Puggy Brown, a hypocritical preacher of the Benjamites (an evangelical religious sect), with whom Lucy had run away. Puggy Brown had been unfaithful to Lucy, though she had relinquished family and position for him, because he claimed that God had told him that he should commit adultery with another of his followers. Young Robert, unlike either parent, wanted to become a farmer. The agricultural possibilities of Tolbrook fascinated him, and he soon got to work, married Ann, and became a successful farmer. Much to Tom's horror, he kept his new threshing machine in the famous and beautiful living room at Tolbrook.

Tom had never been interested in farming. He had wanted to follow a religious career, but because his older brother, Edward the politician, had shown so little interest in the family property, Tom had felt obliged to become a lawyer and handle the family affairs and property. His reverence for the past had caused him to follow a career that did not really interest him. In spite of his objections to Robert's new scientific methods of agriculture, he was happy when he saw his nephew taking a deep interest in the land. Shortly after their marriage, Ann and Robert had a son, named after her father, but called Jan.

Tom, living in his memories, constantly tried to illustrate the value of the past to Ann and Robert. Having sacrificed his own career in order to keep his family home and property, he lived in terms of his old affections. He also had been the family messenger, running after Lucy when she had eloped with Puggy Brown and following along after Edward's mistress, Julie Eeles. Julie Eeles had been a graceful, though not very talented, actress. After Edward left her because she could not help his political career, Tom rather inherited her and she became his mistress. Tom, in other words, had always tidied up after his more striking brother and sister.

Another of Tom's brothers, Bill, was a more settled individual. A stolid military man, Bill had married devoted Amy Sprott. They had two children, Loftus and John. John had been, as a boy, Tom's favorite nephew, but during World War I John became restless and cynical, so that after the war he no longer seemed to care about the family or about any of the concerns for righteous life he had shared with Tom. John, with slack indifference, became a car salesman and married a woman who constantly deceived him with other men. After a while he seemed not to care about living, and one day he was run over in the street and killed. John's death left Ann and Robert the only relatives for whom Tom had any concern.

After a time Robert left Ann for a farm girl named Molly, leaving Tom depressed about the way the present generation of his family was turning out. He felt strongly that the old Victorian virtues, the old allegiance to religion, had made people happier than they were today. Yet he could not hold this point of view strongly, for his own generation had also led unhappy and unfortunate lives. Lucy's evangelist husband was untrue to her, and she, though still charming, had lived a miserable existence; Edward had finally married the woman who became Ann's mother, but she had left him when his political career failed. For all his charm and intelligence, Edward had never really achieved anything. More and more, Tom came to feel that the only person who had really understood and appreciated him was Sara Monday (he often referred to her as Sara Jimson, for he was under the assumption that she had been married to the painter, Gulley Jimson). He was still determined to find her and marry her.

Although Ann and Robert were reconciled to each other (they established a household which included Robert's farm girl), Tom escaped from them and went to London to find Sara. There he discovered that she was living with Fred, a man considerably younger than she. Sara, however, was no longer a woman devoted to Tom and to his feelings toward the past. Not as he had imagined her, she had become coarse, materialistic, interested only in herself.

When Tom suffered another and more serious heart attack, Sara called Ann and Robert, who came quickly and took the old man back to the security of Tolbrook. In his last few days Tom realized that the attempt to find and marry Sara had been a ridiculous gesture. He kept wondering to which of his descendants he should leave his money and property. He pondered about how his family and his values and his home might be most appreciated by a new generation with other concerns and values. Concerned with these matters, he died without leaving a will.

TO THE LIGHTHOUSE

Type of work: Novel
Author: Virginia Woolf (1882-1941)
Type of plot: Psychological realism
Time of plot: c. 1910-1920
Locale: The Isle of Skye in the Hebrides
First published: 1927

Principal characters:

MR. RAMSAY, a professor of philosophy
MRS. RAMSAY, his wife
JAMES, their son
CAMILLA, their daughter
MR. TANSLEY, Mr. Ramsay's guest and friend
LILY BRISCOE, an artist
MR. CARMICHAEL, a poet

Critique:

Set in the out-of-the-way Hebrides Islands, this book has an other-world quality. There is an air of unreality about it, achieved, perhaps, by the odd structure of the book. Virginia Woolf learned a great deal from James Joyce about the psychological novel. Although her stream of consciousness does not get out of hand or lead the story into hidden depths, it does dominate the entire novel and make good its effect. The past has, throughout the novel, an effect upon the present action, and this mingling of past and present is the secret of the book's unity.

The Story:

Mrs. Ramsay promised James, her seven-year-old son, that if the next day were fair he would be taken on a visit to the lighthouse they could see from the window of their summer home on the Isle of Skye. James, the youngest of Mrs. Ramsay's eight children, was his mother's favorite. The father of the family was a professor of philosophy whose students often thought that he was inspiring and one of the foremost metaphysicians of the early twentieth century; but his own children, particularly the youngest, did not like him because he made sarcastic remarks.

Several guests were visiting the Ram-

says at the time. There was young Mr. Tansley, Ramsay's student, who was also unpopular with the children because he seemed to delight in their discomfiture. Tansley was mildly in love with his hostess, despite her fifty-five years and her eight children. There was Lily Briscoe, who was painting a picture of the cottage with Mrs. Ramsay and little James seated in front of it. There was old Mr. Carmichael, a ne'er-do-well who amused the Ramsay youngsters because he had a white beard and a mustache tinged with yellow. There was also Mr. Bankes, a young man in love with Prue, the prettiest of the Ramsay daughters.

The afternoon went by slowly. Mrs. Ramsay went to the village to call on a sick woman. She spent several hours knitting stockings for the lighthouse keeper's child, whom they were planning to visit. Many people wondered how the Ramsays, particularly the wife, managed to be as hospitable and as charitable as they were, for they were not rich; Mr. Ramsay could not possibly make a fortune by expounding Locke, Berkeley, and Hume to students or by publishing books on metaphysics.

Mr. Carmichael, pretending to read, had actually fallen asleep early after lunch. The children, except for James, who was busy cutting pictures out of a catalogue, had busied themselves in a game of cricket. Mr. Ramsay and Mr. Tansley had passed the time in a pointless conversation. Miss Briscoe had only made a daub or two of paint on her canvas. For some reason the lines of the scene refused to come clear in her painting. Prue and Mr. Bankes had gone walking along the shore.

Even the dinner went by slowly. The only occasion of interest to the children, which was one of tension to their mother, came when Mr. Carmichael asked the maid for a second bowl of soup, thereby angering his host, who liked to have meals dispatched promptly. As soon as the children had finished, their mother sent the younger ones to bed. Mrs. Ramsay hoped that Prue would not fall in love with Mr. Bankes, and that Lily Briscoe, who always became seasick. would not want to accompany them in the small sailboat if they should go to the lighthouse the following day. She thought also about the fifty pounds needed to make some necessary repairs on the house.

After dinner Mrs. Ramsay went upstairs to the nursery. James had a boar's skull which his sister detested. Whenever Camilla tried to remove it from the wall and her sight, he burst into a frenzy of screaming. Mrs. Ramsay wrapped the skull in a handkerchief. Afterward she went downstairs and joined her husband in the library, where they sat throughout the evening, she knitting and Mr. Ramsay reading. Before they went to bed it was agreed that the trip for the next day would have to be canceled. The night had turned stormy.

Night followed night. The trip to the lighthouse was never made that summer, nor did the Ramsays return to their summer home for some years. In the meantime Mrs. Ramsay died quietly in her sleep. Prue was married, although not to Mr. Bankes, and died in childbirth. The first World War began. Andrew Ramsay enlisted and was sent to France, where he was killed by an exploding shell.

Time passed. The wallpaper in the house came loose from the walls. Books mildewed. In the kitchen a cup was occasionally knocked down and broken by old Mrs. McNab, who came to look after the house from time to time. In the garden the roses and the annual flowers grew wild or died.

Mr. Carmichael brought out a volume of poems during the war. About the time his book appeared, daffodils and violets bloomed on the Isle of Skye. Mrs. McNab looked longingly at a warm cloak left in a closet. She wished the cloak belonged to her.

At last the war ended. Mrs. McNab received a telegram requesting that the house be put in order. For several days the housekeeper worked, aided by two cleaning women, and when the Ramsays arrived the cottage was in order once more. Several visitors came again to share a summer at the cottage. Lily Briscoe returned for a quiet vacation. Mr. Carmichael, the successful poet, also arrived.

One morning Lily Briscoe came down to breakfast and wondered at the quiet which greeted her. No one had been down ahead of her, although she had expected that Mr. Ramsay and the two youngest children, James and Camilla, would have eaten early and departed for the long-postponed sail to the lighthouse, to which the youngsters had been looking forward with joyful anticipation. Within a few minutes the three straggled down, all having slept past the time they had intended to arise. After a swift breakfast they disappeared toward the shore, their going watched by Lily Briscoe, who had set up her canvas with the intention of once again trying to paint her picture of the cottage.

The journey to the island where the lighthouse stood was not as pleasant as the children had expected. They had never really liked their father; he had taken too little time to understand them. He was short and sharp when they did things which seemed foolish to him, though those actions were perfectly comprehensible to his son and daughter. James, especially, expected to be blamed caustically and pointlessly if the crossing were slow or not satisfactory in some other way, for he had been delegated to handle the sheets and the tiller of the boat.

Mr. Ramsay strode down to the beach with his offspring, each carrying a paper parcel to take to the keepers of the lighthouse. They soon set sail and pointed the prow of the sailboat toward the black and white striped pillar of the lighthouse in the hazy distance. Mr. Ramsay sat in the middle of the boat, along with an old fisherman and his son. They were to take over the boat in case of an emergency, for Mr. Ramsay had little trust in James as a reliable seaman. In the stern sat James himself, nerves tingling lest his father look up from his book and indulge in unnecessary and hateful criticism. But his nervous tension was needless, for within a few hours the little party reached the lighthouse, and, wonderful to relate, Mr. Ramsay sprang ashore like a youngster, smiled back at his children, and praised his son for his seamanship.

TOBACCO ROAD

Type of work: Novel
Author: Erskine Caldwell (1903-   )
Type of plot: Social melodrama
Time of plot: 1920's
Locale: Georgia
First published: 1932

Principal characters:
JEETER LESTER, a poor white
ADA, his wife
DUDE, his son
ELLIE MAY, his daughter
PEARL, another daughter
LOV BENSEY, Pearl's husband
BESSIE, a backwoods evangelist

Critique:

The uproarious, Rabelaisian episodes of *Tobacco Road* make the novel appear to be a burlesque on rural life of the southern United States. Granted the exaggeration for effect, the book deals truthfully, in the main, with a human element which is in evidence in the eastern piedmont from Virginia to Georgia. The character of Jeeter Lester, although repulsive in many respects, is nevertheless a curiously moving one. In creating Jeeter, Caldwell gave the world another minor hero, a man whose futile hopefulness attracts the sympathy of the sentimental and the social-minded.

The Story:

Lov Bensey, husband of Pearl, fifteen-year-old daughter of Jeeter Lester, felt low in his mind when he stopped by the Lester house on his way home with a bag of turnips. Pearl, he complained, refused to have anything to do with him; she would neither sleep with him nor talk to him.

The Lesters lived in a one-room shack which was falling apart. They had nothing to eat but pork-rind soup. Jeeter was trying to patch an inner tube so that the Lester car, a nondescript wreck which had been refused even by the junk dealer, could be used to carry firewood to Augusta. Jeeter's harelipped daughter Ellie May charmed Lov away from his

bag of turnips. While she and Lov were dallying in the yard in front of the shack, the other Lesters pounced upon the bag of turnips. Jeeter grabbed it and ran into the scrub woods, followed by his worthless son Dude. Jeeter ate his fill of turnips. He gave Dude several and even saved a handful for the rest of the family. They returned from the woods to find Lov gone. Sister Bessie, a woman preacher, had come for a visit. Bessie, middle-aged, and Dude, sixteen, were attracted to each other. Bessie, upon leaving, promised to return to take Dude away to be her husband.

The Lesters were starving. Jeeter had long since been unable to get credit at the local stores in order to buy seed, fertilizer, and food. His land was exhausted and there was no chance of reclaiming it because of Jeeter's utter laziness. Jeeter and his wife Ada had had seventeen children. Twelve of them survived, but all except Ellie May and Dude had left home.

Bessie returned and announced that God had given her permission to marry Dude, but Dude refused to listen until Bessie said that she was planning to buy a new car with some money that her late husband had left her. She and Dude went to town and bought a new Ford, the loud horn of which Dude highly approved. At the county courthouse, over the mild protestations of the clerk because of Dude's youth, Bessie got a marriage license. Back at the Lester shack, Bessie, using her authority as preacher, married herself to Dude.

The newlyweds went for a ride in their new car; they returned to the tobacco road at sundown with one fender of the car completely ruined. They had run into a farm wagon on the highway and had killed a Negro whom they left lying by the roadside.

Jeeter, anxious to get food and snuff, persuaded Bessie and Dude to take him to Augusta with a load of firewood. Their arrival in Augusta was delayed, however, by the breakdown of the car. A gallon and a half of oil poured into the crank case enabled them to get to the city, where Jeeter failed to sell one stick of wood. The trio sold the car's spare tire, for which they could see no use, and bought food. They mistook a house of ill-repute for a hotel; Bessie was absent from Jeeter and her young husband most of the night.

During the return trip to the tobacco road, Jeeter unloaded the wood beside the highway and set fire to it. He was about to suggest another trip in the car, but Bessie and Dude rode away before he could stop them.

As the car rapidly fell apart, the warmth between Bessie and her young husband cooled. In a fight between Bessie and the Lesters over Jeeter's right to ride in the car again, Dude sided with his wife. After all, the car still ran a little.

Meanwhile Pearl ran away from Lov; she had managed to escape after he had tied her to their bed. Jeeter advised Lov not to look for Pearl, but to take Ellie May in her place. He asked Ellie May to bring back victuals and clothes from Lov's house. The grandmother, who had been run over by Bessie's Ford, died in the yard.

Jeeter anticipated seeding time by burning the broomsedge off his land. A wind blew the fire to the house while Jeeter and Ada were asleep. The destitute sharecroppers were burned to death on the land that Jeeter's family had once owned as prosperous farmers.

THE TOILERS OF THE SEA

Type of work: Novel
Author: Victor Hugo (1802-1885)
Type of plot: Sentimental romance
Time of plot: The 1820's
Locale: The Isle of Guernsey
First published: 1866

Principal characters:

GILLIATT, a young recluse
MESS LETHIERRY, a shipowner, and Gilliatt's friend
DÉRUCHETTE, Lethierry's niece
SIEUR CLUBIN, captain of Lethierry's steamboat
RANTAINE, Lethierry's former partner
REV. EBENEZER CAUDRAY, Déruchette's lover

Critique:

The Toilers of the Sea is a typical work of the French romantic period. Much of the novel is given over to descriptions of places and people, conveyed with all of Hugo's fidelity to detail. Some critics of the novel have protested against local color emphasized at the expense of conciseness, speed of narration, and credibility of incident and characterization. They forgot that in this novel Hugo's purpose was to present the regional and the romantic, an intention in which he succeeded admirably.

The Story:

In the parish of St. Sampson, Gilliatt was a strange figure. He and his mother had come to the Isle of Guernsey some years before and had made their home in an old house by the shore. Nobody knew where they came from, but most people decided that they were French. When Gilliatt grew to young manhood, his mother died and he was left alone to make his livelihood by fishing and cultivating. To the superstitious people of the town, he was a figure to be feared, for they were sure he had power to communicate with evil spirits and cure strange ailments. The young man went his own way with seeming indifference.

One Christmas Day Gilliatt saw a young woman tracing some letters in the snow. When he reached the spot, he discovered that the letters spelled his own name. The girl was Déruchette, niece of Mess Lethierry, Gilliatt's supporter against the superstitious people of the parish. From that day on Gilliatt was in love with the beautiful Déruchette. Although he stood in her garden and serenaded her with his bagpipe, he lacked the courage to approach her directly. Mess Lethierry heard the music from the garden and thought that it would do the suitor, whoever he was, little good; it was to him the suitor should apply.

Later Gilliatt won a race, the prize being a Dutch sloop. Mess Lethierry thought more highly of him than ever. Lethierry was a good man who loved two things, the sea and his niece. Some time before he had been brought to ruin by the treachery of a man he had trusted. Rantaine, his partner, had run away, not only with his own share of the profits but also with Lethierry's. In an effort to recoup his finances, Lethierry bought a steamboat, an invention the fishermen considered a work of the devil.

The Durande, as the ship was called, shared equal affection with Déruchette in Lethierry's heart. As captain, he engaged Sieur Clubin, a man whose honesty was the pride of the community. Lethierry, despite the opposition to the steamboat, prospered in trade with St. Malo and other points on the French coast.

Meanwhile a new rector, Ebenezer Caudray, had come to the parish. One day, while Gilliatt was fishing from his sloop, he rescued Caudray, who had climbed upon a seat-shaped rock exposed at low tide. The grateful rector gave him a Bible. When Caudray met Déruchette, he fell in love with her, much to Gilliatt's chagrin.

One day the *Durande* did not return from a trip to St. Malo. Lethierry was in despair, the whole parish in an uproar. Some days previously a group of boys had gone prowling near an old and supposedly haunted house. There they had heard men talking in Spanish, discussing payment for taking someone to South America. In St. Malo a man purchased a revolver and spoke mysteriously to various people. A short time before a coast guardsman had been killed. Clubin, encountering Rantaine, had forced him at the point of a gun to return the money stolen from Lethierry. As Rantaine left in a boat, he shouted to Clubin that he would write to Lethierry and tell him that he had given the captain the money.

While Lethierry and the townspeople waited for news of the *Durande*, that ship was in difficulty. The pilot, having discovered a flask of brandy, had got drunk and steered the ship off its course in the fog. The captain cursed the drunken pilot and attempted to avoid a catastrophe. Suddenly there was a crash and the boat began to leak. The passengers took to lifeboats, but the captain remained on board. When they were gone, the captain made his way to the rocks upon which the ship had grounded. Much to his surprise and fear, he discovered that he was not where he had planned to be.

Clubin had deliberately wrecked the ship after placing the brandy where the pilot would find it. In the hope that everyone would believe he had been drowned, he had planned to ground the *Durande* at a spot where he would find some smugglers hired to carry him to South America with the money taken from Rantaine. Now he realized that he had miscalculated, that he was stranded in one of the deathtraps of the sea, that he would drown.

When survivors of the wreck reached St. Sampson and told their story, Sieur Clubin became a hero. But Lethierry was desolate; his fortune was gone. It was not so much the vessel itself that was important, for that could be replaced. But the engine was lost, and he lacked the money to buy another. In his despair Lethierry announced that whoever should regain the engine would have Déruchette for his wife. Gilliatt stepped forward and announced that he would try to salvage the engine.

At the scene of the wreck Gilliatt labored unceasingly against the powerful sea and bad weather. One day he swam into an underwater cave where he was attacked by a monster that he finally managed to kill. He swam farther and in the recesses of the cavern he found the remains of a man and a wallet bearing Clubin's name. The wallet contained many coins. Gilliatt pocketed it and resumed his work.

At last he succeeded in hoisting the engine. Weary and exhausted, he fell into a deep sleep. The next day, after the sun had warmed his tired body, he gained new strength. Then he discovered that part of his work had been undone by the sea. While he attempted to repair the damage, a storm came up and all his work seemed in vain. But he finally got the engine into his boat and sailed for home.

In St. Sampson, with the arrival of Rantaine's letter, Mess Lethierry began to understand Clubin's duplicity. As time passed, Clubin's secret preparations became known, and no one any longer believed that he had gone down with the ship. Lethierry was even more dispirited than ever. One morning, as he looked out at the ocean, he saw Gilliatt's Dutch sloop with the engine aboard. Overjoyed, he sent for Gilliatt, who had slipped away to his own house. Lethierry was ready to make good his promise, with deep gratitude now that Gilliatt had returned not only the valuable engine but also the money recovered from Clubin's wallet. But Déruchette, confronting the unkempt and bedraggled Gilliatt, fainted. Gilliatt, having seen her and Caudray in the garden, knew that she secretly loved the rector.

When the shipowner, unaware of his niece's true affections, pushed the preparations for the wedding, Caudray determined to marry Déruchette without Lethierry's knowledge. The two went off to be married, only to learn that they could not have the ceremony performed without Lethierry's consent. Then Gilliatt arrived with the consent Lethierry had given for the wedding of Gilliatt and Déruchette. To their astonishment, Gilliatt said he would give the bride away. So Caudray and Déruchette were married.

As the newlyweds were embarking upon the *Cashmere,* which was to take them to England, Gilliatt presented Déruchette with a chest of bride's linen he had inherited from his mother. As the ship pulled out, Gilliatt went to the rock seat from which he had once rescued Caudray. On board, Déruchette saw that a man was sitting there, but in her happiness she gave no more thought to him. As Gilliatt watched the ship sail out of sight, the water mounted higher and higher around the rock. Soon the waves washed over it, and nothing could be seen but the sea and the sky.

TOM BROWN'S SCHOOL DAYS

Type of work: Novel
Author: Thomas Hughes (1822-1896)
Type of plot: Didactic romance
Time of plot: Early nineteenth century
Locale: England
First published: 1857

Principal characters:

THOMAS BROWN, a student at Rugby
HARRY EAST, his friend
GEORGE ARTHUR, befriended by Tom Brown
DR. ARNOLD, headmaster of Rugby
FLASHMAN, a bully

Critique:

On the surface a simple recounting of life at an English public school, the story of Tom Brown is in reality a plea for improvement in customs in those institutions. It was the author's hope that the older boys would follow the good example of the splendid headmaster and turn from bullying and cheating to an understanding of the real values to be gained from school life. The author does not ask that young boys give up all their mischief, only that they develop a sense of fitness and charity.

The Story:

Tom Brown was the son of a country squire who believed in letting his children mingle not only with their social equals but also with any children who were honorable. Thus before Tom left home to attend Rugby he had had the advantage of friendship with all types of boys. This training was to be of value to him when he first arrived at the famous school.

When Tom alighted from the coach he was met by Harry East, a lower-school boy who had been at Rugby for a half year. He gave Tom much good advice on how to dress and how to take the hazing and bullying that every new boy must endure. The two boys became immediate friends and were to remain so throughout their years at school. From the first Tom loved the school. He conducted himself with such bravery, both on the playing field and in dormitory scuffles, that he

soon gained popularity among the other boys. One of the sixth-form boys, a leader among the students, made such an impression on Tom with his talks on sportsmanship and kindness to weaker boys that Tom for the first half-year was an almost model student. He did join in some of the mischief and was once sent to Dr. Arnold, the headmaster, but by and large both he and East profited by the lessons they learned in classes and in games.

With the beginning of the second half-year, Tom was promoted into the lower fourth form, a large and unruly class dominated by bullies and ruffians. Formerly he had liked his masters and tried to please them; now he began to believe that they were his natural enemies and to do everything possible to thwart them. He cribbed on his lessons and shirked many of his other duties. He and East disobeyed many rules of the school and often taunted farmers in the neighborhood by fishing in their waters or killing their fowls. All in all, Tom and East and their friends acted in very ungentlemanly ways.

But Tom and East also did some good in the school, for they were basically boys of sound character. Both came from good homes and had received good early training. They finally decided that something must be done about fagging, the custom of running errands for the older boys. Each older boy was allowed two fags, but some of them made every younger lad

3815

in the school wait on them. One particular bully was Flashman. Deciding to strike against his domination, Tom and East locked themselves in their room and defied his demands that they let him in. After attempting to break the door down, Flashman retreated temporarily; but he was not through with the rebels. For weeks he caught them and tortured them at each possible chance, but they held firm and persuaded some of the other lower-school boys to join them. At last Flashman's brutality to Tom and East and their friends so disgusted even the bully's best friends that they began to desert him, and at last his hold on the school was broken forever. Then Tom and East thrashed him soundly, and from that time on Flashman never laid a hand on them. Not long afterward Flashman was caught drunk by the headmaster and was sent away from the school.

Tom and East began to get into trouble in earnest, and the headmaster despaired of their even being allowed to stay in school. But wise Dr. Arnold could see the good in the boys, good which they seemed to try hard to hide, and he arranged for them to be split up. Tom was given a new and shy young boy to live with, one George Arthur. Arthur was a half-orphan and Tom's better nature responded to the homesick younger boy. Arthur was to be the greatest influence to enter Tom's life during his career at Rugby. He was of slight build, but he had moral courage that made Tom ashamed. Arthur did what he thought was right, even when it meant that he must endure the taunts of his housemates. Because Tom could not let a younger boy appear more courageous than he, he reverted to his own former good habits which he had dropped because of fear of hazing. He began again to kneel in prayer morning and night, to read his Bible, and to discuss earnestly the meanings of certain passages. Indeed, as East said, although Tom was seemingly becoming a leader in the school, it was really Arthur who was leading Tom and

thus the other boys. East fought the change as hard as he could. But he too followed Tom, and so in spite of himself he began to change for the better.

When fever struck the school, many of the boys were seriously ill, Arthur among them. One boy died. Arthur remained very weak after his illness and his mother decided to take him out of school until he could recover his strength. Before he left, Arthur spoke to Tom about cribbing. Although Tom, believing that to fool the masters was a schoolboy's duty, scoffed at his friend's views, Arthur as usual prevailed. Tom found it hard to do his lessons honestly, but each time he would weaken the memory of Arthur's face and voice would set him straight again. East did not completely change in this respect, but he did try a little harder on his own before resorting to dishonest translations.

Another result of Arthur's influence was that East took communion. He had never been confirmed. But as a result of a conversation with Tom, at which Tom put forth many of Arthur's beliefs, East talked with Dr. Arnold and received spiritual stimulation. After he began to receive communion East rapidly changed into the good young man he had unknowingly wanted to be.

So the school years passed. East finished up and went off to fight in India. Tom became the leader of the school, and he and Arthur, who had returned after his illness, made many changes in the actions and attitudes of the boys. Tom, graduated, went on to Oxford. While there he learned of the death of his old headmaster, Dr. Arnold. He returned to his old school, to mourn the man who had played such a large part in influencing his life. For it was not until Dr. Arnold was gone that Tom and the others realized how much the good man had done for them. Tom's friends were scattered over the earth, but he knew that his heart would always be with them and chose wonderful days at Rugby.

TOM BURKE OF OURS

Type of work: Novel
Author: Charles Lever (1806-1872)
Type of plot: Historical romance
Time of plot: Early nineteenth century
Locale: Ireland and France
First published: 1844

Principal characters:

TOM BURKE, Irish gentleman and soldier of fortune
ANTHONY BASSET, an unscrupulous estate lawyer
DARBY M'KEOWN, called Darby the Blast, an Irish patriot
CHARLES DE MEUDON, a young French officer
MARIE DE MEUDON, his sister
CAPTAIN BUBBLETON, an English officer
THE MARQUIS DE BEAUVAIS, a French aristocrat
GENERAL D'AUVERGNE, Tom's benefactor
CAPTAIN MONTAGUE CROFTS, Tom's enemy
NAPOLEON BONAPARTE

Critique:

Charles Lever, the most popular of nineteenth-century Irish novelists, was a great admirer of Napoleon, so much so that *Tom Burke of Ours* presents one of the most idealized portraits of that historical personage to be found in any literature. In a preface to this novel Lever called the Napoleonic Period the most wonderful and eventful in modern history. The story proper covers Napoleon's career from the days of the first consulship to the fall of the empire. The plot, although theatrical, is absorbing, and the battle scenes, particularly those of Austerlitz, Jena, and the engagements of the famous "Week of Glory," are presented with dash and brilliance. As a result, the book has the vividness and swift action of a good film. The chief defect of the work is the fact that Lever, intent upon telling a romantic story, maintains no consistent point of view in his presentation of either the history or the society of the period.

The Story:

Tom Burke was only a schoolboy when his father died and the family physician and a rascally estate lawyer conspired to cheat him out of his inheritance as a younger son. Eton, private tutors, fine clothes, and the best horses and dogs had been provided for his older brother George; an obscure Dublin school and hand-me-downs had been considered good enough for fourteen-year-old Tom. On a dark winter day, sitting in the shadows by his dying father's bedside, he overheard the doctor and the lawyer discuss an arrangement to have him articled to Anthony Basset, the lawyer, in return for the five hundred pounds left Tom under his grandfather's will.

The day after the funeral, hoping to escape his dreary prospects as a lawyer's clerk, Tom took to the roads with Darby M'Keown, called by the peasants Darby the Blast, a piper belonging to one of the patriotic secret societies which had survived the disastrous rising of '98. Several times he was almost overtaken by Basset's agents or captured by British soldiers who were everywhere tracking down rebels in those troubled times. By chance he was thrown into the company of Charles de Meudon, a young French officer who had volunteered to aid the cause of Irish independence. The Frenchman taught Tom languages and military science, capturing his boyish imagination with accounts of Napoleon's victories at Marengo, Lodi, Arcola. Knowing that he would never live to return to his own country, the sickly young officer made Tom promise that he would go to France to study at the École Polytechnique and to be like a brother to his friend's sister, Marie de Meudon. Charles died at the country retreat where he and Tom had gone together. Before his death he gave the boy some French money to pay for his journey overseas.

Captured by the British at the time of de Meudon's death, Tom was being taken to Dublin under guard when Darby the Blast appeared and provoked a scuffle with the militia. During the fight Tom escaped. His only hope being to find the quarters of Captain Bubbleton, a bombastic English officer who had been kind to him some time before, he continued on his way to Dublin. There, while searching for the captain, he was caught in a mob rioting before Parliament House. Struck over the head by a musket, he fell unconscious.

When he awoke, Tom found himself in Captain Bubbleton's quarters, where that officer had carried the boy after finding him senseless in the street. Tom tried to tell the captain the true story of his experiences, but his rescuer, who always changed circumstances to suit his fantastic imagination, brushed the explanations aside. To him, Tom was a hero who had been wounded while fighting the Irish rebels and the officers' mess, delighted with the boy's spirit, called him Tom Burke of Ours. Lord Castlereagh himself, the captain added, was concerned for Tom's quick recovery.

Tom's cuts and bruises soon healed under the nursing of the captain and his sister, Miss Anna Maria. One day the captain reported that an officer was coming from the Castle to see the convalescent. To Tom's dismay, the officer was one who was able to recognize him immediately as an associate of rebels. Lodged in jail, the boy was released when Basset appeared at the hearing and claimed his runaway apprentice. But Captain Bubbleton remained Tom's good friend. At his intercession the lawyer was persuaded to accept four hundred pounds of Tom's inheritance money in exchange for the boy's indenture papers.

So Tom did become Tom Burke of Ours for a short time, even though he was still determined to go to France at the first opportunity. The officers of the mess welcomed Captain Bubbleton's charge in friendly fashion. One exception, however, was Captain Montague Crofts, who made little effort to conceal his dislike.

One evening Darby the Blast, disguised as an old woman, came to the barracks to give Tom a packet containing Charles de Meudon's letter of credit and two checks on his banker, papers Tom had dropped while fleeing from the British soldiers. Tom and Darby were interrupted when a group of officers entered and called for a deck of cards to settle a wager between Bubbleton and Crofts. Hearing Bubbleton wagering heavily, and knowing that his friend had not that much money on his person, Tom slipped the captain what he thought was a twenty-pound note. Instead, he gave him one of Charles de Meudon's notes for two thousand livres. After the other officers had gone on duty Crofts threatened to denounce the boy as a traitor and a spy for the French. When Tom stood up against his accuser, the enraged captain drew his sword and tried to run the boy through. Tom was wounded, but before Crofts could strike a second blow Darby the Blast ran into the room and struck the officer to the floor, where he lay as if dead.

Aided by the disguised piper, Tom managed to walk by the sentry and reach a house by the river. There his wound was dressed. Before daybreak he was aboard a smuggler's vessel bound for France.

All went as Charles de Meudon had planned. Tom, enrolled in the Polytechnique, soon distinguished himself at the French military school. One day the famous General d'Auvergne arrived to review the cadets, and Tom led a desperate charge in a mimic battle staged for the occasion. Knocked unconscious, he revived to find a young woman holding a cup of water to his lips. Half-dazed, he had the impression that he had met her somewhere before. At that moment the group about him parted. He saw a short man with a pale, commanding face looking down at him, and he heard Napoleon saying that he should be given his brevet at once. Advanced in rank, Tom moved into new quarters. His roommate was Lieutenant Tascher, the nephew of Madame Bonaparte, from Guadaloupe.

Although he grumbled frequently because his kinsman gave him no preferment, Tascher was generously pleased when Tom received a commission in the Eighth Hussars, a billet the young Creole had also desired. The next day Tom, invited to attend Madame Bonaparte's reception at the Tuileries, went to a fashionable tailor to be fitted for a new uniform. The shop was filled with elegant young dandies who eyed Tom's old cadet uniform with contempt. Taking exception to one lounger's remarks, Tom called him insolent. The young man presented himself as the Marquis de Beauvais, willing to meet Tom with rapiers in the Bois de Boulogne the next morning.

At the reception, which Tom attended in his old uniform, he was graciously received by Madame Bonaparte. A gentleman pointed out the young ladies of the court. One was the girl whom he had found bending over him when he awoke after the mock battle at the Polytechnique. She was Mademoiselle de Rochefort, called the Rose of Provence. While wandering through the Tuileries, Tom overheard a conversation between Napoleon and Talleyrand and learned that the treaties of peace were soon to be broken. He also encountered young Henri de Beauvais, who apologized for his rude behavior of the morning. With his new friend Tom went to a famous restaurant where a gay supper party was in progress. During the evening he indiscreetly revealed the discussion he had overheard. The Rose of Provence, he also learned, was the cousin of de Beauvais. Later, when he was questioned by a police

agent, he got the impression that an attempt might be made to involve him in a political intrigue.

The war with England began, but Tom's squadron remained on duty at Versailles. From time to time he saw the Rose of Provence at a distance. One day the Abbé d'Ervan, whom he had met in the company of de Beauvais, visited him. From his caller Tom learned that de Beauvais was a royalist, also that the Rose of Provence, who had taken her mother's name because of her family's royalist connections, was Charles de Meudon's sister.

About to throw his lot with the rebel Chouans, de Beauvais planned to see his cousin once more and sent the abbé with a request that Tom pass his friend through the sentry lines. At last Tom reluctantly agreed to do so. The next day he encountered the girl in the gardens and revealed himself as her brother's friend. That night he helped de Beauvais to enter the palace grounds. Before he left the young nobleman offered Tom a commission in the royal army; it was refused. Later Marie reproached Tom for his seeming disloyalty in becoming embroiled with the royalists.

Several months later Tom received a note in which Marie begged him to warn if possible a party of Chouans who were to be trapped at the Chateau d'Ancre, de Beauvais among them. He arrived at the chateau, only to be captured when troops surrounded the old castle. Arrested, he was charged with treason.

He was in prison during the reign of terror under the consulate, when the government repressed with harsh measures and bloodshed the royalist uprising for the restoration of the Bourbons, but because of General d'Auvergne's influence with Napoleon he was not among those executed or sent to the galleys. Transferred to a military tribunal, he was released after de Beauvais surrendered and absolved the young Irishman of any part in the conspiracy. Restored to his rank and appointed to d'Auvergne's staff, he was sent to the garrison at Mayence.

Napoleon became emperor. There were reports that the expedition against England would soon sail. In the midst of these warlike preparations General d'Auvergne summoned Tom to Paris. There he revealed his plan to adopt Marie de Meudon as his daughter. But Napoleon, refusing to consent to the plan, insisted that d'Auvergne marry the girl in whom he took so great an interest. Tom, as the general's aide, was forced to witness the hurried wedding of the girl he loved in secret. After the ceremony d'Auvergne left immediately for the front. To Tom he declared that he had made Marie his wife and that his only possible reparation would be to make her his widow.

After the battle of Austerlitz, Tom, now restored to Napoleon's favor, was one of the young officers named to the *compagnie d'élite*. In Paris, during those triumphant days of 1806, his closest friend was the Chevalier Duchesne, an officer who was secretly ready to serve either Bonapartists or Bourbonists to his own advantage. Their friendship cooled eventually because the chevalier suspected Tom of being his rival for the hand of Pauline de Lacostellerie, an heiress related to the empress. When Duchesne swore that he never forgot his debt to a friend or an enemy, Tom expected a challenge to a duel, but before the affair could be arranged he received orders to rejoin the army. At Jena his display of courage and resourcefulness led to his recommendation for the Legion of Honor and a colonelcy.

Meanwhile his enemy was working for his ruin. Shortly after the fall of Prussia he was summoned to Marshal Berthier's quarters at Potsdam. There he was shown an incriminating letter from Duchesne which had been seized in the mails. Duchesne, who had resigned his commission some time before, wrote as if to a fellow conspirator, for the letter, filled with ridicule of the emperor and hints of sedition, was his means of revenging himself upon Tom. Realizing himself disgraced if the nature of the letter were revealed, Tom claimed a foreign officer's privilege of resigning his grade and leaving the service.

With no ideas as to how he was to meet the future he left for Paris. General d'Auvergne and Tascher, his only real friends, were with the army in the field; having resigned his commission under questionable circumstances, he could not turn to them. In Paris he made the acquaintance of a number of royalists and at last consented to travel with an abbé who was going to Ireland on a secret political mission. Instead of the abbé, however, he met his former friend, Henri de Beauvais, who prevailed upon Tom in the name of their former friendship to convey some documents to the Irish patriots. Much as he had left Ireland ten years before, Tom returned on a smuggler's ship at night.

In his delight at being home once more he forgot the circumstances of his departure. He was surprised, therefore, when soon after his return to Dublin he was arrested on an old charge of murderous assault on Captain Crofts. Having survived the blow Darby the Blast had given him, Crofts was still eager for revenge. In the meantime Tom had also encountered Basset and had learned from him that his brother George was dead; he was now the heir to the Burke estates. Tom realized that he was involved in a deep plot, for Crofts, as Basset unintentionally revealed, was a distant kinsman who would inherit the property if Tom were out of the way. But Crofts was completely discredited at the trial. Darby the Blast, who had been transported to Australia some years before, returned in time to tell the true story of the assault and to accuse Crofts of other villainies, so that the judgment of the court turned against Tom's designing enemy and kinsman.

Suddenly possessed of his good name and a fortune, Tom was glad to settle down to the quiet life of a country squire, with old Darby as his loyal pensioner and friend. For a long time he paid no attention to events beyond the boundary of his estate. One day he chanced upon a newspaper and read in it an account of the burning of Moscow. Immediately his interest in Napoleon and his former comrades in arms revived. As disaster followed disaster for the French he brooded more and more upon the falling fortunes of Napoleon. At last he decided to offer his sword again in the emperor's service. Crossing the channel in a fishing boat, he volunteered in the first French unit he encountered. During the fierce fighting at Chaumière he stumbled upon the dead body of General d'Auvergne and with his own hands dug a grave for his old commander. At Montereau his daring in blowing up a bridge won for him the cross of the Legion.

Wounded in that engagement, Tom was invalided at Fontainebleau. One evening he heard hoofbeats and saw a file of dragoons drawn up before a distant wing of the palace. While he was walking in the garden that night, he saw Roustan, the emperor's faithful mameluk, on guard in a lighted apartment. Defeated, his army gone, Napoleon was in retreat. The next morning Tom awoke to find the courtyard filled with troops. From his window he watched the emperor's final farewell to his Old Guard. Napoleon was on his way into exile.

Paris welcomed with wild excitement the restoration of the Bourbons. Tom, who stubbornly continued to wear the Bonapartist tricolor in his hat, was once attacked by an angry mob. He might have been killed if de Beauvais had not appeared to save his life. Later, as Tom was preparing to leave France forever, de Beauvais came to him and offered him a commission in the army of King Louis. Tom refused to renounce his allegiance to the fallen emperor. When they parted the Frenchman handed him a note from Madame d'Auvergne, who asked Tom to call at her hotel that evening.

He found Marie dressed in mourning, but lovelier than ever. Planning to leave France, she wanted to give him some small keepsakes of her brother's and the sword General d'Auvergne had worn at Jena. When she tried to remove from her finger the ring which was to be her own token of remembrance, the band stuck. At that Tom begged her to give it to him where it was. While he stood telling the story of his long-concealed love, she smilingly placed her hand in his.

TOM CRINGLE'S LOG

Type of work: Novel
Author: Michael Scott (1789-1835)
Type of plot: Adventure romance
Time of plot: Nineteenth century
Locale: West Indies
First published: 1833

Principal characters:

TOM CRINGLE, a young midshipman
MARY PALMA, his cousin and wife
OBADIAH, a smuggler and pirate
CAPTAIN TRANSOM, of the *Firebrand*

Critique:

There is almost no plot in *Tom Cringle's Log* and even little connection between episodes. Great numbers of people appear briefly in disconnected incidents and then disappear, for the novel is, as the name implies, a recital of one man's experience as an officer on various British warships during the Napoleonic wars. Although the book gives the reader some first-hand accurate accounts of minor actions in the war with Napoleon and many sidelights on the War of 1812 with America, Scott emphasizes merry bibulous exploits ashore rather than the business of fighting.

The Story:

Tom Cringle, aged thirteen and four feet four inches tall, looked upon himself as a successor to Nelson. In pursuing his aim, he pestered his relative, Sir Barnaby Blueblazes, to such lengths that at last Tom was appointed midshipman aboard the frigate *Breeze* and ordered to report for foreign duty in four days.

Poor Tom had envisioned a period of months ashore after his appointment, time to strut his uniform before all his friends. His time being so short, he hardly knew whether he wanted to go to sea after all, and his widowed mother wept and begged him not to leave. But on the appointed day Tom went aboard his ship, bound for action.

He had a trip to the Bay of Biscay on the *Breeze,* and a tour of duty on the *Kraaken.* Then, an old hand, Tom boarded the *Torch,* an eighteen-gun sloop bound for the North Sea.

Near Cuxhaven the ship's boat was lowered and Tom was put second in command of a party to enter the harbor. The captain was sure no French were near; consequently the party shoved off with light hearts. To their astonishment they were challenged by French sentries. In trying to regain the ship, Tom's boat was hit by a shell from a shore battery, and subsequently he was taken prisoner.

A resident of Hamburg went surety for Tom and took him to his own country house. The next day the Russians advanced and drove out the French. In the confusion Tom and the Hamburg family escaped and safely boarded the *Torch.*

The *Torch* stood off Cork, where Tom played the part of a spy. By a clever tale he induced a group of British seamen to rendezvous in a small tavern. There they were captured and pressed into service. Then with her full complement the *Torch* left for Caribbean waters, where Tom was to spend many years. In the West Indies the French, Spaniards, English, and Americans were all privateering, and there was much work for a British man-of-war, in escorting merchantmen, keeping a lookout for American marauders, and trying to keep slavery and smuggling within bounds.

Tom had an early introduction to the horrors of piracy the day a London merchantman was sighted behaving erratically. With great difficulty a boarding party captured the ship after subduing a pirate crew. In the main cabin of the merchantman the British found a terrifying situation. The captain had been tied on the table, his throat so savagely slashed that he was almost decapitated. Tied in a chair was a prosperous gentleman very nearly hysterical. On the sofa was the man's wife, violated by the pirates. The poor lady was mad with shame and fright and spent her last days in an asylum. The leader of the pirates, who subsequently escaped, was a tall, handsome Spaniard. Tom learned much later that his name was Francesco Cangrejo.

During a violent hurricane the *Torch* went down, and Tom, believing himself the only survivor, spent three terrible days in an open boat. At last thirst and privation overcame him. When he regained consciousness he was on shore, tended by Lieutenant Splinter, the only other crew member to escape. Captain Deadeye, of the *Torch*, was stretched out under a canvas on the beach. Scarcely had Tom recovered his senses when they were taken prisoners by a Spanish platoon. When Tom and Splinter had satisfactorily established their identity, they were freed, but they were stranded in the tiny port of Cartagena, far from the British forces.

On the beach Tom made the acquaintance of a black pilot, Peter Musgrave, who was wanted by the Admiralty for running a British ship aground. Tom agreed to act as Peter's friend at court, and in turn Peter would procure passage to Jamaica.

Peter went aboard a suspiciously decrepit small craft in the harbor and returned with the American mate of the vessel. Obadiah, the mate, took them aboard, and the black captain consented to take the Englishmen to Jamaica for a reasonable fee. As soon as they were at sea, however, some astonishing changes took place. Obadiah assumed the captaincy, and under his directions the villainous but alert crew re-rigged the worn sails and mounted guns on deck. Then the truth dawned on Tom; he was aboard a pirate ship.

Two British men-of-war bore down on the ship, but Captain Obadiah, refusing to heave to, held his course in the face of almost certain suicide. By clever seamanship the pirate craft outran its pursuers, although many of the crew were killed or wounded. Making a landfall in Cuba, the pirates put in to a small river, and after a narrow passage came to anchor in a secluded lagoon a mile in diameter. The lagoon was filled with armed craft of many types. Tom was in the secret den of the West Indian pirates.

When the *Firebrand*, an English warship, engaged a pirate felucca near the river's mouth, Tom escaped with the help of Peter. Going aboard the *Firebrand*, to which he had been assigned by dispatch, Tom took part in the capture of the whole pirate band. Obadiah, who was a renegade Englishman, as Tom learned later, was shot as he tried to swim away. For his bravery in the engagement Tom was promoted to the rank of lieutenant.

Captain Transom of the *Firebrand* proved to be a genial commander with many friends in the islands. Tom spent much time ashore indulging in high jinks. One trip ashore, however, was a somber one. Tom served as interpreter at the trial of the pirates, who were all condemned to death. One of the prisoners, Tom found, was Francesco Cangrejo, who cut a brave figure in the dock in spite of his confessed career of villainy. At the pirate's request, Tom took his miniature and crucifix to deliver to the pirate's betrothed.

In Kingston, where Tom called on his relatives, the Palmas, he was most cordially received. There he met and fell in love with Mary Palma, his cousin. When he was called away on duty, it was with the understanding that they would be married after his next promotion.

At Santiago Tom went ashore to visit Ricardo Campana, a rich merchant. There a priest who met him and Ricardo on the street seemed much upset. Tom could hear the name Cangrejo mentioned and learned that Maria, Francesco's sweetheart, was dying. The party hastened to the Cangrejo house in time for Tom to have a few words with Maria before she died. Tom was saddened when he heard of Francesco's early promise and reflected on the Spaniard's later death for piracy.

On a trip out from Santiago, Tom was ordered to take command of the small schooner *Wave*. At twenty-three, Tom Cringle, lieutenant, became master of his own ship. Sent to patrol for suspicious vessels, Tom sighted a large schooner that failed to heed his signals. After a two days' chase the *Wave* closed with the heavily-armed, larger ship. Displaying great courage at close quarters, the gallant crew of the *Wave* boarded the schooner, which proved to be a slaver. Unable to land the ship with a prize crew, Tom had the slaver shelled until it caught fire and sank. Tom rescued as many slaves as the *Wave* could carry and put them ashore.

Tom was afterward trusted with many missions, including one to Panama. Since he was always diligent in doing his duty and since he had always displayed great courage in battle, he received his second epaulet. Tom Cringle, one time midshipman, became Commander Cringle.

At dinner in Kingston, wearing his two epaulets, Tom was surprised that none of the Palmas remarked on his promotion. Mary herself was quite agitated and left the table. In his embarrassment Tom had the misfortune to drink a glass of catsup. But in spite of all his awkwardness, Tom managed to see Mary alone and win her consent to an immediate marriage.

TOM JONES

Type of work: Novel
Author: Henry Fielding (1707-1754)
Type of plot: Comic epic
Time of plot: Early eighteenth century
Locale: England
First published: 1749

Principal characters:
  TOM JONES, a foundling
  SQUIRE ALLWORTHY, his foster father
  BRIDGET, Allworthy's sister
  MASTER BLIFIL, Bridget's son
  MR. PARTRIDGE, the schoolmaster
  MR. WESTERN, an English squire
  SOPHIA WESTERN, his daughter

Critique:

It is difficult to determine whether greater pleasure is derived from the narrative parts of *The History of Tom Jones, a Foundling,* as Fielding titled his novel, or from the essays written at the beginning of each book. The story itself is a long, involved plot in which Tom finally wins the confidence of those he loves. Most of the humor in this novel lies in Fielding's exaggerated dramatic emphasis and in his lengthy, delicate dissections of the motives of his characters. It must be remembered that Fielding had few examples of the novel form from which to learn, but his novels are so far advanced in development over their predecessors that Fielding must be recognized as a literary innovator. The author knew the follies of human nature, and he attempted to laugh mankind out of its own weaknesses.

The Story:

Squire Allworthy lived in retirement in the country with his sister Bridget. Returning from a visit to London, he was considerably surprised upon entering his room to find an infant lying on his bed. His discovery caused much astonishment and consternation in the household, for the squire himself was a childless widower. The next day Miss Bridget and the squire inquired in the community to discover the baby's mother, and their suspicions were shortly fixed upon Jenny Jones, who had spent many hours in the squire's home while nursing Miss Bridget through a long illness. The worthy squire sent for the girl and in his gentle manner reprimanded her for her wicked behavior, assuring her, however, that the baby would remain in his home under the best of care. Fearing malicious gossip of the neighborhood, Squire Allworthy sent Jenny away.

Jenny Jones had been a servant in the house of a schoolmaster named Mr. Partridge, who had educated the young woman during her four years in his house. Mrs. Partridge, because of Jenny's comely face, was jealous of her. Neighborhood gossip soon convinced Mrs. Partridge that her husband was the father of Jenny's son, whereupon Squire Allworthy called the schoolmaster before him and talked to him at great length concerning morality. Mr. Partridge, deprived of his school, his income, and his wife, also left the country.

Not long afterward Captain Blifil won the heart of Bridget Allworthy. Eight months after their nuptials Bridget bore a son. The squire thought it would be well to rear the foundling and his sister's child together. The foundling had been named Jones, after his mother.

Squire Allworthy became exceedingly fond of the foundling. Captain Blifil died during his son's infancy, and Master Blifil grew up as Squire Allworthy's acknowledged heir. Otherwise, he remained on even terms with the foundling so far as opportunities for advancement were concerned. But Tom was such a mischievous lad that he had but one friend among the servants, the gamekeeper, Black George, an indolent man with a large family. Hired to instruct the lads were Mr. Thwackum and Mr. Square, who considered Tom a wicked soul. Tom's many deceptions were always discovered through the combined efforts of Mr. Thwackum, Mr. Square, and Master Blifil, who as he grew older disliked Tom more and more. It had been assumed by all that Mrs. Blifil would dislike Tom, but at times she seemed to show greater affection for him than for her own son. In turn, the compassionate squire took Master Blifil to his heart and became censorious of Tom.

Mr. Western, who lived on a neighboring estate, had a daughter whom he loved more than anyone else in the world. Sophia had a tender fondness for Tom because of a deed of kindness he had performed for her when they were still children. At the age of twenty, Master Blifil had become a favorite with the young ladies, while Tom was considered a ruffian by all but Mr. Western, who admired his ability to hunt. Tom spent many evenings at the Western home, with every opportunity to see Sophia, for whom his affections were increasing daily. One afternoon Tom had the good fortune to be nearby when Sophia's horse ran away. Tom, in rescuing her, broke his arm. He was removed to Mr. Western's house, where he received medical care and remained to recover from his hurt. One day he and Sophia had occasion to be alone in the garden, where they exchanged confessions of love.

Squire Allworthy became mortally ill. Assuming that he was dying, the doctor sent for the squire's relatives. With his servants and family gathered around him, the squire announced the disposal of his wealth, giving generously to Tom. Tom was the only one satisfied with his portion; his only concern was the impending death of his foster father and benefactor. On the way home from London to see the squire, Mrs. Blifil died suddenly. When the squire was pronounced out of danger, Tom's joy was so great that he became drunk through toasting the squire's health, and quarreled with young Blifil.

Sophia's aunt, Mrs. Western, perceived the interest her niece showed in Blifil, for Sophia, wishing to conceal her affection for Tom, gave Blifil the greater part of her attention when she was with the two young men. Informed by his sister of Sophia's conduct, Mr. Western suggested to Squire Allworthy that a match be arranged between Blifil and Sophia. When Mrs. Western told the young girl of the proposed match, Sophia thought that she meant Tom, and she immediately disclosed her passion for the foundling. But it was unthinkable that Mr. Western, much as he liked Tom, would ever allow his daughter to marry a man without a family and a fortune, and Mrs. Western forced Sophia to receive Blifil under the threat of exposing the girl's real affection for Tom. Sophia met Tom secretly in the garden and the two lovers vowed constancy. Discovering them, Mr. Western went immediately to Squire Allworthy with his knowledge.

Blifil, aware of his advantage, told the squire that on the day he lay near death Tom was out drinking and singing. The squire felt that he had forgiven Tom any wrongs, but his show of unconcern for the squire's health infuriated the good man. He sent for Tom, reproached him, and banished him from his house.

With the help of Black George, the gamekeeper, and Mrs. Honour, Sophia's maid, Tom and Sophia were able to exchange love letters. When Sophia was confined to her room because she refused to marry Blifil, she bribed her maid to flee with her from her father's house. Tom, setting out to seek his fortune, went to an inn with a small company of soldiers. A fight followed in which he was severely injured, and a barber was summoned to treat his wound. When Tom had told the barber his story, the man surprisingly revealed himself to be

Partridge, the schoolmaster, banished years before because he was suspected of being Tom's father. When Tom was well enough to travel, the two men set out together on foot.

Before they had gone far they heard screams of a woman in distress and came upon a woman struggling with a soldier who had beguiled her to that lonely spot. Promising to take her to a place of safety, Tom accompanied the unfortunate creature to the nearby village of Upton, where the landlady of the inn refused to receive them because of the woman's torn and disheveled clothing. But when she heard the true story of the woman's misfortune and had been assured that the woman was the lady of Captain Waters, a well-known officer, she relented. Mrs. Waters invited Tom to dine with her so that she could thank him properly for her rescue.

Meanwhile a lady and her maid arrived at the inn and proceeded to their rooms. They were followed, several hours later, by an angry gentleman in pursuit of his wife. Learning from the chambermaid that there was a woman resembling his wife in the inn, he burst into Mrs. Waters' chambers, only to confront Tom Jones. At his intrusion, Mrs. Waters began to scream. The gentleman, abashed, identified himself as Mr. Fitzpatrick and retreated with apologies. Shortly after this disturbance had subsided, Sophia and Mrs. Honour arrived at the inn. When Partridge unknowingly revealed Tom's relation with Mrs. Waters and the embarrassing situation which Mr. Fitzpatrick had disclosed. Sophia, grieved by Tom's fickleness, decided to continue on her way. Before leaving the inn, however, she had Mrs. Honour place on Tom's empty bed a muff which she knew he would recognize as hers.

Soon after setting out, Sophia overtook Mrs. Fitzpatrick, who had arrived at the inn early the previous evening and who had fled during the disturbance caused by her husband. Mrs. Fitzpatrick was Sophia's cousin, and they decided to go on to London together. In London Sophia proceeded to the home of Lady Bellaston, who was known to her through Mrs. Western. Lady Bellaston was sympathetic with Sophia's reasons for running away.

Unable to overtake Sophia, Tom and Partridge followed her to London, where Tom took lodgings in the home of Mrs. Miller, whom Squire Allworthy patronized on his visits to the city. The landlady had two daughters, Nancy and Betty, and a lodger, Mr. Nightingale, who was obviously in love with Nancy. Tom found congenial residence with Mrs. Miller, and he became friends with Mr. Nightingale. Partridge was still with Tom in the hope of future advancement for himself. Repeated visits to Lady Bellaston and Mrs. Fitzpatrick finally gave Tom the opportunity to meet Sophia during an intermission at a play. There Tom was able to allay Sophia's doubts as to his love for her. During his stay with the Millers, Tom learned that Mr. Nightingale's father objected to his marrying Nancy. Through the kindness of his heart Tom persuaded the elder Nightingale to permit the marriage, to Mrs. Miller's great delight.

Having learned Sophia's whereabouts from Mrs. Fitzpatrick, Mr. Western came to London and took Sophia from Lady Bellaston's house to his own lodgings. When Mrs. Honour brought the news to Tom, he was in despair. Penniless, he could not hope to marry Sophia, and now his beloved was in the hands of her father once more. Then Partridge brought news that Squire Allworthy was coming to London, bringing with him Master Blifil to marry Sophia. In his distress Tom went to see Mrs. Fitzpatrick, but encountered her jealous husband on her doorstep. In the duel which followed, Tom wounded Fitzpatrick and was carried off to jail.

There he was visited by Partridge, the friends he had made in London, and Mrs. Waters, who had been traveling with Mr. Fitzpatrick ever since their meeting in Upton. When Partridge and Mrs.

Waters met in Tom's cell, Partridge recognized her as Jenny Jones, Tom's reputed mother. Horrified, he revealed his knowledge to everyone, including Squire Allworthy, who by that time had arrived in London with Blifil.

In Mrs. Miller's lodgings so many people had praised Tom's goodness and kindness that Squire Allworthy had almost made up his mind to relent in his attitude toward the foundling when news of his conduct with Mrs. Waters reached his ears. But fortunately the cloud was soon dispelled by Mrs. Waters herself, who assured the squire that Tom was no son of hers but the child of his sister Bridget and a student the squire had befriended. Tom's true father having died before his son's birth, Bridget had concealed her shame by putting the baby on her brother's bed upon his return from a long visit to London. Later she had paid Jenny liberally to let suspicion fall upon her former maid.

Squire Allworthy also learned that Bridget had claimed Tom as her son in a letter written before her death, a letter Master Blifil had destroyed. There was further proof that Blifil had plotted to have Tom hanged for murder, although Fitzpatrick had not died. That gentleman recovered sufficiently to acknowledge himself the aggressor in the duel, and Tom was released from prison.

Upon these disclosures of Blifil's villainy, Squire Allworthy dismissed Blifil and made Tom his true heir. Tom's proper station having been revealed, Mr. Western withdrew all objections to his suit. Reunited, Tom and Sophia were married and retired to Mr. Western's estate in the country.

TOM SAWYER

Type of work: Novel
Author: Mark Twain (Samuel L. Clemens, 1835-1910)
Type of plot: Adventure romance
Time of plot: Nineteenth century
Locale: St. Petersburg on the Mississippi River
First published: 1876

Principal characters:

TOM SAWYER
AUNT POLLY, Tom's aunt
HUCKLEBERRY FINN, and
JOE HARPER, Tom's friends
BECKY THATCHER, Tom's girl
INJUN JOE, a murderer
MUFF POTTER, a village ne'er-do-well

Critique:

Rich native humor and shrewd observation of human character make *The Adventures of Tom Sawyer* one of the greatest boys' books ever written. More than a book for boys, it is an idyl of America's golden age, of that pastoral time and scene which had already vanished when Mark Twain re-created St. Petersburg from memories of his own boyhood. Of a lesser greatness and different in purpose from *The Adventures of Huckleberry Finn,* the story of Tom Sawyer's adventures is true to both the fantasies of boyhood and adult nostalgia. Tom's pirate gang, cures for warts, the white-washing of the fence, Jackson's island, Becky Thatcher, Injun Joe, and Huck Finn — American literature would be poorer without them.

The Story:

Tom Sawyer lived securely with the knowledge that his Aunt Polly loved him dearly. When she scolded him or whipped him, he knew that inside her breast lurked a hidden remorse. Often he deserved the punishment he received, but there were times when he was the victim of his tale-bearing half-brother, Sid. Tom's cousin, Mary, was kinder to him. Her worst duty toward him was to see to it that he washed and put on clean clothes, so that he would look respectable when Aunt Polly took Tom, Sid, and Mary to church on Sunday.

A new family had moved into the neighborhood. Investigating Tom saw a pretty, blue-eyed girl with lacy pantalets. She was Becky Thatcher. Instantly the fervent love he had felt for Amy Lawrence fled from his faithless bosom, to be replaced by devotion to the new girl he had just beheld.

She was in school the next day, sitting on the girls' side of the room with an empty seat beside her. Tom had come late to school that morning. When the schoolmaster asked Tom why he had been late, that empty seat beside Becky Thatcher caught Tom's eye. Recklessly he confessed he had stopped to talk with Huckleberry Finn, son of the town drunk. Huck wore castoff clothing, never attended school, smoked and fished as often as he pleased, and slept wherever he could. For associating with Huck, Tom was whipped by the schoolmaster and ordered to sit on the girls' side of the room. Amid the snickers of the entire class, he took the empty seat next to Becky.

Tom first attracted Becky's attention by a series of drawings on his slate. At length he wrote the words, "I love you," and Becky blushed. Tom urged her to meet him after school. Sitting with her on a fence, he explained to her the possibilities of an engagement between them. Innocently she accepted his proposal, which Tom insisted must be sealed by a

TOM SAWYER by Mark Twain. Published by Harper & Brothers.

kiss. In coy resistance she allowed Tom a brief chase before she yielded to his embrace. Tom's happiness was unbounded. But when he mentioned his previous tie with Amy Lawrence, the brief romance ended. Becky left her affianced with a haughty shrug of her pretty shoulders.

That night Tom heard Huck's whistle below his bedroom window. Sneaking out, Tom joined his friend, and the two went off to the cemetery, Huck dragging a dead cat behind him. They were about to try a new method for curing warts. The gloomy atmosphere of the burial ground filled the boys with apprehension, and their fears increased still more when they spied three figures stealing into the graveyard. They were Injun Joe, Muff Potter, and Doctor Robinson. Evidently they had come to rob a grave. When the two robbers had exhumed the body, they began to quarrel with the doctor about money, and in the quarrel Potter was knocked out. Then Injun Joe took Potter's knife and killed the doctor. When Potter recovered from his blow he thought he had killed Robinson, and Injun Joe allowed the poor old man to believe himself guilty.

Terrified, Tom and Huck slipped away from the scene they had just witnessed, afraid that if Injun Joe discovered them he would kill them too.

Tom brooded on what he and Huck had seen. Convinced that he was ill, Aunt Polly dosed him with Pain Killer and kept him in bed, but he did not seem to recover. Becky Thatcher had not come to school since she had broken Tom's heart. Rumor around town said that she was also ill. Coupled with this sad news was the fear of Injun Joe. When Becky finally returned to school, she cut Tom coldly. Feeling that there was nothing else for him to do, he decided to run away. He met Joe Harper and Huck Finn. Together they went to Jackson's Island and pretended to be pirates.

For a few days they stayed happily on the island and learned from Huck how to smoke and swear. One day they heard a boat on the river, firing cannon over the water. Then the boys realized that the townspeople were searching for their bodies. This discovery put a new aspect on their adventure; the people at home thought they were dead. Gleeful, Tom could not resist the temptation to see how Aunt Polly had reacted to his death. He slipped back to the mainland one night and into his aunt's house, where Mrs. Harper and Aunt Polly were mourning the death of their mischievous but goodhearted children. When Tom returned to the island, he found Joe and Huck tired of their game and ready to go home. Tom revealed to them an attractive plan which they immediately decided to carry out.

With a heavy gloom overhanging the town, funeral services were held for the deceased Thomas Sawyer, Joseph Harper, and Huckleberry Finn. The minister pronounced a lengthy eulogy about the respective good characters of the unfortunate boys. When the funeral procession was about to start, Tom, Joe, and Huck marched down the aisle of the church into the arms of the startled mourners.

For a while Tom was the hero of all the boys in the town. They whispered about him and eyed him with awe in the schoolyard. But Becky ignored him until the day she accidentally tore the schoolmaster's book. When the irate teacher demanded to know who had torn his book, Tom confessed. Becky's gratitude and forgiveness were his reward.

After Muff Potter had been put in jail for the murder of the doctor in the graveyard, Tom and Huck had sworn to each other they would never utter a word about what they had seen. Afraid Injun Joe would murder them for revenge, they furtively sneaked behind the prison and brought Muff food and other cheer. But Tom could not let an innocent man be condemned. At the trial he appeared to tell what he had seen on the night of the murder. While Tom spoke, Injun Joe, a witness at the trial, sprang from the window of the courtroom and escaped. For days Tom worried, convinced that Injun Joe would come back to murder him. But as time went by and nothing happened, he gradually lost his fears. With Becky looking upon him as a hero, his world was filled with sunshine.

Huck and Tom decided to hunt for pirates' treasures. One night, ransacking an old abandoned house, they watched, unseen, while Injun Joe and a companion unearthed a chest of money buried under the floorboards of the house. The two frightened boys fled before they were discovered. The next day they began a steady watch for Injun Joe and his accomplice, for Tom and Huck were bent on finding the lost treasure.

When Judge Thatcher gave a picnic for all the young people in town, Becky and Tom were supposed to spend the night with Mrs. Harper. One of the biggest excitements of the merrymaking came when the children went into a cave in the riverbank. The next day Mrs. Thatcher and Aunt Polly learned that Tom and Becky were missing, for Mrs. Harper said they had not come to spend the night with her. Then everyone remembered that Tom and Becky had not been seen since the picnickers had left the cave. Meanwhile the two, having lost their bearings, were wandering in the cavern. To add to Tom's terror, he discovered that Injun Joe was also in the cave. Miraculously, after spending five days in the dismal cave, Tom found an exit that was five miles from the place where they had entered. Again he was a hero.

Injun Joe starved to death in the cave. After searchers had located his body, Tom and Huck went back into the cavern to look for the chest which they believed Injun Joe had hidden there. They found it and the twelve thousand dollars it contained.

Adopted shortly afterward by the Widow Douglas, Huck planned to retire with an income of a dollar a day for the rest of his life. He never would have stayed with the widow or consented to learn her prim, tidy ways if Tom had not promised that he would form a pirates' gang and make Huck one of the bold buccaneers.

TOM THUMB THE GREAT

Type of work: Drama
Author: Henry Fielding (1707-1754)
Type of plot: Farce
Time of plot: Age of chivalry
Locale: King Arthur's court
First presented: 1730

Principal characters:

TOM THUMB THE GREAT, a pocket-size epic hero
KING ARTHUR, Tom Thumb's liege lord
QUEEN DOLLALLOLLA, King Arthur's consort, in love with Tom
PRINCESS HUNCAMUNCA, in love with Tom and Lord Grizzle
LORD GRIZZLE, suitor for Huncamunca's hand
QUEEN GLUMDALCA, a captive giantess, in love with Tom

Critique:

The full title of this play is *The Tragedy of Tragedies, Or, The Life and Death of Tom Thumb the Great.* It is a literary burlesque of the absurd heroic tragedies so popular during the seventeenth and eighteenth centuries, as well as a satire on so-called courtly greatness. The importance of the play lies, however, in the skill with which Fielding parodied the verbal absurdities so common to the heroic tragedies. To add to the satire, Fielding pretended that the play was a newly discovered Elizabethan play, a pretense which permitted him to document the play for the reading public with a host of footnotes showing parallel speeches in the heroic drama to the absurd speeches in his own play. The device left no doubt as to precisely what he was burlesquing. This play was exceedingly popular in Fielding's lifetime; it broke all records for long runs on the stage during the eighteenth century.

The Story:

According to the legends told in his lifetime, Tom Thumb's peasant father and mother were unable to have any children until Tom's father went to Merlin the magician and received from him a charm which resulted in the wife's giving birth to the valiant, but diminutive, Tom Thumb. When he reached manhood, Tom Thumb entered the service of King Arthur, in whose court he accomplished great deeds and earned a vast reputation.

Queen Dollallolla fell in love with Tom Thumb. She loved him, in fact, as much as she loved drinking, but she kept her love a secret from all. Least of all did she tell King Arthur, who was afraid of no one except his queen.

Tom Thumb's greatest achievement was his victory over the giants who dwelt in the land ruled by the amazonian Queen Glumdalca. Tom subdued ten thousand giants and then returned with the surviving foes fastened to his chariot, among them the comely Queen Glumdalca. Because of their size, all the giants except the queen, who was a foot shorter than her subjects, had to be left outside the castle walls. Queen Glumdalca was brought into the castle. As soon as he saw her, King Arthur also fell in love with someone other than his spouse.

Eager to reward Tom Thumb for his great deeds, the king promised him anything within reason. Tom at first replied that permission to serve his king was sufficient reward. When pressed, however, he asked for the hand of Princess Huncamunca, with whom he had long been in love. The queen was furious that her daughter should become the wife of the man she loved. She railed at her husband and swore that the marriage should not take place. But the king, for once holding his own against his virago queen, told her to be quiet. The queen, furious also at her husband, went to Lord Grizzle, a discontented courtier, to secure his aid in preventing the marriage. Lord Grizzle was quite willing to oblige, for he himself was in love with Princess Huncamunca. He promised the queen that he would kill Tom Thumb.

Too late, Queen Dollallolla realized that she did not want Tom killed. She hoped, instead, that King Arthur would die and that she might be free to marry Tom.

In the meantime King Arthur went to tell Princess Huncamunca of his decision to marry her to Tom Thumb. The princess was only too happy to hear of his decision, for she had been in love with Tom for a long time. She had also been afraid that she might die an old maid and, according to old superstition, be doomed to lead apes through hell. After the king had gone, Lord Grizzle came to plead his suit with Princess Huncamunca. She revealed that she loved him, too. Taking her cue from the career of the queen of the giants, who had had twenty husbands, Princess Huncamunca decided that she could love both Tom and Lord Grizzle. She promised to marry Lord Grizzle and he went at once to secure a license for the ceremony.

Shortly after Lord Grizzle had gone on his happy errand, Tom Thumb came to the princess' apartment. Learning of her promise to Lord Grizzle, he paid no attention to it. While he was talking with the princess, Queen Glumdalca came into the room and offered herself to Tom Thumb, who, she said, would take the place of her twenty former husbands. Tom refused, saying he preferred the smaller gold coin of Princess Huncamunca to the large dross coin of the giantess. Queen Glumdalca left in a fury, but her anger abated when she discovered that the king was in love with her.

Tom Thumb hurried Princess Huncamunca off to a parson, who married them quickly and wished them at the same time a long life and many children. Lord Grizzle, returning just after the ceremony, found Princess Huncamunca married to his rival. The princess assured him that there was room in her heart for two husbands and offered to marry him as well. Lord Grizzle, unappeased, rushed out to create a rebellion and kill Tom Thumb.

That night the ghost of Tom Thumb's father appeared to King Arthur and warned him that Tom's life and the king's rule were both endangered by Lord Grizzle and his rebels. After the ghost's departure the king sat meditating on what he had been told, until the queen, rousing from a drunken slumber, came to see what was the matter. She tried, unsuccessfully, to put the king at ease.

The next morning Tom Thumb, in company with the giantess, went forth to subdue the rebels. On the way to the battlefield Merlin's magic vouchsafed Tom Thumb a vision in which he saw that he was doomed to be eaten by a red cow. The vision put him in awe of death, but when Merlin then revealed that Tom would become famous through the medium of the stage, Tom was willing to die.

Lord Grizzle, who had raised an army of rebels under the banner of democracy and freedom, advanced to meet Tom Thumb and the giantess. In a bloody engagement Lord Grizzle killed Queen Glumdalca, and Tom avenged her by killing Lord Grizzle. Their leader dead, the rebels dispersed. Tom cut off Lord Grizzle's head and started a victorious march to the castle.

In the castle, meanwhile, the king, the queen, and the princess awaited the news of the battle, certain that Tom Thumb would triumph and save them from the rebels. Their hopes were confirmed when a courtier ran in to tell them of Tom's success. Their happiness was short-lived, however, for the courtier went on to tell how, on his march back to the castle, Tom Thumb had met a large red cow which had swallowed poor Tom at a gulp.

Queen Dollallolla, outraged at the courtier for bringing news of her loved one's death, seized a sword and killed him. The courtier's mistress then killed the queen. Princess Huncamunca, anxious to avenge her mother's death, slew the courtier's mistress. Another courtier seized the time of strife to kill Princess Huncamunca because of an old grudge he carried against her. The princess' maid then avenged her mistress by killing Huncamunca's murderer. The king, dispensing justice, killed the maid. Then the king, with bodies lying all about him, killed himself, with the thought that his only glory was that he was the last to die.

TONO-BUNGAY

Type of work: Novel
Author: H. G. Wells (1866-1946)
Type of plot: Social criticism
Time of plot: Late nineteenth and early twentieth centuries
Locale: England, West Africa, Bordeaux
First published: 1908

Principal characters:
GEORGE PONDEREVO, a young scientist and the narrato
THE HONORABLE BEATRICE NORMANDY, an aristocrat
EDWARD PONDEREVO, George's uncle
SUSAN PONDEREVO, George's aunt
MARION RAMBOAT, George's wife

Critique:

Tono-Bungay is a spirited novel, interesting from several points of view. The references to early stages of aviation have a quaint charm for the modern reader, and the use of science as a motive of fiction throws light upon the intellectual development of the period. The manufacture and sale of patent medicine becomes a symbol of disintegrating society. Frequently unconvincing, the novel is still good reading, if only for the Dickensian characters it presents. Wells' critical views are always relieved by humor and a shrewd analysis of human motives.

The Story:

George Ponderevo grew up in the shadow of Bladesover House, where his mother was the housekeeper. In that Edwardian atmosphere the boy soon became aware of the wide distinctions between English social classes, each according to their station and degree, for the neighborhood around Bladesover was England in miniature, a small world made up of the quality, the church, the village, the laborers, and the servants. Although George spent most of his time away at school, he returned to Bladesover for his vacations. During one of his vacations he learned for the first time the class he himself represented—the servants.

His lesson came as the result of the arrival at Bladesover House of the Honorable Beatrice Normandy, a child of eight, and her snobbish young half-brother, Archie Garvell. Twelve-year-old George Ponderevo fell in love with the little aristocrat that summer. Two years later their childish romance ended abruptly when George and Archie fought each other. George was disillusioned because the Honorable Beatrice did not come to his aid. In fact, she betrayed him, abandoned him, and lied about him, picturing George as an assailant of his social betters.

When George refused flatly to apologize to Archie Garvell, he was taken to Chatham and put to work in the bakery of his mother's brother, Nicodemus Frapp. George found his uncle's family dull, cloddish, and over-religious. One night, in the room he shared with his two cousins, he told them in confidence that he did not believe in any form of revealed religion. Traitorously, his cousins reported George's blasphemy to their father. As a result, George was called upon in a church meeting to acknowledge his sins. Humiliated and angry, he ran away to his mother at Bladesover House.

Mrs. Ponderevo then took him to live with another uncle, his father's brother, Edward Ponderevo, at Wimblehurst, in Sussex. There George worked in his uncle's chemist shop out of school hours. Edward Ponderevo was a restless, dissatisfied man who wanted to expand, to make money. Aunt Susan Ponderevo was a gentle, patient woman who treated George kindly. His mother died during his years at Wimblehurst.

But George's pleasant life at Wimblehurst was brought suddenly to an end. By foolish investments Edward Ponderevo lost everything of his own, including the chemist shop and also the small fund he was holding in trust for George. The Ponderevos were forced to leave Wimblehurst, but George remained behind as an apprentice with Mr. Mantell, the new owner of the shop.

At the age of nineteen George went up to London to matriculate at the University of London for his Bachelor of Science degree. On the trip his uncle, now living in London, showed him the city and first whispered to him the name of Tono-Bungay, an invention on which the older Ponderevo was working.

When George finally arrived in London to begin his studies he was nearly twenty-two, and in the meantime he had decided to accept a scholarship at the Consolidated Technical Schools at South Kensington instead of the one offered at the university. One day he met an old schoolfellow, Ewart, an artist who exerted a broadening influence on the young man. He also met Marion Ramboat, the girl who was later to become his wife. Because of these influences, George began to neglect his studies. When he saw a billboard which advertised Tono-Bungay, he remembered the hints his uncle had thrown out several years before. A few days later his uncle sent George a telegram in which he offered the young man a job at three hundred pounds a year.

Tono-Bungay was a patent medicine, a stimulant most inexpensive to make and only slightly injurious to the person who took it. After a week of indecision, George joined the firm. One factor that helped to sway him was the thought that Marion Ramboat might be persuaded to marry him if his income were greater. Using new and bold methods of advertising, George and his exuberant uncle made Tono-Bungay a national product. The enterprise was highly successful; both George and his uncle became wealthy. At last Marion consented to marry George but their marriage was unsuccessful. They were divorced when Marion learned that her husband had gone off for the weekend with Effie Rink, one of the secretaries in his office. After his divorce George devoted himself to science and research. He became interested in flying.

Edward Ponderevo, in the meantime, branched out into many enterprises, partly through the influence of the wealthy Mr. Moggs, with whom he became associated. His huge corporation, Domestic Utilities, became known as Do-Ut, and his steady advancement in wealth could be traced by the homes in which he lived. The first was the elaborate suite of rooms at the Hardingham Hotel. Next came a gaunt villa at Beckenham; next, an elaborate estate at Chiselhurst, followed by the chaste simplicity of a medieval castle, Lady Grove, and finally the ambitious but uncompleted splendor of the great house at Crest Hill, on which three hundred workmen were at one time employed. While his uncle was buying houses, George was absorbed in his experiments with gliders and balloons, working in his special workshop with Cothope, his assistant. The Honorable Beatrice Normandy was staying near Lady Grove with Lady Osprey, her stepmother. She and George became acquainted again and after a glider accident she nursed him back to health. Although the two fell in love, Beatrice refused to marry him.

Suddenly all of Edward Ponderevo's world of top-heavy speculation collapsed. On the verge of bankruptcy, he clutched at anything to save himself from financial ruin and the loss of his great, uncompleted project at Crest Hill.

George did his part by undertaking a voyage to Mordet Island in the brig *Maude Mary*, to secure by trickery a cargo of quap, an ore containing two new elements valuable to the Ponderevos largely because they hoped to use canadium—one of the ingredients—tor making a new and better lamp filament. The long, difficult voyage to West Africa was unpleasant and unsuccessful. After the quap had been stolen and loaded on the ship, the properties of the ore were such that the ship sank in mid-ocean. Rescued by the *Portland Castle,* George learned of his uncle's bankruptcy as soon as he came ashore at Plymouth.

To avoid arrest, George and his uncle decided to cross the channel at night in George's airship, and escape the law by posing as tourists in France. The stratagem proved successful, and they landed about fifty miles from Bordeaux. Then Uncle Ponderevo became dangerously ill at a small inn near Bayonne, and a few days later he died, before his wife could reach his side. Back in England, George had a twelve-day love affair with Beatrice Normandy, who still refused to marry him because she said she was spoiled by the love of luxury and the false pride of her class.

George Ponderevo, by that time a severe critic of degeneration in England, became a designer of destroyers.

THE TOWER OF LONDON

Type of work: Novel
Author: William Harrison Ainsworth (1805-1882)
Type of plot: Historical romance
Time of plot: Sixteenth century
Locale: England
First published: 1840

Principal characters:
DUKE OF NORTHUMBERLAND
GUILFORD DUDLEY, Northumberland's son
LADY JANE GREY, Dudley's wife
CUTHBERT CHOLMONDELEY, Dudley's squire
CICELY, in love with Cuthbert
LAWRENCE NIGHTGALL, the jailer
SIMON RENARD, Spanish ambassador
QUEEN MARY
PRINCESS ELIZABETH, Mary's sister
EDWARD COURTENAY, Earl of Devonshire

Critique:

Fictionalized history holds a twofold interest for the reader. First it tells a romantic story; secondly it tells a partly true story. *The Tower of London* brings one more factor to the reader, a lively description of one of the most famous structures in England. The story proper is concerned with Queen Mary's troubled reign, one of the least understood by students of history and literature.

The Story:

At the death of King Edward the Sixth, there were several claimants to the English throne, among them Mary, Elizabeth's older sister, and Lady Jane Grey, wife of Lord Guilford Dudley, who was supported by her father-in-law, the Duke of Northumberland. According to custom, Lady Jane was brought to the Tower of London for her coronation. There the supporters of Mary, while pretending to be in accord with Northumberland, waited to betray Lady Jane.

Among those present was Cuthbert Cholmondeley, Dudley's squire, who having seen a beautiful young girl in the Tower, had fallen in love with her. From inquiries among his servants, Cuthbert learned that she was the adopted daughter of Peter the pantler and Dame Potentia Trusbut, the true circumstances of Cicely's birth being unknown. The chief jailer of the Tower, Lawrence

Nightgall, also loved Cicely. When Simon Renard, the Spanish ambassador, and Lord Pembroke, Mary's supporters, conspired to assassinate Cuthbert because they knew him to be Dudley's favorite, Nightgall eagerly agreed to help them.

Nightgall told Cicely that her new lover had been taken from the Tower and that she would never see him again. Meanwhile, a prisoner in a dungeon below the Tower, Cuthbert was accosted by a strange woman who cried out that she wanted her child to be returned to her. When Nightgall visited Cuthbert, the prisoner asked his jailer about the woman, but Nightgall evaded the question by stating that the woman was mad.

An old woman, Gunnora Broase, had at Northumberland's command administered a dose of poison to the late boy-king, Edward the Sixth. She was directed by a strange man to reveal Northumberland's part in the murder and thus to defeat his intention to place Lady Jane on the throne of England.

Simon Renard and Lord Pembroke had effected a rupture between Lady Jane and Northumberland by convincing Lady Jane that she should not consent to make Dudley a king. Northumberland desired this distinction for his son, but Lady Jane believed that making her husband a king would cause too much dissention in the kingdom. In anger at this slight from his wife, Dudley left the Tower. Surrounded by intrigue, Lady Jane was convinced that Renard and Lord Pembroke were her friends and that Northumberland was her enemy. Lord Pembroke next persuaded Lady Jane to send Northumberland against Mary's forces, which were reported advancing on London. With Northumberland separated from Lady Jane, Lord Pembroke and Renard were certain that they could destroy her rule. Lady Jane was easily persuaded because she did not suspect the treachery of her two advisers.

Cuthbert Cholmondeley escaped from his dungeon. Dudley returned to his wife and his queen in time to convince her of the treachery of Lord Pembroke and Renard, whom Lady Jane ordered imprisoned. Cicely came to Dudley and Lady Jane with the tale of what had happened to Cholmondeley. Soon after the imprisonment of Lord Pembroke and Renard, Nightgall helped them to escape from the Tower. Meanwhile Lady Jane had made Cicely a lady-in-waiting.

Gunnora Broase came to Lady Jane for an audience. The old woman declared that Northumberland had poisoned Edward and that his purpose in marrying his son to Lady Jane was to elevate Dudley to the throne, after which Lady Jane was to be poisoned. Meanwhile Cuthbert had found his way from the lower dungeons and he and Cicely were reunited. He was present when the Duke of Suffolk, Lady Jane's father, urged her to save her head by abdicating. Dudley, however, persuaded his wife not to surrender the crown. Mary was proclaimed queen, and Lady Jane was placed in prison with Cicely and Cuthbert. Dudley was separately confined. Gunnora Broase sneaked into Lady Jane's cell and secreted her from the prison with the promise that Dudley would follow shortly. But when Northumberland disbanded his forces and acknowledged Mary as queen, Lady Jane surrendered herself and returned to her cell in the Tower.

The people acclaimed Mary when she entered London. The new queen's first act was to release all Catholic prisoners and replace them with her former enemies. When Northumberland was arrested and condemned to the scaffold, he pleaded for mercy for Lady Jane because he had been the chief proponent of her pretension to the throne. Although the duke publicly embraced Catholicism in the mistaken belief that his life would be spared, he was executed by Mary's order.

Mary put pressure upon Lady Jane and Dudley to embrace Catholicism as Northumberland had done in order to save their heads, but Lady Jane was determined to die a Protestant.

Released from custody, Cuthbert returned to Dame Trusbut seeking Cicely, but she was nowhere to be found. Cuthbert did find the strange madwoman again. She was lying in a cell, dead.

Among the prisoners Mary had released from the Tower was Edward Courtenay, the Earl of Devonshire. The young nobleman was really in love with Elizabeth, although, covetous of Mary's throne, he pretended to love Mary. Without scruple, he was able to win Mary's promise that she would make him her husband. Renard, however, lurked menacingly in the background. When Courtenay went to Elizabeth with one last appeal of love, Mary and Renard were listening behind a curtain and overheard the conversation. In anger Mary committed Courtenay to the Tower and confined Elizabeth to her room. Then, on Renard's advice, Mary affianced herself to Philip, King of Spain. Later Mary's counselors persuaded her to release Elizabeth.

Moved by compassion for the innocent Lady Jane, Mary issued a pardon for the pretender and her husband. The couple retired to the home of Lady Jane's father, where Dudley began to organize a new plot to place his wife on the throne. Seeing that Dudley was fixed in his design, Lady Jane, faithful to her husband, consented to follow him in whatever he did. Another revolt was led by Sir Thomas Wyat, a fervent anti-Catholic, supported by those who opposed an alliance between

England and Spain. The rebellion was quelled, and Wyat and Dudley were captured. Lady Jane and Cuthbert surrendered themselves to Mary, Lady Jane to plead for the life of her husband in exchange for her surrender. The only condition on which Mary would grant Dudley's life was that Lady Jane should embrace Catholicism. When she refused, she was sentenced to death along with Dudley. Elizabeth was brought to the Tower, Mary planning to do away with Courtenay and her sister after she had completed the destruction of Lady Jane and Dudley.

Nightgall, still suffering from jealousy over Cicely's love for Cuthbert, had held the girl in prison since the fall of Lady Jane. Meanwhile Nightgall had been hired by the French ambassador to assassinate Renard. Renard and Nightgall met in Cuthbert's cell after the squire had been tortured, and in the ensuing fight Cuthbert escaped and ran to find Cicely. Renard succeeded in killing Nightgall, who lived long enough to prove Cicely's noble birth. She was the daughter of the unfortunate madwoman, Lady Grace Mountjoy. Before her execution, Lady Jane requested that Cicely and Cuthbert be allowed to marry. Mary, with strange generosity, pardoned them and granted their freedom.

At the scene of her execution, even the enemies of Lady Jane shuddered at the sight of so good and fair a woman about to die. On the block she reaffirmed her Christian faith as the ax descended upon one of the most ill-fated of English monarchs.

THE TOWN

Type of work: Novel
Author: William Faulkner (1897-1962)
Type of plot: Psychological realism
Time of plot: 1909-1927
Locale: Jefferson, Yoknapatawpha County, Mississippi
First published: 1957

Principal characters:
 FLEM SNOPES, the shrewdest of the Snopes family
 EULA VARNER SNOPES, his wife
 LINDA SNOPES, their daughter
 MANFRED DE SPAIN, the mayor of Jefferson and Eula's lover
 GAVIN STEVENS, a county attorney
 V. K. RATLIFF, a salesman and friend of Gavin Stevens
 CHARLES MALLISON, Stevens' nephew
 MONTGOMERY WARD SNOPES,
 WALLSTREET PANIC SNOPES,
 BYRON SNOPES,
 MINK SNOPES,
 ECK SNOPES, and
 I. O. SNOPES, Flem's cousins

Critique:

In 1940, the novel *The Hamlet* introduced the Snopes family and described the Snopes invasion of the small community, Frenchman's Bend, in fictional Yoknapatawpha County, Mississippi. Seventeen years later *The Town* appeared, reporting further progress of the Snopes clan and of Flem Snopes's rise from restaurant owner to bank president. Faulkner's method of telling the story by means of three narrators (idealistic lawyer Stevens, shrewd and likable salesman Ratliff, and Charles Mallison, Stevens' young nephew) gives the novel unusual depth, and the characters of the book become so well known that readers who missed *The Hamlet* may wish to return to that novel. If Flem Snopes is the symbol of unprincipled thirst for power, then his opponents are symbols for a still existing moral force which can even make a town inhabited by the Snopeses a livable place.

The Story:

The Snopes family, which came out of nowhere after the Civil War, had successfully completed the invasion of Frenchman's Bend. Now Flem Snopes, son of Ab Snopes, a bushwhacker, sharecropper, and horse thief, was ready for the next goal, the domination of Jefferson, county seat of Yoknapatawpha County.

Flem Snopes was ruthless, shrewd, uneducated, and possessed of a fanatic belief in the power of money. The townspeople, who had seen him when he took over Frenchman's Bend and then left it under control of other family members, were wondering about Flem's next move. Among those interested were Gavin Stevens, a young lawyer educated in Heidelberg, and V. K. Ratliff, a good-natured sewing machine salesman, who made up for his lack of education with a great measure of common sense. Stevens felt a moral responsibility to defend the town against the Snopeses, and Ratliff was once the victim of Snopesism when, thinking that it contained a buried treasure, he bought worthless property from Flem for a high price. Another who became an assistant in the fight against Snopes infiltration was Stevens' nephew, Charles Mallison, who watched the

Snopes invasion from his childhood through adolescence.

Flem Snopes realized that more subtle methods for conquering Jefferson were necessary than those he had used in Frenchman's Bend. The greatest advantage for him was his marriage with Eula Varner, daughter of Will Varner, chief property owner in that community. When Eula was pregnant, impotent Flem had married her after making a profitable deal with Varner, who despised Snopes but wanted to save his daughter's honor.

In a small rented house Flem and his wife made a modest beginning in Jefferson by operating a small restaurant of which Ratliff had been a partner before he lost his share in the business deal with Flem. Later the restaurant was transformed into a hotel. The first hint that Flem was aiming even higher came when he was appointed superintendent of the local power plant, before the people even knew that such a position existed.

As the new mayor of Jefferson, Manfred de Spain was not in favor with the town conservatives, but he had won the election in a landslide when he declared himself against an automobile ban imposed by the former mayor. Soon it became known in the town that Eula Snopes and the new mayor were lovers. No one had seen anything, but everybody seemed to know about the affair except her husband.

Shortly after the war, during which Gavin Stevens served overseas, the president of Jefferson's oldest bank was killed in an auto accident. De Spain, named president on account of the bank stock he had inherited, resigned as mayor. The election of a new president made necessary a routine check by government auditors, who uncovered the theft of a large sum of money by a defaulting clerk, Byron Snopes, who fled to Mexico. Announcement was made that the money had been replaced by the new president and that Mr. Flem Snopes had been made a vice president of the bank. Flem's appointment indicated to his opponents a new phase of Snopesism: the search for

money power was now overshadowed by Flem's desire for respectability. This new tactic also became apparent when he rid himself and Jefferson of some undesirable kinsmen, like Montgomery Ward Snopes, who might have destroyed his efforts to make the name Snopes respectable. Montgomery Ward Snopes had returned from the war in France with a rich supply of pornographic pictures. A short time later he opened a photographic studio and gave nightly slide shows for a large part of the male population of Yoknapatawpha County. Flem, not wishing to have his name associated with this shady enterprise, put bootleg whiskey in Montgomery Ward's studio to assure his arrest. When another Snopes, Mink, was jailed for murder, Flem failed to give him any assistance. There was also Eck Snopes, who did not fit into the Snopes pattern on account of his weak intelligence. Flem had no need to bring about his removal, for Eck removed himself. He had been hired to watch an oil tank. While a search was being made for a lost child, Eck, trying to make sure that the child had not climbed into his oil tank, took a lantern and went to look inside the tank. After the explosion only Eck's metal neck brace was available for burial. Meanwhile, the child was found safely somewhere along the road.

Flem's new desire for respectability also made him forget Wallstreet Panic Snopes, who had dared to become a self-made man without his kinsman's help. Wallstreet Panic, a successful grocer, introduced the first self-service store in Jefferson. Flem also disliked the outcome of one of his family projects with I.O. Snopes, who was trained to tie mules to the railroad track in order to collect money from damage law suits against the railroad. When I.O. Snopes was killed during one of these operations, Flem hoped to collect the indemnity. But I.O.'s stubborn wife kept all the money and Flem, in order to avoid complications, was forced to pay off the man who had supplied the mules. Flem also tried to live up to his new social standing by letting a professional decorator furnish his house.

In the meantime Gavin Stevens, who had never been able to rid himself of the attraction Eula Snopes held for him, concentrated his reform efforts on Linda, Eula's daughter. Linda, now in high school, did not know that Flem was not her real father. The lawyer loved Linda and tried to influence her to attend a northern college far away from Snopesism. But Flem, needing a front of outwardly solid family life for his show of respectability, was opposed to the possibility of losing his control of Linda, especially since a will existed which gave the girl a great deal of Will Varner's estate. So Flem disregarded the pleas of his daughter because he still had one more step ahead of him to achieve the position he desired in Jefferson: his scheme to replace de Spain as president of the bank. When he failed in his first attempt to ruin the bank by instigating a run on it, he decided that the time had come to use his knowledge of his wife's adultery as a weapon. Acting as if he had just learned of the eighteen-year-old affair, and armed with a declaration from Linda that she would leave her part of her in-heritance to her father, he visited Will Varner. Once more, in order to save the honor of his daughter and in return for Flem's promise to destroy Linda's note about the inheritance, Varner helped Flem to get rid of de Spain and Flem became president of the bank. Hoping Eula would run away with him, de Spain sold his bank stock, but Eula, hoping to keep her daughter from ever learning of her affairs, remained in Jefferson. She committed suicide after securing from Gavin Stevens a promise that he would marry Linda.

Flem, having reached his goal, agreed to let Linda leave Jefferson. But for a short interval the ghost of old Snopesism came back to Jefferson, when bank thief Byron Snopes sent his four half-Indian children to stay with his kinsfolk. After a series of incidents in which the children terrorized Jefferson and Frenchman's Bend, Flem himself made sure that these last reminders of primitive Snopesism were sent back to Mexico. Meanwhile, he had bought the de Spain house, and workers were busy transforming it into a mansion suitable to Flem Snopes, president of the Bank of Jefferson.

THE TOWN

Type of work: Novel
Author: Conrad Richter (1890-   )
Type of plot: Regional romance
Time of plot: Mid-nineteenth century
Locale: Ohio
First published: 1950

Principal characters:
SAYWARD WHEELER, a pioneer matriarch
PORTIUS, her husband
RESOLVE,
GUERDON,
KINZIE,
HULDAH,
SOOTH,
LIBBY
DEZIA,
MERCY, and
CHANCEY, her children
JAKE TENCH, a steamboat operator
MRS. JAKE TENCH
ROSA TENCH, her child

Critique:

Beginning with *The Trees,* and continuing with *The Fields,* Richter's story of the growth of an Ohio pioneer settlement is completed in *The Town,* the third novel of his trilogy. Although Sayward Wheeler still dominates her family, *The Town* brings to maturity her children, a younger generation having little sympathy for the pioneers' philosophy of work for happiness. Richter's purpose in writing these books was not a historical one. History for its own sake never enters into the story. Richter wanted, instead, to give to the reader the feeling of having lived with his characters, of being familiar with their colloquial speech, their habits, their clothes, their everyday problems, and their struggle for survival against nature, man, and beast. These are satisfying books, full of the love of the land, of earthy wisdom and broad sympathy.

The Story:

Three times in her life Sayward Wheeler had felt that her life was over and done. Not that it frightened her

any; she figured she could do as well in the next world as in this. Once was the day before her father told her the game was leaving Pennsylvania. The next week Sayward and her family traipsed west. The second time was the night she married Portius. This time she was not sure the feeling was more than that she would never have any more babies. She reckoned ten was enough, though one lay in the burying ground.

Her youngest worried her the most. All the others had been hearty enough, but Chancey was so frail folks thought it would have been easier for him to die when he was born. When he was a little fellow his heart flopped so much when he walked that he spent most of his time sitting on a stool in his daddy's office. He looked out of the window for hours, never opening his mouth. Chancey lived in two worlds, the earthy, boisterous one his family loved, and one in which he could float away and do wonderful things.

Sayward had fretted herself to raise him. To harden him, she always had guests sleep with him. She never knew how he shuddered lying next to most of them, but he liked the softness of the bride the time the bridesman got angry up in the loft with all of them and spent the night sitting in the kitchen.

Chancey was his father's favorite because his mind ran as clear as water. Often he rode his father's shoulders into town. He had an uncertain ride the day Portius took him to the hay scales. Portius had just returned from the state capitol where he had put through a bill calling for a new county for the township. With the making of the new county went four judgeships. Portius, because he was an agnostic, did not get an appointment as he had expected. It was given instead to a skinflint tax collector. Portius had come home, drunk and disheveled, minus his horse and saddle. Shortly afterward the new judge came to deliver a load of hay which had to be weighed in town on the new scales. Portius, with Chancey on his shoulders, followed the wavering wagon tracks into town. With one eye on Portius' unsteady gait, the new judge stayed on the wagon while it was weighed in. They clinched their bargain at the inn, the judge demanding cash which Portius produced. When the judge started to leave, Portius claimed that he had bought the judge's person with the load of hay. Before he left the inn the judge had given Portius the hay to avoid being haled to court. Not many could get ahead of Portius; Sayward thought he had too much of the rascal in him himself.

Although he was not yet a judge, he was a popular lawyer, and he was the leader in the fight to have Americus named the county seat. Resolve had studied law with his father and also practiced at the courthouse. Sayward was pleased when he married a girl who was sensible, even if she did have a lot of money. But Sayward felt at the time that things were going along too well and that the Lord would fetch her feet to the ground soon. She was brought around feet first when Huldah disappeared. Sayward knew that

black-eyed minx never fell in the river as some folks thought, but she was taken a little aback when she heard that Huldah had gone to a man's house stark naked, claiming the gipsies had taken her clothing. Sayward went after her. On the way home the ferryman, muttering a coarse remark Sayward only guessed at, made them wait for a second crossing. Sayward would not wait; she drove her horse into the river and forded it instead. Huldah listened respectfully after that.

Her set-to with the ferryman settled in Sayward's mind. Next thing he knew, Portius was arguing for a bridge in town. When it was built, Guerdon worked on it, though he claimed all the while that it was too low for flood time. When the floods came, Chancey, running away, was caught on the bridge and washed down the river. He could not tell whether he was in a dream or not until some men rowed out after him. Guerdon came down the river later to take him home.

Guerdon married a slut and ran away after he killed her lover. Guerdon's daughter Guerda, a sprightly and prophetic child, became Sayward's favorite. Soon after Guerda told Sayward that a good angel was coming for her, the child died suddenly of a throat infection.

Of all the Wheeler children, Chancey always had the hardest row to hoe. He fell in love with Rosa, the child Mrs. Jake Tench had had by Portius. When Rosa realized that all chances were against her, she committed suicide.

After his Aunt Unity died and her Bay State furniture was sent to him, Portius persuaded Sayward that his position in town warranted a mansion on the square. Sayward was proud of the house, but comfortable only in the kitchen and the room where she kept her old cabin furniture. Oh, she never disgraced her family; she could keep up with folks, even when Resolve became state governor. Although she was the richest woman in town, her family said she was so common she spoke to everyone she saw. The things she missed most at the town house were trees. She, who had sworn so often at the big butts, grew lonely for them. The first trees in town were those she planted in her yard.

She enjoyed having Portius' sister come to visit for a month, though the Bay State woman harped mostly on things and folks back east. Sayward could not help laughing when her old bushnipple of a pappy came in to see the woman and praised the old settlers skyhigh.

Her pappy had tracked down their lost Sulie. When Sayward and Genny went out to see her, they found her a squawwoman who would not admit she remembered them.

Chancey left home to become a newspaper editor, blasting the pioneers who slaved for their livelihood and praising the men who advocated the abolition of hardship. Sayward secretly supported Chancey's paper; she thought he had as good a right to say what he pleased as anyone. She missed him, but his newspaper pieces seemed to bring him closer. When he came back for Portius' funeral, Sayward guessed he really came to see if his father had left him any money.

Sayward was lonely. All the folks who had known her kind of life were gone. The children thought her mind wandered a little before she died. She talked to her trees and said in her will that they could not be cut down. When she finally took to her bed, she had it turned toward the trees outside.

THE TRACK OF THE CAT

Type of work: Novel
Author: Walter Van Tilburg Clark (1909-   )
Type of plot: Symbolic allegory
Time of plot: Early twentieth century
Locale: Sierra Nevada Mountains
First published: 1949

> Principal characters:
> ARTHUR BRIDGES, a dreamer
> CURT, and
> HAROLD, his brothers
> GRACE, his sister
> MRS. BRIDGES, the mother
> MR. BRIDGES, the father
> JOE SAM, the Indian hired man
> GWEN WILLIAMS, Harold's girl

Critique:

Like his earlier novel, *The Ox-Bow Incident,* Walter Van Tilburg Clark's *The Track of the Cat* is a tragedy laid in Nevada, his adopted state. It is a long, psychological, and symbolic study of the effect of evil on a ranch family. The black cat means the end of everything to the Indian Joe Sam, whose animism, apparent in his recognition and acceptance of the primitive, mythic nature of Evil, affects the whole Bridges family for whom he works. Clark writes his story with his usual vivid contrasts between dream and fact, white man and Indian, tragedy and hope.

The Story:

Arthur Bridges, dreaming that he was caught in a blizzard in the Sierra Nevadas, could hear a loved one cry out to him, but he could not recognize the voice. He was afraid to move for fear he would fall off an icy cliff. He realized dimly that his left hand was bare and cold. As he put it in the pocket of his red and white cowhide parka, he felt the half-finished carving of a mountain lion that he was making for Joe Sam. Every year he carved a cat for Joe Sam because the old Indian believed a black cat brought death with the first snow unless he could make medicine against it. This year the first snow had come early in October, and

the carved cat was not finished. The black cat must be stalking some prey through the stormy night. As Arthur heard the scream again, he tried to get off the cliff. Falling, he screamed and woke himself up.

Finding himself in the bunk room of the ranch house, Arthur listened for a sound in the wind. When he heard it, he waked his brothers, Curt and Harold. Curt thought Arthur was only dreaming until he also heard the scream of cattle being attacked somewhere in the storm. He rushed into his clothes to go out to the cattle.

The mother, having heard the screams, was making breakfast by the time the boys were dressed. Since it was dark and they could not see what was attacking, they ate while they made plans. Harold, the youngest, was to stay at home. Curt, always the boss, would take charge, but he would take Arthur along because he had dreamed that a black painter was at the cattle.

Arthur got out his whittling as they waited. Harold told him that Joe Sam had been up to his tricks that night. When something worried Joe Sam, he was likely to fall into a trance and go without eating or sleeping for days. Joe Sam always made medicine to his gods before the first snow and carried one of

Arthur's carvings of a mountain lion in a little bag under his chin. The black cat was, to him, the height of evil. Bullets went through it so that it could never be killed. It was as big as a horse. It made no tracks. But it could kill viciously. The early October storm had caught them all unawares, with Joe Sam's cat still unfinished.

The mother had also dreamed something which she would not tell. She wanted Curt to take Harold with him instead of Arthur. But Harold's girl, Gwen Williams, had come to visit the night before and Arthur thought Harold should stay with her. When the mother asked Harold his plans for marrying Gwen, he claimed that he had not gone that far. Arthur figured the valley could hold more stock out of which Harold could take a yearly cut. They all realized that Curt would object if he did not get his own way or if he saw money going outside of the immediate family, even if it were to a brother's family. Harold said he would arrange the matter with Curt when Gwen went home. They all knew the father, who lived now only to drink, would have no say in the matter.

Before Curt and Arthur left, the father and the girls, Grace and Gwen, came to breakfast. The father immediately started drinking. To spite Harold, Curt tried to impress Gwen. Although he made fun of Arthur's half-belief in Joe Sam's black cat, he admitted when he got the horses ready that they were spooky that morning.

Curt and Arthur took only one gun because Curt was sure the cat was in a box canyon where he could easily find and kill it; Arthur would not need a gun for his kind of cat. In the canyon Curt found some of the cattle newly killed, obviously by a mountain lion. There were tracks nearby, but in his highheeled boots he could not follow them through the snow. Leaving Arthur and the gun to hold the trail, Curt went back to the house for tracking boots and food.

Arthur, leading his pony, slowly followed the cat's tracks toward a half-dome where he had often sat, whittling his figures and admiring the view. Suddenly his pony neighed fiercely and jerked, throwing Arthur sprawling into the bushes nearby. As he looked up over his shoulder, Arthur saw the black cat leaping at him.

Curt dawdled at home. Trying to get a rise out of Gwen, he promised to bring her home the skin of the black cat to use as a blanket, or, if it should be a yellow one, to wear as a costume. Harold brought him a frisky horse. Curt, nearly trampling the Indian, asked Joe Sam whether he still believed in the black cat. Joe Sam only replied that hunting would be no good because of the heavy snow.

On the way back to the canyon Curt saw Arthur's horse heading home. Disgusted because he thought Arthur had forgotten the horse as he daydreamed, Curt followed the tracks until he found Arthur's body. While he exchanged his coat for Arthur's heavy parka and packed the body on his own horse, he swore to get the cat if he had to trail it to the Pacific. Then he headed the horse toward home with the body.

Arthur's death greatly upset the mother and Grace. Harold and Gwen had to keep things going at the ranch. The father was drunk and Joe Sam practically hypnotized. A heavy snow settled in, delaying the burial. Afterward they made a huge bonfire in front of the house in case Curt needed direction. He had been out more than two days since Arthur's body had come back on the horse. The mother told Harold he would have to go out after Curt and that he should take Joe Sam along to track.

The horses became spooky when Curt and Joe Sam came near the box canyon. Each man tracked one side of the creek. Harold found dead cattle, one heifer so freshly killed that the blood still spurted. Working carefully, he tracked the cat so closely that he was almost surprised when he saw it. As he shot, Joe Sam's bullet came from across the creek. The cat sprang away with a scream, but the men followed it and finished their job. Although it was almost all black, Joe Sam said that the cat was not his black painter. His was a devil killing all the time.

Harold found Curt's crumpled body under a cliff. Tracing back from the place above the body where the snow had been broken off, he guessed that Curt had rushed wildly about after leaving a fire and a pile of cut boughs higher up. There, where the fire had been, Harold found Curt's gun and snowshoes, but he could find no tracks except Curt's in all the clearing. Puzzled and a little terrified, Harold guessed that the dead black painter might as well be blamed for Curt's death after all.

THE TRAITOR

Type of work: Drama
Author: James Shirley (1596-1666)
Type of plot: Tragedy of blood
Time of plot: c. 1480
Locale: Florence, Italy
First presented: 1631

Principal characters:
ALEXANDER, Duke of Florence, enamored of Amidea
LORENZO, his kinsman and the next in succession
AMIDEA, betrothed to Pisano and scornful of the duke
SCIARRHA, and
FLORIO, her brothers and avengers
PISANO, enamored of Oriana, though engaged to Amidea
COSMO, his friend, engaged to Oriana
ORIANA, loved by Pisano, formerly by Cosmo
MOROSA, her mother
PETRUCHIO, Pisano's servant, in Lorenzo's hire
DEPAZZI, an informer for Lorenzo

Critique:

James Shirley was one of the first playwrights to learn his trade from the printed page rather than in the theater. *The Traitor* displays a talent carefully nurtured on Marlowe, Shakespeare, and Jonson, but at the same time capable of original, powerful poetry. In his own day his position in the theater was that of competent journeyman playwright, yet his works graced the boards for generations. *The Traitor*, which remained in theatrical repertoire for over a hundred and fifty years, was attributed falsely in the late seventeenth century to a Jesuit who died in Newgate Prison. Shirley's reputation has only recently been rescued from critical neglect.

The Story:

The reign of Alexander, the young Duke of Florence, began in a cloud of conspiracy, for his cousin Lorenzo had played the role of the loyal kinsman to seat the duke and was now playing the villain to unseat him, under the pretext of establishing a republic. For this purpose he appealed through pressures and persuasion to Cosmo, beloved of Oriana, to give over his suit in favor of Pisano, who had become enamored of the girl through the influence of his servant Petruchio, secretly in the hire of Lorenzo.

Pisano, in turn, was to break his engagement to Amidea so that the duke might have her later for his lustful purposes.

From a man exiled at Lorenzo's request, the duke received a message which told of the prince's treachery. Confronted with this evidence, Lorenzo denied everything and cleverly reinstated himself and even strengthened his plot by recounting the examples of his loyalty to his kinsman. Restored to favor, Lorenzo undertook to procure the beautiful Amidea for the duke. By design, he attempted to accomplish his purpose through the offices of her brother, the hot-headed Sciarrha.

Sciarrha, reacting as Lorenzo had expected, renounced the duke and, acting on hints from Lorenzo, agreed to murder his ruler in Amidea's chamber that night. Sciarrha, in the presence of his brother Florio, tested his sister's chastity by advocating the assignation. She rejected his proposal, however, and her other brother threatened Sciarrha's life should such degradation be visited upon them. Her devotion to virtue and Florio's threat to murder Sciarrha were greeted with great elation, but before a pact could be made Pisano arrived to declare that Amidea was no longer paramount in his affections, and that he was in love with and desired to marry another. This news was withheld from Sciarrha for fear that he would embark on a reckless course of revenge harmful to them all.

Meanwhile, Cosmo's attempts to place his friend Pisano in Oriana's affection proved unsuccessful. In spite of her mother's pleadings, Oriana remained, for the time being, loyal to Cosmo.

The plans for the assignation which was supposed to end in murder were well laid. In order to arouse the populace, Depazzi, picked because of his political innocence, was to spread the news of the ruler's death even before the murder. Lorenzo would then quiet the citizens and the uneasy nobles by consenting to act as interim ruler until the state could be delivered from tyranny and be proclaimed a republic.

Sciarrha made sure that nothing was lacking in his lavish entertainment of the duke. A masque which depicted the downfall of treachery was portrayed before the youthful ruler, but he remained unmoved, so intent was he on the lovely Amidea. When Amidea received the duke in her chambers, her brothers were concealed behind the arras as she pleaded with him to abandon his wicked pursuits. Threatened with her suicide before his eyes, the duke repented and declared his determination to be a ruler worthy of her esteem. The brothers then appeared to congratulate their revered leader and urged him to hide in order to discover the author of the traitorous plot against him.

Lorenzo, when told the duke had died according to the plans made, cleverly accused the brothers of treachery and denied any complicity in the plot. The duke attempted a reconciliation of the plotters, but without success.

After the people had been quieted by the duke's appearance before the mob, Lorenzo claimed repentance equal to the duke's, much to Sciarrha's anger and disgust. Lorenzo, continuing to play the villain, told Sciarrha that Pisano had broken off his marriage contract with Amidea and that Oriana was to be led to the altar by her mother's duplicity. Infuriated by this news, Sciarrha once again became Lorenzo's ally. Pisano would die and Sciarrha would also be a willing tool in the conspiracy against the duke. Lorenzo released the former conspirator, Depazzi, from his service.

But the duke's repentance was short-lived when he received assurances from Lorenzo that Amidea would soon be more tractable in order to save her brother, who seemed bound for his own destruction. Amidea tried in vain to persuade Pisano to take his wedding party elsewhere that he might escape Sciarrha's fury, and she even pleaded with Oriana, who was more than willing to return Pisano to his rightful loved one; but Pisano refused to be moved. He refused to fight back, however, when Sciarrha demanded satisfaction, and so he was murdered before Lorenzo's watchful eyes and guard. Further supplication to Sciarrha to deliver his sister to the duke's lust proved useless until Lorenzo pointed out that the brother's execution would only make Amidea's ruin more certain. At last Sciarrha agreed to send his sister to the duke's bed that very night.

Amidea, in double mourning for a lover lost and a brother's life forfeited, begged to die rather than suffer ignomiy. Sciarrha again tested her chastity with his unacceptable proposals. Amidea knelt in prayer for her brother's soul when she realized he must kill her in order to protect her. Later Florio promised Lorenzo that he would bring his sister to the duke—in secret, however, to spare her shame.

After the corpse of Amidea had been prepared, the duke entered his chamber and cried out in horror when he kissed her cold lips. In Lorenzo's presence he wished that he too might die, and Lorenzo killed him with Petruchio's help. Though he protested that only his grief spoke out, the duke died in full knowledge of the treachery his kinsman had planned. He was placed in bed with his intended victim. Though Sciarrha had pretended to share in Lorenzo's plans, he fought and killed Lorenzo, receiving in the struggle his own death wound. Petruchio was sent to the torture chamber. Cosmo assumed the rule of the city and promised to make what amends he could to Oriana and Florio.

TRAVELS IN ARABIA DESERTA

Type of work: Record of travel
Author: Charles M. Doughty (1843-1926)
Time: 1876-1878
Locale: Northwestern Arabia
First published: 1888

Travels in Arabia Deserta has been recognized, almost since its publication in 1888, as one of the greatest travel books in the English language. Doughty spent almost two years traveling, going on pilgrimages, and living with various nomad tribes in northwestern Arabia, then a land almost completely unknown to Europeans and Americans. His account is a thoroughly realized document, a comprehensive understanding and treatment of every aspect of the life of the nomadic Arabs. Written with grace, fullness, and enormous insight, *Travels* in *Arabia Deserta* has become a classic of travel literature and a necessary book of instructions for anyone interested in that part of the Moslem world. T. E. Lawrence, in his introduction to the 1921 edition of this work, acknowledged that Doughty was the first and greatest of all European writers on Arabia.

Travels in Arabia Deserta is also an objective treatment of life among the nomads. Doughty was content to observe, to understand, to record, without leveling judgments against a civilization so different from his own. This objectivity allowed him to see and report the Arabs as they lived, to understand fully their customs, their prejudices, and their attitudes.

In several ways, Doughty was extremely well equipped to be one of the first Europeans to visit the Arabian peninsula and explore it extensively. A geologist, he was able to draw geological maps of uncharted territory and determine the nature of the terrain. As a scientist he was also enormously interested in the climate of Arabia, and he filled his book with observations on climate and topography. Doughty drew, and included in his work, some of the first maps of the area he visited. He was also interested in and knowledgeable about architecture

and archaeology. He captured a keen sense of Arabic design and often used one of the designs as a chapter heading. Because of his interest in many phases of scientific learning, he was able to use many of the skills of Western civilization, for the first time, on the Arabian peninsula. In addition, Doughty was an able medical practitioner. He attempted to use his medical knowledge to help the Arabs among whom he lived. Although, later, he did help enormously during epidemics of tropical diseases such as cholera and leprosy, the Arabs were often inclined to distrust him. Doughty points out that in their love for certainty and complete assurance they were likely to judge a medical practice by a single case and they were not appreciative of the tentative conclusions of honest medical science.

Although Doughty had great respect and affection for the nomad tribes among whom he traveled, he did not sentimentalize them or the conditions in which they lived. Long passages in *Travels in Arabia Deserta* describe their filth, poverty, and ignorance. Frequently they could get little food; often, even the chief of the tribe could not get enough water for his wife to make him a cup of coffee. They wore thin cotton robes, even though the desert nights frequently became very cold. The Arabs met with frequent rival tribes who might steal their camels and their meager possessions, and they were suspicious of any stranger. Their life, as depicted by Doughty, was not the life of romantic adventure; rather it was one of poverty, hardness, insecurity, and want.

Travels in Arabia Deserta gives a complete picture of the social life and customs of the nomad tribes. Men, ruling the family tyrannically, decided also the affairs of the tribe. Women were servants, and girl children were not looked on with favor. In the tribes Doughty visited he found little evidence of the notion of the harem that Europeans and Americans have idealized. There was no moral feeling against polygamy, but most of the men, even the chiefs, could not afford to keep more than one woman. The woman, if she found the arrangement not to her liking, could run away and settle herself in a place more congenial to her. And those men who had two wives with them on their travels frequently found the jealousy between the two women not worth the extra pleasure of a second wife. Women were slaves in the family itself, but they had some choice as to whether or not to submit to slavery. Doughty also discussed the notion of justice in the Arab society. Although the men ruled the family firmly and there were frequent wars between different tribes, justice within the tribe was fairly humane and understanding. Thieves were not hanged but, rather, were forced to make amends. Doughty contrasted these notions of a merciful concept of justice with the ideas of divine wrath and fearful justice in the Old Testament.

Doughty did not simply chronicle the social customs of the Arabs. He also discussed their religion fully and attempted to relate both their religion and their customs to the kind of life the climate and the economic circumstances forced them to lead. In their difficult desert existence, the leniency of their justice was an expression of their sympathy for others caught in the same way of life, but, according to Doughty, they would never have articulated such a feeling, for their life made such practical demands upon them that they had neither the time nor the inclination for any introspection or analysis. They simply went about the difficult task of keeping themselves alive.

They were a deeply religious people. Although the open and barren nature of their terrain made them suspicious of enemies, forthright and direct in manner and speech, and little inclined to subtle thought, this same open terrain, this area

that showed only earth and sky, seemed to make them feel closer to God and feel their religion with enormous intensity. They often embraced religious causes, and they followed the dictates of their religion with a fierce intensity that was not necessarily moral or reasoned, but rather a product of the closeness they felt with God. They accepted death and disaster easily (too easily, at times, for Doughty), for these people, trying to live in the enormous, barren desert, felt themselves subject to the will of an all-powerful God. When they could build structures, they built towers, expressions of their desire both to relieve the flatness of their surroundings and to approach God more closely. The towers were also useful in posting watchmen to warn the tribe of any possible enemy attack. Doughty points out also that the tower is the natural expression of the tribe used to desert existence, the natural attempt to put the relationship between God and man in a vertical sphere.

Doughty discusses, too, the fanatical quality of the nomad's religion, his willingness to sacrifice anything, including his life, for a cause he believes sacred. This fanaticism is, again, a product of the singleness, the open nature of his desert surroundings. Man finds little in nature to divert him, little to draw his attention from his home and his God, so in his allegiance to his cause he finds little qualification or sophistication to divert his faith.

Doughty conveyed his observations in a rich, full style. He managed to use this fullness as a splendid means of carrying the entire range of his observations and inferences about Arab life. At times, to contemporary ears, his style seems stilted and archaic. For example, he writes sentences like this: "We were to depart betimes by the morrow." This style was deliberately archaic even in the 1880's, yet it helps to produce the flavor of a different and more primitive culture. The archaic richness of the style completes the contrast between our world and the world of the Arab nomad. Doughty, fully aware of the differences between these worlds, has managed to create a comprehensive and understanding portrait of the nomad world, to produce, in *Travels in Arabia Deserta*, a history of the beliefs, the experiences, the essential conditions of life, of the nomadic peoples of northwestern Arabia.

THE TRAVELS OF MARCO POLO

Type of work: Record of travel
Author: Marco Polo (1254-1324), as set down by the scribe, Rustigielo
Type of plot: Adventure romance
Time of plot: 1260-1295
Locale: Greater Asia
First transcribed: Fourteenth-century manuscript

> Principal characters:
> NICOLO POLO, a Venetian merchant
> MAFFEO POLO, his brother
> MARCO POLO, Nicolo's son
> KUBLAI KHAN, Emperor of China

Critique:

The story of Marco Polo's Asiatic journey is the most astounding of all travel books of Western civilization. One reason for its popularity is that Marco Polo did not mind mixing some real facts with his fiction. Another is that he possessed in high degree a quality few travelers have ever had; he was able to see more objectively than the many who have described lands visited only in terms of their home countries. His book is the record of a merchant-gentleman who sets forth his own observations and at the same time reveals the medieval viewpoint — its interest in alchemy and enchantments, its concern with mystery, and its sound, logical way of thinking beneath the surface superstition and credulity of the age.

The Story:

Marco Polo's father and uncle set forth on their first trip East in 1260, with a cargo of merchandise for Constantinople. From there Nicolo and Maffeo Polo ventured on into the lands of the Tartar princes. Having at last reached the court of Kublai Khan, they managed to ingratiate themselves into his highest favor. During their stay the khan questioned them about the Catholic faith and asked them to return to Europe and to request the Pope to send missionaries to his distant land. In the year 1269, the two Polos arrived in Venice, to learn that Pope Clement was dead and that Nicolo Polo's wife had also died after giving birth to a son, Marco Polo.

There was a long delay in the naming of a new Pope. At last the Polos decided to return to Kublai Khan and to take young Marco with them. Scarcely had they left Italy, however, when word followed them that Gregory the Tenth had been elected in Rome. The Polos at once asked the new Pope to send missionaries to Kublai Khan, and Gregory appointed two priests to accompany the merchants. Before their arrival at the khan's court, the priests turned back when confronted by strange lands and unknown dangers. Young Marco Polo remembered that the journey to the land of Kublai Khan took three and a half years.

Kublai Khan received them graciously and appointed Marco one of his attendants. In a short time Marco Polo had learned four different languages and he was sent by Kublai Khan on various important missions.

For seventeen years the Polos remained at the court of Kublai Khan before they finally expressed a desire to return to their own country with their wealth. They felt that if the great khan should die they would be surrounded by envious princes who might harm them. The khan was unwilling to part with the Polos, but they managed to get his permission by offering to transport some barons to the East Indies. Fourteen ships were made ready for the homeward voyage. The expedition arrived at Java after about three months. Eighteen months more were required for the voyage to the territory

THE TRAVELS OF MARCO POLO by Marco Polo. Published by Doubleday & Co., Inc.

of King Argon in the Indian seas. During the voyage six hundred of the crew were lost as well as two of the barons. From there the Polos took an overland route to Trebizond. En route they learned that the great Kublai Khan was dead. The three arrived home safely in 1295, in possession of their wealth and in good health.

When the time came for him to dictate to the scribe, Rustigielo, the story of his travels, Marco Polo remembered that Armenia was divided into two sections, the lesser and the greater. In Armenia Major was the mountain said to have been Mount Ararat, where Noah's ark came to rest. Near this place was a fountain of oil so great that caravans of camels hauled away the oil, which was used for an unguent as well as for heat and light.

At the boundaries of the province of Georgiania, Alexander the Great had caused a gate of iron to be constructed. This gate, though not all of iron, was commonly said to have enclosed the Tartars between two mountains.

At Teflis was a fountain wherein hundreds of fish made their appearance from the first day of Lent until Easter Eve. During the remainder of the year they were not to be seen.

Baudas, or Baghdad, anciently known as Babylon, lay along the river that opened out upon the Sea of India. The city was one of the great cities of the world, and its ruler one of the richest men of all time. He lost his life through his unwillingness to spend a penny of his wealth for its protection. His captor locked him up in his tower where he starved to death surrounded by gold. In that region also a Christian cobbler had caused a mountain to move and by his miracle converted many Arabs to Christianity.

In Irak Marco Polo visited a monastery in which the monks wove woolen girdles said to be good for rheumatic pains. He also visited Saba, from whence were said to have come the three Magi who adored Christ in Bethlehem. At Kierman, on the eastern confines of Persia, Marco saw the manufacture of steel and products in which steel was used. Much rich embroidery was also found there as well as splendid turquoises. The Karaunas of the region had learned the diabolical art of producing darkness in order to obscure their approach to caravans they intended to rob.

At Ormus he encountered a land-wind so hot that people exposed to it died. A whole army was once wiped out by the wind and the inhabitants, seeking to bury the invaders, found the bodies baked so hard that they could not be moved. Bitter, undrinkable water, the tree of the sun, and the old man of the mountain were all of that region. The old man of the mountain used to administer drugs to young men to make them think they were truly in Paradise. At his orders they assassinated any one not of the true faith. His followers held their own lives of little worth, convinced that they would return to Paradise upon their deaths.

On the overland route to Cathay, Marco met Nestorian Christians as well as people who were part Christian and part Mohammedan. There too he found a miraculous pillar said to remain upright without any visible means of support. In Peyn he discovered chalcedony and jasper and also peculiar marriage customs. Passing over a desert, he heard the strange sounds attributed to evil spirits but since explained as the sounds of shifting sand dunes. At Kamul he discovered the primitive hospitality of turning over houses and wives for the entertainment of strangers. At Chinchitalas he discovered the use of material which would not burn; it was asbestos.

On the borders of the Gobi the Polos gathered supplies for their trip through the desert. They passed close to the land of Prester John and heard the history of the war between Prester John and Genghis Khan. He saw the land of Tenduk, governed by the princes of the race of Prester John.

Kublai Khan was a great king who had rewarded generously those who had aided him in the conquest of other nations. Each noble so favored received a golden tablet inscribed by the khan for the protection of its wearer. Kublai Khan had four principal wives, plus a number of women who were given to him each year. He had some fifty sons, all of whom were appointed to high places in the empire. In the winter the khan lived in Peking, in a magnificent palace that was eight miles square. His personal bodyguard consisted of twelve thousand horsemen.

Greatest in interest among his people were the Tibetans, who produced the scent of musk, used salt for money, and dressed in clothes of leather. Gold dust was found in their rivers and among their inhabitants were many said to be sorcerers. Karazan was known for its huge serpents, or crocodiles, which the natives killed for hides and gall. This gall was a medicine for bites from mad dogs.

In Kardandan, Marco observed fathers who took over the nursing of babies. In the city of Mien he saw two towers, one of silver and one of gold. Bengal he found rich in cotton, spikenard, galangal, ginger, sugar, and many drugs. The region also supplied many eunuchs.

For a time Marco Polo held the government of the city of Yan-Gui upon orders of the khan. Nicolo and Maffeo Polo aided the khan in overcoming the city of Sa-Yan-Fu, the two Venetians having designed a catapult capable of hurling stones weighing as much as three hundred pounds.

Marco thought the city of Kin-sai, or Hang-chau, so beautiful that the inhabitants might imagine themselves in Paradise. There were twelve thousand bridges over the canals and rivers of the city, and the houses were well-built and adorned with carved ornaments. The streets were paved with stone and brick. The people were greatly concerned with astrology. Moreover, the inhabitants had provided for fire fighters who kept a constant guard throughout the city. From it the khan received revenue of gold, salt, and sugar.

In the kingdom of Kon-cha, Marco found people who ate human flesh. He also found there a kind of chicken covered with black hair instead of feathers. He observed with much interest the manufacture of Chinese porcelain.

In his travels he saw the merchant ships of India, which were large and built in sections so that if one section sprang a leak, it could be closed off while repairs were made. On the island of Java he obtained pepper, nutmegs, spikenard, galangal, cubebs, cloves, and gold. Idolators lived there as well as cannibals. Elephants, rhinoceroses, monkeys, and vultures were in abundance. He also discovered the practice of the natives which was to pickle certain monkeys so that they resembled dead pygmies. These creatures were then sold as souvenirs to sailors and merchants.

In Lambri he saw what he thought were men with tails. He also saw the sago tree from which the natives made flour. On the island of Nocueran he visited people living like naked beasts in trees. They possessed the red and white sandal wood, coconuts, sapanwood, and cloves. At Angaman he saw more cannibals. In Ceylon he found rubies, sapphires, topazes, amethysts, and garnets. The grave of Adam was believed to be on a high mountain in Ceylon.

Marco thought India the noblest and richest country in the world. Pearls were found in abundance. The kingdom of Murphili was rich in diamonds. In the province of Lac he heard that people often lived to the age of one hundred and fifty years and managed to preserve their teeth by a certain vegetable they chewed. In Kael he found people chewing a leaf called tembul, sometimes mixed with camphor and other aromatic drugs as well as quicklime. At Cape Comorin he found apes of such a size as to appear like men. At Malabar he found gold brocades, silk, gauzes, gold, and silver. At Guzzerat he discovered pirates of the worst character. In Bombay he bought incense and horses.

Marco visited the island of Madagascar, where the inhabitants reported a bird so large it was able to seize an elephant in its talons. He thought the women of Zanzibar the ugliest in the world. The people did business in elephant teeth and tusks.

Marco recalled how Kublai Khan and his nephew, Kaidu, fought many battles for the possession of Great Turkey. Over a hundred thousand horsemen were brought to fight for each side. At first Kaidu was victorious. Kaidu had a mannish daughter, Aigiarm, who battled with any man who wanted her for a bride. At last she seized the man of her choice from the hosts of enemies in battle.

Marco believed that Russia was a region too cold to be pleasant. He spoke of trade in ermine, arcolini, sable, marten, fox, silver, and wax among the natives, who were included in the nation of the king of the Western Tartars.

Marco Polo gave thanks to God that the travelers were able to see so much and return to tell about the marvels of many lands.

TRAVELS WITH A DONKEY

Type of work: Record of travel
Author: Robert Louis Stevenson (1850-1894)
Type of plot: Sketches and impressions
Time of plot: 1878
Locale: The Cévennes, French Highlands
First published: 1879

Principal characters:
ROBERT LOUIS STEVENSON, the traveler
MODESTINE, a donkey
FATHER APOLLINARIS, a Trappist monk

Critique:

Stevenson said that every book is a circular letter to the friends of him who wrote it. *Travels with a Donkey in the Cévennes* takes much of its merit from the warm-hearted spirit of Stevenson himself. Throughout the narrative the reader is led by Stevenson's voice as if Stevenson were talking in the same room for the enjoyment of his reader. More vivid than either his account of the people or his account of the history made in the Cévennes is Stevenson's way of describing the countryside and its variations in mood.

The Story:

In twelve days, from September 22, 1878, until October 3, 1878, Robert Louis Stevenson walked from Le Monastier to St. Jean du Gard in the Cévennes. His only companion was Modestine, a donkey. He traveled as his fancy led him, stopping to sleep whenever occasion offered. One morning after a night's sleep out of doors Stevenson scattered coins along the road upon the turf in payment for his night's lodging.

Modestine, the donkey, demanded that her owner exercise all his ingenuity. At first he loathed her for her intractable differences of opinion displayed concerning the rate of travel to be maintained. Repeated blows seemed not to influence her until he learned to use the magical word "Proot" to get her moving. Later he obtained a real goad from a sympathetic innkeeper at Bouchet St. Nicolas. Modestine was dainty in her eating. She seemed to prefer white bread, but she learned to share half of Stevenson's brown loaves with him.

Modestine and her owner quarreled about a short cut. She hacked, she reared; she even brayed in a loud, aggrieved tone. However, he forced her to give in. A few days later Stevenson began to understand his strong-willed donkey; he came to understand her stupidity, and he overlooked her flights of ill-judged light-heartedness.

Stevenson, like many who buy at the insistence of others and sell at their own pleasure, was eager to dismiss the matter of Modestine's cost. He had paid sixty-five francs and a glass of brandy for her, but he sold her for thirty-five francs. Stevenson commented that the pecuniary gain was not obvious, but that he had bought freedom into the bargain.

More absorbing than the pleasure with which Stevenson contrasted his vagabond life and that of deeply-rooted monks and peasants was his interest in long-remembered, local conflicts. Such a conflict was that struggle at Pont de Montvert where Camisards, led by Pierre Seguier, murdered the Archpriest of the Cévennes. Seguier was soon taken and his right hand cut off. He himself was then burned alive. Stevenson also identified the characteristic elements in the landscape as he went along. He thought the Cévennes remarkably beautiful.

Stevenson's account of the local peasantry was less appreciative than his account of the landscape. He described two mishaps. In the first place, the peasants looked with suspicion upon a traveler wandering on their bleak high hills with very little money and no obvious purpose other than to stare at them. At his ap-

3860

proach to one village the people hid themselves. They barricaded their doors and gave him wrong directions from their windows. Secondly, two girls whom he termed "impudent sly sluts" bade him follow the cows. For these reasons, Stevenson came to feel sympathy for the infamous beast of Gevauden, who, according to tradition, ate about a hundred children of the district.

During his travels he visited Our Lady of the Snows Monastery. Approaching the monastery, he encountered Father Apollinaris, who, clad in the white robe of his order, greeted him and led him to .the entrance of the monastery. He felt the atmosphere of his environment and portrayed it in descriptions of the monks at their duties, the feel of the highland wind on his face, the cheerless, four-square buildings which were bleak and too new to be seasoned into the place.

The belfry and the pair of slatted gables seemed plain and barren. When he departed after a day of quiet repose, the lonely Trappist, Father Apollinaris, accompanied him, holding Stevenson's hands in his own.

Stevenson continued on to St. Jean du Gard. He lost his way and found it again. Modestine learned to wait patiently when he wanted to stop to talk with someone. The procession of days took him through gullies, along river beds, and over high ridges. At St. Jean du Gard he parted from Modestine. Then, seated by the driver en route to Alais through a rocky gully past orchards of dwarf olive trees, Stevenson began to reflect what Modestine had become in his life. She had been patient and she had come to regard him as a god. She had eaten from his hand. He felt that he had parted from his best friend.

TREASURE ISLAND

Type of work: Novel
Author: Robert Louis Stevenson (1850-1894)
Type of plot: Adventure romance
Time of plot: 1740's
Locale: England and the Spanish Main
First published: 1883

Principal characters:

JIM HAWKINS, cabin boy of the *Hispaniola*
DR. LIVESEY, a physician and Jim's friend
SQUIRE TRELAWNEY, a wealthy landowner
MR. SMOLLETT, captain of the *Hispaniola*
LONG JOHN SILVER, leader of the mutineers
BEN GUNN, a pirate

Critique:

Since its publication, this novel has been a favorite of boys everywhere. With action moving swiftly from beginning to end, the story is told in the first person for the most part by the boy hero; the rest is told in the person of Doctor Livesey. The character of John Silver dominated Stevenson so completely that the outcome is not entirely acceptable from a conventionally moral point of view. The book, according to Stevenson, was born out of his fascination with a water-color map he himself drew of an imagined treasure island.

The Story:

Young Jim Hawkins always remembered the day the strange seaman, Bill Bones, came looking for lodgings at his father's inn, the Admiral Benbow. He came plodding up to the inn door, where he stood for a time and looked around Black Hill Cove. Jim heard him singing snatches of an old sea song:

"Fifteen men on the dead man's chest,
Yo-ho-ho, and a bottle of rum."

When he learned from Jim's father that the inn was a quiet one with little trade, he declared it was just the berth for an old seaman. From that time the strange guest—a retired captain he called himself—kept watch on the coast and the land road by day and made himself free in the taproom of the inn at night. There he drank and sang and swore great oaths while he told fearsome tales of the

Spanish Main. Wary of all visiting seamen, he paid Jim Hawkins to be on the lookout for a one-legged sailor in particular. He was so terrible in his speech and manners that Jim's father, sick man that he was, never had the courage to ask for more than the one reckoning Bill Bones had paid the day he came to the inn. He stayed on without ever clinking another coin into the inn till for his meals and lodging.

The one-legged sailor never came to the inn, but another seaman named Black Dog did. The two men fought in the inn parlor, to the terror of Jim and his mother, before Captain Bones chased his visitor up the road and out of sight. He fell down in a fit when he came back to the inn, and Doctor Livesey, coming in to attend Jim's father, cautioned Captain Bones to contain himself and drink less.

Jim's father died soon afterward. On the day of the funeral a deformed blind man named Pew tapped his way up to the door of the Admiral Benbow. The man forced Jim to lead him to the captain. Bill Bones was so terrified when the blind man gave him the Black Spot, the pirates' death notice, that he had a stroke and died.

Jim and his mother took the keys to his sea chest from the dead man's pocket and opened it to find the money due them. As they were examining the contents, they heard the tapping of the blind man's stick on the road. Jim pocketed an oilskin packet and he and his mother left hurriedly by the back door of the inn as a gang of men broke in to search for Captain Bones' chest. Mounted revenue officers arrived and scattered the gang. Blind Pew was trampled to death by the charging horses.

Jim gave the packet to Dr. Livesey and Squire Trelawney. The three discovered that it contained a map locating the hidden treasure of the bloody buccaneer, Captain Flint. Squire Trelawney, intrigued, decided to outfit a ship in which to sail after the treasure. The doctor threw in his lot and invited Jim to come along as cabin boy.

In Bristol Trelawney purchased a schooner, the *Hispaniola*, and hired one Long John Silver as ship's cook. Silver promised to supply a crew. Jim went to Bristol and met Silver, who had but one leg. He was alarmed when he saw Black Dog again in the inn operated by Silver, but Silver's smooth talk quieted Jim's suspicions.

After the *Hispaniola* had sailed, Captain Smollett, hired by Squire Trelawney to command the ship, expressed his dislike of the first mate and the crew and complained that Silver had more real authority with the crew than he did. One night Jim, in a barrel after an apple, overheard Silver discussing mutiny with members of the crew. Before Jim had a chance to reveal the plot to his friends, the island was sighted.

The prospects of treasure on the island caused the disloyal members of the crew to pay little heed to Captain Smollett's orders; even the loyal ones were hard to manage. Silver shrewdly kept his party under control. Wisely, the captain allowed part of the crew to go ashore; Jim smuggled himself along in order to spy on Silver and the men on the island. Ashore, Silver killed two of the crew who refused to join the mutineers. Jim, alone, met Ben Gunn, who was with Captain Flint when the treasure was buried. Gunn told Jim that he had been marooned on the island three years before.

While Jim was ashore, Dr. Livesey went to the island and found Captain Flint's stockade. Hearing the scream of one of the men Silver murdered, he returned to the *Hispaniola*, where it was decided that the honest men would move to the fort within the stockade. Several dangerous trips in an overloaded boat completed the move. During the last trip the mutineers aboard the ship unlimbered the ship's gun. Squire Trelawney shot one seaman from the boat.

In the meantime the gang ashore saw what was afoot and made efforts to keep Jim's friends from occupying the stockade. The enemy repulsed, Squire Trelawney and his party took their posts in the fort. The mutineers on the *Hispaniola* fired round shot into the stockade, but did little damage.

After leaving Ben Gunn, the marooned seaman, Jim made his way to the stockade. The *Hispaniola* now flew the Jolly Roger skull and crossbones. Carrying a flag of truce, Silver approached the stockade and offered to parley. Admitted by the defenders, he demanded the treasure chart in exchange for the safe return of Squire Trelawney's party to England. Captain Smollet would concede nothing and Silver returned to his men in a rage. The stockade party prepared for the coming battle. A group of the pirates attacked from two sides, swarmed over the paling and engaged the defenders in hand-to-hand combat. In the close fighting the pirates were reduced to one man, who fled back to his gang in the jungle. The loyal party was reduced to Squire Trelawney, Dr. Livesey, Captain Smollett, and Jim.

During the lull after the battle, Jim sneaked off and borrowed Ben Gunn's homemade boat. In this he rowed out to the *Hispaniola* under cover of darkness and cut the schooner adrift. In trying to return to shore, he was caught offshore by coastal currents. Daylight having come, Jim saw that the *Hispaniola* was also aimlessly adrift. When the ship bore down upon him, he jumped to the bowsprit. Ben Gunn's little boat was smashed. Jim found himself on board alone with pirate Israel Hands, wounded in a fight with another pirate. Jim took command and proceeded to beach the ship. Pursued by Hands, he climbed quickly to a crosstree just before Hands threw his knife into the mast not more than a foot below Jim as he climbed. Jim had time to prime and reload his pistols, and he shot the pirate after he had pinned the boy to the mast with another knife throw.

Jim removed the knife from his shoulder, made the ship safe by removing the sails, and returned to the stockade at night, only to find it abandoned by his friends and now in the hands of the pirates. When Silver's parrot, Captain Flint, drew attention to the boy's presence, the pirates captured him. Silver's men, dissatisfied with the buccaneer's methods of gaining the treasure, grumbled. One attempted to kill Jim, who had bragged to them of his exploits in behalf of his friends. But Silver, for reasons of his own, took the boy's side and swore he would take the part, also, of Squire Trelawney. Silver's disaffected mates met and gave Silver the Black Spot, deposing him as their chief. The pirate leader talked his way out of his difficulty by showing them, to Jim's amazement and to their delight, Captain Flint's chart of Treasure Island.

Dr. Livesey came under a flag of truce to the stockade to administer to the wounded pirates. He learned from Jim that Silver had saved the boy's life. And Jim heard, to his mystification, that the doctor had given Captain Flint's chart to Silver.

Following the directions of the chart, the pirates went to find the treasure. Approaching the hiding place, they heard a high voice singing the pirate chantey, "Yo ho ho, and a bottle of rum." Also, the voice spoke the last words of Captain Flint. The men were terrified until Silver recognized Ben Gunn's voice. Then the pirates found the treasure cache opened and the treasure gone. When they uncovered only a broken pick and some boards, they turned on Silver and Jim. At this moment Jim's friends, with Ben Gunn, arrived to rescue the boy.

Early in his stay on the island Ben Gunn had discovered the treasure and carried it to his cave. After Dr. Livesey had learned all this from Gunn, the stockade was abandoned and the useless chart given to Silver. Squire Trelawney's party moved to Gunn's safe and well-provisioned quarters.

The *Hispaniola* having been floated by a tide, the group left Treasure Island, leaving on it three escaped buccaneers. They sailed to a West Indies port where, with the connivance of Ben Gunn, John Silver escaped the ship with a bag of coins. A full crew was taken on, and the schooner voyaged back to Bristol. There the treasure was divided among the survivors of the adventure. "Drink and the devil had done for the rest."

A TREE GROWS IN BROOKLYN

Type of work: Novel
Author: Betty Smith (1904-   )
Type of plot: Domestic romance
Time of plot: Early twentieth century
Locale: Brooklyn, New York
First published: 1943

Principal characters:
> FRANCIE NOLAN, a Brooklyn girl
> NEELEY NOLAN, her brother
> KATIE NOLAN, her mother
> JOHNNIE NOLAN, her father

Critique:

A Tree Grows In Brooklyn is the story of a young girl affected by the realities and mysteries of life. The setting of Brooklyn tenement life in the early 1900's makes full use of local color. Francie's struggles to overcome poverty and to obtain an education in a world in which only the fittest survive make absorbing reading.

The Story:

For their spending money Francie and Neeley Nolan relied on a few pennies they collected from the junkey every Saturday. Katie, their mother, worked as a janitress in a Brooklyn tenement, and the money she and their father earned —he from his Saturday night jobs as a singing waiter—was barely enough to keep the family alive and clothed.

After their Saturday morning trips with the rags, metal, and rubber they had collected during the week, Francie would visit the library. She was methodically going through its contents in alphabetical order by reading a book each day, but on Saturdays she allowed herself the luxury of breaking the sequence. At home, sitting on the fire escape, she could look up from her book and watch her neighbors' preparations for Saturday night. A tree grew in the yard; Francie watched it from season to season during her long Saturday afternoons.

At five o'clock, when her father came home, Francie would iron his waiter's apron and then go to the dry-goods store to buy the paper collar and muslin dickey which would last him for the evening. It was her special Saturday night privilege to sleep in the front room, and there she could watch the people in the street. She got up briefly at two in the morning when her father came home, and was given a share of the delicacies he had salvaged from the wedding or party at which he had served. Then, while her parents talked far into the night, Francie would fix Saturday's happenings in her mind and gradually drift off to sleep.

Johnnie Nolan and Katie Rommely had met when he was nineteen and she was seventeen, and they were married four months later. In a year's time Francie was born. Johnnie, unable to bear the sight of Katie in labor, had got drunk, and when the water pipes burst at the school in which he was janitor, he was discharged. Neeley was born soon after Francie's first birthday. By that time Johnnie was drinking so heavily that Katie knew she could no longer rely on him for the family's support. In return for free rent, the Nolans moved to a house in which Katie could be janitress.

Francie was not sent to school until she was seven, and Neeley was old enough to go with her. In that way the children were able to protect each other from would-be tormentors. Seated two-at-a-desk among the other poverty-stricken children Francie soon grew to look forward to the weekly visits of her art and music teachers. They were the sunshine of her school days.

By pretending that Francie had gone to live with relatives, Johnnie was able to have her transferred to another school which Francie had seen on one of her walks. A long way from home, it was, nevertheless, an improvement over the old one. Most of the children were of American parentage and were not exploited by cruel teachers, as were those from immigrant families.

Francie noted time by holidays. Beginning the year with the Fourth of July and its firecrackers, she looked forward next to Halloween. Election Day, with its snake dances and bonfires, came soon after. Then followed Thanksgiving Day, on which the children disguised themselves with costumes and masks and begged trifles from storekeepers. Soon afterward came Christmas. The year Francie was ten and Neeley nine, they stood together on Christmas Eve while the biggest tree in the neighborhood was thrown at them. Trees unsold at that time were thrown at anyone who volunteered to stand against the impact. Bruised and scratched, Francie and her brother proudly dragged their tree home.

The week before Christmas, when Francie had just become fourteen, Johnnie staggered home drunk. Two days later he was found, huddled in a doorway, ill with pneumonia. The next day he was dead. After the funeral, Neeley was given his father's ring and Francie his shaving mug, his only keepsakes aside from his two waiter's aprons. To his wife Johnnie left a baby, due to be born the following spring.

In March, when their funds were running low, Katie cashed the children's insurance policies. The twenty-five dollars she received carried them through until the end of April. Then Mr. McGarrity, at whose saloon Johnnie had done most of his drinking, came to their rescue. He hired Neeley to help prepare free lunches after school and Francie to do housework, and the money the children earned was enough to tide them over until after Katie's baby was born.

Laurie was born in May. In June, after their graduation from grade school, Francie and Neeley found their first real jobs, Neeley as errand boy for a brokerage house and Francie as a stemmer in a flower factory. Dismissed two weeks later, she became a file clerk in a clipping bureau. She was quickly advanced to the position of reader.

In the fall there was not money enough to send both her children to high school, and Katie decided that the more reluctant Neeley should be chosen.

With the money Francie earned and with Neeley's after-school job at McGarrity's saloon, the Nolans had more comforts that Christmas than they had ever known before. The house was warm; there was enough food; and there was money for presents. Fourteen-year-old Neeley received his first pair of spats, and Francie almost froze in her new black lace lingerie when they went to church on Christmas morning.

When the clipping bureau closed with the outbreak of the war, Francie got a job as teletype operator. By working at night, she was able to take advanced college credits in summer school that year. With the help of a fellow student, Ben Blake, she passed her chemistry and English courses.

Francie was eighteen when she had her first real date, with a soldier named Lee Rhynor. The evening he was to leave to say goodbye to his parents before going overseas, Lee asked her to marry him when he returned. Francie promised to write to him every day. Three days later she received a letter from the girl he married during his trip home.

Katie also had a letter that day. Officer McShane had long been fond of Katie. Now retired, he asked her to marry him. To this proposal all the Nolans agreed. As the time approached for the wedding, Francie resigned her job. With

Katie married, she intended to go to Michigan to college, for with Ben Blake's help she had succeeded in passing the entrance exams.

The day before Katie was to be wed, Francie put the baby in the carriage and walked down the avenue. For a time she watched the children carting their rubbish into the junk shop. She turned in her books at the library for the last time. She saw another little girl, a book in her hand, sitting on a fire escape. In her own yard the tree had been cut down because the tenants had complained that it was in the way of their wash. But from its stump another trunk was growing.

THE TREE OF THE FOLKUNGS

Type of work: Novel
Author: Verner von Heidenstam (1859-1940)
Type of plot: Historical romance
Time of plot: Eleventh and thirteenth centuries
Locale: Sweden
First published: 1905-1907

Principal characters:
FOLKE FILBYTER, founder of the Folkung line
INGEMUND,
HALLSTEN, and
INGEVALD, his sons
FOLKE INGEVALDSSON, his grandson
ULF ULFSSON, a pagan udalman
KING VALDEMAR, descended from Folke Filbyter
DUKE MAGNUS, his brother
QUEEN SOPHIA, wife of Valdemar
LADY JUTTA, her sister
GISTRE HÄRJANSON, a minstrel
YRSA-LILL, a goat-girl
ARCHBISHOP FULCO, prelate of Upsala

Critique:

Like Sigrid Undset in Norway, Verner von Heidenstam drew inspiration from the history of his native Sweden in medieval times. *The Tree of the Folkungs* is a historical novel of imaginative freedom and dramatic vigor. There are two parts to the story. The first deals with the period at the end of the eleventh century, a barbaric, brutal age which in the North saw heathenism and Christianity in conflict. In the second half of the novel the Folkung family, proud descendants of an ancient peasant freebooter, have pushed their way to the Swedish throne by the middle of the thirteenth century. Here are all the pageantry, heroism, humility, superstition, cruelty, and greed of the Middle Ages. The effect is not one of antiquarianism, however, for von Heidenstam is interested in a living past, the growth of a culture, with its mixture of good and evil, nobility and baseness. The writer tells his story with a variety of styles and techniques, mingling myth, legend, history, saga, and fantasy. The result is a literary work of racial significance and tragic power. The author was awarded the Nobel Prize in Literature in 1916.

The Story:

Folke Filbyter planted the seed from which grew the mighty Folkung tree. Homeward returning after long sea-roving, he brought his ship to shore near a shield-maiden's grave-ground in the land of Sveas and Goths. Dwarf Jorgrimme, a Finnish sorcerer, prophesied terror would darken the land and Thor's image tremble.

For two nights Folke tramped inland, his sack of booty on his back. The third night he came to Jorgrimme's cave, where the sorcerer gave him drink from the horn Månegarm, treasure of the gods. Then the dwarf cut the sack so that some of the gold fell out. Discovering the leak, Folke swore he had sown the ground with riches he would also reap. There he built his mighty hall, Folketuna.

Before long Folke had land and thralls but no sons. One morning his men found Jorgrimme's daughter trapped in a wolf-pit, and Folke took her home to his bed. Three sons she bore him, Ingemund, Hallsten, and Ingevald, but she got no honor and crouched in the straw like the scurviest thrall. Ingemund and Hallsten went sea-roving. Ingevald stayed by his

THE TREE OF THE FOLKUNGS by Verner von Heidenstam. Translated by Arthur J. Chater. By permission of the publishers, Gyldendalske Boghandel, Nordisk Forlag, A/S, Copenhagen, Denmark. Copyright, 1925, by Alfred A. Knopf, Inc. Renewed, 1953, by Alfred A. Knopf, Inc.

father's side.

Folke, wanting a good marriage for his son, spoke for Holmdis, Ulf Ulfsson's daughter. Meanwhile old Jakob, a begging friar, preached a new faith in the region. When Ingevald tumbled the dwarfs' one-eyed god, his mother gave him sacred Månegarm, stolen from Jorgrimme's burial-cairn. Folke swore bloodbrotherhood with the king of outlaws and got great riches. Then Holmdis proudly spurned a match with the thrall-woman's son, but Ingevald carried her by force to his father's hall. There, waiting in vain for her kinsmen to rescue her, she brought one son to Folketuna before she died. After her funeral Folke had no good of Ingevald. Folke Ingevaldsson was his grandfather's heir.

When Jakob came again, Ingevald, hoping to save his son from the lawless life at Folketuna, gave the child to the priest. For years old Folke rode from hearth to hearth looking for his lost grandchild. Thrall and thane alike knew of the grim old man's search.

King Inge traveled through the land with his bodyguards, and wherever he stopped men died or else were baptized in the new faith. When Ulf Ulfsson spoke for the old gods, the king's earl and chief adviser, a ruthless, priest-trained young man, left him bound to perish in the forest. Ingemund and Hallsten, homewardbound, were in Ulf's hall that night and joined the king's guard.

Folke was at Upsala when the sacred grove burned and people cried out against Inge and called Blot Sven king. There Folke saw the king's earl, on his hand the star-shaped mark of the child stolen from Folketuna years before. Although the old outlaw offered his riches to help the king's need, young Folke and his uncles were proud men with little wish to have a name as unsavory as Folke Filbyter's associated with them, now that they were counted among the greatest of the king's thanes. They took the treasure he offered to advance themselves, but they visited him seldom in the bare hall where he sat in the dirty straw. At last

he opened his veins and died as unwanted old men had done in ancient times.

Two hundred years later King Holmger lay dead, with the sacred sword Gråne on his grave, and Earl Birger of the Folkungs ruled in Sweden, although it was his young son Valdemar who wore the crown. Valdemar grew up weak and soft, a lover of pleasure and women. From his far ancestor, Folke Filbyter, he inherited a yeoman's love of the land and a liking for serfs and outlaws. There were many who thought that his brother, Junker Magnus, should have been king, for he was bold and cunning and the better knight. When Magnus unhorsed his brother at a great tournament at Belbo, and Valdemar laughed at his tumble without shame or regret, Earl Birger was so angry with his son that he collapsed from a stroke and died soon afterward. At the division of the earl's estate his sons quarreled over a missing drinking horn, Månegarm, an heirloom of the old days.

Valdemar's bride was Sophia, daughter of Denmark's king. Lady Jutta was her sister. Sometimes Valdemar talked with the maid apart and she became frightened. Valdemar also spent much time in the hut of Yrsa-lill, a goat-girl, to whom Gistre Härjanson had carried Månegarm. The company drank from it when Valdemar went to the hut to carouse with herdsmen and outcasts. Meanwhile the land knew confusion. Peasants paid no taxes and robbers roamed the highways. Valdemar would allow no wrongdoer to be punished.

When Jutta wished to return to Denmark, Magnus and Sir Svantepolk, a worthy knight, set out to escort her. Valdemar overtook them at the goat-girl's hut, where the party had stopped to rest. After convincing Jutta that Magnus was a trickster, Valdemar accompanied her to the border, and on the way they became lovers. Sir Svantepolk, renouncing his allegiance, rode off to join Duke Magnus. Queen Sophia had Yrsa-lill thrown into a cage filled with snakes. Gistre, the minstrel, rescued the girl, who afterward lay speechless in the convent at Vreta.

When Jutta bore a son beyond the marches, Valdemar gave the child into the keeping of Archbishop Fulco of Upsala. Then the king threatened to take away his brother's titles. Magnus had the sword Gråne brought from King Holmger's tomb and fastened it to his own belt. At Vreta, Yrsa-lill regained her speech and prophesied that whoever would get St. Eirik's banner from a man-maiden's hands would rule Sweden.

Jutta, now prioress at Roskilde, went to Upsala for a holy festival honoring St. Eirik. There she found her son and saw Valdemar surrounded by his wild body-guard. Moved by her old love, she took off her religious habit and dressed in the robes of one of the king's favorites. Together she and Valdemar stood on the balcony of the king's house while the people howled disapproval and insults. Queen Sophia ordered Jutta sent to a convent in the archbishop's keeping.

Archbishop Fulco gave St. Eirik's banner to some maidens who carried it to Duke Magnus. Afterward there was war between the brothers. Crafty, vain, Magnus battled Valdemar and his army of peasants and outlaws. Valdemar seemed indifferent to the outcome, however, and sat feasting at Ramundeboda while his army was defeated at Hofva. From that time on Magnus had the crown, but the war did not end with his victory, for Valdemar fought and then fled from lost villages and provinces. At last the outlawed king had nothing left but a jeweled riding-whip borrowed from Lady Luitgard, the last friend to share his misfortunes, and he gave that to Gistre and told the minstrel to go look for Yrsa-lill. Alone and unarmed, Valdemar then surrendered to his brother.

King Magnus, old and sick by that time, gave the country peace. Valdemar lived a prisoner at Nyköpingshus, Luitgard his only company, but in his captivity he found such contentment that Magnus died envying him.

THE TREES

Type of work: Novel
Author: Conrad Richter (1890-   )
Type of plot: Regional romance
Time of plot: Late eighteenth and early nineteenth centuries
Locale: Old Northwest Territory
First published: 1940

> Principal characters:
> WORTH LUCKETT, a woodsy
> JARY, his wife
> SAYWARD,
> GENNY,
> ACHSA,
> WYITT, and
> SULIE, their children
> LOUIE SCURRAH, Genny's husband
> PORTIUS WHEELER, Sayward's husband
> JAKE TENCH, a white runner

Critique:

The Trees is the first of three novels Conrad Richter has written to trace the growth of a pioneer settlement in the old Northwest Territory west of the Alleghenies and north of the Ohio River. Considered with the other two, *The Fields* and *The Town*, these novels are actually a trilogy telling the story of Sayward Luckett from the time she left Pennsylvania to enter the deep woods in the Ohio wilderness. One of the most interesting characteristics of the books is the use Richter has made of early pioneer language as it was spoken, not as it was written. This is only one proof of the authenticity of the facts he used in writing a new and effective type of regional story. No other novel conveys so realistically what the first settlers must have felt when they faced the timbered wilderness on the frontier, the barrier of trees that shut out the sky and gave protection to animals and human enemies. *The Trees* is a pioneer story of simple human warmth and vigor.

The Story:

Worth Luckett was a woodsy with an itching foot. By the time he had five growing children and one left in its infant grave, he was ready to take off again. He had already been west when he was a boy with Colonel Bouquet. Jary, his wife, had never wanted to leave the settlements, but game was growing scarce in Pennsylvania; without food brought down by his gun, Worth could not see how he could feed his family. He was wary of telling Jary outright that he wanted to move on, but she knew what he wanted and was half resigned to it when she heard that the animals were clearing out of places where men lived.

Because Jary had the slow fever, the care of the younger children fell on Sayward's shoulders. She was nearly fifteen, a strapping girl scared of neither man nor beast. It was not beyond her strength to drown a white-faced buck when Worth had neglected to bring meat home. The girls, Genny, Achsa, and baby Sulie, and the boy Wyitt knew they had to step when Sayward spoke.

Worth led his family across the Ohio River and on until they came to a wilderness of trees that reached as far as the eye could see. Near a spot covered with deer antlers Worth laid out a place for a cabin. He was handy enough with tools to have the shell of a cabin up quickly, but the game in the woods drew him away so often that fall came before the cabin was finished. The darkness under the big trees had disheartened Jary so much that she did not even speak of the cabin until one fall day when the leaves had fallen so that she could look up through the branches and see the sky again. Then she felt like a human being who wanted to live in a house. She sent Worth back to his job. The snow fell the day after they moved into their cabin.

A few Indians still followed the trace by the house. One came on a night when Worth was away. Sayward hid the ax under her bed to fell him if he made a move toward the children in the loft or came toward her bed. He got up at night to cook some of his own meat at the fire. Worth was disturbed when he came home and found the Indian still there, but he and the Indian roared with delight when Sayward showed them the hidden ax.

Jary had such a hankering after some bread that Worth walked six days to bring back some white flour. But she could not eat the bread after Sayward made it; the slow fever had nearly finished her. When she died, they buried her under one of the big trees outside the cabin. Worth went away for a while, leaving Sayward to take care of the others.

One day, for the first time since they had lived there, they heard another ax in the woods. The young ones investigated and found a cabin going up, a man and a boy working on it. The man was a tom thumb, Sayward thought, when he asked her father for Sayward as a wife. Sayward thought he might be the first around there to ask her to marry him, but probably not the last.

Before long a trading post was set up by the river. Wyitt could hardly wait to trade off some of his skins for a knife. Indians and whites were whooping it up while he was there. He never forgot the sight of the wolf they skinned alive and set free.

More people raised cabins nearby until the Lucketts had several neighbors within walking distance. Worth blamed them and their cutting of the trees for the swamp pestilence that brought down Achsa, who was as brown and tough as an Indian. While the fever was on her Achsa begged for water, but that was the one thing she was not supposed to have. Late one night Sayward awoke to see Achsa crawling into the cabin with the kettle. She had drunk her fill from the run and had brought water back in the kettle. After that Achsa got well.

Louie Scurrah as a child had acted as decoy for Delawares on the warpath. When he came back to a small cabin nearby, the Lucketts expected to steer clear of him. He charmed Worth first with his woodsy tales, then Genny and Achsa, but there was always unspoken enmity between him and Sayward.

Sulie never returned after the day she was separated from Wyitt as they drove in the neighbor's cows. Worth was away at the time and the trail was cold when he and Louie gathered some neighborhood men to beat the woods. They found Sulie's tracks leading to a bark playhouse in a grove of trees, with a bit of her dress as a cover for a play trencher, but they could not find tracks leading out. Close by there were Indian trails, but they were also cold.

With Sulie gone, Worth went too. He thought he might follow the Indian tracks west.

The feeling between Louie and Sayward was not softened when Sayward, after finding Louie with Genny in the woods, told him it was time for him to marry Genny. He took Genny down the river and married her with good grace, but before long his itching foot took him off more and more often.

Louie got Wyitt a rifle to help kill meat for Sayward's cabin. The first day he had it, Wyitt wounded a buck. Standing over the animal to slit its throat, he suddenly found himself hoisted aloft. The deer tried to shake him loose, but Wyitt was able to kill it when it tired. His clothes were torn to ribbons and he was badly cut. Sayward, realizing that she had another woodsy on her hands and thankful for the meat he brought, said nothing.

Finally Louie went off to the English lakes with Achsa. Sayward did not know until later that they left the very night the painter tried to claw his way down Genny's chimney. Genny burned everything in the house that night to keep the painter from coming into the cabin. When Wyitt and Sayward found her, she did not recognize them. At last, under Sayward's care, Genny came back to her senses.

At a sober wedding of old folks, Jake Tench decided it was time to get a wife for solitary Portius Wheeler, a former Bay State lawyer. When the girl Jake picked shied off, Sayward told Jake that she would marry Portius. Jake brought Portius to Sayward's cabin where, under the influence of brandy, Portius went through the marriage ceremony. But when neighbors tried to put him to bed with Sayward, he turned tail and ran. Jake brought him back at dawn. Although Sayward told him she would not hold him against his will, Portius stayed with her.

Together they cut down trees for a garden patch. The neighbors brought teams to snake out the logs and to plow. Portius treated Sayward with gentle deference, and she was happy when she looked forward to her first-born.

THE TRIAL

Type of work: Novel
Author: Franz Kafka (1883-1924)
Type of plot: Fantasy
Time of plot: Twentieth century
Locale: Germany
First published: 1925

Principal characters:
JOSEPH K., a bank employee
THE ADVOCATE
TITORELLI, a painter
LENI, the Advocate's servant

Critique:

The Trial is one of the most effective and most discussed works to come out of Central Europe between wars. To many, perhaps most, readers it is a highly engaging comedy filled with buffoonery and fantasy. More serious students of literature see in it, however, a vast symbolism and a first rate psychological study of a system whose leaders are convinced of their own righteousness. To some the court is a symbol of the Church as an imperfect bridge between the individual and God. To others the symbolism represents rather the search of a sensitive Jew for a homeland that is always denied him. At any rate The Trial is a powerful and provocative book.

The Story:

Perhaps some one had been telling lies about Joseph K., for one morning he was arrested. The landlady's cook always brought him his breakfast at eight o'clock, but this morning she failed to appear. Joseph looked out of the window and noticed that the old lady across the way was peering into his room. Feeling uneasy, he rang the bell. At once a man entered dressed like a tourist. He advised Joseph to stay in his room, but Joseph failed to obey. In the next room he saw another strange man reading a book. The missing breakfast was explained by the empty dishes he saw. The two strangers had eaten it.

The two strangers had come to notify Joseph he was under arrest. They were so sure of themselves and yet so considerate that Joseph was at a loss as to the attitude he should take toward them. They tried to take his underwear, saying it was of too good quality, but when he objected they did not press him. They refused to tell him the reason for his arrest, saying only that he would be interrogated. Finally, after Joseph had dressed according to their choices of his wardrobe, they led him to another room to be questioned by the Inspector.

To his dismay Joseph saw that the Inspector was occupying Fräulein Bürstner's room. The Inspector gave no further hint as to the reason for the arrest, nor did he inquire into Joseph's defense. The latter at one point said that the whole matter was a mistake; but under pertinent if vague questioning, Joseph admitted that he knew little of the law. All he learned, really, was that some one in high authority had ordered his arrest.

Then Joseph was told that he could go to work as usual. His head fairly aching from bewilderment, Joseph went to the bank in a taxi. Arriving half an hour late, he worked all day long as diligently as he could. He was, however, frequently interrupted by congratulatory callers, for this day was his thirtieth birthday.

He went straight home at nine-thirty to apologize for using Fräulein Bürstner's room. She was not in, however, and he settled down to anxious waiting. At eleven-thirty she arrived, tired from an evening at the theater. In spite of her uninterested attitude he told her the whole story very dramatically. At last Fraülein Bürstner sank down exhausted on her bed. Joseph rushed to her, kissed her passionately many times, and returned to his room.

A few days later Joseph received a brief note ordering him to appear before the court for interrogation on the following Sunday. Oddly enough, although the address was given, no time was set for the hearing. By some chance Joseph decided to go at nine o'clock. The street was a rather mean one, and the address proved to be that of a large warehouse.

Joseph did not know where to report, but after trying many doors he finally reached the fifth floor. There a bright-eyed washerwoman seemed to be expecting him and motioned him through her flat into a meeting hall. Joseph found the room filled with old men, most of them with long beards. They all wore badges.

When the judge asked Joseph if he were a house painter, he snappishly rejoined that he was the junior manager of a bank. Then the judge said he was an hour and ten minutes late. To this charge Joseph replied that he was present now, his appearance in court being the main thing. The crowd applauded. Encouraged, Joseph launched into a harangue damning the court, its methods, the warders who had arrested him, and the meeting time and place.

The judge seemed abashed. Then an interruption occurred. At the back of the room a man clasped the washerwoman in his arms and screamed, all the while looking at the ceiling. Joseph dashed from the room, loudly refusing to have any more dealings with the court.

All that week Joseph awaited another summons. When none came, he decided to revisit the meeting hall. The washerwoman again met him kindly and expressed her disappointment that the court was not in session. She told him a little about the court and its methods. It seemed that the court was only a lower body which rarely interfered with the freedom of the accused people. If one were acquitted by the court, it meant little, because a higher court might rearrest the prisoner on the same charge. She seemed to know little of Joseph's particular case, although she said she knew as much as the judge. As she was speaking, a law student seized the washerwoman and carried her up the stairs.

The woman's husband kindly offered to lead Joseph up to the law offices, the inner sanctum of the court located in the attic. There Joseph found a number of people waiting for answers to petitions. Some of them had been waiting for years, and they were becoming a little anxious about their cases. The hot room under the roof made Joseph dizzy and he had to sit down. The hostess tried to soothe him and the director of public relations was very pleasant. Finally some one suggested that Joseph ought to leave and get some fresh air.

On his uncle's advice, Joseph hired an Advocate, an old man who stayed in bed most of the time. His servant, Leni, took a liking to Joseph and would often kiss him while he was conferring with the Advocate. Joseph liked best to dally with her in the kitchen. After some months, all the Advocate had done was to think about writing a petition. In desperation Joseph discharged him from the case.

Leni was heartbroken. She was in her nightgown entertaining another client. This man, a businessman, Leni kept locked up in a small bedroom. The Advocate warned Joseph of his high-handed behavior and pointed to the businessman as an ideal client. Disgusted, Joseph left the house.

Then Joseph went to see Titorelli, the court painter. Titorelli told him he could hope for little. He might get definitive acquittal, ostensible acquittal, or indefinite postponement. No one was ever really acquitted, but sometimes cases could be prolonged indefinitely. Joseph bought three identical paintings in return for the advice.

Even the priest at the cathedral, who said he was court chaplain, offered little encouragement when consulted. He was sure that Joseph would be convicted of the crime charged against him. Joseph still did not know what that crime was, nor did the priest.

At last two men in frock coats and top hats came for Joseph at nine o'clock on the evening before his thirty-first birthday. Somehow they twined their arms around his and held his hands tightly. They walked with him to a quarry. There one held his throat and the other stabbed him in the heart, turning the knife around twice.

TRIAL BY JURY

Type of work: Comic opera
Author: W. S. Gilbert (1836-1911)
Type of plot: Humorous romance
Time of plot: Nineteenth century
Locale: England
First presented: 1875

> Principal characters:
> THE LEARNED JUDGE
> ANGELINA, the plaintiff
> EDWIN, the defendant
> COUNSEL FOR THE PLAINTIFF
> FOREMAN OF THE JURY
> FIRST BRIDESMAID

Critique:

A gentle satire on the due processes of law, *Trial by Jury* is a short and delightful play by the Gilbert half of the famous team of Gilbert and Sullivan. It was the second operetta on which these two talented men collaborated, the forerunner of many more well-known and well-loved musicals. It is the only Gilbert and Sullivan comic opera without spoken dialogue.

The Story:

The court was assembled, waiting for the learned Judge, the plaintiff, and the defendant. The jurymen were warned that they must set aside all prejudice and view the case in a judicial state of mind. The usher, who warned them to be fair, went into raptures over the beauty and the heartbreak of the plaintiff, ending each bit of praise, however, with the reminder to be free of bias.

When Edwin, the defendant, entered, the jurymen chanted to him to beware their fury. The defendant thought this a very strange proceeding and begged them to hear his story. The jury, after consultation, agreed that they should hear his plea. Then the defendant told how his heart had leaped with joy when he first knew his old love. He had laid his heart and his riches at her feet. He had moped and sighed just like a lovesick boy. But then the joy had turned to boredom. The flame of love had burned out, and so one morning he had awakened to be another's lovesick boy.

The jurymen then confessed that when they were young lads they had behaved in much the same fashion and acted as regular cads. Now that they were respectable men, they had not a scrap of sympathy for the defendant.

The learned Judge entered, but before he would hear the case he felt obliged to tell the court how he had become judge. When he was first called to the bar, he was, like most barristers, an impecunious lad, and he had almost despaired of ever trying a case before an English jury. Tiring at last of this third-class living, he had married a rich attorney's old and ugly daughter. The rich attorney had rewarded him for his sacrifice, after assuring him that he would soon grow used to his bride's looks. Cases then came fast to the young attorney and he restored many thieves and burglars to freedom. At last he became rich enough to throw over his elderly, ugly bride. Now he was a judge, and a good judge too, ready to hear this case of breach of promise.

The jurymen, sworn in, promised to weigh the case carefully. Angelina, the plaintiff, was then called in, preceded by her bridesmaids. The Judge took an immediate fancy to the first bridesmaid and sent her a note, which she kissed and placed in her bosom. But when the plaintiff entered, the learned Judge, trans-

3877

ferring his affection to Angelina, had the note taken from the first bridesmaid and given to the plaintiff. She too kissed it and placed it in her bosom as the Judge and the jurymen took turns praising the plaintiff.

The plaintiff stated her case. She had been basely deceived by the defendant, who had wooed her without ceasing. When she had tried to name a day for their wedding, however, he had framed excuses and at last deserted her. His act was doubly criminal because she had already bought her trousseau. The plaintiff reeled, and the foreman of the jury and the Judge vied with each other to support her. At last Angelina fell sobbing on the Judge's chest. The jurymen shook their fists at the defendant and warned him again to dread their fury.

Edwin, although admitting that he had trifled with the lady, held himself blameless. No one should be censured for changing appetites. To atone, however, he would marry this lady today, his other love tomorrow. The Judge thought that a reasonable proposition, but the Counsel submitted that such a deed would be Burglaree. The Judge considered this a fine dilemma, calling for all their wits.

The plaintiff went to the defendant and embraced him, vowing that she loved him with unceasing fervor. She reminded the jury to remember her great loss when they assessed the damages the defendant must pay. The defendant then extolled his vices, stating that she could not abide him for a day. They should remember that when they assessed the damages.

The Judge, tossing aside his books and papers, said that he could not stay there all day. He would marry the lady himself. As he embraced her the others agreed that he was indeed a good judge—of beauty.

A TRICK TO CATCH THE OLD ONE

Type of work: Drama
Author: Thomas Middleton (1580-1627)
Type of plot: Comedy of intrigue
Time of plot: First years of seventeenth century
Locale: London
First presented: c. 1604

Principal characters:

WITGOOD, a young prodigal of good family
A COURTESAN, Witgood's mistress and accomplice
PECUNIUS LUCRE, Witgood's miserly uncle
WALKADINE HOARD, a rival miser to Pecunius Lucre
TAVERNER, Witgood's friend and accomplice
JOYCE, Walkadine Hoard's niece, pretty and wealthy

Critique:

Thomas Middleton, next to Ben Jonson, was the greatest realist among the dramatists writing during the reign of James I. The realism is not reinforced in Middleton's work by a close attention to the structure of the drama, as is so noteworthy in the Jonsonian plays. Middleton, a commoner himself and holder of a post for many years under the Lord Mayor of London, was exceedingly interested in the life of the people who lived within the city, rather than in the people of the court and the fashionable world. Where Middleton got the plot for this play is not known; possibly he gathered it out of incidents that actually occurred in London. On the other hand, the influence of this play on Philip Massinger's *A New Way to Pay Old Debts* is obvious. The greatest merits of the Middleton play are its intrigues, its hustle and bustle of incident, and its propensity to give good fun.

The Story:

Theodorus Witgood, a young man of quality, had been so prodigal with his fortune that he had lost it all. Even his country estate had been mortgaged to his uncle, Pecunius Lucre, a miserly man. The cause of Witgood's downfall was a Courtesan, a young woman on whom he had wasted his fortune after seducing her. Fortunately for Witgood, the girl really liked him and was anxious to help him. When Witgood conceived

a plan to regain his fortunes, a plan that required her help, she readily promised to help her lover.

Witgood's plan was to take the Courtesan to London and pass her off as a rich widow. With the aid of a tavern-keeper, who gave Witgood his services as a servant and the use of his horses, the plan was put into execution. Witgood even hoped to get back the mortgage from his uncle. As soon as Uncle Lucre heard about the rich widow, his miserly instincts were aroused. Taken in by his nephew's story, he hoped to promote the marriage and eventually gain the widow's money and estates.

Uncle Lucre invited Witgood and the supposed wealthy widow to his home, where in spite of his real feelings toward Witgood he praised the young man to the skies. In addition to his uncle, the creditors to whom Witgood owed money were anxious to help his marital efforts, for the creditors realized that a good marriage would enable them to collect the money he owed them.

When word of the wealthy widow spread through the town, many suitors came to woo her. Among them was Walkadine Hoard, a rival miser who was pleased at the prospect of wooing a widow of fortune and so keeping that fortune from falling into the hands of Uncle Lucre. The situation was to Witgood's advantage, and he filled his uncle's ears with talk of the jointures that other suitors were willing to give the widow. His hope was that his uncle would take the hint and restore his estates and money to him in the belief that he should shine as well as the other suitors in the supposed widow's eyes. The plan was only a ruse, however. for Witgood had no intention of marrying the Courtesan and making an honest woman of her. Witgood's real love was Joyce, the daughter of Hoard's rich brother. Lest Joyce think he had forsaken her, Witgood sent her a letter telling her to keep faith with him. They had to keep their love secret, for Witgood's wild ways and prodigality, plus the enmity between their respective uncles, prevented their marriage.

In the meantime Hoard plotted to get the widow for himself. Accompanied by several gentlemen. he went to her and told her the truth about young Witgood. His friends also represented Hoard as an ardent suitor. Witgood, in another room, heard all that was said. At his first chance he advised the Courtesan to go ahead with her deception and marry old Hoard, a marriage which would give her a place in the world and restore her lost reputation. Hoard's proposal was a piece of luck that the plotting pair had not foreseen. She promised to meet Hoard at a tavern and elope with him. When she confessed that she had no estates, Hoard, thinking she was only teasing him, refused to believe her.

The Courtesan went to the tavern, where the old miser met her. To entertain his uncle, Witgood then went and told him that Hoard was being married off to a prostitute. Uncle Lucre was immensely pleased. Discreet Witgood did not tell the uncle that the prostitute was the supposed wealthy widow.

Witgood's creditors, getting wind of what was happening, secured a bailiff and had him arrested for debt. After much talking he persuaded them to take him first to Hoard's house. When they arrived there, Witgood informed Hoard that he had an earlier marriage contract with the widow, a contract which could not be nullified until both parties agreed

to break it. Old Hoard was horrified, for the bond meant that his new wife's property, if any, was not his. Pretending to save the day, the woman suggested that Hoard buy off Witgood by paying the young man's debts. The creditors, paid by Hoard, went their way. Then Witgood and the widow confessed the woman's true identity. The bridegroom fumed, realizing too late that the supposed widow had told him in the presence of witnesses that she had no fortune. Hoard had been gulled into taking another man's mistress as his wife.

Meanwhile the tavernkeeper, acting as servant for Witgood and the Courtesan, had convinced Uncle Lucre that his nephew could marry the widow only if he had a fortune or an estate. The uncle, hoping to use the young man to get the supposed widow's fortune in his hands, gave up the mortgage on Witgood's estates. The tavernkeeper hastened with the papers to Witgood, who was extremely pleased with the way his plans were working out.

Before he left Hoard's house, Witgood, once more in control of his estates, received a message in which Joyce told him that she would meet him a short time later.

Old Hoard tried to pass off his wife as she had been passed on to him. He ordered a great wedding supper and invited, among other guests, his rival and also his brother. Everything went off well until Hoard's brother recognized the bride as Witgood's former mistress. In the confusion that followed the bride fell on her knees and asked forgiveness, telling her husband that she repented her previous sins and would make him a good wife. She pointed out that it was better for a man to have a wife whose sins were behind her instead of before her. Witgood also helped her reputation by saying that he had been her seducer and only lover.

Witgood himself then declared that he, too, had reformed. He promised to put aside his old habits of prodigality as the first step in winning consent to his marriage with Joyce, the girl he truly   loved.

THE TRICKSTER

Type of work: Drama
Author: Titus Maccius Plautus (c. 255-184 B.C.)
Type of plot: Comedy of intrigue
Time of plot: Late third century B.C.
Locale: Athens
First presented: 191 B.C.

Principal characters:
SIMO, an old Athenian gentleman
CALIDORUS, his son
PSEUDOLUS, Simo's servant
BALLIO, a procurer, owner of Phoenicium
HARPAX, a messenger
SIMIA, servant of one of Calidorus' friends
PHOENICIUM, loved by Calidorus

Critique:

The Trickster (*Pseudolus*) shares both the deficiencies and the excellences of most of Plautus' plays. The comedy displays what might be called an absolute unity of place and time: the whole of the action occurs before a single house in Athens in precisely the time it would have occupied in reality. The result, while attesting strongly to the dramatist's ingenuity, tends to violate what is perhaps the most important unity of all, that of action. The plot is crowded with irrelevant events introduced primarily to provide time for other more essential events to take place off stage, and the characters are sometimes given improbable speeches to account for their presence in this place at this time when another place and time would have appeared more suitable. Nevertheless, Plautus seems not oblivious of these incongruities, and he presents them with a sufficient hint of irony to make them entertaining, even if they are not dramatically integrated.

The Story:

Pseudolus, a servant of the Athenian Simo, observed one day that his master's son Calidorus was deeply despondent about something. Questioning him on the matter, Pseudolus was given a letter from Phoenicium, a slave girl with whom Calidorus was in love. She had written that Ballio, her master, had sold her to a Macedonian military officer for the sum of twenty minae. However, the transac-

tion was not yet complete; the officer had given Ballio fifteen minae to seal the bargain and had arranged that Phoenicium was to be delivered to a servant of his who would bring the remaining five minae and a letter bearing a seal to match the one the officer had made with his ring and left in Ballio's keeping. This servant was to arrive on the festival of Bacchus, now being celebrated.

Calidorus was naturally and thoroughly upset by this news, for he had no money with which to buy Phoenicium and no prospect of getting any. At loose ends, he appealed to the wily Pseudolus for help. With great self-confidence, the servant promised to trick Calidorus' father, Simo, out of the money.

Before any plan could be formulated, Ballio appeared, cursing and beating some of his slaves. Calidorus and Pseudolus approached him and begged him to reconsider his bargain, pointing out that Phoenicium had been promised to Calidorus as soon as the young man could find the money to pay for her. But the unscrupulous Ballio remained unmoved. taunting Calidorus with his poverty and his inability to get money from his father. Before they parted, however, he craftily pointed out that today was the day on which the officer had agreed to send his final installment of the payment for Phoenicium and that if the promised money were not received, Ballio would be free to sell her to any other bidder.

As Pseudolus was revolving his plans in his mind, he overheard Simo talking to a friend and learned that the old man had already heard of Calidorus' plight and had steeled himself in advance against any plea for money that his son might make. Finding his task thus complicated, Pseudolus stepped forward and brazenly admitted his commission, telling Simo that he intended to get the twenty minae from him and that Simo should consequently be on his guard. The slave told his master in addition that he intended to trick Ballio out of the slave girl. Simo was skeptical, but Pseudolus finally goaded him into promising to pay for the girl if Pseudolus proved successful in getting her away from the procurer.

Soon afterward Pseudolus was fortunate enough to overhear a newcomer identify himself as Harpax, the Macedonian captain's messenger, come to conclude the dealings for Phoenicium. Accosting the messenger, Pseudolus identified himself as one of Ballio's servants and persuaded Harpax to allow him to deliver the sealed letter that was to identify the rightful purchaser. Then he induced Harpax to go to an inn to rest from his journey until Pseudolus came to get him.

When the messenger had gone, Calidorus appeared in the company of a friend, and in the conversation that followed, the latter agreed to lend five minae for the execution of Pseudolus' plot. He agreed, moreover, to allow his servant Simia to be used in the enterprise.

These arrangements made, the three left to conclude their preparations. Then Ballio appeared in the company of a cook, and it was disclosed that today was the procurer's birthday and that he was preparing a feast for his customers. Before Ballio went into his house, it was disclosed also that Simo had met him in the market place and had warned him to be on his guard against Pseudolus' plot.

Immediately after Ballio went in, Pseudolus appeared in the company of Simia. During their conversation Simia revealed himself to be shrewd and wily, and in

the ensuing confrontation with Ballio he proved as apt a dissembler as Pseudolus himself. For when Ballio came out of his house, Simia approached and asked directions to find the procurer. Ballio identified himself, but, suspicious, he asked Simia the name of the man who had sent him. For a moment, the eavesdropping Pseudolus was afraid that his plot had collapsed, for Simia had not been told the name of the Macedonian captain. Simia adroitly evaded the trap, however, by pretending suspicion on his part and refusing to give Ballio the sealed letter until the procurer had himself identified Phoenicium's purchaser. Ballio did so, received the letter and the money and released Phoenicium into Simia's custody.

After Simia and Phoenicium had gone, Ballio, congratulating himself on having outwitted Pseudolus, chuckled at the prospect of the servant making his tardy effort to obtain the girl. When Simo appeared, the procurer expressed his certainty that Pseudolus had been foiled and declared that he would give Simo twenty minae and relinquish his right to the girl as well if Pseudolus were successful in his plot.

At that moment Harpax entered, grumbling that Pseudolus had not come to get him as he had promised to do. Confronting Ballio, he learned the procurer's identity and set about to close the bargain his master had made. Ballio, convinced that Harpax was in the employ of Pseudolus, did his best to humiliate the messenger, until Harpax mentioned having given the sealed letter to a "servant" of Ballio. From the description, Ballio realized with great chagrin that he had been thoroughly duped. Simo held him to his word regarding the twenty minae and the relinquishing of his rights to Phoenicium, and Harpax, learning that the girl was no longer available, insisted on the return of the fifteen minae that the captain had already deposited.

Meanwhile, Pseudolus, Calidorus, and Phoenicium were celebrating their victory with wine. Pseudolus later met Simo and demanded the twenty minae which the old man owed him for having successfully tricked Ballio. Simo gave the money with good will since it was not ultimately coming out of his pocket. Pseudolus returned half the sum and took his master off to drink to their good fortune.

TRILBY

Type of work: Novel
Author: George du Maurier (1834-1896)
Type of plot: Sentimental romance
Time of plot: Nineteenth century
Locale: Paris and London
First published: 1894

Principal characters:
TRILBY O'FERRALL, an artist's model
SVENGALI, a Hungarian musician
GECKO, another musician
TAFFY,
SANDY, and
LITTLE BILLEE, English art students

Critique:

This novel has had an astonishing success both in its original form and in a dramatic version for stage presentation. Its chief merit lies in its picture of student life in the Latin Quarter of Paris. Du Maurier, who wrote the book from recollections of his own youth, seems to have set down only the glamorous elements. The result is delightful reading so long as the reader remembers that the account of Bohemian life is idealized and sentimentalized.

The Story:

In the large Latin Quarter studio which Taffy, Sandy, and Little Billee shared, the three students were hosts to Svengali, an unconventional musician, and Gecko, a fiddler. Suddenly there was a knock on the door. An artist's model came in; she had heard music and decided to stop by. She wore a mixture of clothing—a soldier's coat, a pair of men's shoes, a frilled petticoat—and she carried her lunch. When she began to sing, her voice was so flat that the listeners did not know whether to be amused or embarrassed. Only Svengali realized the quality of her untrained voice.

Svengali went one morning to borrow money from Sandy. Trilby was in the studio when he arrived. Because she complained of a headache, Svengali

hypnotized her. Sandy, thinking of the control Svengali might have over Trilby, was alarmed.

Trilby came more often to the studio. She cooked for the three Englishmen, darned their clothing, joined in their meals and parties. In return they taught her how to speak correct English and treated her as a highly respected sister. When Sandy fell ill, Trilby refused to let anyone else look after him.

Svengali had a stroke of luck when he was hired to appear in concerts. He was anxious to hypnotize the model again, but the three Englishmen would not permit it.

Because Trilby posed in the nude, Little Billee, who had fallen in love with her, became angry and left Paris. Trilby, unhappy at this turn of events, became a laundress. She began to take care of her appearance, so that when Little Billee returned he was completely charmed by her. At Christmas time Trilby promised to marry Little Billee. But a few days later his mother and a clergyman arrived and made Trilby promise that she would not marry Little Billee. Trilby left Paris. Little Billee became ill and with his mother and sister returned to England.

Five years passed. Little Billee achieved success in London. Sandy and Taffy traveled on the continent. When the three friends met again at a ball in London, there was much talk of old days in Paris. Word went around that Svengali had found a great pupil, that he had married her and was making a famous singer of her. Little Billee painted more pictures and fell in and out of love with a girl named Alice. The other two friends went their ways.

At last the three met in Paris. During their stay they attended the first performance of the famous La Svengali in Paris and discovered that the singer was their Trilby of earlier days. Under the hand of her master she had gained a great voice that thrilled her audience. The three Englishmen were overcome.

The next day, when they saw Trilby and Svengali in the park, Little Billee ran up to greet her. She looked at her old friends vaguely, listened to something which Svengali said to her, and then to their surprise glanced coldly at them as if she had never seen them before.

The next day Little Billee encountered Svengali, who spat on him. A fight began in which the tall musician was more than a match for the small artist. Then Taffy appeared. With one hand he seized Svengali's nose and with the other he slapped Svengali on the cheek. Svengali was only too glad to escape. A few days later the Englishmen left for home.

When Svengali brought his star to London, she was the talk of the city. Little Billee and his friends bought tickets for Trilby's first concert.

At the last minute the concert was canceled. Svengali had scolded Trilby past the limit of Gecko's endurance, and Gecko had attacked Svengali with a knife. At that moment Trilby became imbecile in her manner. While her husband remained ill she was incapable of speech, and she spent all her time with him. Svengali would not permit her to leave him either to practice or to sing her concert without him.

At last Svengali recovered. Not well enough to conduct the orchestra, however, he was compelled to occupy a seat in a box facing Trilby as she sang. When Little Billee and his friends arrived, they saw Svengali rise from his place with a look of unalterable hatred on his face. Then he slumped forward. Trilby, led from the wings, took her place somewhat mechanically. She seemed to be looking for Svengali. The orchestra began her number. She remained indifferent, refusing to sing. Again and again the orchestra began to play. At last she demanded, in her old gutter French, what they wanted of her. When they said she was to sing, she told the orchestra to be quiet; she would sing without an accompaniment. Then she began in the same flat voice with which she had sung for Little Billee and his friends years before. At once catcalls shook the house. Terrified, Trilby had to be led away. The confusion increased when someone shouted that Svengali was dead in his box.

The three friends went to Trilby's dressing-room. Finding her frightened, they took her to Little Billee's lodgings, where the next day he and his friends called on her. Trilby knew nothing of her career as a singer, and she remembered Svengali only as the kindest man in her life. She was pale and seemed vastly aged.

She told them that Svengali had offered to look after her when she left Paris. He had not married her, however, for he already had a wife and three children. As Trilby talked, her mind seemed disturbed beyond recovery, and a doctor was called in. She gradually became weaker and weaker. There seemed little that could be done for her.

Gecko went to prison for striking Svengali. Svengali's money, which Trilby had earned, went to his wife and children. Each afternoon the three friends went to visit Trilby. She became more and more emaciated, and could no longer rise from her chair. Only by

3886

smiles and gestures could she reveal to them the gay, carefree Trilby of other days in Paris.

One day a large life-like photograph of Svengali was shown her. She began to sing and charmed her listeners to tears with the sadness of her song. Then she fell asleep. A doctor, summoned immediately, said she had been dead for a quarter of an hour or more.

Years later Taffy and his wife, Little Billee's sister, met Gecko in a café in Paris and he told them of Svengali's influence over Trilby. Svengali had hypnotized the girl, had made her a singing automaton of matchless voice. When the spell was broken, there was no Trilby, Gecko claimed, for Svengali had destroyed her soul. Taffy and his wife told him how Little Billee had died shortly after Trilby's death. There was little any of them could say. They could only wonder at the strangeness and sadness of Trilby's story.

TRISTAN AND ISOLDE

Type of work: Poem
Author: Gottfried von Strassburg (fl. late twelfth and early thirteenth centuries)
Type of plot: Romantic tragedy
Time of plot: The Arthurian period
Locale: Northern Europe, Ireland, England
First transcribed: c.1210

Principal characters:
RIVALIN, a lord of Parmenie
BLANCHEFLEUR, his wife
TRISTAN, their son
RUAL THE FAITHFUL, Tristan's foster father
MARK, King of Cornwall, Tristan's uncle
ISOLDE THE FAIR, King Mark's bride, loved by Tristan
BRANGENE, Isolde's companion
ISOLDE OF THE WHITE HANDS, Tristan's bride

Critique:

Those who know Richard Wagner's opera of the same title are familiar with the basic plot of Gottfried von Strassburg's version of this widespread tale. The version Wagner chose, 19,000 or so lines of which are attributed to Gottfried, the medieval German court poet, is the finest extant and the most extensive telling of one of the most famous love stories of all times. This metrical romance, which belongs to the tradition of German *Minnesang,* does not follow the line of chivalric romance developed by other writers, and there is no deadly repetition of knightly deeds of valor in war and tournaments. Instead, Gottfried celebrates romantic love deeper than chivalric love with its strict but conventional code of behavior; his conception of love is more inward, at once enchanting and enthralling, bewildering and ecstatic, one that sways the soul and makes martyrs of those who have partaken of love's sacrament. The landscape against which Tristan and Isolde move often suggests an inner dream world of motivation and compulsion.

The Story:

Rivalin, a lord of Parmenie, tired of baiting Duke Morgan, the wicked ruler, signed a year's truce and set off for Britain where King Mark of Cornwall was establishing peace and order. Badly wounded while fighting in the defense of Cornwall, Rivalin was pitied and nursed back to health by Mark's sister Blanchefleur, whom he took back to Parmenie as his bride. Later, hearing of Rivalin's death at Duke Morgan's hand, Blanchefleur went into labor, and died during the birth of her son. Rual, Rivalin's faithful steward, and his wife reared the boy out of loyalty to their dead lord and mistress and to thwart Duke Morgan's vindictiveness. The boy was named Tristan, in keeping with the sad events preceding his birth and a prophecy of grief to come.

Tristan's education was courtly, both at home and abroad; it included music, art, literature, languages, falconry, hunting, riding, knightly prowess with sword and spear, and jousting. These accomplishments he used to great advantage throughout his short life. He was loved deeply by his foster parents, his stepbrothers, and the people of Parmenie as well.

Kidnapped by Norwegians, Tristan managed to make his way to Cornwall after an eight-day storm at sea. He immediately attached himself to King Mark's court as a hunter, later the master of the hunt. When his royal lineage was revealed, he became his uncle's knight and vassal.

Known far and wide as a doughty knight, Tristan returned to avenge his father's death by defeating and killing

Duke Morgan; his lands he gave to Rual and his sons. Meanwhile, Duke Morolt of Ireland, who had exacted tribute from King Mark, demanded further payment or a fight to the death in single combat with the Cornish king. Tristan acted as King Mark's emissary to the Irish court, where his efforts to have Duke Morolt recall his demand for tribute were unsuccessful. Duke Morolt did agree, however, to let Tristan fight in King Mark's place. They met and fought in Cornwall. After wounding Tristan in the hip, Duke Morolt suggested that the young knight yield so that his sister Isolde, Queen of Ireland, could nurse him back to health. This offer was refused, and the fight waved fiercely again. Tristan finally sliced off Duke Morolt's head and hand.

Tristan, disguised as a beggar, went to Ireland to be cured. Calling himself Tantris, he ingratiated himself with Queen Isolde, who cured him of his hurt. Afterward he became the tutor in music and languages to her daughter, Isolde the Fair. When the young Isolde learned that he was the murderer of her uncle, the queen mother forgave him and allowed him to return to Cornwall.

In Cornwall, Tristan sang the praises of the Irish princess. Because King Mark had made the young knight his heir, some jealous noblemen, hoping to have Tristan slain, suggested that he return to Ireland and bring Isolde back as King Mark's bride. On his arrival in Ireland Tristan killed a dragon which had long ravished the kingdom. In gratitude, Queen Isolde entrusted her beautiful daughter to Tristan's care.

On the return voyage, Brangene, the faithful companion and cousin of Isolde the Fair, failed to guard carefully the love potion intended by the queen for Isolde and King Mark on their nuptial day. Tristan and the princess drank the potion and were thenceforth enslaved by love for each other. They both experienced conflicting duty and desire, turned red then white, became both depressed and exalted, and finally gave in to love. To deceive King Mark, Brangene stole into Isolde's bed so that Tristan and Isolde might meet in secret.

After some time had passed, Isolde grew apprehensive lest Brangene betray her, and she ordered her companion's death. Fortunately, the queen relented before Brangene could die, and all went on as before until the king was at last informed of Tristan's treachery. King Mark made many attempts to trap the lovers, meanwhile vacillating between trust and angry jealousy. Each time a trap was set, Tristan and Isolde proved their false innocence by some cunning ruse.

Finally the lovers were exiled. The king invited them to return, however, when he discovered them innocently asleep in a cave, a sword between them. Although King Mark urged propriety on their return to court, Tristan and Isolde almost immediately abandoned all caution, driven as they were by the caprices of love. Knowing that the king would have them killed if they were discovered, Tristan set out from Cornwall after accepting a ring from his beloved as a token of their fidelity to each other.

During his travels Tristan performed deeds of knightly valor in Germany, Champagne, and Normandy. In gratitude for his services in Normandy the duke gave him his daughter Isolde, called Isolde of the White Hands to distinguish her from Isolde the Fair, as his bride. Lovesick and dejected, Tristan accepted his bride in name only—the name Isolde.

(At this point Gottfried's narrative breaks off abruptly. From his source materials and from related versions, it is likely that Tristan was fatally wounded by a poisoned spear and that Isolde the Fair, summoned from Cornwall, arrived after her lover had died. Shock and grief caused her death also. King Mark, learning of the love potion, forgave them and ordered the lovers buried side by side in Cornwall.)

TRISTRAM

Type of work: Poem
Author: Edwin Arlington Robinson (1869-1935)
Type of plot: Chivalric romance
Time of plot: Arthurian period
Locale: England and Brittany
First published: 1927

Principal characters:
TRISTRAM, Prince of Lyonesse
MARK, his uncle, King of Cornwall
HOWEL, King of Brittany
ISOLT OF THE WHITE HANDS, Howel's daughter
ISOLT, Princess of Ireland
GOUVERNAIL, Tristram's friend
ANDRED, Mark's minion
QUEEN MORGAN, the wily queen

Critique:

The old Breton lay of *Tristram and Yseult* is here reworked with happy results. In Robinson's version the romance loses some of its air of remoteness and its rather stereotyped romantic convention, and we have, instead, a genuine love story with little except the names to remind us of the Middle Ages. The characters talk and think in a plausible manner which adds to the ease of reading. More than the modernization, however, Robinson tells the story with real lyric power. The use of symbolism, as in the quiet ship on a still ocean at the death of Tristram, brings vividness and appeal to the tale.

The Story:

Isolt of the white hands was too pensive and preoccupied for a young girl. Always she looked to the north, toward England, and her father, King Howel of Brittany, loved his daughter too much to let her attitude go unquestioned.

Isolt told her father she was waiting for Tristram, who some time before had made a visit to the Breton court. Fond of Isolt as a man is fond of a child, he had given her on his departure an agate for a keepsake and had promised to come back. Now Isolt was a woman of eighteen and she waited for Tristram as a woman waits for her lover. King Howel tried to tell her that Tristram thought of her as a child, and that he probably would not return; but Isolt would not be convinced.

In Cornwall it was the wedding day of old, lecherous King Mark and the dark and beautiful Isolt of Ireland, his bride. With the wedding feast in full swing, the wine cup was often passed. Sick of the drunken merriment and sicker with inner torment, Tristram, nephew of the king, left the feast and wandered in the fresh night air.

King Mark, displeased by his nephew's absence, sent Gouvernail, Tristram's preceptor and friend, to ask him to return. Tristram said only that he was sick. Then feline Queen Morgan came to talk to Tristram. She used all her arts and blandishments on the brooding knight, and they were cunning indeed, for Queen Morgan, much experienced in the arts of love, was more than a little attracted to Tristram. But Tristram repeated stubbornly that he was sick.

Then there was a soft step on the stair, as Brangwaine came, followed a moment later by dark-caped, violet-eyed Isolt of Ireland herself. She looked at Tristram but said nothing as he took her in his arms. Memories hung about them like a cloud.

King Mark was old and unattractive,

and he had wanted a young wife in his castle. Yearning for Isolt of Ireland, he had sent as emissary his gallant nephew, Tristram, to plead his cause. Tristram had to fight even to get to the Irish court. After he had slain the mighty Morhaus, Isolt's uncle, he made a bargain of state with the Irish king and took Isolt back to Cornwall in his boat. One night they were alone with only the sea and the stars to look upon them. Isolt waited in vain for Tristram to speak. If he had, she would have loved him then, and there would have been no marriage of convenience with King Mark. But bound by knightly fealty Tristram kept silent and delivered Isolt to his uncle. Now he looked at her and regretted bitterly that he had not spoken on the boat.

Andred stole behind them to spy on their love-making. He was a faithful servitor of King Mark, but jealousy of Tristram and love for Isolt motivated him as well. But Tristram saw Andred skulking in the shadow, seized him, and threw him heavily on the rocks. When King Mark himself came out to inquire about his absent guests, he stumbled over Andred's unconscious body and stood unseen long enough to hear the passionate avowals of Tristram and Isolt.

Since Tristram was his nephew, King Mark did not have him killed, but he banished Tristram forever from Cornwall on pain of burning at the stake.

The sick Tristram wandered in a fever. When he recovered, he found himself the captive of Queen Morgan in her castle. Queen Morgan eventually gave up her siege of Tristram's heart and let him go.

Next Tristram went to Brittany, where a griffin, giant scourge of the Breton land, was threatening King Howel and his court. Knightly Tristram, fierce in battle although sick for love, slew the griffin and put his hosts to flight. As a hero, Tristram had a secure place at King Howel's court, and there he married Isolt of the white hands. He pitied her and she loved him, although she

knew of his sorrow. For two years Tristram was a faithful husband and reigning prince.

Then from the north came another ship with Gawaine aboard bringing a message from King Arthur. For his deeds Tristram was to become a Knight of the Round Table; hence his summons to Camelot. Isolt watched her husband go with quiet despair, for she feared he would not come back. She had little dread of King Mark, for Gawaine had told her in secrecy that King Mark was in prison. The Cornish king had forged the Pope's signature on a paper ordering Tristram to go fight the Saracens, and his forgery had been detected. But somehow Isolt knew that Tristram's danger lay in Cornwall.

Guinevere, Arthur's queen, and her lover, Lancelot, plotted to bring Irish Isolt and Tristram together. Lancelot took Tristram to Joyous Guard, his trysting castle, and Guinevere brought Isolt of Ireland secretly out of Cornwall. So the lovers were together again, while King Mark was in prison.

They had a happy summer together and as autumn drew near Tristram lost a little of his apprehension. Early one morning he went out on the sea while Isolt slept. When he returned, there were strangers in Joyous Guard and Isolt was gone. King Mark, released from prison, had abducted his wife and carried her off to Cornwall.

Tristram moped in silence until he had a letter from Queen Morgan. She chided him for his lovesickness and urged him to see his Isolt once more. Goaded by the wily queen, Tristram rode to Cornwall prepared to fight and die for a last look at Isolt. But when he arrived at his uncle's castle, he entered easily and in surprised joy sought out Isolt. She told him that she was near death. King Mark, in pity for her wasting figure and sick heart, had given her permission to receive her lover. Isolt and Tristram, sad in their love because Isolt was to die, sat on the shore and gazed out at a still ship on the quiet ocean. While they sat thus, the jealous Andred crept up behind them and stabbed Tristram in the back. So Tristram died before Isolt after all. King Mark finally realized that Andred was also in love with Isolt, and he regretted that his lecherous lust for a young queen had brought sorrow and death to many lives.

Gouvernail went back to Brittany to convey the grievous news of Tristram's death to Isolt of the white hands, who divined the truth when he disembarked alone. He told her only part of Tristram's sojourn in England, only that Tristram had seen the dying Isolt of Ireland a last time with King Mark's consent, and that Andred had killed Tristram by treachery. Isolt was silent in her grief; no one could know what she was thinking, nor how much she divined of Tristram and the other Isolt.

Now Isolt looked no more for a ship from England. On the white sea the white birds and the sunlight were alive. The white birds were always flying and the sunlight flashed on the sea.

TRISTRAM SHANDY

Type of work: Novel
Author: Laurence Sterne (1713-1768)
Type of plot: Humorous sensibility
Time of plot: 1718-1766
Locale: Shandy Hall in England
First published: 1760-1767 (published in several books)

Principal characters:
TRISTRAM SHANDY, who tells the story
MR. WALTER SHANDY, his father
MR. TOBY SHANDY, his uncle, an old soldier
CORPORAL TRIM, Uncle Toby's servant
MR. YORICK, a parson
DR. SLOP, a medical quack
WIDOW WADMAN, a romantic widow

Critique:

The Life and Opinions of Tristram Shandy, Gentleman is one of the most amusing books ever written. In part, its humor derives from Sterne's delight in oddities of material and method. His pleasure in the unexpected creates surprise on almost every page. Memory and an intense sensibility combine to create the first true psychological novel in English literature. The organization of the novel is based on little more than Sterne's whims. Diagrams, unusual uses of type, and strange numbering of the pages are amusing pranks played by the author.

The Story:

Tristram Shandy, in telling the story of his earliest years, always believed that most of the problems of his life were brought about by the fact that the moment of his conception was interrupted when his mother asked his father if he had remembered to wind the clock. Tristram knew the exact date of his conception, the night between the first Sunday and the first Monday of March, 1718. He was certain of this date because, according to his father's notebook, Mr. Shandy set out immediately after this date to travel from Shandy Hall up to London. Before this date Mr. Shandy had been seriously inconvenienced by an attack of sciatica.

Another complication of Tristram's birth was the marriage settlement of his parents. According to this settlement,

quoted in full by Tristram, Mrs. Shandy had the privilege of going to London for her lying-in. But, if Mrs. Shandy were to put Mr. Shandy to the expense of a trip to London on false pretenses, then the next child was to be born at Shandy Hall. The circumstance of a needless trip to London having occurred some time before, Mr. Shandy stoutly insisted that Tristram should be born at Shandy Hall, the birth to be in the hands of a country midwife, rather than in those of a London doctor.

On the night of Tristram's birth, his father and his Uncle Toby were sitting in the living-room engaged in one of their interminable discussions and debates. Informed by Susannah, the maid, that Mrs. Shandy was about to be delivered of a child, they sent for the midwife. As an extra measure of safety, they sent also for Dr. Slop, a bungling country practitioner whom Mr. Shandy admired because he had written a five-shilling book on the history of midwifery. While the midwife attended Mrs. Shandy, the doctor would, for a fee of five guineas, drink a bottle of wine in the back parlor with Mr. Shandy and his brother, Toby.

Uncle Toby, who had been called the highest compliment ever paid human nature, had been a soldier until he was wounded during the siege of Namur in 1695. The wound, the exact position of which was to play such a large part in Tristram's story later on, forced him to retire to the country. There at the suggestion of his faithful servant, Corporal Trim, he had built, on a bowling green behind Shandy Hall, a large and complicated series of model fortifications and military emplacements. Uncle Toby's entire time was spent playing soldier and thinking about this miniature battlefield. It was his hobbyhorse, and he rode it continually with the greatest of pleasure. Mr. Shandy was not at all taken with his brother's hobby, and had to keep him from discussing it by violent interruptions so that he could himself continue, or start, one of his long and detailed digressions on obscure information.

As the two brothers sat awaiting the arrival of the midwife and her rival, Dr. Slop, Mr. Shandy made a rhetorical question of the subject of Mrs. Shandy's preference for a midwife rather than a male doctor. Uncle Toby suggested naïvely that modesty might explain her choice. This innocent answer led Mr. Shandy into a long discussion of the nature of women, and of the fact that everything in the world has two handles. Uncle Toby's innocence, however, always made it impossible for him to understand such affairs.

Dr. Slop, with his bag of tools, finally arrived. The midwife was already in attendance when he went up to see about the birth of the child. Meanwhile, to pass the time, Corporal Trim read a sermon aloud. Dr. Slop, in attending Mrs. Shandy, unfortunately mistook Tristram's hip for his head. In probing with his large forceps, he flattened what Tristram always referred to as his nose. This mistake Tristram blamed essentially on the affair of the winding of the clock mentioned earlier. This, and a later incident concerning the falling of a window sash when Tristram, still a little boy, was relieving himself through a window, brought about a problem in his anatomy which he mentioned often in his story of his life.

Between Tristram's birth and almost immediate baptism, Mr. Shandy entertained the company with a long story he had translated from the Latin of the old German writer, Slawkenbergius, a tale telling of the adventures of a man with an especially long nose. By the time Mr. Shandy had recovered from the bad news of the accident with the forceps, and had asked about his child, he learned that it was very sickly and weak; consequently he summoned Mr. Yorick, the curate, to baptize the child immediately. While rushing to get dressed to attend the ceremony, Mr. Shandy sent word to the parson by the maid, Susannah, to name the child Trismegistus, after an ancient philosopher who was a favorite of Mr. Shandy. Susannah forgot the name, however, and told Mr. Yorick to name the child Tristram. This name pleased the old man because it happened to be his own as well. When Mr. Shandy, still half unbuttoned, reached the scene, the evil had been done. Despite the fact that Mr. Shandy thought correct naming most important, his child was Tristram, a name Mr. Shandy believed the worst in the world. He lamented that he had lost three-fourths of his son in his unfortunate geniture, nose, and name. There remained only one fourth—Tristram's education.

Tristram managed to give a partial account of his topsy-turvy boyhood between many sidelights on the characters of his family. Uncle Toby continued to answer most of his brother's arguments by softly whistling Lillibullero, his favorite tune, and going out to the little battlefield to wage small wars with his servant, Corporal Trim. The next important event in the family was the death of Master Bobby, Tristram's older brother, who had been away at Westminster school. To this event Mr. Shandy reacted in his usual way by calling up all the philosophic ideas of the past on death and discoursing on them until he had adjusted himself to the new situation. The tragic news was carried to the kitchen staff and Susannah, despite a desire to show grief, could think of nothing but the wonderful wardrobe of dresses she would inherit when her mistress went into mourning. The vision of all Mrs. Shandy's dresses passed through her mind. Corporal Trim well demonstrated the transitory nature of life by dropping his hat, as if it had suddenly died, and then making an extemporaneous funeral oration.

After many more digressions on war, health, the fashions of ancient Roman dress, his father's doubts as to whether to get Tristram a tutor, and whether to put him into long trousers, Tristram proceeded to tell the history of his Uncle Toby, both in war and in love. Near Shandy Hall lived the Widow Wadman, who, after laying siege to Uncle Toby's affections for a long period, almost got him to propose marriage to her. But the gentle ex-soldier, who literally would not kill a fly, finally learned the widow's purpose when she began to inquire so pointedly into the extent and position of his wound. First he promised the widow that he would allow her to put her finger cn the very spot where he was wounded, and then he brought her a map of Namur to touch. Uncle Toby's innocence balked her real question until Corporal Trim finally told his master that it was the spot on his body, not the spot on the surface of the world where the accident took place, that was the point of the Widow Wadman's interest. This realization so embarrassed the old man that the idea of marriage disappeared from his mind forever. Tristram concluded his story with Parson Yorick's statement that the book had been one of the cock and bull variety, the reader having been led a mad, but merry, chase through the satirical and witty mind of the author.

THE TRIUMPH OF DEATH

Type of work: Novel
Author: Gabriele D'Annunzio (1863-1938)
Type of plot: Psychological romance
Time of plot: Nineteenth century
Locale: Italy
First published: 1894

Principal characters:
GEORGE AURISPA, a young Italian of wealth and family
SIGNOR AURISPA, George's materialistic father
HIPPOLYTE, George's mistress

Critique:

To a person of sensitivity, this novel by D'Annunzio may seem overdrawn. Because of its subject matter and florid style, sale of the book was prohibited in some countries. The result was to give D'Annunzio a tremendous underground reputation. Some critics have argued that the characters, except for Hippolyte, are types, particularly among the minor figures of the novel. The hero is the romantic Byronic hero in modern dress, a man who has never grown up because he has never had to take on responsibility or worry, because he has never had to methodize his life in any way. There are times when the story resembles a case history of one whose emotions have never matured with the body, a case history for the psychiatrist's notebook as much as a novel. Yet the book holds a power of its own. The lives of Hippolyte and George Aurispa represent both a triumph of romantic individualism and a failure of humanity and civilization.

The Story:

George Aurispa, a young Italian of old family and sufficient money to enjoy life without working, had fallen in love with a lovely married woman named Hippolyte. She had lived with her husband only a few weeks, for she had fallen ill shortly after her marriage. When the affair with George began, she left her husband and returned to her family. Marriage was out of the question for the lovers; because of religious reasons they could not marry as long as one or the other had a living spouse.

Infatuated, both George and Hippolyte often wished they could spend even more time together. But on the second anniversary of their first meeting an incident occurred which both regarded as an ill omen and which cast a pall over their minds. As they walked in Rome's Pincio gardens they came to a terrace where a man had just committed suicide. Blood and a lock of blond hair were still in evidence.

The suicide of the unknown young man in the Pincio affected the lovers even more than they realized at the time. George began to feel that materialism and sensuality, fostered by his love for Hippolyte, had taken too firm a hold upon him. Hippolyte, on the other hand, was warned again of her own mortality and the fact that she had a tendency toward epilepsy.

Soon afterward George was called home. His father and mother did not live together, and George had known for some time that his father kept a mistress. During the visit he learned for the first time the full story of his father's conduct. His mother told him that his father had despoiled the family fortune, refused a dowry for their daughter, and lived openly with his mistress and two illegitimate children. George disliked the financial entanglements of the situation; his own money he had inherited from an uncle. When George did visit his father to intercede for his family, the young man did nothing to help his mother and sister. Instead, he agreed to sign a note as surety for his father, who was trying to borrow money from a bank. George was struck, however, by the way his father had surrendered completely to a life of gross materialism.

Before he left his mother to return to Rome, George visited the apartment in the mansion where his uncle had lived. His uncle had committed suicide. The realization of his uncle's deed filled him with curiosity and melancholy, and he almost decided to kill himself with the same dueling pistol the uncle had used.

Returning to Rome, George again fell under the spell of Hippolyte, even though he was now haunted by his fear of gross sensuality, the thought of suicide, and a friend's warning that Hippolyte was coarse beneath her beauty and would someday find a richer lover.

In order to escape from his fears, George searched for a place where he and Hippolyte could be away from the world. He thought that in a small village on the Adriatic coast they could live in peace and he could work out his emotional and psychological problems.

But their new secluded life left George in even more of a quandary. There were times when he felt great happiness in being with his mistress day and night. At other times he saw in her only the embodiment of the same animal nature that was slowly but surely ensnaring him as it had ensnared his father. In order to escape, to achieve idealism, George once more considered taking his own life.

The Church offered no solution to his problem. Both he and Hippolyte were, in their way, devout. They visited shrines, but the mobs of humanity, the beggars with their sores and ills, only repulsed the lovers. Hippolyte's spell continued to work its way with George. She, proud of her power to awaken his desires, used this power constantly. George loved her and hated her at the same time, but he knew that he himself was not without blame. When their affair had begun, she was modest and almost frigid. Her husband, to whom she had been married by her family, had been brutal, and she had been ill. George, the first to stir her emotions, had helped to shape her personality.

Like all people living together, they discovered some irritating traits in each other. George was displeased with Hippolyte's feet, which he regarded as too common-looking. She, on the other hand, thought he was often too morbid. Both of them tried too hard, as they readily admitted, to escape into a world of pleasure and ideality.

Trying by all means to keep from antagonizing each other, they continued to make short excursions away from the village. George had a piano and music sent from Rome to their retreat. Still George found himself thinking not only of his death but of Hippolyte's as well. He sometimes believed that he could escape from sensuality only through the loss of his beloved. Death was the means he knew he must take to banish her irrevocably. She, for her part, seemed to realize what was in his mind. She had dreams in which she saw him dead or taking threatening attitudes toward her. Again, in George's mind, she was the most beautiful and fascinating of women, for her power over him continued to grow. Often, when he was emotionally distressed, she could draw him from that state of mind with nothing more than a kiss.

One afternoon, while they were swimming, George had an impulse to drown Hippolyte. She seemed to sense his mood and refused to go bathing with him again. One night they had a pleasant meal together. Later that evening, with great effort on his part, so strong was her physical charm at such a time, George persuaded his mistress to take a walk down to the rocky coast where fishermen were working at their nets. When they came to a one-plank bridge over which they had to walk, Hippolyte, growing dizzy at the sight of waves and rocks below, refused to cross. But George, feeling that he had found the time and place for his despairing deed, swept Hippolyte into his arms and plunged both of them to death on the rocks many feet below.

TROILUS AND CRESSIDA

Type of work: Drama
Author: William Shakespeare (1564-1616)
Type of plot: Realistic comedy
Time of plot: Trojan War
Locale: Troy
First presented. 1601-1602

> Principal characters:
> PRIAM, King of Troy
> HECTOR, and
> TROILUS, his sons
> AGAMEMNON,
> ACHILLES,
> ULYSSES,
> AJAX, and
> DIOMEDES, Greek commanders
> PANDARUS, a Trojan lord
> CRESSIDA, his niece

Critique:

The apparent last-minute inclusion of *The History of Troilus and Cressida* in the First Folio (1623), between the histories and the tragedies, has tended to put this play in an anomalous position in the opinion of commentators ever since. *Troilus and Cressida* has been called a satire, a comedy, a history, and a tragedy. The truth probably is that it is a little of all of these. Certainly, it is a comedy of disillusionment and bitterness. It would seem clear, however, that Shakespeare, in his unusual handling of the traditional elements of the *Iliad*, was in his own way, perhaps, commenting on the fading splendor of the Age of Elizabeth. Shakespeare knew the story from the pages of Chaucer and Henryson; but, where Chaucer and Henryson gave the story medieval color, Shakespeare transferred his Troy to the decadent days of the late Renaissance.

The Story:

During the Trojan War, Troilus, younger son of Priam, King of Troy, fell in love with the lovely and unapproachable Cressida, daughter of Calchas, a Trojan priest who had gone over to the side of the Greeks. Troilus, frustrated by his unrequited love, declared to Pandarus, a Trojan lord and uncle of Cressida, that he would refrain from fighting

the Greeks as long as there was such turmoil in his heart. Pandarus added to Troilus' misery by praising the incomparable beauty of Cressida; Troilus impatiently chided Pandarus, who answered that for all it mattered to him Cressida could join her father in the Greek camp.

Later, Pandarus overheard Cressida and her servant discussing Hector's anger at having received a blow in battle from Ajax, a mighty Greek warrior of Trojan blood. Pandarus extolled Troilus' virtues to Cressida, who was all but indifferent. As the two discoursed, the Trojan forces returned from the field. Pandarus praised the several Trojan warriors—Aeneas, Antenor, Hector, Paris, Helenus—as they passed by Cressida's window, all the while anticipating, for Cressida's benefit, the passing of young Troilus. When the prince passed, Pandarus was lavish in his praise, but Cressida appeared to be bored. As Pandarus left her to join Troilus, Cressida soliloquized that she was charmed, indeed, by Troilus, but that she was in no haste to reveal the state of her affections.

In the Greek camp, meanwhile, Agamemnon, commander of the Greek forces in Ilium, tried to put heart into his demoralized leaders. Old Nestor declared that the seven difficult years of the siege of Troy had been a real test of

Greek stamina. It was the belief of Ulysses that the difficulties of the Greeks lay in a lack of order and discipline, not Trojan strength. He reminded his fellow Greek leaders that the disaffection of mighty Achilles and the scurrilous clowning of Patroclus, a Greek leader, had provoked disorder in the Greek ranks. Even Ajax, usually dependable, had become fractious, and his follower, deformed Thersites, embarrassed the Greeks with his taunts.

As the Greek leaders conferred, Aeneas delivered to them a challenge from Hector, who in single combat would defend the beauty and the virtue of his lady against a Greek champion. When the leaders went their several ways to announce the challenge to Achilles and to other Greeks, Ulysses and Nestor decided that the only politic action to take, the pride of Achilles being what it was, was to arrange somehow that Ajax be chosen to fight Hector. Ajax, Achilles, and Patroclus heard of the proclamation, but tended to disregard it. Their levity caused the railing Thersites to break with them.

In Troy, meanwhile, Hector was tempted to concede to a Greek offer to end hostilities if the Trojans returned Helen to her husband, King Menelaus. Troilus chided his brother and Helenus for their momentary want of resolution. As the brothers and their father, Priam, discussed the reasons for and against continuing the war, Cassandra, prophetess and daughter of Priam, predicted that Troy would be burned to the ground by the Greeks. Hector heeded her warning, but Troilus, joined by Paris, persisted in the belief that the war, for the sake of honor, must be continued. Hector, although aware of the evil the Trojans were committing in defending Paris' indefensible theft of Helen from her husband, conceded that for reasons of honor the fighting must go on.

The Greek leaders approached Achilles, who had kept to himself since his quarrel with Agamemnon. Refusing to confer with them, Achilles retired into his tent and sent his companion, Patroclus, to make his apologies. At Achilles' persistent refusal to deal with the Greek commanders, who sought in him their champion against Hector, Ulysses played on the pride of Ajax with subtle flattery and convinced this Greek of Trojan blood that he should present himself as the Greek champion in place of Achilles.

In the meantime Pandarus had prepared the way for a tryst between Troilus and Cressida by securing the promise of Paris and Helen to make excuses for Troilus' absence. He brought the two young people together in his orchard, where the pair confessed to each other their undying love. Cressida declared that if she were ever false, then all falsehood could forever afterwards be associated with her name. Pandarus witnessed these sincere avowals of faith and himself declared that if Troilus and Cressida did not remain faithful to each other, then all go-betweens would be associated with his name. These declarations having been made, Pandarus led the young people to a bedchamber in his house.

In the Greek camp, Calchas, Cressida's father, persuaded Agamemnon to exchange Antenor, a Trojan prisoner, for Cressida, whose presence he desired. Diomedes, a Greek commander, was appointed to effect the exchange.

Planning to ignore Achilles, the Greek leaders passed the warrior with only the briefest recognition. When he demanded an explanation of that treatment, Ulysses told him that fame was ephemeral and that great deeds were soon forgotten. Fearful for his reputation, now that Ajax had been appointed Greek champion, Achilles arranged to play host to the unarmed Hector after the contest.

Diomedes returned Antenor to Troy, and at dawn he was taken to Pandarus' house to escort Cressida to the Greek camp. When Troilus and Cressida learned of Diomedes' mission, Troilus appealed unsuccessfully to the Trojan leaders to allow Cressida to remain in Troy. Heartbroken, he returned to Cressida and the young couple repeated their vows in their farewells. Troilus then escorted Cressida and Diomedes, who commented on Cressida's beauty, as far as the city gates. When Diomedes and Cressida encountered the Greek leaders outside the walls, Cressida was kissed by Agamemnon, Menelaus, Nestor, Patroclus, and others. Ulysses observed that she appeared wanton.

Warriors of both sides assembled to watch Hector and Ajax fight. The two companions clashed for only a moment before Hector desisted, declaring that he could not harm Ajax, his cousin. Ajax accepted Hector's magnanimity and invited the Trojan to join, unarmed, the Greek commanders at dinner. Hector, accompanied by Troilus, was welcomed among the Greeks with many warm compliments, but Achilles, meeting Hector, rudely mentioned that part of Hector's person in which he would one day inflict a mortal wound. Stung by Achilles' pride and lack of manners, Hector declared hotly that he would destroy all of Achilles at one stroke. The result was an agreement to meet in combat the next day. Ajax managed to calm heated tempers, however, and the feasting began.

Troilus, anxious to see his beloved Cressida, asked Ulysses where he might find Calchas, and Ulysses promised to be his guide. After the banquet they followed Diomedes to Calchas's tent, where Cressida met him and in affectionate overtures toward Diomedes revealed to the hidden Troilus that she had already all but forgotten him. As she gave Diomedes, as a token of her love, a sleeve that had belonged to Troilus, compunction seized her for a moment. But she quickly succumbed to Diomedes' charms and promised to be his at their next meeting. Diomedes left, vowing to kill in combat the Trojan whose sleeve he would be wearing on his helmet. Troilus, unable to believe that Cressida was the girl whom he loved so passionately, returned to Troy. He vowed to take the life of Diomedes.

As the new day approached, Hector was warned by Andromache, his wife, and by his sister Cassandra not to do battle that day; all portents foretold disaster. When their words proved ineffectual, King Priam tried vainly to persuade Hector to remain within the walls. During the battle Diomedes unhorsed Troilus and sent the horse as a gift to Cressida. Despite his overthrow, Troilus continued to fight heroically. Hector appeared to be, for his part, invincible. When Patroclus was severely wounded in the action, Achilles, enraged, ordered his followers, the Myrmidons, to stand by. As the action subsided, and Hector was unarming himself at the end of the day, the Myrmidons, at Achilles' command, closed in on brave Hector and felled him with their spears.

Troilus announced to the retiring Trojan forces that Hector had been killed by treachery and that his body, tied to the tail of Achilles' horse was being dragged around the Phrygian plain. As he made his way to the gates, he predicted general mourning in Troy and expressed his undying hatred for the Greeks. He encountered Pandarus, whom he abruptly dismissed as a cheap pander, a man whose name would be infamous forever.

TROILUS AND CRISEYDE

Type of work: Poem
Author: Geoffrey Chaucer (1340?-1400)
Type of plot: Chivalric romance
Time of plot: Trojan War
Locale: Troy
First transcribed: c. 1382

Principal characters:
TROILUS, young prince of Troy
CRISEYDE, a young widow
PANDARUS, Troilus' friend and Criseyde's uncle
DIOMEDES, a Greek warrior

Critique:

Troilus and Criseyde, the only long work completed by Chaucer, is based on the legend of the Trojan War. The characters, however, behave in the best tradition of the medieval court of love. As an incomparable teller of tales, and as a great poet, Chaucer combined his two talents to produce this almost perfectly constructed narrative poem. The effective depiction of character and its development in the poem forecast the shrewd observations of human nature made by Chaucer in the prologue to The Canterbury Tales.

The Story:

Calchas, a Trojan prophet, divining that Troy was doomed to defeat, fled to the Greeks. He left behind him his beautiful daughter, Criseyde, a young widow.

One day in April the citizens of Troy were observing the rites of the spring festival. Among those in the temple was Troilus, a younger son of King Priam of Troy. Troilus, scornful of the Trojan swains and their lovesickness at this season, saw Criseyde for the first time and fell deeply in love with her. Sick with the love malady he had always scorned, Troilus invoked the god of love to have pity on him. Feeling that he had no hope of winning Criseyde, he became the scourge of the Greeks on the battlefield.

Pandarus, friend of Troilus, offered his advice and help when he learned that Troilus had lost his heart to a beauti-ful Trojan. When Troilus at length disclosed that his lady was the fair Criseyde, Pandarus offered to become a go-between, a service he was well able to perform since he was Criseyde's uncle.

Pandarus called on his niece to gossip with her. They discussed Priam's sons and Pandarus praised the bravery of Troilus. Subtly he disclosed to Criseyde that young Troilus was dying for love of her. Criseyde, suspecting that the intentions of neither Troilus nor Pandarus were honorable, cried out in distress at this information, but Pandarus soon convinced her that Troilus' love was pure. She felt herself drawn to the prince when she beheld his modesty as he rode past her house after a day of battle outside the walls of Troy. She decided, after much inner turmoil, that it would not be dishonorable to show friendship to Troilus in order to save the young man's life.

At the suggestion of Pandarus, Troilus wrote a letter to Criseyde. Impressed, she wrote a restrained letter in return. When Troilus, wishing to be with Criseyde, soon tired of this correspondence, Pandarus arranged a meeting by asking Deiphobus, brother of Troilus, to invite the pair to his house for dinner. After the dinner Criseyde gave the miserable prince permission to be in her service and to adore her.

Pandarus, eager to bring about a private meeting of the lovers, studied the stars and decided on a night which would be propitious for their tryst. He

3901

invited Criseyde to dine with him on that evening. Troilus was already hidden in his house. As the lady prepared to take her leave, it began to rain and Pandarus persuaded her to stay. So through Pandarus' wiles the lovers were brought together. After yielding, Criseyde gave Troilus a brooch as a token of their love.

About that time a great battle was fought between the Greeks and the Trojans and several of the Trojan leaders were captured. In an exchange of prisoners Calchas persuaded the Greeks to ask for Criseyde in return for Antenor, a Trojan warrior. The Trojan parliament, after much debate, approved of the transaction. Hector, another brother of Troilus, argued that Criseyde should remain in Troy, but without success. Troilus was in despair, and Criseyde prepared to be separated from her lover.

Pandarus brought the lovers together secretly after plans for the exchange had been made. Criseyde, broken-hearted, told the prince that their separation would not be for long, and that she would remain faithful to him.

Troilus and his party accompanied Criseyde to the place appointed for the exchange. There they met Antenor and conducted him to Troy, while Diomedes, a young Greek warrior, led Criseyde away to the Greek camp. Troilus returned to Troy to await the passing of ten days, at the end of which time Criseyde had promised she would return. But Diomedes had seduced the fair Criseyde by the tenth day. She gave him a brooch she had received from Troilus at their parting; Diomedes gave her a horse he had captured from Troilus in battle.

After several weeks of anxious waiting, Troilus wrote to Criseyde. She answered him, avowing weakly her love for him and saying that she would return to Troy at the earliest opportunity. Troilus, sensing that something was amiss, grieved. One day he saw the brooch which he had given Criseyde on a piece of armor taken from Diomedes on the battlefield. Knowing that Criseyde had forsaken him for another, Troilus sought out and fought Diomedes indecisively many times. Eventually the unhappy Troilus was killed by mighty Achilles.

THE TROJAN WOMEN

Type of work: Drama
Author: Euripides (c. 485-c. 406 B.C.)
Type of plot: Classical tragedy
Time of plot: Age of the Trojan War
Locale: Before the ruined walls of Troy
First presented: 415 B.C.

Principal characters:
POSEIDON, god of the sea and patron of Troy
PALLAS ATHENA, goddess of wisdom
HECUBA, Queen of Troy
CASSANDRA, her daughter, a prophetess
ANDROMACHE, wife of Hector, prince of Troy
HELEN, Queen of Sparta abducted by Paris
MENELAUS, King of Sparta
TALTHYBIUS, herald of the Greeks
CHORUS OF THE CAPTIVE TROJAN WOMEN

Critique:

The Trojan Women (the *Troades*) has more pathos and emotional tension than any other play by Euripides. It is not, strictly speaking, an Aristotelian tragedy, for it has no central tragic figure; neither is it simply a tragic pageant. The Greek warriors collectively constitute the tragic hero in that they commit *hubris* by defiling the Trojan temples and brutally murdering the innocent. At the end of the play their doom awaits them. This compelling presentation of the utter folly of mass warfare and genocide speaks eloquently to the twentieth century. No doubt Euripides was moved to write the play in protest against the Athenian massacre of all the males and the enslavement of the women and children of Melos in 415 B.C., when that unfortunate city sought to remain neutral in the war against Sparta. The *Troades* is the only surviving play of a trilogy that included *Alexandros* (another name for Paris), which dealt with the refusal of Priam and Hecuba to murder the infant Paris as commanded by the oracle's prediction that he would be the ruin of Troy, and *Palamedes*, which dealt with the treachery of the Greek leaders who murdered Palamedes before Troy. In the *Troades* the Greek and Trojan lines of tragedy are merged.

The Story:

On the second morning after the fall of Troy and the massacre of all its male inhabitants, Poseidon appeared to lament the ruins and vow vengeance against the Greeks. To his surprise, Pallas Athena, the goddess who had aided the Greeks, joined him in plotting a disastrous homeward voyage for the victors who had despoiled her temple in Troy. They withdrew as Hecuba rose from among the sleeping Trojan women to mourn the burning city and her dead sons and husband. The chorus joined her in chanting an anguished lament.

Talthybius, the herald of the Greeks, arrived to announce that Agamemnon had chosen Cassandra to be his concubine and that the other royal women of Troy had been assigned by lot—Polyxena to the tomb of Achilles, Andromache to Achilles' son Neoptolemus, and Hecuba herself to Odysseus, King of Ithaca and conceiver of the wooden horse that had led to the fall of the city. Amid the cries of the grieving women Cassandra appeared, bearing a flaming torch in each hand. The chorus was convinced that she had gone mad as she danced and prayed to Hymen, god of Marriage, that Agamemnon take her soon to Argos as his bride, for there she would cause his death and the ruin of his entire family. As for Odysseus, she foretold that he would suffer for ten more years on the seas before reaching his homeland. As Talthybius led her off, he observed that Agamemnon himself must have been mad to fall in love with the insane Cassandra.

Hecuba, broken with grief, collapsed to the ground. From the city came a Greek-drawn chariot loaded with the spoils of war and bearing Andromache and her infant son Astyanax. Cursing Helen, the cause of all their woe, Andromache called upon the dead Hector to come to her and announced enviously that Polyxena had just been killed upon the tomb of Achilles as a gift to the dead hero. Drawing upon her last remaining strength, Hecuba tried to comfort the distraught Andromache and urged that instead of mourning for Hector she win the love of Neoptolemus so that her son might grow to manhood and perhaps redeem Troy. At this point the reluctant herald Talthybius announced the Greeks' order that the son of so distinguished a warrior as Hector must not be permitted to reach manhood but must be killed at once by being hurled from the battlements of Troy. As Talthybius led away Andromache and her son, a fresh lament and cursing of Helen went up from the grieving women of Troy.

Suddenly King Menelaus came striding in the sunlight with his retinue to demand that his faithless wife Helen be dragged to him by her blood-reeking hair. Hecuba pleaded with him to slay Helen at once, lest her beauty and feminine wiles soften his will, but Menelaus remained determined to take her back to Greece, where the relatives of those who died for her sake might have the pleasure of stoning her to death. Helen approached, calm and dignified. Her plea for the right to speak being supported by Hecuba, she argued that she was not responsible for the fall of Troy. The first blame must be attributed to Priam and Hecuba, who refused to kill the infant Paris as the oracle commanded; the second to Aphrodite, who bewitched her into submitting to Paris; the third to Deiphobus and the Trojan guards who prevented her from escaping to the Greeks after she had come to her senses. Goaded on by the chorus of Trojan women, Hecuba jeered at these claims, insisting that the gods would not have been so foolish as Helen would have them believe, that her own lust drove her into Paris' arms, and that she could always have escaped Troy and her own shame by way of suicide. Helen, falling to her knees, pleaded with Menelaus not to kill her. Hecuba also knelt to beg Helen's immediate death and to warn Menelaus against taking her aboard his ship. Menelaus compromised: Helen would return to Greece on another ship and there pay for her shameful life. As Menelaus led her away, the chorus wailed that Zeus had forsaken them.

Talthybius then returned, bearing the crushed body of Astyanax on Hector's shield. He told Hecuba that Andromache, as she was being led aboard Neoptolemus' ship, had begged that the infant be given proper burial. The performance of that rite was more than Hecuba could bear, and she had to be restrained by force from throwing herself into the flames of the city. As the captive women were led off to the Greek ships, the great crash of Troy's collapsing walls was heard and the city was engulfed in smoke and darkness.

THE TRUE HISTORY

Type of work: Prose romance
Author: Lucian (c. 120-c. 200)
Type of plot: Satiric fantasy
Time of plot: Second century
Locale: The universe
First transcribed: Second century

Principal characters:
  LUCIAN
  ENDYMION, King of the Moon
  PHAETHON, King of the Sun
  SCINTHARUS, an inhabitant of the whale's belly

Critique:

Poking fun at exaggerated travel books like Antonius Diogenes' *The Marvels of Ultima Thule* and others now lost, Lucian, called by Macaulay "the last great master of Attic eloquence and Attic wit," wrote in *The True History* a two-part parody that greatly influenced Rabelais and Swift. Because Lucian was also known as a writer of satirical dialogues mocking many beliefs of the people, the story originated that he was torn to pieces by dogs in Egypt. In an explanatory prologue to this work Lucian declared that athletes alternate severe exercise with relaxation. Intellectuals should do the same, he maintained, and alternate serious reading with that which is witty and entertaining. And so he wrote *The True History*, "with a novelty of subject and excellence in design," and for the purpose of telling lies in a plausible way and parodying the exaggerations of certain writers that he "need not name because the enlightened reader could easily recognize the originals." Because the creatures he was going to describe could not possibly exist, he hoped all his readers would disbelieve him.

The Story:

Heading westward from the Pillars of Hercules, Lucian in his sloop with a crew of fifty finally reached the Atlantic Ocean. Filled with a thirst for adventure and an intellectual restlessness to see what was on the other side of the world, he found the first day of the voyage delightful. Then came a terrible storm that drove the ship before it for seventy-nine days. On the eighteenth day the adventurers came to a lofty wooded island and went ashore.

After resting, twenty sailors accompanied Lucian on an exploration of the island. They discovered a bronze tablet announcing that Hercules and Dionysius had been there, and they saw two huge footprints. They also discovered that the river had its source in a grape arbor and contained Chian wine. Eating the fish that swam in it made them drunk.

The inhabitants of the island were women, human from the waist up, but growing on vines. When several of the crew became too friendly with these creatures, the sailors soon found themselves tangled in the vines and taking root; and so they had to be left behind.

Filling their casks with wine and water, the survivors set sail, only to run into a whirlwind that whipped the sloop hundreds of miles into the air. A week later the ship was thrown upon the moon, which was inhabited by men riding vultures. The king, Endymion, enlisted the service of the Greeks in his war against Phaethon and his people of the sun.

The mighty invasion force was made up of eighty thousand vulture-riding cavalry and twenty thousand troops riding birds covered with grass and having lettuce leaves for wings. This vegetarian force had armor of vegetable husks, but Greek swords. Among their allies were fighters from other constellations astride monster fleas.

The army of the sun rode flying ants, gnats, and mosquitoes. Some hurled radish bombs, others wielded asparagus spears. But they were no match for the lunar troops until centaur reinforcements arrived, so numerous that the number could not be set down for fear of creating incredulity. When the moon army was put to flight, Lucian and his friends were captured and bound with spiderwebs.

To bring the Moon People to terms, Phaethon erected a cloud screen. Cut off from sunlight, the moon troops soon surrendered. The terms of capitulation were inscribed on a slab of electrum. With the coming of peace, Lucian had time to explore the moon and note its wonders.

Homeward bound, the Greeks paused at Lamptown, inhabited by lanterns, and at Cloud-Cuckooland, where Lucian verified the details of Aristophanes' comedy, *The Birds*. Finally the travelers reached the ocean again, only to have their sloop swallowed by a huge whale. In its belly, amid a clutter of wrecked ships, they found Scintharus, who was raising vegetables on an island. He had lived there for twenty-seven years, ever since leaving Cyprus.

There were many other inhabitants, all quarrelsome and unjust. Some had eel eyes and lobster faces; others were half men and half animals. Since their only weapons were fishbones, Lucian decided to attack them. The creatures were all slain in two battles in which the Greeks suffered only one casualty; the sailing master was stabbed with a mullet spine.

One day, after living in the whale for a year and eight months, the Greeks heard a loud uproar in the outside world.

Peering between the whale's teeth, they watched a naval battle of giants who manned floating islands and fought with oysters and sponges.

At last the Greeks conceived a scheme to gain their liberty. They set fire to the forest inside the whale; then, as the creature was about to suffocate, they wedged open his jaws and sailed out, with Scintharus as pilot. But they did not get far, for a north wind froze the ocean. They lived in a cave they hollowed in the ice until, after a month, it occurred to them to hoist the sails and let the ship glide across the smooth ice to open water.

Sailing in a sea of milk, they took on provisions at a cheese island. They stopped at the Isle of the Blessed and watched a lawsuit between Theseus and Menelaus for the custody of Helen. While the hearing was in progress, Helen ran off with a new sweetheart, aided by some of Lucian's crew; and the tourists were deported. Lucian, however, did have time to consult Homer on moot points concerning his life and writing, and to catalogue the famous Greeks who inhabited the isle. Also, he witnessed a prison break by the damned and watched the heroic exploits of Achilles in recapturing them.

Again voyaging, the travelers passed a place of punishment for liars. Herodotus was there, but Lucian knew he was safe because he had never written anything but the truth. The company spent a month at the Port of Dreams, and also paused briefly to take Calypso a note from Odysseus. Pirates attacked them several times, but the travelers finally reached safety in a land which Lucian recognized as the continent facing his world.

TRUTH SUSPECTED

Type of work: Drama
Author: Juan Ruiz de Alarcón (c. 1581-1639)
Type of plot: Thesis comedy
Time of plot: Seventeenth century
Locale: Madrid
First published: 1628

> *Principal characters:*
> DON GARCÍA, a young man given to lying
> DON BELTRÁN, his father
> TRISTÁN, his servant
> JUAN DE SOSA, a friend, in love with Jacinta
> JACINTA, niece of Don Sancho, Don Beltrán's friend
> LUCRECIA, her friend

Critique:

Mexican-born, Juan Ruiz de Alarcón became one of the leading dramatists of the Golden Age in Spain. The twenty-six plays now identified as his are divided into two groups. His early plays, in keeping with the romantic tradition, are marked by complicated plots. His later works are more concerned with the human qualities of his characters and less with dramatic situations; some critics attribute to his Mexican background this departure from the current conventions of the theater. His two best plays belong to his second period. *Walls Have Ears* attacks slander, and *Truth Suspected* presents an excellent character study of a congenital liar. The latter play inspired Corneille's *Le Menteur* (1643).

The Story:

When Don García returned home from studies at the University of Salamanca, he learned that on the death of his brother Gabriel he had become the heir to the family estates and fortune. His father also provided him with a shrewd and cynical servant, Tristán. Don García's tutor had already reported that the young man was given to one great vice: lying. Later his discerning servant agreed. The son's habit naturally worried his father, himself a man of great honor. Though he admitted that regard for truth was uncommon at the court of Spain, he hated the vice of lying above all others, and he vowed to break his son of the habit.

During his first day in Madrid, Don García indulged in his practice after meeting two attractive women in the shopping center of the city. Taking his cue from Tristán's remark that the women of Madrid were money-mad, the young gallant told them that he was a wealthy man from the New World. Though he had been in Madrid hardly a day, he assured one of the women that he had worshiped her from afar for a year. Unfortunately, he had misunderstood the information bought from their coachman by Tristán; he thought the girl he wanted to marry was Lucrecia, but the object of his attentions was really her friend Jacinta.

More lying followed when Don García met his friend, Juan de Sosa, a young man in love with Jacinta but rejected by her uncle until he acquired a knighthood. This time, falsely claiming responsibility for a serenade and banquet the preceding night, Don García found himself challenged to a duel by Juan.

In the meantime, hoping to get his son married off before Madrid learned of his habit of lying, Don Beltrán, after giving him a lecture on the value of truth, told him he had arranged for his marriage to Jacinta, niece of his old friend, Don Sancho. Since Don García thought it was Lucrecia whom he loved, he promptly invented a prodigious lie about his marriage to a lady of Salamanca. He declared that while visiting her one night, he had been

3907

discovered by the lady's father; to save her reputation and life, he had agreed to marry her.

Lucrecia, to help Jacinta decide which of her suitors she preferred, signed her name to a note inviting Don García to wait beneath her balcony. During his talk with the veiled ladies, his earlier story about a wife in Salamanca and his uncertainty as to which of the veiled women was the one he loved resulted in their ridicule and scorn. Rudely dismissed, he received from Tristán a lecture on the evils of lying.

More lying was necessary when Don Beltrán attempted to send for his son's wife. She could not travel, Don García told him; she was going to have a baby. Although he laughed at Tristán's warning that "one who lies needs a quick wit and a good memory," his punishment had already begun. When Lucrecia invited him to another meeting at a convent, he found himself trapped in a mesh of deceit, and the veiled ladies showed how unsuccessful had been his wooing. Tristán contributed to his unhappiness by many quotations from Latin and Greek writers. The servant also remarked that he could see no sense to his master's lies when they were so easily discovered.

But even Tristán was fooled by Don García's account of his supposed duel with Juan de Sosa; actually he had placated his former friend by telling more lies. It would have been better had he silenced his challenger on the dueling field, for Juan now appeared to tell Don Beltrán that no one with the name of Don García's supposed wife lived in Salamanca. So incensed was the father that he was about to disinherit his son. Even by telling the truth, Don García could not convince him without corroboration from Tristán. The word of a servant was more trustworthy than the oath of a nobleman, the ashamed father pointed out.

When Juan's attainment of knighthood cleared away that obstruction to his suit, Don Sancho gladly arranged for the young man's marriage to Jacinta; and that lady, disillusioned and dubious of a lying suitor, was happy to agree with her uncle's decision. Don Beltrán, too, was won over, and he agreed to arrange for his son's delayed marriage. But when the suitors were paired off, Don García saw his lady go to his rival. Even though the whole affair had been based on misunderstanding, it was now too late to correct the mistake. Don García must in honor bound marry Lucrecia.

Tristán again underlined a moral when he assured his master that if he had told the truth instead of lying he would now be happy with Jacinta. However, Lucrecia was also beautiful.

TURCARET

Type of work: Drama
Author: Alain René Le Sage (1668-1747)
Type of plot: Social comedy
Time of plot: Seventeenth century
Locale: Paris
First presented: 1709

Principal characters:
    M. TURCARET, a financier, in love with the Baroness
    MME. TURCARET, his wife
    THE BARONESS, a young widow and a coquette
    FRONTIN, the Knight's valet
    THE KNIGHT, a coxcomb
    THE MARQUESS, another coxcomb
    MARINE, and
    LISETTE, maidservants to the Baroness
    MME. JACOB, a dealer in toilette necessaries, sister to M. Turcaret
    FLAMAND, M. Turcaret's valet

Critique:

In *Turcaret, or, The Financier* action never lags; lines never drag. This type of French satirical comedy is marked by the main features of earthy realism, an almost didactic purpose, and photographic characterizations, and *Turcaret* is a classic of its kind. The satire is founded both in personalities and in national conditions. The title character is the profiteer, whose altruism is nonexistent and whose wealth is his only merit. Those who ingratiate themselves for favors from this parvenu are no more admirable than he is. Through the relationships of the various characters, Le Sage presents a clear picture of the social disintegration which began in the last years of Louis XIV, of the clumsy fiscal system of seventeenth-century France, and of the demoralized attitude of the French resulting from the military disasters of the war with England and Austria.

The Story:

M. Turcaret lavished gifts and immense sums of money upon the Baroness, whom he had asked to marry him. The Baroness in turn poured equal amounts into the pockets of the wheedling Knight. Marine admonished her mistress to use her reasoning. The discerning Marine knew the Baroness' motivation in keeping the Knight. He had been the first to offer her, a widow, love. Marine outlined a judicious pattern for the Baroness: drop the Knight, because M. Turcaret might not like the idea of her having "friends" and accept M. Turcaret's gifts. Then, should he not want to marry her, she would have wealth and possessions and could marry some needy gentleman. To be sure, the world might talk a little about her rejection by M. Turcaret, but a husband, needy or not, could restore her reputation by marriage.

An early gift was a small coffer, delivered by Flamand, M. Turcaret's valet. It contained two notes: one a bill of exchange for ten thousand crowns and written by M. Turcaret; the other a quatrain, dedicated to the Baroness. Marine was anxious to read the verse of the second to see whether it was as good as the prose of the first.

Enraged by her mistress' gullibility with the Knight, Marine quit her job with the Baroness. She announced, in quitting, that she would report to M. Turcaret that the Baroness was little more than the middleman for his money, as it passed from M. Turcaret to the Knight.

Frontin quipped that such a servant as Marine with all her righteousness was worse than a mother. As to her exposing them to M. Turcaret, Frontin added that waiting maids were like pious ladies performing their charitable deeds as a means of avenging themselves. Frontin knew exactly the young woman, Lisette, to replace Marine as the Baroness' maid.

To show her animosity for M. Turcaret and her kind thoughts for the Knight, the Baroness gave the Knight the ten-thousand-crown note given her by M. Turcaret to redeem her diamond ring (also a gift from M. Turcaret), which she had given the distraught Knight to pawn so that he might pay a gambling debt.

Frontin gave a succinct summary of the life of the times, when he traced the source of income. He and the Knight had a coquette who milked the man of affairs who made his money pillaging the taxpayers. It made, he thought, a diverting circumstance of trickery.

The Knight returned the ring, but not the change from the note. His action was timely, as M. Turcaret, having heard Marine's story of the Baroness' generosity toward the Knight, appeared and asked to see the ring. When the Baroness produced it, Marine's report to M. Turcaret was undermined. The ring incident served as *prima facie* evidence that the Baroness had the note also. M. Turcaret became putty in the Baroness' hands as she reprimanded him for believing Marine's report.

M. Turcaret's undisciplined character was demonstrated fully, just prior to this scene of abject apology, as he went about the Baroness' room smashing her largest mirror and her finest porcelains. This outburst, he said, gave him a little relief. He restored the damage with costly replacements.

Taking full advantage of M. Turcaret's subservience, the Baroness told him that she wished Frontin to replace Flamand in his service. M. Turcaret observed that Frontin's countenance was marked by honesty; he asked Frontin whether he had principles. Asked what he meant, M. Turcaret explained that he meant clerk's principles—such as knowledge of the single entry system. Frontin stated his qualifications as adeptness at two handwritings, ability with double

entry, and a knowledge of preventing frauds or countenancing them—as M. Turcaret's advantage would require.

When Lisette reported as the Baroness' maid, it was apparent that she would be active in the financial intrigue. Frontin, having coached her in the finances and relationships among the various people, gave Lisette her cardinal responsibility to the Baroness: indefatigable compliance and unceasing flattery of the Baroness' infatuation for the Knight. Lisette was most capable in exercising her duties.

The Knight explained to Frontin that he had not been able to find the usurer to cash the ten-thousand-crown note, that Frontin was to find a moneychanger to effect the transaction so that the Baroness would not learn that they had not pawned her diamond. Further, the valet was to go to the restaurateur to make the arrangements for that night's dinner which the Knight was giving in honor of the Baroness and M. Turcaret.

Frontin's first move as M. Turcaret's valet was to maneuver, with Lisette's assistance, his employer into an outlay of sixty pistoles, the amount to be payment on a coach and horses for the Baroness. His second move involved his coming to the Baroness with a bailiff who had a deed signed by the Baroness and her late husband (Frontin's handwriting ability had been put to early use), assigning ten thousand livres to a horse merchant. The visit was well-timed. M. Turcaret was present and paid the sum due, rather than have the Baroness discomfited.

A countess from the country, whom the Marquess—the son of M. Turcaret's former master—brought to the Baroness' dinner, was Mme. Turcaret, who had not lived with her husband for ten years because of his meanness and ill manners. Mme. Turcaret had come to Paris to collect five quarters' support owed her by M. Turcaret. The Knight recognized her as the lady with whom he had had an affair. Mme. Jacob, who came on reference from one of the Baroness' friends to sell her a fashionable headdress, was M. Turcaret's sister.

In the midst of abuses and insults among the Turcarets and Mme. Jacob, M. Turcaret was called away to discuss a business matter with his partners. Sensing Turcaret's fiscal embroilments, the Baroness announced that she would give up M. Turcaret for his and Mme. Turcaret's happiness; the Marquess followed suit in severing connections with Mme. Turcaret. Frontin brought the news that the bailiffs had apprehended M. Turcaret, he being responsible for a pay-officer who had defaulted on two hundred thousand crowns. Mme. Jacob went to her brother's aid, not forgetting she was his sister. Mme. Turcaret went to him to bombard him with insults, not forgetting she was his wife.

Frontin reported that he had been searched by the bailiffs, who had confiscated the ten-thousand-crown note, which he had not yet been able to cash, and the ten-thousand-livre note which M. Turcaret had issued to relieve the Baroness of her debt on the bond. The Baroness, aware then that her diamond had never been pawned and that the note would never be returned to her, put the duping Knight and Frontin out of her life forever. The Knight denied Frontin future employment with him. Then he went off with the Marquess, to resume their old comradely habit of drinking all night and sleeping all day.

Left alone with Lisette, Frontin confessed that he had not been searched by the bailiffs. He had cashed the notes and had the forty thousand francs safely put away. If Lisette's ambition were satisfied with such a sum, Frontin proposed, they should start a stock of honest children. He was taking over in finances where M. Turcaret had left off.

Type of work: Novelette
Author: Henry James (1843-1916)
Type of plot: Moral allegory
Time of plot: Mid-nineteenth century
Locale: England
First published: 1898

Principal characters:
THE GOVERNESS
MRS. GROSE, housekeeper at Bly
MILES, and
FLORA, the two children of the house
MR. QUINT, and
MISS JESSEL, two apparitions

Critique:

The Turn of the Screw is more than a ghost story. Of all James' work, it best exemplifies his power to understand and depict moral degradation. The real evil lies not in the horror of the apparitions themselves, but in what is happening to change the children from examples of sweetness and innocence to flagrant liars and hypocrites. Certainly there are few stories in literature which embody as much unspoken horror as The Turn of the Screw. It is the sense of dreadful and unguessable things which gives the tale its elegance and tone, raising it above the cheapness of melodrama. As James himself said in the preface to the original edition, it is the reader's own intensified imagination which supplies the particulars in abundance.

The Story:

It was a pleasant afternoon in June when the governess first arrived at the country estate at Bly where she was to take charge of Miles, aged ten, and Flora, eight. She faced her new position with some trepidation because of the unusual circumstances of her situation. The two children were to be under her complete care, and the uncle who had engaged her had been explicit in the fact that he did not wish to be bothered with his orphaned niece and nephew. Her uneasiness dis-appeared, however, when she saw her charges, for Flora and Miles seemed incapable of giving the slightest trouble.

The weeks of June passed uneventfully. Then, one evening, while she was walking in the garden at twilight, the governess was startled to see a strange young man at a distance. The man looked at her challengingly and disappeared. The incident angered and distressed the young woman, but she decided the man was a trespasser.

On the following Sunday evening the young woman was startled to see the same stranger looking in at her through a window. Once again he stared piercingly at her for a few seconds and then disappeared. This time the governess realized that the man was looking for someone in particular and that perhaps he boded evil for the children in her care. A few minutes later the governess told the housekeeper, Mrs. Grose, of the incident and described the appearance of the man. Mrs. Grose told her that it was a perfect description of Peter Quint, the valet to the governess' employer, but that Mr. Quint was dead.

One afternoon shortly afterward, a second apparition appeared. This time the ghost of Miss Jessel, the former governess, appeared in the garden to both the governess and the little girl, Flora. The strange part of the situation was that the little girl refused to let the governess know that she had seen the figure and knew who it was, though it was obvious that she had understood the appearance fully.

From the housekeeper the governess learned that the two apparitions had been lovers while alive, though the girl had been of a very fine family and the man had been guilty of drunkenness and worse vices. For what evil purpose these two spirits wished to influence the seemingly innocent children, neither the housekeeper nor the governess could guess. The secrecy of the children about seeing the ghosts was maddening to the two women.

They both felt that the boy was continuing to see the two ghosts in private and concealed that fact, just as he had known of the illicit affair between the valet and the former governess in life and had helped them to conceal it. Yet, when in the presence of the children, the governess sometimes felt that it would be impossible for the two children to be influenced into evil.

The third time the ghost of Quint appeared to the governess inside the house. Unable to sleep, she had sat reading late at night. Hearing someone on the stairs, she went to investigate and saw the ghost, which disappeared when faced by her unflinching gaze. Each night after that she inspected the stairs, but she never again saw the ghost of the man. Once she glimpsed the apparition of Miss Jessel as it sat dejectedly on the lowest stair. Worse than the appearance of the ghosts was the discovery that the children had left their beds at night to wander on the lawn in communication with the spirits who were leading them to unknown evil. It became apparent to the governess that the children were not good within themselves. In their imaginations they were living in a world populated by the evil dead restored.

In such an atmosphere the summer wore away into autumn. In all that time

the children had given no sign of awareness of the apparitions. Knowing that her influence with the children was as tenuous as a thread which would break at the least provocation, the governess did not allude to the ghosts. She herself had seen no more manifestations, but she had often felt by the children's attitude that the apparitions were close at hand. What was worse for the distressed woman was the thought that what Miles and Flora saw were things still more terrible than she imagined, visions that sprang from their association with the evil figures in the past.

One day Miles went to her and announced his desire to go away to school. The governess realized it was only proper that he be sent to school, but she feared the results of ghostly influences once he was beyond her care. Later, opening the door of the schoolroom, she again saw the ghost of her predecessor, Miss Jessel. As the apparition faded the governess realized that her duty was to stay with the children and combat the spirits and their deadly influence. She decided to write immediately to the children's uncle, contradictory to his injunction against being bothered in their behalf. That night before she wrote she went into Miles' room and asked the boy to let her help him in his secret troubles. Suddenly a rush of cold air filled the room, as if the window had been blown open. When the governess relighted the candle blown out by the draft, the window was still closed and the drawn curtain had not been disturbed.

The following day Flora disappeared. Mrs. Grose and the governess found her beside the garden pond. The governess, knowing she had gone there to see the ghost, asked her where Miss Jessel was. The child replied that she only wanted to be left alone. The governess could see the apparition of Miss Jessel standing on the opposite side of the pond.

The governess, afraid that the evil influence had already dominated the little girl, asked the housekeeper to take the child to London, and to request the uncle's aid. In place of the lovable angelic Flora there had suddenly appeared a little child with a filthy mind and filthy speech, which she used in denouncing the governess to the housekeeper. The same afternoon Mrs. Grose left with the child as the governess had requested.

That evening, immediately after dinner, the governess asked Miles to tell her what was on his mind before he left the dining-room. When he refused, she asked him if he had stolen the letter she had written to his uncle. As she asked the question she realized that standing outside the window, staring into the room, was the ghost of Peter Quint. She pulled the boy close to her, shielding him from any view of the ghost at the window, while he told her that he had taken the letter. He also informed her that he had already been expelled from one school because of his lewd speech and actions. Noting how close the governess was holding him, he suddenly asked if Miss Jessel were near. The governess, angry and distraught, shrieked at him that it was the ghost of Peter Quint, just outside the window. When Miles turned around, the apparition was gone. With a scream he fell into the governess' arms. At first, she did not realize that she had lost him forever—that Miles was dead.

TWELFTH NIGHT

Type of work: Drama
Author: William Shakespeare (1564-1616)
Type of plot: Romantic comedy
Time of plot: Sixteenth century
Locale: Ilyria
First presented: 1600

Principal characters:
VIOLA (CESARIO), twin sister of Sebastian
OLIVIA, a countess
MARIA, her maid
SEBASTIAN, twin brother of Viola
ANTONIO, Sebastian's friend
ORSINO, Duke of Ilyria
SIR TOBY BELCH, Olivia's uncle
SIR ANDREW AGUECHEEK, Olivia's ancient suitor
MALVOLIO, Olivia's steward

Critique:

Because of its title, it is assumed that this play was intended to be performed as a feature of the Twelfth Night festivities observed in Shakespeare's day. One of Shakespeare's most delightful comedies, the principal charm of *Twelfth Night, Or, What You Will* lies in the comic characters: Malvolio, Sir Toby Belch, Sir Andrew Aguecheek, and Maria. Viola, the heroine, ranks with Portia and Rosalind in intelligence and wit. The original source of the plot was an Italian *novella* by Bandello, based on an earlier work by Cinthio, but the story was translated into various secondary sources which Shakespeare probably used. In the character of Malvolio the playwright pokes sly fun at the Puritans of his day.

The Story:

Viola and Sebastian, twin brother and sister who exactly resembled each other, were separated when the ship on which they were passengers was wrecked during a great storm at sea. Each, thinking the other dead, set out into the world alone, with no hope of being reunited.

The lovely and charming Viola was cast upon the shores of Ilyria, where she was befriended by a kind sea captain. Together they planned to dress Viola in men's clothing and have her take service as a page in the household of young Duke Orsino. This course was decided upon be-

cause there was no chance of her entering the service of the Countess Olivia, a rich noblewoman of the duchy. Olivia, in deep mourning for the death of her young brother, would admit no one to her palace and would never think of interviewing a servant. So Viola, dressed in man's garb, called herself Cesario and became the duke's personal attendant. Orsino, impressed by the youth's good looks and pert but courtly speech, sent him as his envoy of love to woo the Countess Olivia.

That wealthy noblewoman lived in a splendid palace with a servant, Maria, a drunken old uncle, Sir Toby Belch, and her steward, Malvolio. These three made a strange combination. Maria and Sir Toby were a happy-go-lucky pair who drank and caroused with Sir Andrew Aguecheek, an ancient nobleman who was much enamored of Olivia. In return for the grog supplied by Sir Andrew, Sir Toby was supposed to press Sir Andrew's suit of love with Olivia. Actually, however, Sir Toby never sobered up long enough to maintain his part of the bargain. All these affairs were observed with a great deal of disapproval by Malvolio, the ambitious, narrow-minded steward. This irritable, pompous individual could brook no jollity in those about him.

When Cesario arrived at the palace, Olivia finally decided to receive a messenger from Orsino. Instantly Olivia

3915

was attracted to Cesario and paid close attention to the page's addresses, but it was not love for Orsino that caused Olivia to listen so carefully. When Cesario left, the countess, feeling in a flirtatious mood, sent Malvolio after the page with a ring. With an abrupt shock, Viola, who enjoyed playing the part of Cesario, realized that Olivia had fallen in love with her in her man's garb.

Meanwhile Maria with Sir Toby and Sir Andrew decided to stop Malvolio's constant prying into their affairs. Maria devised a scheme whereby Malvolio would find a note, supposedly written by Olivia, in which she confessed her secret love for the steward and asked him to wear yellow stockings tied with cross garters and to smile continually in her presence. Malvolio, discovering the note, was overjoyed. Soon he appeared in his strange dress, capering and bowing before the countess. Olivia, startled by the sight of her usually dignified steward behaving in such a peculiar fashion, decided he had lost his wits. Much to the amusement of the three conspirators, she had him confined to a dark room.

As the days went by in the duke's service, Viola fell deeply in love with that sentimental nobleman, but he had eyes only for Olivia and pressed the page to renew his suit with the countess. When Cesario returned with another message from the duke, Olivia openly declared her love for the young page. Cesario insisted, however, that his was a heart that could never belong to any woman. So obvious were Olivia's feelings for Cesario that Sir Andrew became jealous. Sir Toby and Maria insisted that Sir Andrew's only course was to fight a duel with the page. Sir Toby delivered Sir Andrew's blustering challenge, which Cesario reluctantly accepted.

While these events were taking place, Sebastian, Viola's twin brother, had been rescued by Antonio, a sea captain, and the two had become close friends. When Sebastian decided to visit the court of Duke Orsino at Ilyria, Antonio, although

he feared that he might be arrested because he was the duke's enemy and had once fought a duel with Orsino, decided to accompany his young friend. Upon arrival in Ilyria, Antonio gave Sebastian his purse for safekeeping, and the two men separated for several hours.

During his wanderings about the city Antonio happened upon the trumped-up duel between the unwilling Cesario and Sir Andrew. Mistaking the page for Sebastian, Antonio immediately went to the rescue of his supposed friend. When police officers arrived on the scene, one of them recognized Antonio and arrested him in the name of the duke.

Antonio, mistaking Viola in disguise for Sebastian, asked for the return of his purse, only to be surprised and hurt because the page disclaimed all knowledge of the captain's money. As Antonio was dragged protesting to jail, he shouted invectives at "Sebastian" for refusing him his purse. Thus Viola learned for the first time that her brother still lived.

The real Sebastian, meanwhile, had been followed by Sir Andrew, who never dreamed that the young man was not the same Cesario with whom he had just been fighting. Egged on by Sir Toby and Maria, Sir Andrew engaged Sebastian in a duel and was promptly wounded, along with Sir Toby. Olivia then interfered and had Sebastian taken to her home. There, having sent for a priest, she married the surprised but not unwilling Sebastian.

The officers were escorting Antonio past Olivia's house as Duke Orsino, accompanied by Cesario, appeared at the gates. Instantly Orsino recognized Antonio and demanded to know why the sailor had returned to Ilyria, a city filled with his enemies. Antonio explained that he had rescued and befriended the duke's present companion, Sebastian, and because of his deep friendship for the lad had accompanied him to Ilyria despite the danger his visit involved. Then, pointing to Cesario, he sorrowfully accused the supposed Sebastian of violating their friendship by not returning his purse.

The duke was protesting against this accusation when Olivia appeared and saluted Cesario as her husband. The duke also began to think his page ungrateful, especially so since Cesario had been told to press Orsino's suit with Olivia. Just then Sir Andrew and Sir Toby came running in looking for a doctor because Sebastian had wounded them. Seeing Cesario, Sir Andrew began to rail at him for his violence. Olivia dismissed the two old men quickly. As they left the real Sebastian appeared and apologized for the wounds he had given the old men.

Spying Antonio, Sebastian joyfully greeted his friend. Antonio and the rest of the amazed group, unable to believe what they saw, stared from Cesario to Sebastian. Viola then revealed her true identity, explained her disguise, and told how she and her brother had been separated. The mystery cleared up, Sebastian and Viola affectionately greeted each other. The duke, seeing that the page of whom he had grown so fond was in reality a woman, asked that Viola dress again in feminine attire. She was unable to do as he desired, she explained, because the kind sea captain to whom she had entrusted her own clothes was held in prison through the orders of Malvolio. This difficulty was cleared up quickly, for Olivia's clown, Feste, pitying Malvolio, visited him in his confinement and secured a long letter in which the steward explained the reasons for his actions. The plot against him revealed, Malvolio was released. Then followed the freeing of the sea captain, the marriage of Viola and Orsino, and also that of Sir Toby and Maria. Only Malvolio, unhappy in the happiness of others remained peevish and disgruntled.

TWENTY THOUSAND LEAGUES UNDER THE SEA

Type of work: Novel
Author: Jules Verne (1828-1905)
Type of plot: Adventure romance
Time of plot: 1866-1867
Locale: The Seven Seas
First published: 1870

Principal characters:
PROFESSOR PIERRE ARONNAX, a French scientist
CONSEIL, his servant
NED LAND, his friend and companion
CAPTAIN NEMO, captain of the *Nautilus*

Critique:

Many writers have had vivid and penetrating imaginations which permitted them to speculate about things to come. Jules Verne was one of these, and his book is in the tradition that has given us Utopian stories of revealed discoveries and inventions yet to occur. In this instance Verne was really prophetic. The submarine and most of the inventions conceived by Captain Nemo have become realities. Books of this nature are seldom great, but they are always interesting.

The Story:

In different parts of the ocean, a number of ships had sighted a mysterious monster, gleaming with light, such as no man had ever seen before. After this monster had attacked and sunk several vessels, people all over the world were both amazed and alarmed. Finally an American frigate, the *Abraham Lincoln,* was fitted out to track down and destroy the mysterious sea creature. Among its passengers was Pierre Aronnax, Professor of Natural History in the Museum of Paris, who had published his opinion that the monster was a giant narwhal. One of the crew was Ned Land, an expert harpooner. For quite a while the ship sailed without sighting anything even remotely resembling the reported terror of the seas.

The creature was sighted at last. When an opportunity presented itself, Ned Land threw his harpoon, but the monster was uninjured and Land realized that it was protected by a thick steel-like armor. During a pursuit in the darkness, a terrific explosion rocked the ship. Professor Aronnax, Ned Land, and Conseil found themselves floundering in the water. Aronnax fainted. Regaining consciousness, he discovered that they were aboard some sort of underwater craft. Later two men came to greet them. The survivors from the ship spoke to them in various languages, but the men appeared not to understand. Then the captain of the vessel appeared and spoke to them in French. He revealed that his name was Nemo, that the vessel was a submarine, that they were, in effect, prisoners who would have every liberty aboard, except on occasions when they would receive orders to retire to their cabins.

The submarine *Nautilus,* Aronnax learned, had been built in a complicated manner. Parts of it had been secured from various places and secretly assembled on a desert island. Then a fire had been set to destroy all traces of the work done there. The ship manufactured its own electricity, had provisions for quantities of oxygen which allowed it to remain submerged, and was as comfortable as any home. All food came from the ocean. There was fish, but fish such as Aronnax had never before tasted. There was clothing made from some sort of sea fibres. There were cigars, not of tobacco but of a special seaweed. Captain Nemo showed them air guns which allowed him and the crew to go hunting, as well as a device that permitted the crew to walk the ocean floor.

In the Pacific, Captain Nemo invited the three survivors to a hunt in the marine forest of Crespo, where Ned Land saved Captain Nemo's life by killing a creature which was about to put an end to the captain. Later, the captain saved Land's life. In Ceylon they watched the pearl divers in the oyster beds. There Nemo saved an Indian from the jaws of a shark.

Off the coast of Borneo the three survivors decided to go ashore in the hope of bagging some land game. While they were hunting, they were attacked by natives. Although they managed to get back to the Nautilus, the savages remained clustered about the ship. Aronnax was alarmed, certain that the natives would board the submarine when the hatches were opened for oxygen the next morning. He took his problem to Captain Nemo, who was not at all worried. Instead he told the professor about an eighteenth-century ship that had sunk with a full cargo of gold. The next morning, when the hatches were opened, the natives did try to come aboard, but the few who touched the rails let out a shriek and retreated in terror. Ned Land touched the rail and was paralyzed with shock; the rail was electrified.

The captain announced suddenly that he would enter the Mediterranean. Aronnax supposed that he would have to circle the Cape of Good Hope. To his astonishment, he learned that the captain had discovered a passage under the Isthmus of Suez. The submarine entered the Mediterranean through the underwater passage.

On one occasion the three companions were ordered to go to their cabins. Some sort of encounter occurred, and later Aronnax was called upon to treat a crew member who had been injured. When the sailor died, he was buried in a coral forest on the ocean floor. By that time the survivors had discovered that Captain Nemo had a tremendous fortune in gold salvaged from sunken vessels. Although the captain had some mysterious hatred against society, he nevertheless used the money to benefit his unfortunate fellow men.

Ned Land grew to dislike the captain very much. He told Aronnax that he would escape as soon as an opportunity presented itself. They thought such an opportunity had come when they rounded Spain, but their plan did not materialize. When they came close to Long Island, they thought the time for escape had come. But a sudden hurricane blew the ship off its course, toward Newfoundland.

On another occasion the captain astonished them by heading toward the South Pole. There the ship was endangered by an iceberg, and for several days passengers and crew were in danger of their lives. Escaping, they headed northward. As the Nautilus approached the coast of Norway, it was suddenly drawn into the notorious maelstrom, the deathtrap for so many ships. Shortly before, the submarine had encountered a mysterious ship which had attacked it. The submarine succeeded in sinking the unknown vessel. Aronnax believed that in this incident there was a clue to Captain Nemo's hatred of society.

The professor never knew what actually happened after the Nautilus was drawn into the maelstrom. When he awoke, he and his companions were safe and sound on a Norwegian island. They also had no idea how they had reached the island. They were the only men who now knew the secrets of the ocean —if Captain Nemo and his crew had perished.

TWENTY YEARS AFTER

Type of work: Novel
Author: Alexandre Dumas, father (1802-1870)
Type of plot: Historical romance
Time of plot: Mid-seventeenth century
Locale: France and England
First published: 1845

Principal characters:
D'ARTAGNAN,
ATHOS,
PORTHOS, and
ARAMIS, Musketeers of the Guard
CARDINAL MAZARIN, Minister of State
MORDAUNT, Cromwell's agent

Critique:

The most appealing factor in this Dumas novel is the clever use made of history. It is an intriguing pastime to speculate upon what might have happened had not the fictional Mordaunt dogged the footsteps of the real Charles of England, or had not the real Mazarin relied upon the fictional shrewdness of D'Artagnan. Intricate in plot, though not so much so as *The Count of Monte-Cristo,* this sequel to *The Three Musketeers* is in some ways a less original work than its predecessor. Dumas was repeating himself in his infallibly clever D'Artagnan and his persistently saintly Athos. Furthermore, the four musketeers behave for Mazarin, after the passage of twenty years, very much as they did for Richelieu in the earlier novel; the only change that twenty years wrought was that of names and places. But in spite of these defects the novel has perennial interest as a sequel to *The Three Musketeers.*

The Story:

When the powerful Richelieu had died and Cardinal Mazarin, whose name gossip coupled with that of Queen Anne, had seized control of the French government; and while Oliver Cromwell was overthrowing Charles I of England, D'Artagnan, a lieutenant in the Musketeers, pined for intrigue and adventure.

Politically, France was in turmoil, with revolt impending. High taxes, coupled with the evident avarice and extravagance of the rulers who levied them, had aroused the people. Also stirred, but motivated by loyalty to the throne, were some of the powerful nobles.

Queen Anne was under Mazarin's thumb. She, in turn, acted as protector for her son, King Louis XIV, then only ten years old. The boy despised Mazarin. Mazarin, beset on all sides by enemies and harassed by fears for his personal safety, summoned D'Artagnan, whose earlier fame with the King's Musketeers had been obscured by time.

Twenty years had passed since D'Artagnan, the Gascon adventurer, and the other three musketeers, Athos, Porthos, and Aramis, had performed doughty deeds for their country and their king. Now, separated by time and interests, they had all but lost touch with one another. Ordered by Mazarin to recruit the three musketeers, D'Artagnan found himself confronted by mystery in the conduct of his former comrades in arms.

First he found Aramis, the dandy, a monk who lived in luxury. The former musketeer declined D'Artagnan's proposal on the pretense that such activity would interfere with his monastic vows. Porthos was a more willing adventurer. Living on a large estate with a sufficient income, he was unhappy because of his lack of a title. He wished to be a baron. This D'Artagnan promised him. Athos, who had adopted a son, Raoul, lived on another luxurious estate. He also refused to ally

3920

himself with D'Artagnan. The adopted son of Athos was in reality his true son, begotten illegitimately, but Athos did not want to acknowledge the boy as his own and reveal the circumstances of his birth.

When the Duke de Beaufort, a political prisoner, escaped from his prison at Vincennes, Mazarin ordered the faithful adventurers, D'Artagnan and Porthos, to recapture the duke and the man who had helped his escape. D'Artagnan and Porthos, attempting to overtake the fugitives, found themselves confronted by Aramis and Athos. The four comrades dropped their weapons, exchanged vows of eternal friendship and love, and then parted, both pairs to carry on according to their own alliances.

Athos and Aramis were members of the Fronde, a political force composed of two factions: the rebellious commoners of Paris, who hoped to overthrow the king, and the nobility, who wished to replace the king. D'Artagnan and Porthos had sworn allegiance to Mazarin, who represented the king.

The first outbreak of the revolt found Mazarin and the queen unprepared. The mob, after tearing up the streets of Paris, surrounded the palace, and Mazarin called upon D'Artagnan to save him. No obstacle was too great for the clever Gascon. He smuggled Mazarin away from the palace and out of Paris. Then he returned and gave similar assistance to the queen and the young king.

During the early days of their exploits the four musketeers and an Englishman named de Winter had executed a vicious woman referred to simply as Milady; she was de Winter's sister-in-law. Mordaunt, Milady's son, a young man sworn to revenge his mother's death and an agent in the service of Oliver Cromwell, returned to France in a dual role: to search for and to murder those who had caused his mother's execution and to serve as an emissary for Cromwell, who hoped to learn how great was French sympathy for deposed Charles I of England. Lord de Winter had also gone to France to assist Henrietta Maria, the wife of Charles, and to ask that the king be given sanctuary in France should he escape Cromwell's forces.

The Fronde came to Henrietta Maria and Lord de Winter in the persons of Athos and Aramis. They departed secretly for England in de Winter's company, but not before they had learned that Milady's embittered son was on their trail.

When Mordaunt presented his case for Cromwell before Mazarin, the cardinal decided to send a message to the Puritan leader. His messengers were Porthos and D'Artagnan, who unwittingly placed themselves in the hands of their enemy when they set out for England with Mordaunt, whose identity was as yet unknown to them.

At a battle near Newcastle, King Charles was taken by Cromwell's troops. When D'Artagnan and Porthos discovered Aramis and Athos in the defeated army, they tried to save their friends by taking them prisoners, with the feigned excuse of holding them for ransom. The cruelty of the Puritans, coupled with the personal courage of the fallen Charles I, so influenced D'Artagnan that he consented to do everything he could to help the king escape to France.

As the victorious army of Cromwell made its way back to London, D'Artagnan maneuvered himself into the good graces of the soldier who guarded Charles. As the four musketeers were about to kidnap the king, their plans were thwarted by an unlucky interruption instigated by Mordaunt. In London, D'Artagnan began to lay the groundwork for snatching Charles to safety. As the time for the execution approached, the plans of D'Artagnan one by one toppled under the vigilant efforts of Mordaunt. At last D'Artagnan kidnaped the executioner, sent his comrades in disguise as gallows builders, and awaited his chance to free the royal prisoner. His attempt failed, however, when Charles was beheaded by a volunteer executioner, who, it was later discovered, was the vicious Mordaunt.

Fearing for their own lives, the four comrades plotted to escape from England.

Mordaunt followed them to the coast, mined their ship, and bought off the crew. But fortune was with the heroes, who discovered the casks filled with gunpowder. When Mordaunt blew up the ship, they were waiting to seize him. Athos stabbed the Englishman as the two men struggled in the water.

Back in France, Mazarin, angry because they had attempted to aid King Charles, arrested D'Artagnan and Porthos. Athos was arrested while trying to aid them. Porthos, using his great strength, overcame their guards, seized Mazarin in his country retreat, and forced him to release Athos. With Mazarin in their power, they compelled him to pardon them and grant their demands.

When the Frondist revolt was over and Paris restored to order, the royal household returned to the palace. The musketeers, twenty years older but forever the same, were again in good standing. D'Artagnan was awarded a captaincy in the Musketeers and Porthos was granted the title of baron. Athos went back to his estate and Aramis back to his amours. None of the four knew when they would ever meet again.

TWO GENTLEMEN OF VERONA

Type of work: Drama
Author: William Shakespeare (1564-1616)
Type of plot: Romantic comedy
Time of plot: Sixteenth century
Locale: Italy
First presented: 1594

Principal characters:
VALENTINE, and
PROTEUS, two gentlemen of Verona
JULIA, beloved of Proteus
SILVIA, beloved of Valentine
THURIO, in love with Silvia
THE DUKE OF MILAN, Silvia's father

Critique:

Written before Shakespeare's complete dramatic maturity, *Two Gentlemon of Verona* is a play of no great depth. True, it is romantic, witty, gay, but the incidents are too pat to be believable. Some of the characters seem superficial, playing roles in which they have no real concern. Also, the hero's quick and sympathetic forgiveness of the friend who had betrayed him so grossly strikes a false note. Nevertheless the comedy is charming and engrossing and worthy of the reader's time. For, in spite of the faults, some of the bard's magic is there.

The Story:

Valentine and Proteus, two long-time friends of great understanding, disagreed heartily on one point. Valentine thought the most important thing in life was to travel and learn the wonders of the world. Proteus, on the other hand, thought love the only thing worthwhile. The two friends parted for a time when Valentine traveled to Milan, to seek advancement and honor in the palace of the duke. He pleaded with Proteus to join him in the venture, but Proteus was too much in love with Julia to leave her side for even a short time. Julia was a noble and pure young girl, pursued by many. But Proteus at last won her heart and the two were happy in their love.

Valentine journeyed to Milan, and there he learned his friend had been right in believing love to be all that is worth-while. For Valentine met the duke's daughter Silvia and fell instantly in love with her. And Silvia returned his love. But her father wanted her to marry Thurio, a foolish man who had no charm but owned much land and gold. Valentine longed for Silvia, but he saw no chance of getting her father's consent to his suit. Then he learned that his friend Proteus was soon to arrive in Milan, sent there by his father, who, ignorant of Proteus' love affair, wished his son to educate himself by travel.

The two friends had a joyful reunion. Valentine proudly presented his friend to Silvia, and to Proteus he highly praised the virtue and beauty of his beloved. When they were alone, Valentine confided to Proteus that he planned to fashion a rope ladder and steal Silvia from her room and marry her, for her father would give her to no one but Thurio. Valentine, asking his friend to help him in his plan, was too absorbed to notice that Proteus remained strangely silent. The truth was that, at the first sight of Silvia, Proteus had forgotten his solemn vows to Julia, sealed before he left her with the double giving of rings, and he had forgotten too his oath of friendship with Valentine. He determined to have Silvia for his own. So, with protestations of self-hatred for the betrayal of his friend, Proteus told the duke of Valentine's plan to escape with Silvia from the palace and carry her away to be married in another land. The duke, forewarned, tricked Valentine into revealing the plot and banished him from Milan, on penalty of his life should he not leave at once.

While these events were taking place, Julia, thinking that Proteus still loved her and grieving over his absence, disguised herself as a page and traveled to Milan to see her love. She was on her way to Milan when Valentine was forced to leave that city and Silvia. Valentine, not knowing that his one-time friend had betrayed him, believed Proteus' promise that he would carry letters back and forth between the exile and Silvia.

With Valentine out of the way, Proteus next proceeded to get rid of Thurio as a rival. Thurio, foolish and gullible, was an easy man to trick. One night Proteus and Thurio went to Silvia's window to serenade her in Thurio's name, but Proteus sang to her and made love speeches also. Unknown to him, Julia, in the disguise of a page, stood in the shadows and heard him disown his love for her and proclaim his love for Silvia. But Silvia scorned him and swore that she would love no one but Valentine. She also accused him of playing false with Julia, for Valentine had told her the story of his friend's betrothal.

Calling herself Sebastian, Julia, still in the dress of a page, was employed by Proteus to carry messages to Silvia. One day he gave her the ring which Julia herself had given him and told her to deliver it to Silvia. When Silvia refused the ring and sent it back to Proteus, Julia loved her rival and blessed her.

Valentine, in the meantime, had been captured by outlaws, once honorable men who had been banished for petty crimes and had taken refuge in the woods near Mantua. In order to save his own life, Valentine joined the band and soon became their leader. A short time later Silvia, hoping to find Valentine, escaped from the palace and with the help of an agent arrived at an abbey near Milan.

There she was captured by the outlaws. When her father heard of her flight, he took Thurio and Proteus, followed by Julia, to the abbey to look for her. But Proteus, arriving first on the scene, rescued her from the outlaws before they were able to take her to their leader. Again Proteus proclaimed his love for her. When she scornfully berated him, he seized her and tried to force his attentions upon her. Unknown to Proteus, however, Valentine had overheard all that was said. He sprang upon Proteus and pulled him away from the frightened girl.

Valentine was more hurt and wounded by his friend's duplicity than by anything else that had happened. But such was Valentine's forgiving nature that when Proteus confessed his guilt and his shame over his betrayal, Valentine forgave him and received him again as his friend. In order to prove his friendship, he gave up his claim on Silvia. At that moment Julia, still disguised, fainted away. When she was revived, she pretended to hand over to Silvia the ring Proteus had ordered her to deliver. But instead she offered the ring Proteus had given her when they parted in Verona. Then Julia was recognized by all, and Proteus professed that he still loved her.

The outlaws appeared with the duke and Thurio, whom they had captured in the forest. Thurio gave up all claim to Silvia, for he thought a girl who would run off into the woods to pursue another man much too foolish for him to marry. Then her father, convinced at last of Valentine's worth, gave that young man permission to marry Silvia. During the general rejoicing Valentine begged one more boon. He asked the duke to pardon the outlaws, all brave men who would serve the duke faithfully if he would return them from exile. The duke granted the boon, and the whole party made its way back to Milan. There the two happy couples would share one wedding day and mutual joy.

THE TWO NOBLE KINSMEN

Type of work: Drama
Authors: William Shakespeare (1564-1616) and John Fletcher (1579-1625)
Type of plot: Chivalric romance
Time of plot: Age of legend
Locale: Athens and Thebes
First presented: c. 1613

Principal characters:
THESEUS, Duke of Athens
HIPPOLYTA, his wife
EMILIA, her younger sister
PALAMON, and
ARCITE, cousins, nephews of Creon, King of Thebes

Critique:

The Two Noble Kinsmen was a joint production of the aging Shakespeare and his protégé, John Fletcher. Specific scenes have been attributed, on the basis of stylistic traits, to each dramatist. That many scenes cannot be specifically assigned would suggest intimate collaboration. The main plot was taken from Boccaccio's *Teseide*, which, in turn, was derived from Statius' *Thebaid*. Shakespeare had already used the Theseus-Hippolyta theme in *A Midsummer Night's Dream*. Chaucer had used the same story in "The Knight's Tale." The underplot of this play is marked by a sentimentality that betokened the end of the golden age of Tudor and Stuart drama.

The Story:

During the marriage ceremony of Theseus, Duke of Athens, and Hippolyta, Queen of the Amazons, three widowed queens begged Theseus' aid. Creon, King of Thebes, had slain their husbands in battle and would not permit their bodies to receive decent burial. Theseus commiserated with the queens, but provided small comfort for their grief when he directed that his nuptial ceremonies be continued. The queens persisting in their pleas, Theseus conceded to the extent of ordering an expeditionary force to be readied to march against Thebes. Not to be denied, the distracted queens finally persuaded him to champion their cause. He appointed Pirithous, an Athenian nobleman, to stand in his place for the remainder of the ceremony, kissed Hippolyta farewell, and led the queens away toward Thebes.

Meanwhile, in Thebes, the cousins Palamon and Arcite, nephews of Creon, found their uncle's tyranny unbearable and stultifying, and decided to leave Thebes. But no sooner had they made this decision then they learned that Thebes was threatened by Theseus. The cousins, loyal to Thebes if not to Creon, deferred their departure in order to serve their city.

When the opposing forces met, Palamon and Arcite fought with great courage, but the Athenians were victorious in the battle. Theseus, triumphant, directed the three widowed queens to bury their dead in peace. Palamon and Arcite, having been wounded and left for dead on the battlefield, were taken by the Athenians.

The cousins, healed of their wounds and finding themselves in a prison in Athens, impressed their jailers with their seeming unconcern at being incarcerated. In their cell, however, they sadly bemoaned their fate to each other. Resigned to spending the rest of their lives in prison, they recalled with grief the joys of battle and the hunt, and they grieved at the thought of a future without marriage. Even so, they made some attempt to reconcile themselves to imprisonment by declaring that in their cell they had each other's excellent company and that they were insulated from the infinite number of evils that beset free men.

Emilia, Hippolyta's beautiful sister, entered the prison garden. Palamon saw her and fell in love at once. When Arcite beheld her, he too fell in love. Palamon declared that Arcite must not love her, but Arcite answered that Palamon, who had called her a goddess, might love her spiritually; he, Arcite, would love her in a more earthly manner. Palamon maintained that this goddess they had beheld was his to love because he had seen her first. Arcite, in turn, insisted that he too must love her because of the propinquity of the pair. Palamon, enraged, wished for liberty and weapons so that he and Arcite might decide the issue in mortal combat.

The jailkeeper, on orders, took Arcite to Theseus. Palamon, meanwhile, was filled with despair at the thought that Arcite was now free to win Emilia. The keeper returned to report that Arcite had been sent away from Athens and that Palamon must be moved to a cell in which there were fewer windows. Palamon writhed in the knowledge that Arcite now seemed certain to win the hand of Emilia.

But Arcite, in the country near Athens, felt no advantage over his cousin. Indeed, he envied Palamon, who he believed could see Emilia every time she visited the prison garden with her maid. Desperate, he assumed a disguise and returned to Athens to participate in athletic games in honor of Emilia's birthday. Excelling in the games, he admitted that he was of gentle birth; but Theseus did not penetrate his disguise. Theseus, admiring Arcite's athletic prowess and his modesty, designated him to be a serving-man to Emilia.

In the meantime the daughter of the jailkeeper fell in love with Palamon and effected his escape. In the forest, where the court had gone a-Maying, Arcite came upon the escaped prisoner. In spite of Palamon's harsh words to him, Arcite promised to supply his cousin with food. Two days later he brought food and drink. When he left, he promised to return the next time with armor and weapons, that the two might decide their quarrel by combat.

Arcite having returned with armor and weapons, the two youths armed themselves and fought. At the same time Theseus and his party, hunting in the forest, came upon the struggling pair. Theseus condemned them to be executed straightway, one for having defied banishment, the other for having broken out of prison. But Hippolyta, Pirithous, and Emilia begged Theseus for mercy. The duke then declared that they might live if they would forget Emilia. When both refused, Theseus resolved that the youths should go free, but that in a month they must return to Athens, both accompanied by three knights of their own choice, and determine this problem in the lists. The victor would be awarded the hand of Emilia; the loser and his companions would be executed on the spot.

A month passed. As Emilia admired likenesses of Palamon and Arcite and despaired at her inability to choose one or the other as her favorite, the cousins, with six knights, returned to Athens. Arcite and his knight-companions invoked Mars, the god of war; Palamon and his cohorts invoked Venus, the goddess of love; Emilia, in her role as a priestess of Diana, invoked the goddess of chastity to bring victory to the youth who loved her best. In the tournament which followed Arcite was the victor.

Palamon now laid his head on the block in anticipation of execution, but Pirithous interrupted the beheading to announce that Arcite had been thrown and mortally trampled by a black horse that Emilia had given him. Before he died, Arcite, brought before his cousin, relinquished his claim upon Emilia to Palamon. Palamon, reconciled with his cousin, observed sorrowfully that he had lost a great love in order to gain another.

TWO YEARS BEFORE THE MAST

Type of work: Record of travel
Author: Richard Henry Dana, Jr. (1815-1882)
Type of plot: Adventure romance
Time of plot: 1834-1836
Locale: California and the high seas
First published: 1840

Principal character:
RICHARD HENRY DANA, JR.

Critique:

The author wrote this realistic account of the life of a common sailor to make the public aware of the hardships and injustices to which American sailors were subjected. In his narrative, chiefly in the form of a journal, Dana explains life at sea at great length. The book also reveals much about life in Spanish California in the early nineteenth century. Dana was a careful observer, and his story has the ring of authenticity throughout.

The Story:

In August, 1834, Richard Henry Dana, Jr., shipped aboard the brig *Pilgrim* out of Boston for a voyage to California. He went as an ordinary seaman, hoping to relieve his eye trouble by the journey; upon his return he planned to reënter Harvard College.

Since Dana was a completely green hand, he was forced to bunk in the steerage instead of in the forecastle with the other sailors. At first his duties were confusing, doubly so during the first two days, for he was violently seasick. But he soon found his sea legs and quickly learned shipboard routine. He and his companions were kept busy all day cleaning and repairing the ship. At night they took turns standing watch.

The voyage was uneventful until October, when the *Pilgrim* passed near the mouth of the River Plate. Here Dana encountered his first real storm at sea. The weather then began to get cold, and all the crew prepared to round Cape Horn.

The seas at the Horn were high, and they encountered snow and hail. Everyone's clothing was perpetually wet. By the middle of November the ship rounded the Horn and headed northward.

The first mishap of the voyage occurred soon afterward, when a young sailor was swept overboard. A boat lowered to search for him found no trace of the lost man. Following the custom of the sea, the captain auctioned off the dead man's clothing.

Near the end of November the brig made the island of Juan Fernandez and dropped anchor for the first time since her departure from Boston. Dana was glad to see land and managed to get on shore for a short time. As soon as the ship had taken on water, however, it weighed anchor and headed for California.

Shortly after Christmas Dana was acknowledged by the crew to be experienced enough to move into the forecastle with them. Now he was a real seaman.

By the middle of January the *Pilgrim* made her first California port at Santa Barbara. There Dana learned that his work for the next year would be loading cattle hides into the ship. The sailors carried the stiff, undressed hides out through the surf on their heads and deposited them in a boat. Then the crew of the boat took the hides to the ship and stowed them away.

The *Pilgrim* next sailed northward to Monterey with some passengers. At that port Mexican customs officers inspected the cargo. Then the company agent aboard the ship set up a store in order to trade with the townspeople. The crew was kept busy on a shuttle service between ship and shore. Because he had some knowledge of languages, Dana became the interpreter for the *Pilgrim,* and he was sent ashore on errands which required a knowledge of Spanish. In this way he became acquainted with the town and its people. He found the Spaniards to be pleasant but lazy, with most of the trade carried on by foreigners. Everyone owned horses; they were so numerous that the price of a fine animal was very low.

When business began to fall off, the *Pilgrim* returned to Santa Barbara. There the crew again began the work of collecting cattle hides from shore. At the time trouble was brewing aboard the ship. Captain, mate, and crew were all at odds. One day the captain began to flog a sailo unjustly; when one of his shipmates stood up for him, the captain flogged the second sailor also. The sailors were angry, but they had no higher power to which they could appeal, for the captain's word was law. Her hold filled with hides, the *Pilgrim* sailed for San Diego.

In San Diego, Dana got his first shore leave. After drinking for a time with the rest of the crew, he and a friend hired horses and rode to a nearby mission, where they were able to get a good Mexican meal, a welcome change from the salt beef served aboard ship.

The undressed hides were unloaded from the *Pilgrim* and placed in a large shed on the beach, where they were to be dressed and stored until enough hides had been collected for the voyage home. Just as the ship had finished unloading and was ready to set sail, a man deserted ship. After an unsuccessful search, the brig put to sea without him.

The *Pilgrim* took on more hides at San Pedro and then continued on to Santa Barbara. It was the Lenten season, and Dana saw the celebrations ashore. The ship gathered more hides at several places and returned to San Diego. After the hides had been unloaded, the captain sent Dana and another man ashore to assist with the dressing of the hides.

Then the ship sailed northward on another coastal voyage.

Dana became acquainted with some Sandwich Islanders who lived on the beach and worked with him; he found them to be generous men and true friends. Some of his spare time he spent reading books and studying navigation. Each day he had to perform a certain amount of work on a certain number of hides, which had to be cleaned, soaked in brine, scraped, dried, beaten, and then stored away.

When the ship *Alert* arrived at San Diego, Dana, anxious to be at sea again, exchanged places with a boy aboard the ship. The *Alert* belonged to the same company as the *Pilgrim;* she was to take aboard the hides collected by the brig and carry them to Boston. The *Pilgrim* was not to sail for home until later. The two vessels had exchanged captains, and Dana was under the same master as before. However, the first mate of the *Alert* was a good officer, and Dana found conditions much more pleasant in his new berth.

Loading hides, the *Alert* moved up and down the coast for several months. In the middle of November, 1835, she left Santa Barbara with some passengers bound for Monterey. However, such a gale came up that the ship could not put in at Monterey but went on up the coast to San Francisco.

The ship then continued working up and down the coast until there were enough hides at San Diego to make her full cargo. In May she headed southward for Cape Horn.

Rounding the Horn on the return journey was even worse than on the way out. Dana became sick with a toothache at the time he was needed most on deck. For days everyone had to work extra hours because of the danger from icebergs. Finally, however, the *Alert* got clear of the ice and ran before a strong wind around the Horn.

Once the ship entered the Atlantic tropics, the weather was fair except for occasional violent storms. Some of the men began to come down with the scurvy, but they were soon cured after the crew obtained fresh vegetables from a passing ship.

On September 21, 1836, the *Alert* anchored in Boston harbor. Hurriedly the crew performed their last duties in bringing her to the wharf. Within five minutes after the last rope had been made fast, not one of the crew was left aboard.

TYPEE

Type of work: Novel
Author: Herman Melville (1819-1891)
Type of plot: Adventure romance
Time of plot: Mid-nineteenth century
Locale: Marquesas Islands
First published: 1846

Principal characters:
HERMAN MELVILLE (TOM), an American sailor
TOBY, his friend
MEHEVI, chief of the Typees
KORY-KORY, a native servant
FAYAWAY, a native girl
MARNOO, a native taboo man

Critique:

Typee is a fictionized narrative of actual adventures of young Herman Melville. Although most of the narrative is based upon the capture and escape of Tom and Toby, much of the book is devoted to a description of the life of the Typee cannibals. In spite of its somewhat antiquated style, the book makes fascinating reading. *Typee* has historical interest because it is the first romance of the South Seas.

The Story:

The whaler *Dolly* had been long at sea, and the men were discontented and restless when the captain finally gave orders to put in at Nukuheva, one of the Marquesas Islands. This was the chance Tom and Toby, two young sailors, had been waiting for. Even though the natives of the island were known to be cannibals, Tom and Toby deserted the ship and fled inland, planning to hide until the *Dolly* sailed. Then they hoped to sign aboard another ship where they would get better treatment.

Tom and Toby began their flight with only a few biscuits for food. On the first night away from the ship Tom contracted some disease which caused his leg to swell, and he was in much pain. Nevertheless, he and Toby went on. At last, when their food was all gone, they realized that they could stay alive only by giving themselves up to one of the savage tribes that inhabited the island.

They discovered too late that the natives to whom they surrendered themselves were the Typee tribe, the most ferocious cannibals on Nukuheva. Tom and Toby were treated with respect, however, and were given food and comfortable quarters. All the natives came to see the strangers. Mehevi, the king of the Typees, appointed Kory-Kory as personal servant to Tom. The captives went to live in the home of Tinor, Kory-Kory's mother. Mehevi had a medicine man examine Tom's swollen leg, but the native remedies had no effect on the disease.

Tom, unable to walk, spent most of his time reclining in the house while Kory-Kory attended to his needs. A beautiful young maiden, Fayaway, was also his constant companion. She, among all the Typees, seemed to understand the painful situation of the two captives.

Toby convinced the Typees that he should be allowed to return to the main harbor on the island to seek medical aid for Tom. On the trail he was attacked by hostile warriors from a neighboring tribe, and he returned to the Typees with an ugly head wound.

A few days later Toby discovered a boat offshore. He was allowed to go down by the beach, but Tom was detained in his house. Toby promised to bring medical aid to Tom within three days. But the three days passed without the return of Toby. Tom could learn nothing from the natives; he realized that now he was the single captive of the Typees. Somewhat recovered, he was allowed to roam almost at will within

3931

the country of the Typees. But he was always accompanied by Kory-Kory; there was no chance for escape.

As Tom's leg improved, he began to indulge in the pleasures allowed him and to observe the native life with interest. The Typees seemed to exist in a perpetual state of happiness, interrupted only by skirmishes with neighboring tribes.

One of Tom's greatest pleasures was to paddle a canoe about a small lake in company with Fayaway. For the privilege of taking Fayaway with him he had to ask special permission, since entering a canoe was ordinarily taboo for a woman.

One day a handsome stranger appeared among the Typees bearing news from other parts of the island. He was Marnoo, a taboo man, who was free to go among all the tribes without harm. When Tom learned that Marnoo knew English, he asked the native to help him escape. This Marnoo could not do for fear of arousing the anger of the Typees.

The daily life of the natives was extremely regular. Each morning they bathed and ate breakfast. After the meal they smoked their pipes. The rest of the morning they spent sleeping, conversing, or doing odd jobs about their houses. The men often spent the afternoon in the large meeting house of Mehevi; there they relaxed and joked in a sort of bachelors' club. Before the evening meal they bathed again. After the meal the young girls entertained the rest with dancing. Everyone retired at an early hour.

Tom was present at the Feast of the Calabashes. It seemed to have some religious significance, but most of the time was spent in eating and drinking. During the two days of the festival Tom decided the natives did not take their religion seriously. They possessed many idols not treated with any high degree of respect. The most universal religious observance was that of tattooing; everyone was tattooed upon the face, even the women. The bodies of some of the men were completely covered with intricate designs.

Since the men outnumbered the women in the tribe, the women often had two or three husbands. But the men never had more than one wife. All in the tribe seemed happy with the various aspects of their social organization. Private property was limited to household goods, food was common property. All understood and followed the laws and customs of the tribe; there were never disputes among the Typees.

One day a battle was fought between the Typees and a neighboring tribe. Afterward the bodies of the dead enemies were taken to the ceremonial feasting place. For the next day or two Tom was not allowed to leave the vicinity of his house. He suspected that the Typees were making a meal of their dead enemies. Later he discovered the remains of the meal and found that he was correct, though the Typees denied they were cannibals.

A few days later Marnoo again appeared among the Typees. This time he told Tom to try to escape by means of the same path by which he left. Tom was unable to leave the village, however, for Kory-Kory kept close watch on him day and night.

Not many days after Marnoo had left, the Typees excitedly announced the approach of a boat. Tom argued with the natives and finally persuaded them to let him go to the beach. He had some difficulty in getting there, since his leg had begun to swell again.

At the beach Tom found a boat from an Australian ship standing just outside the surf. Marnoo had told the Australian captain of Tom's trouble, and he had sent a boat loaded with presents to obtain Tom's release. The Typees, however, had no wish to release their captive. In desperation, Tom broke away from the guard which had been placed around him and plunged into the surf. He managed to reach the boat, and the sailors pulled away from shore.

Thus ended Tom's captivity among

3932

the Typees. His only regret was in leaving the faithful Kory-Kory and the beautiful Fayaway.

Many years later Tom again met Toby and learned from him that he had intended to return to the aid of his injured friend, but he had been tricked into boarding a vessel which sailed from Nukuheva the following day. It was only long after Toby had given Tom up for lost that the two friends learned of each other's fate after their separation.

THE UGLY DUCHESS

Type of work: Novel
Author: Lion Feuchtwanger (1884-   )
Type of plot: Historical chronicle
Time of plot: Fourteenth century
Locale: Central Europe
First published: 1926

Principal characters:
DUCHESS MARGARETE
PRINCE JOHANN, her husband
CHRÉTIEN DE LAFERTE, aide to Prince Johann
MARGRAVE KARL LUDWIG, Margarete's second husband
PRINCE MEINHARD, Margarete's son
KONRAD VON FRAUENBERG, Margarete's adviser
AGNES VON FLAVON, Margarete's rival

Critique:

Although this historical novel relies mainly on interesting events to keep the story going, the characters are well developed and credible. To some readers, however, the book may seem confusing, because the plot is complicated by the rivalries of various monarchs and the political situations of the fourteenth century. In spite of these difficulties, the character of the ugly duchess gives the novel a proper center at all times.

The Story:

Heinrich, King of Bohemia, Duke of Carinthia, and Count of Tyrol, was an important person to three people—King John of Luxemburg, Albert of Austria, and Ludwig of Wittelsbach. Though most of the king's hereditary territory had long been taken by others, the Tyrol and other lands he still owned were valuable. The three rival monarchs sought, by various means, to control them in order to extend their respective empires.

John of Luxemburg persuaded Heinrich to agree that his daughter, Princess Margarete, should marry John's son, Prince Johann of Luxemburg, and that Princess Margarete should be declared Heinrich's heir. It was not likely that Heinrich himself should have another heir, despite the fact that his wife, Princess Beatrix, was still young.

Princess Margarete and Prince Johann were married in childhood. At the wedding feast, Margarete took a fancy to the prince's page, Chrétien de Laferte, and insisted that he be made a knight. Johann refused, but Margarete had her way when the prince's father agreed.

Margarete was undoubtedly one of the ugliest women ever born. To compensate for her lack of charm, she concentrated upon becoming a good ruler and achieving power. Always she had to be vigilant against the encroachments of other nations, even against her own barons and nobles, who were despoiling the land. When her father died and John of Luxemburg was killed in battle, she and Johann were the joint heirs of their principalities, but it was Margarete who ruled, governing so cleverly that her fame spread throughout Europe.

She and Chrétien had become close friends. When Heinrich's mistress died, she left three daughters. One of these, Agnes von Flavon, appealed to Margarete and Johann to be permitted to retain the two fiefs which Heinrich had granted her mother. Johann was willing, but the princess declared that one of the estates should go to Chrétien. When a group of barons, including her illegitimate brother, Albert, plotted to drive the Luxemburgers from the country, Margarete consented to the revolt

THE UGLY DUCHESS by Lion Feuchtwanger. Translated by Willa and Edwin Muir. By permission of the publishers, The Viking Press, Inc. Copyright, 1928, by The Viking Press, Inc.

and urged that Chrétien be made leader of the rebels. Then Johann informed Margarete that Agnes was to marry Chrétien. Margarete sent anonymous letters telling of the planned revolt, and the rebellion was put down. Chrétien's head was sent to her by Johann, who did not know that Margarete herself had revealed the conspiracy.

A Jew named Mendel Hirsch came to the castle to ask for permission to settle in the Tyrol. Margarete granted his petition and the country prospered from the industry and crafts which the Jews brought to the area. Mendel Hirsch became her confidant. Meanwhile another rebellion was brewing. Jacob von Schenna, a friend from her youth, brought the news of the plot to Margarete. She consented to it listlessly, for her spirit had been broken because of a pogrom which resulted in the death of Hirsch and the other Jews. When Prince Johann returned to the castle, he found it barred to him. Margarete had their marriage annulled.

Margarete and Margrave Karl, son of Emperor Ludwig, were married. As a result, Luxemburgers close to the Pope influenced the pontiff to excommunicate Margarete and Karl and to place the land under an interdict. John's son was elected Holy Roman Emperor in place of the excommunicated Ludwig. The years that followed were not happy ones, and plagues and destructive fires ravaged the country. Margarete was blamed because the people thought these visitations a punishment for her illegal marriage. She and Karl had a son, Prince Meinhard, who grew up easy-going and not intelligent. Conditions of the country were so perilous that Margarete, in an effort to secure money, entered into an agreement with Albert of Austria, who promised financial assistance in return for a treaty by which Tyrol should go to Austria if she died without heirs.

In the meantime Prince Johann wished to remarry. Accordingly, he went to Margarete and made an agreement with her. When a new Pope was elected, the marriage of Margarete and Karl was solemnized and Prince Meinhard was declared their rightful heir. Later the interdict was lifted and church bells pealed as services were resumed.

One day, as the margrave was setting out on a trip, Konrad von Frauenberg, Margarete's unscrupulous adviser, went to her to say goodbye and hinted that his death might occur at any moment since Karl detested him. But it was the margrave who died, mysteriously poisoned, leaving Margarete the undisputed ruler of the principality. Then Prince Meinhard and another young prince formed the Arthurian Order, which pillaged the community. Later the order was put down, but Prince Meinhard stayed in Munich, the pawn of a rival prince. Agnes von Flavon was also in Munich and plotting against Margarete.

At the castle a group led by Konrad von Frauenberg had organized a council for the control of the state. Margarete wanted her son back, sure that her position would be stronger if he could be married to an Austrian princess. Von Frauenberg went to Munich and after some time succeeded in persuading Prince Meinhard to return home. But as they were crossing the mountains, von Frauenberg pushed Meinhard off a cliff. He told the pursuers that the prince's death had been an accident.

Agnes von Flavon returned to Tyrol, where she was promptly imprisoned by Margarete. Tried for crimes against the state, she was convicted. Margarete insisted that Agnes be executed, but the council refused to pass the death sentence. Balked, Margarete was willing to free Agnes if the prisoner would acknowledge her crimes against the state, promise to plot no more, and leave Tyrol. Agnes, believing that Margarete would not order her execution, refused. A few days later Konrad von Frauenberg slipped into her cell and poisoned Agnes.

Her funeral took place on the same day that Prince Meinhard was buried. All the nobles and barons went to Agnes' funeral; no one went to that of the prince. Even in death Agnes had won. A few days later Margarete was called upon to honor her agreement with Austria. Accordingly, she signed a proclamation to the effect that her territories were now the property of the Austrian duke. Then Margarete went into exile, to spend the rest of her days in a peasant's hut. A greedy, ugly old woman, she sniffed hungrily whenever she smelled fish cooking for dinner.

ULYSSES

Type of work: Novel
Author: James Joyce (1882-1941)
Type of plot: Psychological realism
Time of plot: June 16, 1904
Locale: Dublin
First published: 1922

Principal characters:
STEPHEN DEDALUS, a young Irish writer and teacher
BUCK MULLIGAN, a medical student
LEOPOLD BLOOM, a Jewish advertising salesman
MARION TWEEDY BLOOM (MOLLY), his wife
BLAZES BOYLAN, Mrs. Bloom's lover

Critique:

Ulysses is an attempt at the complete recapture, so far as it is possible in fiction, of the life of a particular time and place. The scene is Dublin, its streets, homes, shops, newspaper offices, pubs, hospitals, brothels, schools. The time is a single day in 1904. A continuation of the story of Stephen Dedalus as told in *A Portrait of the Artist as a Young Man,* the novel is also a series of remarkable Homeric parallels, the incidents, characters, and scenes of a Dublin day corresponding to those of the Odyssean myth. Leopold Bloom is easily recognizable as Ulysses; Molly Bloom, his wife, as Penelope, and Dedalus himself as Telemachus, son of Ulysses— in Joyce's novel Bloom's spiritual son. The book is written in a variety of styles and techniques, the most important being the stream of consciousness method by which Joyce attempts to reproduce not only the sights, sounds, and smells of Dublin, but also the memories, emotions, and desires of his people in the drab modern world. Ulysses is the most widely discussed novel of our time, the most influential for technique and style.

The Story:

Buck Mulligan mounted the stairs of the old tower and prepared to shave himself on that morning of June 16, 1904. A moment later Stephen Dedalus came to the stairhead and stood looking out over Dublin Bay. When Mulligan spoke of the sea glinting in the morning sunlight, Stephen had a sudden vision of his own mother, to whose deathbed he had been called back from Paris a year before. He remembered how she had begged him to pray for her soul and how he, rebelling against the churchly discipline of his boyhood, had refused.

After breakfast Stephen and Mulligan went off with Haines, a young Englishman who also lived in the old tower. In spite of the Englishman's attempts to be friendly, Stephen disliked Haines, who was given to night-long drunken sprees. Stephen felt that his own life was growing purposeless and dissolute through his association with Mulligan and other medical students.

Stephen was a teacher. Because it was a half-holiday at school, the boys were restless. One of his pupils was unable to do his simple arithmetic problems, and in the boy Stephen saw for a moment an image of his own awkward youth. He was relieved when he could dismiss the class.

Later he walked alone on the beach. He thought of literature and his student days, of his unhappiness in Dublin, his lack of money, his family sinking into poverty while his shabby-genteel father made his daily round of the Dublin pubs. He saw the carcass of a dead dog rolling in the surf. Stephen remembered how a dog had frightened him in his childhood; he was, he thought wryly, not one of the Irish heroes.

Meanwhile Leopold Bloom had crawled out of bed to prepare his wife's breakfast. He was a Jewish advertising salesman, for sixteen years the patient, uncomplaining husband of Marion Tweedy Bloom, a professional singer of mediocre talent. He was vaguely unhappy to know that she was carrying on an affair with Blazes Boylan, a sporting Irishman who was managing the concert tour she was planning.

Munching his own breakfast, Bloom read a letter from his daughter Milly, who was working in a photographer's shop in Mullingar. Her letter reminded Bloom of his son Rudy, who had died when he was eleven days old. Bloom read Milly's letter again, wondering about a young student his daughter mentioned. For a moment he was afraid that Milly might grow up like her mother.

Bloom set out on his morning walk. At the post-office he stopped to pick up a letter addressed to Henry Flower, Esq., a letter from a woman who signed herself Martha. Bloom, unhappy at home and under another name, was carrying on a flirtation by mail. Idly he wandered into a church and listened to part of the mass. Later he joined a party of mourners on their way to the funeral of an old friend, Paddy Dignam, who had died suddenly of a stroke. During the service Bloom watched Father Coffey. He thought again of little Rudy and of his own father, a suicide.

The day's business for Bloom was a call at a newspaper office to arrange for the printing of an advertisement. While he was there, Stephen Dedalus also came to the office. The two men saw each other, but they did not speak.

Leaving the newspaper building, Bloom walked across the O'Connell bridge. He met Mrs. Breen and gave her an account of Dignam's funeral. She told him that Mrs. Purefoy was in the maternity hospital in Holles Street. Bloom walked on, watching the sights of Dublin on a summer day. At last he entered Davy Byrne's pub and ordered a cheese sandwich. Later he went to the National Library to look at some newspaper files. There Stephen, flushed with the drinks he had taken at lunch, was expounding to Buck Mulligan and some literary friends his own ingenious theory of Shakespeare's plays and the second-best bed of Shakespeare's will. Again Bloom and Stephen saw one another but did not speak.

Bloom went to the Ormond Hotel for a late lunch. Blazes Boylan came into the bar before he went off to keep an appointment with Molly.

Late in that afternoon Bloom got into a brawl in a pub where the talk was all about money Blazes Boylan had won in a boxing match. Escaping from the jeering crowd, Bloom walked along the Sandymount shore and in the dimming twilight watched young Gertie MacDowell. The moon rose. Bloom decided to stop by the hospital to ask about Mrs. Purefoy. As he walked slowly along the strand a cuckoo-clock struck nine in a priest's house he was passing. Bloom suddenly realized that he had been cuckolded again, while he sat dreaming his amorous fantasies on the Dublin beach.

At the hospital he learned that Mrs. Purefoy's baby had not yet been born. There he saw Stephen Dedalus again, drinking with Buck Mulligan and a group of medical students. Bloom was disturbed to find the son of his old friend, Simon Dedalus, in that ribald, dissolute company.

Bloom went with the medical students to a nearby pub, where Stephen and Buck Mulligan began a drunken argument over the possession of the key to the old tower. When the group broke up Stephen and one of the students went on to a brothel in the Dublin slums, Bloom following them slowly. All were drunk by that time. Bloom had a distorted, lurid vision of his wife and Blazes Boylan together. Stephen, befuddled, thought that his dead mother suddenly appeared from the grave to ask him again to pray for her soul. Running headlong into the street, he was knocked down in a scuffle with two British soldiers. Bloom took Stephen home with him. Stephen, exhausted by his wild night, remained silent and glum while Bloom talked about art and science. Bloom had begged him to spend the night, to leave Mulligan and his wild friends and come to live with the Blooms, but Stephen refused. The bells of St. George's Church were ringing as he walked off down the silent street.

Bloom went slowly to bed. As he drifted off to sleep he told Molly firmly that she was to get up and prepare his breakfast in the morning.

Molly Bloom lay awake thinking of Blazes Boylan. She thought of the mysteries of the human body, of people she had known, of her girlhood at a military post on Gibraltar. She considered the possibility that Stephen Dedalus might come to live with her and her husband. Stephen was a writer, young, refined, not coarse like Boylan. She heard a far, shrill train whistle. She recalled the lovers she had had, Bloom's courtship, their years together, the rose she wore in her hair the day Bloom had asked her to marry him as they stood close under a Moorish arch. So wakeful, earthy Penelope's thoughts flowed on, while her tawdry Ulysses, Bloom, the far wanderer of a Dublin day, snored in the darkness by her side.

THE UNBEARABLE BASSINGTON

Type of work: Novel
Author: Saki (Hector Hugh Munro, 1870-1916)
Type of plot: Social satire
Time of plot: Early 1900's
Locale: London
First published: 1912

Principal characters:
COMUS BASSINGTON, the "unbearable" Bassington
FRANCESCA BASSINGTON, his mother
ELAINE DE FREY, an heiress
COURTNEY YOUGHAL, a young M. P.
HENRY GREECH, Mrs. Bassington's brother

Critique:

H. H. Munro, who wrote under the pen name of Saki, belongs to the tradition of the social satirists, including Oscar Wilde and Evelyn Waugh. *The Unbearable Bassington* represents the essence of the inimitable Saki: his amusing dialogue, his skillful use of poetic figures, his sharp wit. This short novel is a brilliant piece of satire, excellent in its character studies and pungent dialogue. Though it has been said that the discovery about the painting at the end of the volume is an unnecessary feature, the fake masterpiece represents a typical Saki touch.

The Story:

Francesca Bassington was a successful member of London society who was able to make a little money go a long way. Her greatest interest in life was the drawing-room in her small, perfect house on Blue Street. Foremost of her treasures was a famous Van der Meulen masterpiece, which hung in the paneled place of honor in that charming room. She also had a son Comus who presented a serious problem to his mother because of his casual attitude toward life. Francesca had come to the conclusion that there was only one solution for her son's future. He must marry a wealthy girl. Her first choice was Emmeline Chetrof, who would eventually come into a comfortable fortune and, most important of all, would upon her marriage inherit the house in which Francesca lived.

During the time Comus was at school Francesca wrote her son, asking him to show special kindness to Emmeline's brother Lancelot. That suggestion on the part of his mother caused Comus to treat the child even more cruelly, and her plans for a match between Comus and Emmeline Chetrof ended dismally.

Two years later, when Comus was turned loose in his mother's fashionable world of Mayfair and Ascot, she persuaded her brother, Henry Greech, to secure a position for the young man as a secretary to Sir John Jull, the governor of an island in the West Indies. Because he did not want to leave England, Comus sent to a newspaper an article criticizing Sir John. This scurrilous attack was written by Courtney Youghal, a young politician whom Comus knew and admired. Printed over Comus' signature, it had the desired result. Comus lost the position Sir John had promised.

At a dinner given by Lady Caroline Benaresq, Francesca Bassington first learned that her son was interested in Elaine de Frey, a wealthy girl who resembled a painting by Leonardo da Vinci. At the same party Francesca learned that Courtney Youghal was also interested in the young heiress.

One summer afternoon Elaine de Frey entertained her two suitors, Comus and Courtney, at tea in her garden. Elaine,

THE UNBEARABLE BASSINGTON by Saki, from THE NOVELS AND PLAYS OF SAKI. By permission of the publishers, The Viking Press, Inc. Copyright, 1930, by The Viking Press, Inc.

an earnest and practical young lady, had analyzed her suitors carefully, but even though she realized that Comus was both frivolous and undependable she found herself falling in love with him and making excuses for his shortcomings. Courtney, as a rising member of Parliament, also interested her and seemed to her practical mind a better risk than Comus. When the tea was served, Comus snatched up a silver basket containing the only bread and butter sandwiches and dashed off to feed the swans. Returning with the basket, an heirloom of the de Frey family, Comus asked permission to keep it as a souvenir of a delightful tea party. Elaine did not wish to part with the piece of silver, but Comus made such a scene that she finally gave in to his wishes.

One fine June morning all of London society had turned out to ride, walk, or sit in the chairs along the Row. Courtney Youghal was there discussing the theater with Lady Veula Croot. In a secluded part of the Row, Elaine and Comus had rented chairs. The two had drifted apart slightly because of small unrepaid loans which Comus had requested and because of the affair of the silver basket. That morning Comus again asked Elaine to lend him money —five pounds to pay a gambling debt. She promised to send him two pounds by messenger and curtly asked to be excused. He had hurt her pride and alarmed her practical sense of caution. As she was leaving the Row she met Courtney. Over the luncheon table they became engaged.

At an exhibition at the Rutland Galleries Comus learned of Elaine's engagement. Elaine had intended to write Comus a gracious but final note, but instead she went to call on her cousin Suzette, to break the news of her engagement. When Elaine returned home after her call, she found a letter from Comus awaiting her. In the letter he thanked her for the loan, returned the money, and promised to return the silver basket in lieu of a wedding gift.

Francesca Bassington learned of the engagement, a blow to her elaborate plans, from that inveterate gossip, George St. Michael. She informed Comus that he must take a position in West Africa, for which Henry Greech had made arrangements. With his eyes on the Van der Meulen masterpiece, Comus asked his mother if she could not sell something. Mrs. Bassington was fiercely angry at such a suggestion and scolded him severely.

That night, as lonely Comus watched the play from the stalls of the Straw Exchange Theatre, he envied Courtney and Elaine and their circle of friends. Francesca learned from St. Michael, her usual source, that Emmeline Chetrof was to be married but only after a long engagement. Thus her beloved house on Blue Street was safe for a time. Francesca entertained at a dull dinner party in honor of her son's departure—a party to which none of Comus' friends was invited.

In the meantime, Courtney and Elaine were taking their wedding trip on the continent. During their honeymoon they soon discovered that neither loved the other, that the marriage was not likely to be highly successful. Comus Bassington, exiled to West Africa, was bored and unhappy. Shortly before Christmas Francesca received a cablegram saying that Comus was dangerously ill. To calm herself, she walked in the park, for the first time realizing how selfish her love for her possessions, especially the Van der Meulen, had been. During the time she was walking, her brother brought an eminent critic to inspect the masterpiece. Returning to the house, she found a cablegram announcing the death of Comus. A few minutes later George Greech arrived to inform her that the Van der Meulen masterpiece was not an original, but only a good copy. While his voice buzzed on and on, Francesca sat stricken among her prized pieces of silver, bronze, and porcelain—all of them as beautiful and soulless as Francesca herself.

UNCLE SILAS

Type of work: Novel
Author: Joseph Sheridan Le Fanu (1814-1873)
Type of plot: Mystery romance
Time of plot: Nineteenth century
Locale: England
First published: 1864

Principal characters:
MAUD RUTHYN, an English heiress
AUSTIN RUTHYN, her father
SILAS RUTHYN, her uncle and guardian
MILLY, Silas' daughter
DUDLEY, his son
LADY MONICA KNOLLYS, Maud's cousin
DR. BRYERLY, a trustee of the Ruthyn estate
LORD ILBURY, another trustee
MADAME DE LA ROUGIERRE, a governess
MEG HAWKES, a servant

Critique:

Uncle Silas is more than the sentimental, nineteenth-century story of the designing uncle and the lovely heiress driven almost insane by terror. It is a well-constructed novel, rambling in the Victorian fashion but highly effective in the mechanics of atmosphere and suspense. Le Fanu, in fact, protested against the labeling of his novels as examples of the sensational school of fiction popularized by Wilkie Collins and Charles Reade. In his view, his fiction was a continuation of that type of tragic romance exemplified in *The Bride of Lammermoor* and other novels by Sir Walter Scott. The fact remains that Le Fanu has never lost a following of readers to keep his name alive, and this novel is an example of his fiction at its best. Most notable is his handling of character and scene as we sometimes see them in old Dutch paintings, with certain figures prominently in the foreground, others in the middle distance, and still others in the background, all clearly visualized, however, and busy with whatever happens to be at hand. Uncle Silas and Madame de la Rougierre are creatures of terror in the foreground, but equally relevant are Dudley Ruthyn, Dr. Bryerly, Lady Monica, Milly, and Meg Hawkes, figures successively removed from the center of the action but no less necessary for atmosphere and plot.

The Story:

Maud Ruthyn had spent a lonely childhood in the great old house at Knowl. Her mother had died when the girl was very young, and her father, Austin Ruthyn, had become a recluse who seldom left the grounds of his estate. Disappointed in Parliament many years before, he had retired from public life to devote himself to scientific and literary studies. These had led him to Swedenborgianism, a doctrine suited to his eccentric and moral tastes. His daughter knew him only as a kindly but solitary and taciturn man.

For this reason she never questioned him about her uncle Silas, whose portrait as a handsome young man hung in the oak room at Knowl. From vague hints and the whispers of the servants she knew that some mystery overshadowed this relative she had never met, a scandal which had clouded her father's life as well. Uncle Silas, a younger brother, lived at Bartram-Haugh, a Derbyshire estate owned by Austin Ruthyn.

One of the few visitors at Knowl was Dr. Bryerly, a tall, ungainly man who dressed always in black and wore an untidy scratch wig. Like Maud's father, he was a Swedenborgian. The girl was greatly in awe of him, but she knew that he had her father's confidence. On one occasion Mr. Ruthyn showed her the key to a locked cabinet in his study. He was soon to go on a journey, he said, and after his departure she was to give the key to Dr. Bryerly and to no other.

Maud was a little past seventeen when her father employed a new governess, Madame de la Rougierre, a tall, masculine-looking woman who was smirking and sly in her speech and manners. Maud hated her from the first. On every possible occasion the governess questioned her charge about Mr. Ruthyn's will and business affairs; sometimes Maud thought that the woman was deliberately spying on the household. One day Madame de la Rougierre and her pupil walked to a ruined abbey near Knowl. While the woman was exploring the ancient churchyard, a strange young man accosted Maud. The girl was frightened by his coarse appearance and offensive manner, but Madame de la Rougierre ignored the incident.

Maud forgot the whole affair in her excitement over the arrival of Lady Monica Knollys, her father's cousin from Derbyshire. Madame de la Rougierre pretended to be ill during Lady Monica's visit. When that brisk, sensible noblewoman went to the governess' room, the conversation revealed that they had previously known each other under circumstances distasteful to Lady Monica. When she told Mr. Ruthyn that the governess was not a suitable companion for his daughter, he accused her of prejudice, and a lively dispute followed. The result was that Lady Monica left Knowl abruptly, but not before she had warned Maud against Madame de la Rougierre and cautioned her always to be on guard against her. Lady Monica also told Maud that at one time her uncle Silas had been suspected of murder, but that nothing had been charged. Later Silas had interested himself in religion. Lady Monica, it was plain, did not like him.

A short time later Maud had another strange adventure. While she was walking with Madame de la Rougierre in the park, they saw on an unfrequented road a carriage with one woman as its only passenger. Continuing on their way, they met three men, among them the coarse young stranger who had approached Maud near the ruins of the abbey. All were tipsy and addressed the governess with rough familiarity. When one of the men tried to seize Maud, her screams attracted two gamekeepers. In a scuffle with the intruders one of the gamekeepers was shot. Mr. Ruthyn and the servants tried to intercept the strangers at the park gates, but the men and their woman companion had disappeared.

Madame de la Rougierre was discharged not long afterward. One night Maud fell asleep in her father's study. She awoke to find the governess going through his private papers. Informed of the midnight search, Mr. Ruthyn discharged the woman at once. Maud was glad to see the last, as she supposed, of her sly, simpering governess.

When Mr. Ruthyn died suddenly of a heart attack, Maud understood at last the journey he had contemplated. She learned also that Dr. Bryerly had been her father's physician as well as his friend. With the key she gave him the doctor unlocked the cabinet which contained Mr. Ruthyn's will. Its provisions disturbed Dr. Bryerly and filled Lady Monica with dismay. After varying bequests to relatives, friends, and servants, the remainder of Mr. Ruthyn's great estate was given to Maud, under the trusteeship of Dr. Bryerly, Lord Ilbury, Sir William Aylmer, and Mr. Penrose Cresswell. In addition, Silas Ruthyn was appointed Maud's guardian, with the stipulation that the girl was to live with him at Bartram-Haugh until her twenty-first birthday. Lady Monica immediately recalled the strange circumstances under which Mr. Charke, a turfman to whom Silas Ruthyn owed large gambling debts, had been found dead at Bartram-Haugh;

only the fact that the body had been discovered in a bedroom locked from the inside had kept Silas from being charged with murder. Dr. Bryerly, in turn, was disturbed by the knowledge that Silas would inherit her fortune if Maud died before her majority, and he advised that an attempt be made to have the provisions of the wardship put aside. Silas, however, refused to relinquish his guardianship. Maud, who interpreted the will as her father's wish that she vindicate her uncle's name by becoming his ward, announced that she would go to live with Silas in Derbyshire.

With her maid, Mary Quince, Maud traveled by carriage to Bartram-Haugh. The house was old and rambling, with many of the rooms closed and locked. The grounds were wild and neglected. Although Silas welcomed his niece courteously and with many pious sentiments, it seemed to Maud that he was secretly laughing at her at times. His own rooms were furnished in great luxury. The quarters Maud shared with her cousin Milly were shabby and bare. Milly was a loud, good-humored girl at whom her father sneered because of her hoydenish manners. Maud took an immediate liking to her young relative. There was also a son, Dudley, but Milly said that her brother was seldom at home.

The first morning after her arrival Maud went with her cousin for a walk through the grounds. To their surprise they found the gate leading into Bartram Close locked and guarded by Meg Hawkes, the miller's rough-tongued daughter. When Meg refused to let them pass, the girls entered the park by a little-traveled path that Milly knew. There they met a pleasant young gentleman who introduced himself as Mr. Carysbrook, a tenant at the nearby Grange. Maud felt that he paid her particular attention; she, in turn, was attracted to the amiable and pleasant young man.

Maud had Milly as her only companion. She saw little of her uncle. Addicted to laudanum, Silas passed many of his days in a coma. Sometimes the girls were summoned to sit in his room while he lay quietly in bed. One day Dr. Bryerly appeared unexpectedly to transact some business with Silas. To the doctor's questions Maud replied that she was happy at Bartram-Haugh. Dr. Bryerly gave her his address in London and told her to communicate with him if the need should ever arise.

Early in December, Lady Monica Knollys opened her house at nearby Elverston and invited Maud and Milly to visit her. To Milly's surprise, Silas gave his consent. Among the guests at dinner was Mr. Carysbrook. Lady Monica told Maud that he was in reality Lord Ilbury, one of her trustees.

In the meantime Dudley Ruthyn had returned to Bartram-Haugh. Summoned to her uncle's room to meet him, Maud realized that he was the same vulgar young man she had encountered twice before, at Knowl. When she told of those meetings, Silas brushed the matter aside. The spirits of youth, he declared, ran high at times, but Dudley was a gentleman. Maud was relieved to learn that Milly disliked and feared her brother, and the girls avoided him as much as possible. Meg Hawkes, brutalized by her father, became ill. Maud supplied her with medicines and delicacies and so won the strange girl's devotion.

Lord Ilbury called at Bartram-Haugh and expressed the hope that Maud would be allowed to visit his sister at the Grange. Dr. Bryerly also appeared and accused Silas of misusing his ward's property. Infuriated, Silas ordered him out of the house. When the invitation from the Grange arrived, Silas angrily refused his consent to the visit. A short time later Maud was made unhappy when Milly was sent to study in a French convent, but her situation became even more unbearable when Dudley began to persecute her with his proposals of marriage. Silas refused to listen to her protests. She should, he said, give the matter her serious attention for a fortnight. Before that time passed, however, Dudley's unwelcome attentions abruptly ended when his secret marriage to Sarah Mangles, a barmaid, was revealed. Sarah was the woman Maud had seen in the carriage at Knowl. In his rage Silas sent Dudley and his bride away. Before his departure Dudley offered to conduct Maud safely to Lady Monica for twenty thousand pounds. Convinced that this was another of his schemes, she refused. A few days later she saw in the paper an announcement stating that Dudley and his wife had sailed for Melbourne.

Silas confessed to his ward that he faced final and complete ruin. To elude his creditors, he said, he would be forced to send Maud to join Milly in France; he himself would travel by another route to join them there. Maud grew apprehensive, however, when she learned that her companion on the journey was to be Madame de la Rougierre, her former governess. Confined like a prisoner, she tried to communicate her plight to Lady Monica, but the servant she bribed to carry her letter returned the message to his master. With reproaches for her ingratitude and accusations against him, Silas told her that she was to leave for France immediately with Madame de la Rougierre; Mary Quince, the maid, would follow with him in a few days.

Maud, guarded by her grim companion, traveled to London and spent the night in an obscure hotel. The next night they entrained, as Madame de la Rougierre informed her, for Dover. Maud was so dull and sleepy on their arrival that she paid little attention to the house to which they were driven. The next morning she awoke and found herself, not in a Dover inn, but in one of the upper chambers at Bartram-Haugh. Madame de la Rougierre said only that there had been a change in plans. Maud realized that everything told her had been lies, that she was to die. Her only hope was that Meg Hawkes, who had unexpectedly

appeared, would carry word of Silas' villainy to Lady Monica at Elverston.

That night Madame de la Rougierre drank some drugged wine intended for Maud and fell asleep on the girl's bed. Crouched in the shadows of an old press, Maud was surprised to see the window of the room swing inward and a man suspended by a rope clamber over the sill. The intruder was Dudley; the announcement of his departure for Australia had been another of Silas' fabrications. Dazed, she saw him raise a spiked hammer and strike at the figure on the bed. When old Silas entered by the doorway and the two began to open a trunk containing the girl's jewelry, she took advantage of the noise and ran from the room. As she left the house she encountered Tom Brice, a servant in love with Meg Hawkes. The man, cursing his master's villainy, drove her to safety at Elverston.

So shaken was she by her experience that Lady Monica hurried her off to France at once, and two years passed before she learned what had happened after her flight. Silas had killed himself with an overdose of opium. Dudley had disappeared. Madame de la Rougierre's body had been found buried in the courtyard, its whereabouts disclosed by Meg Hawkes' brutal old father. Subsequent investigation had also revealed that Maud's room was the chamber in which Charke had been found dead; the peculiar construction of the window frame explained how his murderer had been able to enter a room locked from the inside. But those grim discoveries were forgotten as time passed. Milly became the wife of a worthy clergyman. Meg Hawkes married Tom Brice and the two, with capital provided by Maud, emigrated. Dr. Bryerly gave up his practice and undertook the management of the Ruthyn estates. As for Maud, she married Lord Ilbury and found new happiness as a wife and mother.

UNCLE TOM'S CABIN

Type of work: Novel
Author: Harriet Beecher Stowe (1811-1896)
Type of plot: Sentimental romance
Time of plot: Mid-nineteenth century
Locale: Kentucky and Mississippi
First published: 1852

Principal characters:
UNCLE TOM, a Negro slave
EVA ST. CLARE, daughter of a wealthy Southerner
SIMON LEGREE, a planter
ELIZA, a runaway slave
TOPSY, a black imp

Critique:

A sentimental but powerful document in the controversy over slavery, *Uncle Tom's Cabin, or, Life Among the Lowly* is a novel whose political and humanitarian pleading is now outdated. The highly exaggerated Legree and the highly exaggerated Eva, however, have become properties of the American imagination. The novel seems linked to two popular traditions. It incorporates all the sentimental elements of the novel of feeling, and in its horror scenes it suggests the Gothic novels of Mrs. Radcliffe and Horace Walpole.

The Story:

Because his Kentucky plantation was encumbered by debt, Mr. Shelby made plans to sell one of his slaves to his chief creditor, a New Orleans slave dealer named Haley. The dealer shrewdly selected Uncle Tom as part payment on Mr. Shelby's debt. While they were discussing the transaction, Eliza's child, Harry, came into the room. Haley wanted to buy Harry too, but at first Shelby was unwilling to part with the child. Eliza listened to enough of the conversation to be frightened. She confided her fears to George Harris, her husband, a slave on an adjoining plantation. George, who was already bitter because his master had put him to work in the fields when he was capable of doing better work, promised that some day he would have his revenge upon his hard masters. Eliza had been brought up more indulgently by the Shelbys and she begged him not to try anything rash.

After supper in the cabin of Uncle Tom and Aunt Chloe, his wife, the Shelby slaves gathered for a meeting. They sang songs, and young George Shelby, who had eaten his supper there, read from the Bible. In the big house Mr. Shelby signed the papers making Uncle Tom and little Harry the property of Haley. Eliza, learning her child's fate from some remarks of Mr. Shelby to his wife, fled with her child, hoping to reach Canada and safety. Uncle Tom, hearing of the sale, resigned himself to the wisdom of providence.

The next day, after Haley had discovered his loss, he set out to capture Eliza. However, she had a good start. Moreover, Mrs. Shelby purposely delayed the pursuit by serving a late breakfast. When her pursuers came in sight, Eliza escaped across the Ohio River by jumping from one floating ice cake to another, young Harry in her arms.

Haley hired two slave-catchers, Marks and Loker, to track Eliza through Ohio. For their trouble she was to be given to them. They set off that night.

Eliza found shelter in the home of Senator and Mrs. Bird. The senator took her to the house of a man known to aid fugitive slaves. Uncle Tom, however, was not so lucky. Haley made sure Tom would not escape by shackling his ankles

UNCLE TOM'S CABIN by Harriet Beecher Stowe. Published by Houghton Mifflin Co.

before taking him to the boat bound for New Orleans. When young George Shelby heard Tom had been sold, he followed Haley on his horse. George gave Tom a dollar as a token of his sympathy and told him that he would buy him back one day.

At the same time George Harris began his escape. White enough to pass as a Spaniard, he appeared at a tavern as a gentleman and took a room there, hoping to find before long a station on the underground railway.

Eliza was resting at the home of Rachel and Simeon Halliday when George Harris arrived in the same Quaker settlement.

On board the boat bound for New Orleans, Uncle Tom saved the life of young Eva St. Clare, and in gratitude Eva's father purchased the slave. Eva told Tom he would now have a happy life, for her father was kind to everyone. Augustine St. Clare was married to a woman who imagined herself sick and therefore took no interest in her daughter Eva. He had gone north to bring back his cousin, Miss Ophelia, to provide care for the neglected and delicate Eva. When they arrived at the St. Clare plantation, Tom was made head coachman.

Meanwhile Loker and Marks were on the trail of Eliza and George. They caught up with the fugitives and there was a fight in which George wounded Loker. Marks fled, and so the Quakers who were protecting the runaways took Loker along with them and gave him medical treatment.

Unused to lavish Southern customs, Miss Ophelia tried to understand the South. Shocked at the extravagance of St. Clare's household, she attempted to bring order out of the chaos, but she received no encouragement because the slaves had been humored and petted too long. Indulgent in all things, St. Clare was indifferent to the affairs of his family and his property. Uncle Tom lived an easy life in the loft over the stable. He and little Eva became close friends with St. Clare's approval. Sometimes St. Clare

had doubts regarding the institution of slavery, and in one of these moods he bought an odd pixie-like child, Topsy, for his prim New England cousin to educate.

Eva grew more frail. Knowing that she was about to die, she asked her father to free his slaves, as he had so often promised. After Eva's death St. Clare began to read his Bible and to make plans to free all his slaves. He gave Topsy to Miss Ophelia legally, so that the spinster might rear the child as she wished. Then one evening he tried to separate two quarreling men. He received a knife wound in the side and died shortly afterward. Mrs. St. Clare had no intention of freeing the slaves, and she ordered Tom sent to the slave market.

At a public auction he was sold to a brutal plantation owner named Simon Legree. Legree drank heavily, and his plantation house had fallen to ruin. He kept dogs for the purpose of tracking runaway slaves. At the slave quarters Tom was given his sack of corn for the week, told to grind it himself and bake the meal into cakes for his supper. At the mill he aided two women. In return they baked his cakes for him. He read selections from the Bible to them.

For a few weeks Tom quietly tried to please his harsh master. One day he helped a sick woman by putting cotton into her basket. For this act Legree ordered him to flog the woman. When Tom refused, his master had him flogged until he fainted. A slave named Cassy came to Tom's aid. She told Tom the story of her life with Legree and of a young daughter who had been sold years before.

Then she went to Legree's apartment and tormented him. She hated her master and she had power over him. Legree was superstitious. When she talked, letting her eyes flash over him, he felt as though she were casting an evil spell. Haunted by the secrets of his guilty past, he drank until he fell asleep. But he had forgotten his fears by the next morning, and he knocked Tom to the ground with his fist.

Meanwhile, far to the north, George and Eliza and young Harry were making their way slowly through the stations on the underground railway toward Canada.

Cassy and Emmeline, another slave, determined to make their escape. Knowing the consequences if they should be caught, they tricked Legree into thinking they were hiding in the swamp. When Legree sent dogs and men after them, they sneaked back into the house and hid in the garret. Legree suspected that Tom knew where the women had gone and decided to beat the truth out of his slave. He had Tom beaten until the old man could neither speak nor stand.

Two days later George Shelby arrived to buy Tom back, but he came too late. Tom was dying. When George threatened to have Legree tried for murder, Legree mocked him. George struck Legree in the face and knocked him down.

Still hiding in the attic, Cassy and Emmeline pretended they were ghosts. Frightened, Legree drank harder than ever. George Shelby helped them to escape. Later, on a river boat headed north, the two women discovered a Madame de Thoux, who said she was George Harris' sister. With this disclosure, Cassy learned also that Eliza, her daughter, was the Eliza who had married George and with him and her child had escaped safely to Canada.

These relatives were reunited in Canada after many years. In Kentucky George Shelby freed all his slaves when his father died. He said he freed them in the name of Uncle Tom.

UNCLE VANYA

Type of work: Drama
Author: Anton Chekhov (1860-1904)
Type of plot: Impressionistic realism
Time of plot: Nineteenth century
Locale: Russia
First presented: 1899

Principal characters:
ALEXANDR SEREBRYAKOV, a retired professor
YELENA ANDREYEVNA, his wife, aged twenty-seven
SONYA ALEXANDROVNA, his daughter by his first wife
MARYA VOYNITSKY, widow of a Privy Councillor and
mother of his first wife
IVAN VOYNITSKY (UNCLE VANYA), her son
MIHAIL ASTROV, a doctor
MARINA, an old nurse

Critique:

Chekhov's plays were meant to be acted by people who immersed themselves so deeply in the parts that they infected their audiences with strong emotions and moods suggested simply or subtly. It is more difficult to read these plays, but a great deal of satisfaction can be derived from them if they are read with a sympathy for characters who are perhaps ordinary in themselves, though they really speak for the whole world. In *Uncle Vanya* we feel the hopelessness of Sonya and Uncle Vanya, who have dedicated their lives to a mistaken ideal in supporting Professor Serebryakov, and yet we feel at least Sonya's faith that they will have eventual rest for their troubles.

The Story:

Astrov, the doctor, called to minister to retired Professor Serebryakov, who had complained all night of pains in his legs. To the annoyance of the doctor, however, the professor had gone for a long walk with his wife Yelena and Sonya, his daughter. Astrov told the old nurse, Marina, that he felt a hundred years old, overworked as he was. Too, he felt that, having worked with weak, discontented people for years, he had become as strange as they. Caring for nothing and no one,

he wondered if people living a hundred years hence would remember men like him who had struggled to beat out a road for them.

Marina explained that the professor had completely changed the routine of the house, so that everyone waited on him and everyday work was sandwiched in if possible. Ivan Voynitsky enviously described the fortunate life the professor had, living on the fruits of his first wife's estate, with her mother doting on his every word, retired now and writing as he pleased, with a new and beautiful young wife to cater to him. But it had been Ivan, Uncle Vanya to Sonya, who worked with him, who had blindly followed his mother's ideals and made the estate a splendidly productive place to supply extra money for the professor. Only recently had he realized how selfish the professor had been in treading over everybody. Ivan told his mother that he could no longer bear to hear of the pamphlets which had been her life for the last fifty years.

When the professor came in, he immediately excused himself to get to his writing. Yelena, apologizing to the doctor, said that her husband was well again. Both Ivan and the doctor admired her ex-

UNCLE VANYA by Anton Chekhov, from PLAYS BY ANTON TCHEKOFF. Translated by Marian Fell. By permission of the publishers, Charles Scribner's Sons. Copyright, 1912, by Charles Scribner's Sons. Renewed, 1939, by Charles Scribner's Sons.

travagantly, and the doctor invited her and Sonya to come to his estate to see his trees. A crank on the subject of trees, the doctor wanted to restore the countryside to its former state before the peasants cut down forests indiscriminately. Yelena realized Sonya was attracted to the doctor. Yelena was bored with everything, even Ivan's love for her.

Again the professor complained of pains in his legs, this time keeping his wife awake for two nights. Believing that he had earned the right to be disagreeable and tyrannical at his age, and feeling that he was in a vault with stupid people who made foolish conversation, he refused to see the doctor he had summoned. He begged not to be left with Ivan, who would talk him to death. Only Marina seemed to be able to handle him; she led him away so that the others could rest.

Yelena asked Ivan to try to reconcile everyone, since all seemed to be involved in hatred or petty wrangling. When Ivan made love to her again, she left him. Ivan realized he could have fallen in love with her ten years before and might even have married her if he had not been wrapped up in the ideal of fulfilling the professor's wishes. He felt cheated in the realization that the professor, retired, was a nonentity.

Ivan and the doctor continued the drinking they had started while the doctor waited to see the professor. Sonya asked them both to stop; Ivan because he was living on illusions, the doctor because she did not want him to destroy himself. She tried to tell him obliquely that she loved him, but he felt his reactions had been blunted. He would never be able to love anyone, though Yelena might be able to turn his head.

Yelena and Sonya effected a reconciliation when Yelena explained that she had married Sonya's father in the belief that she loved him, only to find she was in love with an ideal. Having lost that illusion, she found herself very unhappy. Sonya, glad to make friends with her, was happy about everything; she had

spoken at last to the doctor, even if he had not understood her.

While waiting for the hour at which the professor had asked all the family to join him, Yelena complained of being bored. Sonya suggested that she help on the estate. When Yelena declined all suggestions, Ivan told her she was too indolent to do anything. To make matters worse, her indolence was catching, for he had stopped work to follow her, as had Sonya and the doctor, who used to come once a month but now came daily. Since Yelena seemed to have mermaid blood in her veins, he said, she should let herself go for once and fall in love with a watersprite. Yelena was indignant. Ivan, as a peace offering, went to get her some autumn roses.

Sonya asked Yelena's help. She knew the doctor came to see Yelena, not even realizing Sonya was there. Yelena decided to speak to him in Sonya's behalf. When she did, he laughed at her for pretending she did not know why he came. Then he kissed her. Yelena halfheartedly held him off until she saw Ivan returning with the roses.

The professor, not content with country living but unable to live in the city on the income from the estate, suggested that they sell the estate, invest most of the money, and buy a small place in Finland with the remainder. His plan was greeted with horror, particularly by Ivan, who was driven almost mad as he felt the estate slipping away from Sonya, the work of twenty-five years undone. He explained how the estate had been bought for Sonya's mother and handed on to Sonya; how he had paid off the mortgage and made the place productive; how Sonya and he had slaved on the property by day and over books by night with only the professor in mind. Feeling cheated, he rushed away while the professor declared that he could no longer live under the same roof with Ivan. Yelena begged him to leave the place immediately, but to apologize to Ivan before they left. When the professor tried to make amends, Ivan shot at him twice, missing both times.

Marina, pleased with the arrangement, hoped that matters would settle down after the professor and his wife left. Astrov refused to go home before Ivan had given back the morphia he had taken from the doctor's bag. Ivan, saying he was a madman, begged for a way out, but the doctor laughed and said that both of them, the only well-educated men in the district, had been swamped in the trivialities of country life and that they were both cranks, a very normal condition of man. After reconciliations all around, the professor and Yelena left, followed by Astrov. Marina rocked away with satisfaction, Ivan's mother went back to her pamphlets, and Sonya assured Ivan that after work to rest their minds they would find life happier.

UNDER FIRE

Type of work: Novel
Author: Henri Barbusse (1874-1935)
Type of plot: Social criticism
Time of plot: 1914-1915
Locale: France
First published: 1917

> Principal characters:
> VOLPATTE,
> EUDORE,
> POTERLOO, and
> JOSEPH MESNIL, French soldiers

Critique:

Barbusse ranks in time with the first of the writers who deglorified war. To him war in the trenches was a saga of mud, lice, and death. When they had to, the poilus worked and fought with a will, but anyone who had a wound severe enough for hospitalization was considered lucky. The characters have neither illusions nor glamour, but they do appreciate the necessity of stamping out war. To most of them the essence of war means killing Germans, but a few look on the enemy as people like themselves. Under Fire has no thread of plot; it is a mere series of incidents with only the war to connect them. The merit of the book lies in the vivid pictures it presents.

The Story:

High up in the mountains, the rich old men had every medical care at their sanatorium. When an obsequious servant softly told them that war had begun, they took the news in various ways. One said France must win; another thought it would be the last war.

Far down on the plain one could see specks, like ants, hurrying to and fro. Those thirty million men, in their common misery, held great power in their hands. When they became miserable enough, they would stop wars.

That morning they came out of the dugouts to the sound of rifle fire and cannonading. They were in fantastic dress against the cold, the damp, the mud; and all were incredibly dirty. As they stumbled out into the trenches, they reached inside their clothes to scratch their bare skins. As they walked along the trench, the oozy mud released each foot with a sticky sigh. Bertrand's squad, holding a secondary trench in the reserve line, was getting ready for another day. Lamuse, the ox-man, was puffy around the eyes; he had been on fatigue duty during the night.

Three breathless fatigue men brought up the breakfast. One of the squad asked what was in the cans; the mess man merely shrugged. Paradis looked in the cans; there were kidney beans in oil, bully beef, pudding, and coffee.

Cocon explained to his neighbor the arrangement of the trenches, for Cocon had seen a military map and had made some calculations. There were over six thousand miles of trenches on the French side and as many more on the German side. The French front was only an eighth part of the total world front. Just to think about it made one more insignificant, and it was terrible to imagine so much mud. The only possible way to look at the whole matter was to concentrate on dislodging the Boches in the opposite lines.

Tirloir had once seen a captured German officer, a Prussian colonel, who was being led along the communication trench when Tirloir kicked him. The colonel nearly had a seizure when he realized that a mere private had touched him. The squad agreed that the German officers were the real evil.

There was a disturbance just ahead; some important people were coming to visit. One could hear oaths and grunts when it became known that they were civilians. One of the visitors was so bold as to ask if the coffee were good. The squad remembered the saying that winning a war is certain if the civilians can hold out.

When the mail came around, rumors flew fast. Many were sure that their squad was soon to be sent to the Riviera for a long rest; another had heard they were going to Egypt. The troops stopped their gossip as a company of African soldiers moved by; they decided an attack had been planned. The Africans were notoriously ferocious fighters.

During a sharp attack, Volpatte had both of his ears almost cut off. At the dressing station the doctors bandaged his head. Volpatte was happy to be going to the rear, for at last he could rest. After a long while he came back to the trenches with his ears nicely sewed. When his comrades asked him about the hospital he was so angry he could scarcely speak. Then it all came out; the hospital was swarming with malcontents, malingerers, and general shirkers. The worst were those assigned to the hospital for duty; they seemed to think they ran the whole war. The squad soothed Volpatte; let those who could, get by easily.

When the squad retired for a brief rest, they were billeted in a village where for an outrageous sum they rented a cow shed without walls. For a table they had a door on some boxes and a plank for a bench. But it was a wonderful experience to be above ground once more. The woman who ran the house sold them wine for twenty-two sous, although the established price was fifteen sous a bottle. Everywhere they went they heard the same story; the civilians had all the hardships.

Eudore got a fourteen-day leave. His wife, a practical person, applied well in advance for a permit to go to the village of her husband's people. She herself ran a tiny inn with only one room, where she would have no privacy to entertain her man, and Eudore's people had a big house. Eudore arrived in his village after much delay with only seven days left of his furlough, but his wife was not there; her permit had not arrived. Fearing to miss her, he stayed with his parents and waited. Then she wrote to say that no permits were allowed for civilian travel. Eudore went to the mayor and got permission to go to his wife. It was raining very hard when he got off the train to walk the several additional miles to his home. On the way he fell in with four poilus returning from leave. They tramped along together in the rain until they came to the inn. But Eudore and his wife could not turn out the four poilus in the rain, and so all six of them spent the night on chairs in the tiny room. Early in the morning Eudore left; his furlough was over.

Fraternization with the Boche was strictly forbidden. While out looking for bodies, Poterloo took a chance and fell in with some German privates, jolly fellows who offered to go with Poterloo to a nearby Alsatian village so that he could see his wife. Poterloo put on some great boots and a Boche coat and followed his friends behind the German lines. They reached the village safely. That night Poterloo walked twice past the house where his wife was staying with relatives. Through the lighted window he could see his wife and her sister at dinner with a group of German non-coms. They were laughing and eating well. Poterloo carried back to the trenches a disheartening picture of his wife laughing up into the face of a German sergeant.

There were six Mesnil brothers, four of them already killed by 1915. Joseph and André were pessimistic about their own chances. On reconnaissance, one of Bertrand's squad discovered André propped upright in a shell crater. At first they were afraid to tell Joseph, but he did not seem much affected by the news. Bertrand was killed. Then Joseph was wounded in the leg and taken to the dismal dressing station, a large dugout. There were many men in the dugout, most of them resigned to death, all of them given to spiritless discussion. It was agreed that to stop war you had to kill the spirit of war. That appeared to be a difficult job. It came as a new thought to some of them that they were the masses, and the masses had the power to stop war. But it was just too much to do. Many men thought only in terms of killing Boches. It hardly mattered anyway. Nearly all of them would be dead soon. The war went on.

UNDER THE GREENWOOD TREE

Type of work: Novel
Author: Thomas Hardy (1840-1928)
Type of plot: Regional romance
Time of plot: Nineteenth century
Locale: Rural England
First published: 1872

Principal characters:
REUBEN DEWY, a carrier
DICK DEWY, his son
MR. SHINER, a farmer
MR. MAYBOLD, the vicar
FANCY DAY, a schoolmistress

Critique:

Unlike the stark realism and philosophical pessimism found in most of the novels of Thomas Hardy, Under the Greenwood Tree is almost pure romance. It is a gentle story, full of whimsical, simple humor. The characterizations, in particular those of the Wessex rustics, are delightful, even though often so simplified as to appear to be caricatures. This book, one of his early novels by a great English master, deserves a place with those of his maturity.

The Story:

On Christmas Eve the village choir prepared to go about its annual caroling. In fine voice, mellowed by generous mugs of cider, the men and boys gathered at the home of Reuben Dewy. Then with their fiddles and the cello of Grandfather Dewy, they departed on their rounds. The first stop was at the schoolhouse, to serenade the new schoolmistress, Fancy Day. At first there was no indication that she had heard them, but at last she appeared, framed, picturelike, in a window. Later the men missed young Dick Dewy. When they found him he was leaning against the school, staring up listlessly at the now darkened window.

At church, on the following morning, Fancy Day caused quite a stir of excitement. For three men she was the primary attraction—Dick Dewy, Farmer Shiner, and the new vicar, Mr. Maybold. To many other men in the congregation, the members of the choir, Fancy Day was

not endeared. She committed what amounted almost to blasphemy. For as long as anyone could remember the male choir had provided music for the service, but the young woman, on her first day in church, led the young girls in singing along with the men. Some of the older and wiser ones foresaw more trouble from a girl so froward.

Mr. Dewy, the carrier, called by everyone the tranter, gave his annual party on the afternoon and evening of Christmas Day. During the dancing, Dick was alternately delighted and depressed by Fancy. When he could claim her for a dance, he was transported with joy. But when she danced with Farmer Shiner, a handsomer, wealthier man, Dick was downcast. And when Farmer Shiner escorted the lady home, the evening was ruined for young Dick.

Using a handkerchief left behind by Fancy as his excuse, Dick a few days later found courage to call at the schoolhouse. Being a very inexperienced lover, he simply returned the handkerchief, stammered a good day, and departed. It was not until spring that he made any real progress in his silent love affair. By that time Dick was a wan and shadowy figure of a man. He spoke to no one of his love, but it was obvious to all but Fancy and her other two admirers that Dick was not himself.

But before Dick could declare himself, a delegation from the choir waited on the new vicar, Mr. Maybold. Having heard disquieting rumors that they were to be

3956

displaced by an organ, played by Fancy Day, they learned from the vicar that their fears were well founded. He had brought an organ to the church, since he preferred that instrument to a choir. He agreed that the choir was fine, but an organ would be better. In order to spare the feelings of the faithful choir members, however, he agreed to wait for a time before deposing them. They were to have the dignity of leaving on a special day, not on any ordinary Sunday.

Dick's big day came when he was allowed to bring Fancy and some of her belongings from the home of her father. He was dismayed to find Farmer Shiner also present at the house, but when Fancy allowed him to touch her hand at the dinner table Dick's spirits rose perceptibly. On the ride home he could not find the words that were in his heart; he felt, nevertheless, that he had made some progress with his lady. Then in the weeks that followed rumors of her friendliness with the vicar and with Farmer Shiner drove him to desperation. One day, screwing up his courage, he penned her a letter, asking bluntly whether he meant anything to her. When he received no answer from Fancy, he resolved that he would have it out with her the next Sunday.

Before Sunday came, however, he had to go on an errand for the vicar's mother, an errand which would take him to a neighboring town. As he was about to leave this village, he saw Fancy waiting for the carrier to take her home. Seizing the opportunity, Dick helped her into his cart and triumphantly carried her off. On the way home he finally made his proposal and was equally surprised and overjoyed to hear her acceptance.

They kept their betrothal a secret since they could not marry for some time. Also, Fancy's father had told her that he hoped she would accept Farmer Shiner for a husband. One trait of Fancy's character troubled Dick. She seemed to take undue pleasure in dressing to please others than himself, but whenever he prepared to punish her by letting her worry about him for a change, Fancy would go to him and apologize for her vanity. The young lover, unable to resist her shamefaced tears, would take her back into his heart before she knew she was gone.

On the day he was at last to meet her father to ask for her hand, Dick prepared himself carefully. In spite of his precautions, her father told him bluntly that he was not good enough for Fancy, that she was too cultured, too well educated, and too wealthy for a plain carrier. Sadly Dick agreed, and sadly he turned toward home.

But Fancy was not so easily defeated. When tears failed to move her father, she resorted to the age-old trick of languishing away for love. She did not eat, at least not so that her father could notice, but merely pined and sighed. The ruse worked, and her father reluctantly found himself begging her to marry her young lover. The date was set for the coming midsummer.

On the day that Fancy was installed at the organ, the day the choir died a disillusioned death, Dick went away to serve at the funeral of a friend. Fancy had put her hair in curls and in other ways dressed more lavishly than ever before. Dick was sorry to see her dress so beautifully when she knew he would not be present to see her, but she put him off brusquely. On his way home that night, Dick walked through the rain to get one last glimpse of his love before he retired. She would not even lean out her window far enough to give him a kiss. Later, when she saw the vicar approaching through the rain, she greeted him warmly. The vicar too had been enchanted with her appearance of the morning. Knowing nothing of her betrothal to Dick, he had decided to ask for her hand in marriage. Surprising even herself, Fancy accepted him.

The next morning the vicar met Dick on the road. Dick, still thinking himself betrothed, shyly told the vicar of his coming marriage to Fancy. The vicar kept his shocked silence, leaving Dick ignorant of Fancy's faithlessness. Then the vicar sent a note to the young lady, telling her that she could not honorably forsake Dick. Before it was delivered, he in turn received a note from Fancy, stating that she had been momentarily swayed by the prospect of a more cultured, more elegant life; now she begged to withdraw her acceptance of his proposal because she had loved and still loved another.

In summer the wedding day came. It was a great celebration, marred only by the vicar's refusal to perform the ceremony. Puzzled, Dick could not think of any way in which he might have offended the vicar. And when, after the ceremony, Dick told his bride that they would never have a secret between them, Fancy replied that they never would, beginning from that day forth.

UNDER THE YOKE

Type of work: Novel
Author: Ivan Vazov (1850-1921)
Type of plot: Romantic tragedy
Time of plot: 1875-1876
Locale: Bulgaria
First published: 1889

Principal characters:
KRALICH, a revolutionary
RADA, his sweetheart
SOKOLOV, a doctor
MARIKA, a young girl

Critique:

Under the Yoke was published after Bulgaria had won her independence from Turkish rule. Translated, the novel brought to Western readers a fresh and vivid insight into the affairs of that troubled country. Although the story is tragic, the treatment of the theme is romantic in the manner of Scott, and through fictitious characters and events the trials of the Bulgarians are faithfully re-created. Critically, the novel has been called one of the finest romances to come out of Eastern Europe.

The Story:

One day Marko, a substantial family man, sat down to his evening meal. His children and his relatives were a noisy crowd, but over the din they heard an alarming noise in the yard. The females all shrieked, because they were afraid of robbers. Marko took a pistol and went to investigate. In the stable he found a spent and furtive man cowering in the dark.

Ivan Kralich, the fugitive, had returned to the village of Bela Cherkva after escaping from a Turkish prison. The Turks were harsh rulers of Bulgaria, and anyone suspected of revolutionary tendencies was either killed outright or imprisoned. But eight years of confinement had failed to quench Kralich's spirit. Having made his getaway, he asked for sanctuary because the Turks were on his trail. Marko, a patriot who had known Kralich's family, told the fugitive to remain in hiding in his stable. As he returned to the house, however, Turkish

policemen knocked at the door. They had heard the women shrieking and had come to see what the trouble was.

As soon as Marko could get rid of the Turks he hurried back to the stable, but Kralich had disappeared. Hearing the police, he had climbed the wall and run. Unfortunately, he ran into a patrol and escaped them only after leaving his coat in the hands of the Turks. They shot at him, but the fugitive escaped into the countryside.

It was raining, and at last he took refuge in a mill. As he crouched in a dark corner, the miller came in with his daughter Marika, an innocent girl of fourteen. Kralich watched unobserved as they made beds on the floor. Then two Turkish policemen knocked and forced their way into the mill. One of them was a notorious lame man who had cut off a girl's head a short while before. The miller was terror stricken when the Turks ordered him to get them some raki. Knowing that they wanted Marika, the miller bravely refused to leave. Throwing aside all pretense, the Turks seized him and started to bind him. Kralich was moved to action when the despairing miller called to Marika for help. He took an ax and after a brief struggle killed the Turks. After Kralich and the miller had buried the bodies, the grateful miller led Kralich to a good hiding place in a nearby monastery.

While Kralich was resting, Sokolov, the village doctor, found himself in trouble. Called a doctor, though he had re-

3959

ceived no training and prescribed few medicines, he was regarded with suspicion by the Turks because he was a patriotic Bulgarian and because his peculiar habits included keeping a pet bear. That night, as he was playing with the bear, the Turks arrested him on a charge of treason.

What had happened was that Kralich had asked Sokolov the way to Marko's house, and the compassionate doctor had given Kralich his coat. When Kralich lost the coat during his escape from the patrol, the police recognized Sokolov's garment. In the pockets they found revolutionary documents. The arrest created a sensation in the district. Kralich, hearing of Sokolov's trouble, started to the village to clear him. Marko cleverly fooled the police, however, by substituting a harmless newspaper for the incriminating documents when the official messenger stopped for a drink in a tavern. Because the evidence had disappeared, the easygoing Turkish bey released Sokolov.

Kralich changed his name and found a job teaching school. He maintained contact with the revolutionaries, however, and soon welcomed to the cause his friend Mouratliski, who had also fled from the Turks. Mouratliski, passing as an Austrian photographer, soon became a familiar figure in the village. Kralich, continuing to discuss the cause of liberty, won many converts. He also fell in love with Rada, a gentle orphan who taught in the girls' school.

Once the townspeople gave a play in which Kralich took a leading role. The bey, who understood no Bulgarian, was an honored guest. At the end of the play Kralich led the cast in singing patriotic and revolutionary songs. The audience was much moved. The quick-witted Bulgarian who was translating for the bey assured that Turkish official that the songs were part of the drama.

Kralich finally came under suspicion when a spy informed the Turks that the schoolmaster was working for Bulgarian independence. A detachment of police surrounded the church while the villagers were at worship, but Kralich got through the cordon by assuming a disguise. Taking to the mountains and the woods, for months he led a wandering life sheltered by patriotic Bulgars. He preached continually the need for revolution. One day, when he attended a party in a small village, Turks came and beat an old man to death. Kralich led a small group, including the giant Ivan Kill-the-Bear, out along a trail and waited in ambush. The Bulgars succeeded in killing the Turks and left their bodies to be eaten by wolves.

Meanwhile, in Bela Cherkva, Rada led an uneasy life. The village, knowing of her love for Kralich, twitted her on her hopeless affair after his disappearance. In particular, a student named Kandov made her life miserable by following her about. At last Kralich slipped into the village to visit her. Because Rada, overjoyed, was reluctant to part from him again, Kralich invited her to go to Klissoura, a nearby village, where he was busy organizing a revolt. Soon afterward she set out, but Kandov followed her and found the house where she was staying. When Kralich appeared, he was already a little jealous because he had received an anonymous letter accusing Rada of intimacies with Kandov. As soon as he saw Kandov with her, Kralich became angry and left.

The inhabitants of Klissoura, under the fiery leadership of Kralich, prepared to revolt. On the day for the rising the little garrison proclaimed its independence of Turkey, and the citizen soldiers, after setting their wooden cannon on the trail, prepared to battle the Turks. Bela Cherkva did not revolt as planned, however, and the whole Turkish strength was concentrated on Klissoura. The Bulgarians were quickly overwhelmed. When the victors began pillaging the town, Rada was lucky enough to get back to Bela Cherkva with the help of Ivan and his wife.

A fugitive once more, Kralich wandered hungry and cold through the Balkans. He took shelter at last in the mill and sent the faithful Marika into town with a letter asking Sokolov to bring him clothes. Marika could not find the doctor, who had also become a fugitive, but by chance the letter fell into Rada's hands. She made up a bundle of clothing and started off to the mill.

Sokolov, meanwhile, had joined Kralich. When Rada arrived, the lovers had a brief and tearful reunion before pursuing Turks attacked the mill. Kralich and Sokolov were both armed, and for a time they held their stronghold against the enemy. Rada was the first to be killed by gunfire. Kralich kissed her cold lips and returned to the battle. The Turks quickly closed in on the two Bulgarians when the defenders' ammunition gave out. Kralich's head was mounted on a pole and carried in triumph back to the village.

UNDER TWO FLAGS

Type of work: Novel
Author: Ouida (Marie Louise de la Ramée, 1839-1908)
Type of plot: Sentimental romance
Time of plot: Early nineteenth century
Locale: London and environs, the continent, Algeria
First published: 1867

Principal characters:
THE HONORABLE BERTIE CECIL, a young Guardsman
BERKELEY, his younger brother
LORD ROCKINGHAM (THE SERAPH), Bertie's friend
RAKE, Bertie's servant
CIGARETTE, a French patriot
COLONEL CHATEAUROY, Bertie's enemy
PRINCESS CORONA D'AMAGÜE, the Seraph's sister

Critique:

Under Two Flags is a tale written by a master of her craft. As a novel it combines two popular traditions of English fiction, the adventure and the sentimental romance. Ouida was a widely read writer of her generation, and her books are still popular with those who have a fondness for a story of heroic adventure and characters of moral virtue.

The Story:

The Honorable Bertie Cecil, of the First Life Guards, although a fashionable member of his London set and an admirable fellow in every other respect, was uncommonly hard put to it for money. No money-lender in London would accept his note after he had mortgaged his whole inheritance. In those circumstances he depended upon winning a race with his six-year-old, Forest King, and he had staked everything on the race. Nevertheless with good-humored generosity he lent his younger brother, Berkeley, fifty pounds. The following day he rode Forest King to victory over a difficult course and received the praise of his lady, a fashionable peeress who had worn his scarlet and white.

His father, Lord Royallieu, who lived in the same mortgaged splendor that he had taught his sons to enjoy, loved his sons with the exception of Bertie, who looked too much like his dead wife's lover and, to the old viscount's detestation, carried the dead lover's name. The

old man took every occasion to sneer at Bertie's extravagance, and one day revealed his suspicions that Bertie was really the son of Alan Bertie.

Bertie was petted by the world. Sought after by half the women in London, he carried on flirtations with many. Lady Guenevere was one of his conquests. Rake, his valet, was devoted to him. Bertie had salvaged Rake from a bad affair and had treated him as he treated others, with friendly decency.

While he was disturbed by his financial affairs, his head groom had promised to dope Forest King for a fee. When it was learned that Forest King had been doped before a race, his friends, far from blaming him, pretended to agree that the horse was merely ill, but Bertie felt himself disgraced.

While Bertie's best friend, Lord Rockingham, known to his comrades of the Guards as the Seraph, was attempting to discover the mystery of Forest King's condition, he received a report that Bertie Cecil had forged the Seraph's name to a note. Bertie could not deny the charge, for the note had been presented at a time when he had been dining with Lady Guenevere. Wishing to protect her name from scandal, Bertie allowed himself to be accused. Knowing that his brother had forged the note and hoping to protect Berkeley's name as well, he left London suddenly in

3962

order to escape arrest.

Bertie, accompanied by Rake, made his escape on Forest King. Rake had discovered that the groom had doped Forest King, and he had pummeled him for it. He and his master rode to a place of safety; then Bertie ordered Rake to take Forest King to Lord Rockingham. He waited in hiding for a time, in the hope Lady Guenevere would save him by telling of his whereabouts when the forged note was presented. She chose to keep silent, however, holding her reputation at greater worth than Bertie's name.

At last, by a throw of the dice, Bertie decided to cast his lot with the French Foreign Legion. The faithful Rake accompanied him. Back in England people believed Bertie dead as well as ruined. Rockingham had Forest King; the old viscount burned Bertie's picture.

As Louis Victor, Bertie made his mark with his new companions in the Foreign Legion. They marveled at his skill with the horses, at his bravery, at his brilliance at dancing or cards. Bertie was a veteran Legionnaire when he received, six months late, the news that his father had died at the age of ninety. His older brother inherited the title.

Cigarette, a woman of independent spirit, a dancer and singer for the troops, came to understand and like Bertie. She warned him against Colonel Chateauroy, who hated Bertie because of his gallant record and popularity, and asked him never to disobey any of the colonel's unreasonable commands. Partly because he pitied her, Bertie promised. Shortly afterward Cigarette saved Bertie's life from some drunken Arabs. She was in love with him, but he was indifferent to her.

Bertie spent his spare time carving chessmen of ivory and through this occupation he met the lovely Princess Corona d'Amagüe, a woman who had been unhappily married to a man injured while saving her brother's life. Her husband had died soon after, and the princess had felt ever since a feeling

of responsibility for his death. Bertie soon fell in love with Princess Corona.

Colonel Chateauroy made it clear that he would never permit Bertie to be promoted above the rank of corporal. Bertie learned that Rake was purposely getting himself into trouble to prevent his own promotion, for he did not wish to outrank his master.

One day, in an old English journal, Bertie read that his older brother had died suddenly and that Berkeley had become Viscount Royallieu.

The regiment was ordered out. In the fighting that followed, Cigarette saved the day when she arrived at the head of a fresh squadron of cavalry. She found Bertie, badly wounded, on the battlefield. In the tent to which she had him carried, Bertie began to talk incoherently while Cigarette sat beside him. All she heard him say made her more jealous of the princess. She also learned that Bertie was English. No French person ever hated the English more than she. At her request Bertie was not told who had brought him back from the battlefield and cared for him during his sick ravings.

Three weeks later Bertie was startled when the Seraph came as an English tourist to visit the Legion camp. Not wishing to encounter his former friend, Bertie asked for and received permission to carry dispatches through hostile territory to another legion post. With faithful Rake, he rode away on a mission that meant almost certain death. Rake was killed in an Arab ambush, but Bertie delivered his dispatches safely. On his return trip he stopped at a way station and there saw his brother Berkeley, who was one of a party of tourists traveling with Princess Corona. Bertie gave no sign of recognition but spurred his horse and rode on.

Berkeley followed Bertie. When he caught up with his older brother, he revealed his fear that Bertie might claim the title. Indifferent to all except Berkeley's selfishness, Bertie asked his brother to leave Algeria at once.

Shortly afterward he discovered that Princess Corona was really the younger sister of the Seraph. She also became aware of Bertie's real name, and insisted that he make himself known to her brother. She begged him to claim his title, but he refused.

Cigarette went to Princess Corona, who requested her to tell Bertie that the Seraph was looking for his former friend. In another interview with Bertie, the princess asked him to tell his story and let the world be the judge. As he left her tent Colonel Chateauroy intercepted him and insulted the princess. In sudden rage Bertie struck his superior officer. Colonel Chateauroy arrested him. Bertie was sentenced to death.

When Cigarette heard Bertie's fate, she forced Berkeley, whom she met accidentally, to acknowledge that Bertie was in reality his brother, an exile for Berkeley's crime, and the true heir to the estate of Royallieu. She carried her story to a marshal of France, demanding that Bertie's honor be saved even though his life were already forfeited. With a stay of execution signed by the marshal she rode at full speed to reach the Legion camp before the hour set for Bertie's execution.

The Seraph, not Cigarette, reached Bertie first. But in spite of the Seraph's entreaties, Colonel Chateauroy refused to delay the time of execution.

Cigarette reached the spot just as the volley was fired. With her own body she took the bullets intended for Bertie. She died, the marshal's order safely delivered. A child of the army and a soldier of France, she gave her life to save a comrade. It was a sacrifice that Bertie and Princess Corona, happily reunited, were never to forget.

UNDER WESTERN EYES

Type of work: Novel
Author: Joseph Conrad (Teodor Józef Konrad Korzeniowski, 1857-1924)
Type of plot: Psychological realism
Time of plot: Early twentieth century
Locale: St. Petersburg, Russia, and Geneva, Switzerland
First published: 1911

Principal characters:
RAZUMOV, a Russian student
VICTOR HALDIN, a revolutionist
NATHALIE HALDIN, his sister
MRS. HALDIN, mother of Victor and Nathalie
THE ENGLISH PROFESSOR, a friend of the Haldins

Critique:

In the later years of Joseph Conrad, increasing recognition accorded him as a novelist of genius tended to identify him almost exclusively as a writer of sea tales. This tendency distressed Conrad because he felt that the nature of his writing ran the risk of being obscured by only one part of his material. He himself called attention to those novels which turn away from exotic places and deal with various aspects of Europe before World War I. Occupying a conspicuous place among the latter is *Under Western Eyes*. Despite its initial failure to impress the public, its clearness of judgment and its picture of prewar Russia were later confirmed by its reception in that country and by the events of the Russian Revolution. Razumov is one of those lonely figures so absorbing to Conrad. In his loneliness Razumov keeps a journal which eventually falls into the hands of an elderly Englishman in Geneva, the friend and adviser of the girl Razumov loves. Under this Englishman's "western eyes" the whole episode involving Razumov is scanned and evaluated. The fictional result is an interpretation of the Russian mind and temperament which has seldom been surpassed for sharpness of perception and objectivity of treatment.

The Story:

A student, at the St. Petersburg University, Razumov, while not talkative or gregarious, had been generally respected by the other students. His silences were attributed to profundity of thought, and his behavior was such as to inspire confidence and good opinion. Razumov, absorbed in his studies, remained largely indifferent to the impression which he made on his fellow students. He dreamed of winning scholarly honors, and he had no wish to become involved in the revolutionary activities which occupied minds of such acquaintances as Victor Haldin, a youth in whose company he had occasionally spent some time. Razumov's mother was dead; his father, Prince K——, acknowledged his illegitimate son only to the extent of sending him money secretly, through an intermediary. As a result, the unspent feeling which Razumov was unable to direct toward parents or family found its way into other channels. He lavished much of it on his country and felt, in his loneliness, that if he were not a Russian, he would not be anything.

By a strange turn of circumstances the uneventful pattern of Razumov's life was abruptly altered. On a certain snowy morning in St. Petersburg, a sensational event occurred—a political terrorist assassinated a prominent government official and then escaped. An hour or two later, the unsuspecting Razumov returned to his apartment to find a visitor awaiting him. The guest was Victor Haldin. Presuming on his casual acquaintance with

Razumov, Haldin had selected the latter's quarters as a place of temporary refuge. Pressed for an explanation, he confessed that he was the killer being sought by the police. He asked Razumov to help him in making his escape from the city.

Razumov, dismayed, knew he could be compromised and ruined by Haldin's visit if it ever became known. However, he went in search of a sledge-driver who might spirit Haldin away, but he found the man helplessly drunk. His dismay and despair deepening, Razumov decided that he could not continue to shield Haldin. In his extremity, he broke an unwritten rule by calling on Prince K—— to ask his advice and beg his protection. Prince K—— immediately contacted the authorities, with the result that Haldin was promptly apprehended and executed. Razumov, after extended interrogation by General T—— and Councilor Mikulin, was released, but not before he had been marked down, by the councilor's sharp eyes, as a tool of great potential usefulness to the government.

Meanwhile, in Geneva, Haldin's mother and sister waited anxiously for news of him. When word of his execution arrived, they were grief-stricken and bewildered; but their efforts to find out the exact circumstances of his end were blocked by the mystery and vagueness which shrouded the whole affair. Nathalie, Victor Haldin's sister, was relieved when she heard that a Russian named Razumov had arrived in Geneva. According to the rumors which had been circulating, this man was an escaped colleague of her brother's, a fellow conspirator and revolutionist. Surely he, better than any other, would be able to solve the puzzle of her brother's arrest and execution.

To the Haldins, Razumov proved to be an elusive and enigmatic quarry. He lost himself at once in a circle of revolutionists in exile, including the celebrated Peter Ivanovitch, the legendary Madame de S——, and the sinister Nikita. Among them he was admired as a hero. This role Razumov found increasingly difficult to maintain, especially after he met Nathalie Haldin and fell in love with her.

Razumov finally broke under the strain of keeping up his twofold deception. Through his journal, which he sent to Nathalie Haldin, she learned his true relationship to her brother. Then, on an impulse, he confessed to the revolutionists the fact that he was a government spy. Brutally beaten by Nikita, with his hearing destroyed, he stumbled in front of a tramcar. Suffering from two broken limbs and a crushed side, he was picked up by passers-by and carried to a hospital.

The tragic story of Razumov might have ended there, but his will to live proved too strong. Nursed back to partial health by a motherly revolutionist, he eventually returned to his homeland. There, in the south of Russia, he shared a two-room cottage with his Good Samaritan friend, the devoted Tekla. Ironically, some of the revolutionists came to regret the cruel treatment Razumov had received at their hands. Periodically they visited his cottage to be stimulated by his intelligent and original views on politics, society, and morality.

THE UNDERDOGS

Type of work: Novel
Author: Mariano Azuela (1873-1952)
Type of plot: Social and historical chronicle
Time of plot: 1914-1915
Locale: Zacatecas, northern Mexico
First published: 1915

Principal characters:
  DEMETRIO MACÍAS, a poor Indian of Jalisco
  LUIS CERVANTES, an opportunist journalist and political turncoat
  CAMILA, a village girl
  LA PINTADA, "The Painted Lady," a prostitute and camp follower
  "WHITEY" MARGARITO, a sadistic soldier

Critique:

Mariano Azuela knew at first hand the materials of this novel, for he had served as a military doctor with Pancho Villa's Golden Boys. His vivid account of revolutionary Mexico was first published serially in a small El Paso newspaper. Almost forgotten, it was revived in 1924 and won immediate fame for its author. Pessimism marks this story of those coming up from below—*Los de abajo*—at the beginning of the Mexican Revolution. This is no overall picture of the struggle, but a blending of excitement, cruelty, and beauty as seen through the eyes of a man practically pushed into the struggle, a soldier who fought because the enemy was in front of him. Best known of Azuela's sixteen novels, *The Underdogs* has appeared in dozens of Spanish editions and has been translated into eight languages.

The Story:

Demetrio Macías was a peaceful Indian who knew nothing about revolutions. When as a follower of Madera he was hounded by the political leader of Jalisco, he fled with his wife and child to the mountains. There some Federal soldiers came upon the fugitives at breakfast and sent Demetrio flying. Wild and lawless, they would have raped his wife if he had not returned with a gun. Being no killer, the Indian let them go free, only to have them come back with reinforcements and burn his fields. Demetrio

then joined a band of sixty sharpshooting rebel outlaws and helped them to drive off twice that many soldiers. During the fighting two of the rebels were killed and Demetrio was shot in the leg.

For two weeks the outlaws remained hidden in a native village, looked after by Indians who hated the government. Venancio, a barber-surgeon, tended Demetrio's wound. The village women also used poultices of laurel and fresh pigeon blood to heal him. An attractive young girl named Camila was his nurse.

One day the psuedo-intellectual Luis Cervantes blundered into the village and explained that he had deserted the government forces because his commanding officer had assigned him to menial duty. Distrusting Cervantes' glib tongue and big words, the rebels pretended to condemn him to death. One outlaw dressed in a priest's robes and pretended to hear the deserter's last confession in order to determine whether he was a spy. Accepted eventually as a revolutionist, Cervantes then urged the rebels to join the great revolutionary leaders of Mexico. Camila fell in love with him. Although she made her feelings evident, Cervantes never encouraged her, not even on the night of the outlaws' departure. The girl had never responded to Demetrio's love making; he was only an Indian.

Hearing from messengers that Huerta's Federalists had fortified the city of Zaca-

THE UNDERDOGS by Mariano Azuela. Translated by E. Munguía, Jr. By permission of the publishers, Coward-McCann, Inc. Copyright, 1929, by Coward-McCann, Inc.

tecas, Cervantes urged the band to hurry to join the besiegers and be in at the capture. He also flattered Demetrio by telling the Indian that he was more than a common rebel, that he was a tool of destiny to win back the rights of the people.

Demetrio planned a surprise attack on one of the towns along their march, but an Indian guide betrayed the scheme and the Federalists were prepared to resist. A friendly citizen showed the rebels a back way into the town, however, and the garrison was overwhelmed. The rebels found and stabbed the treacherous guard and killed the Federal soldiers who had survived the attack.

By the time General Natera arrived in the district, Demetrio's reputation had grown so great that he was made a colonel in the revolutionary army. Failing to take Zacatecas, the rebels were forced to retreat, discarding their booty along the road. Demetrio thought of going back to Camila, until news of Villa's coming excited the rebels and gave them a fresh incentive.

During the next battle Cervantes and Solis, an idealist, took refuge in a place where they thought they would be safe. While they discussed the significance of the revolution, a stray bullet killed Solis. Demetrio's gallant charge turned the tide of battle for Villa and won him promotion to the rank of general.

While drinking and boasting in a tavern after the battle, Demetrio met Whitey Margarito and La Pintada, a prostitute with whom he went looking for a hotel room. Her insistence that as a general he should occupy a house of his own made him decide to commandeer a fine residence. During the ransacking Cervantes found a valuable diamond ring. The soldiers tore the pictures from books in the library and sold the ruined volumes. Whitey, joining Demetrio's forces, ran off with Cervantes' girl while Demetrio was arguing the matter of taking her instead of La Pintada, of whom he had tired.

Soon afterward the rebels raided the house of Don Mónico, Demetrio's land-owning enemy, and burned the estate. Cervantes, having collected much loot, suggested that he and Demetrio hide it in case they were forced to leave the country. Demetrio wished to share it with others still an idealist, he believed the rebel cause would triumph. Because he wanted only Camila, Cervantes promised to get her for his leader.

Cervantes went to the village and persuaded the girl to return with him. Believing that Cervantes was in love with her, she was surprised to find herself in Demetrio's bed. The next morning La Pintada discovered Camila and offered to help her escape. Camila refused. She had found that she liked Demetrio and she decided to stay with him and the army.

During the march against General Orozco at Jalisco, Whitey showed his cruelty when he tortured a prisoner by tightening a rope around the man's neck until his eyes bulged. Later, when kind-hearted Camila persuaded Demetrio to return ten bushels of confiscated corn to a starving villager, Whitey gave the man ten lashes instead. Camila's protests at the incident won her the enmity of La Pintada, who had taken up with Whitey after Demetrio and Cervantes had discarded her. When Demetrio, siding with Camila, ordered the camp follower away, La Pintada became enraged and stabbed Camila.

By the time Demetrio and his men reached Aguascalientes they found Villa and Carranza, once allies, fighting each other. The Federal forces, taking advantage of the disunity, defeated Villa at Celaya. The defeat was a terrible shock to Demetrio's followers, who could not bring themselves to believe that their idol had been beaten. The rebels were forced to retreat.

Cervantes escaped safely across the border. From El Paso he wrote to Venancio, the barber-surgeon. He said that Whitey had shot himself, and he invited Venancio to join him in Texas, where with the barber's money they could open a Mexican restaurant.

After Villa's defeat Demetrio found the villagers no longer willing to help the rebels. To them, he and his followers had become outlaws once more. Somewhat discouraged, he decided to return home. He had been away two years and had seen much, but he could not answer his wife's questions when she asked him why he kept on fighting. He lacked Cervantes' glib tongue to put his true feelings into words.

Trying to pacify the landowners of the region, the government sent troops into the uplands after the outlaw band. Once more the rebels and the Federal troops clashed. Outnumbered, the outlaws perished on the spot where two years before they had won their first victory. After the fighting had ended the soldiers found the body of Demetrio Macías. His eyes, forever fixed, still sighted along the barrel of his gun.

UNDINE

Type of work: Novel
Author: Friedrich de La Motte-Fouqué (1777-1843)
Type of plot: Symbolic allegory
Time of plot: The Middle Ages
Locale: Austria
First published: 1811

Principal characters:
UNDINE, a water spirit
SIR HULDBRAND, a knight
KÜHLEBORN, Undine's uncle
BERTALDA, loved by Sir Huldbrand

Critique:

Essentially a fairy tale, Undine is a highly imaginative and romantic narrative. Told simply but well, it is in the tradition of German folklore, and for that reason it is interesting and enjoyable even to grownups.

The Story:

Near a forest in Austria there lived an old fisherman, his wife, and their foster daughter, Undine. The nearby wood was said to be inhabited by spirits who were enemies of the mortal human beings who lived outside the forest.

One day a young knight, Sir Huldbrand of Ringstetten, was traveling through the forest when a storm broke. As he rode through the gloomy wood he was pursued by spirits and tormented by other manifestations of unearthly folk. At last he came to the edge of the forest and took refuge in the fisherman's cottage, where he was given food and shelter.

Sir Huldbrand was amazed by the beauty of young Undine, who asked him to tell the story of his adventures in the forest. The fisherman forbade the telling, however, and cautioned that it was unwise to talk of spirits at nighttime. Undine, rebellious, mischievous, and untamed, disappeared into the night when reproved by her foster father.

The fisherman and the knight cried for her to return, but their voices were lost in the noise of the wind and rain. As the storm increased they became more worried, and finally they set out in search of her. It was Sir Huldbrand who found her, safe and sound in the leafy bower where she was hiding. When he returned with her to the fisherman's cottage, he told her of his adventures in the forest. Meanwhile the storm raged so furiously that the cottage had become isolated and the four people were cut off by the encircling floods.

Sir Huldbrand then told how he had happened to be traveling through the forest. He had fallen in love with Bertalda, a haughty lady who insisted that he prove his love and courage by a journey through the dreadful wood. At that point in his tale Undine, jealous of the lady, bit the knight's hand. A few days later, a priest, his boat lost in the swirling stream, took refuge on the island. That night he married Undine and Sir Huldbrand. The marriage changed the girl completely. She became submissive, considerate, full of affection. She had gained a soul.

After the flood waters had subsided, the couple left for the knight's domain, Castle Ringstetten. On their way they went to pay homage to the duke of the domain, and in his hall they met Bertalda. Undine took Bertalda to her bosom and announced that she had a surprise for her. Shortly before, Undine had told her husband that she really was a water spirit, that she could live on earth only until he rejected her love; then Kühleborn, who ruled the waters, would call her back to her water home. She had lived with the fisherman and his wife since she had been a mere child, for she had appeared at

3970

their cottage on the evening of the day when their own child had, apparently, been drowned.

Undine's surprise, arranged with the help of Kühleborn, the river spirit, was revealed. Bertalda was the long-lost child of the fisherman and his wife. But the proud lady at first refused to accept them as her true parents. When she demanded proof of the story, she was identified by a birthmark on her body. Bertalda's foster parents were disgusted with her shameless behavior, and they cast her off. The next day Bertalda accosted Undine and Sir Huldbrand outside the duke's castle. Dressed as a mean fishing girl, she had been ordered to sell food to learn humility and the dignity of toil so that she could rejoin her real parents. Pitying her, Undine and Sir Huldbrand insisted that she live with them at Castle Ringstetten.

Life did not always go smoothly at the castle. One day Undine, who was loved by the servants, ordered the well to be sealed. But Bertalda, who wanted the water from it to remove her freckles, ordered the seal removed. Sir Huldbrand insisted that Undine was mistress of the castle and the well remained sealed. Bertalda then decided to go to the fisherman's cottage. She went through the Black Valley, where Kühleborn, who hated her, put all sorts of difficulties in her way. At last she was rescued by Sir Huldbrand and Undine, who had followed her flight.

Later the three started down the Danube to visit Vienna. Everything went wrong, and the sailors thought the boat was bewitched. Finally, in exasperation, Sir Huldbrand forgot Undine's advice not to remonstrate with her whenever they were close to water. He told her that he was tired of her and her spirit relatives and ordered her to return to her watery home. Although he was sorry as soon as he had spoken those words, he could not recall them; Undine had already disappeared beneath the waves.

At first Sir Huldbrand grieved, but as time passed he thought less often of Undine. At length he and Bertalda decided to be married. But the priest who had married Sir Huldbrand to Undine refused to perform the ceremony, and so they were married by another. Bertalda then commanded the workmen to remove the stone from the well which Undine had ordered sealed. All were terrified when a white figure emerged from it. It was Undine. She went into the castle and told Sir Huldbrand that he must die.

Sir Huldbrand expired while he looked upon her face, and Undine vanished. There were some who said that she reëntered the well. At the funeral Undine joined the mourners kneeling by the grave, but at the end of the service she disappeared. Then on the spot where she had knelt water sprang forth and a stream appeared to flow about the knight's grave. It was Undine surrounding her lover in death.

THE UNFORTUNATE TRAVELLER

Type of work: Novel
Author: Thomas Nash (1567-1601)
Type of plot: Picaresque romance
Time of plot: Reign of King Henry VIII
Locale: England and Europe
First published: 1594

Principal characters:
 JACK WILTON, a page for King Henry VIII and a soldier of fortune
 DIAMANTE, a rich widow, later Jack's wife
 THE EARL OF SURREY, Jack's friend and benefactor
 HERACLIDE DE IMOLA, hostess to Jack and Diamante in Rome

Critique:

The Unfortunate Traveller, Or, The Life of Jack Wilton was written almost a hundred and fifty years too early to be classified as a novel. Not a novel in the generally accepted sense of that term, the book is, however, an important forerunner of the English novel as it was to develop in the eighteenth century. The Unfortunate Traveller, along with Sir Philip Sidney's Arcadia, was one of the high points of the literature of the last years of the sixteenth century. Nash's realism in this work is high, yet he catered also to the Elizabethan taste for the romantic and far-fetched, especially in dealing with Italy and the Italians. Seldom has a work, even in the twentieth century, described in such detail the horrors of public torture and execution, and the incidents of a rape and a looting. Throughout life a very witty satirist, Nash could not, even in this work, resist the opportunity to find fault; he does so with the stupidity of professional military men and with the inability of the universities to entertain royalty satisfactorily.

The Story:

Jack Wilton was a page serving in the army of King Henry VIII of England when his adventures began. While the English troops were encamped near Turwin, in France, Jack, pretending that he had overheard the king and his council planning to do away with a certain sutler, convinced the sutler that he ought to give away all his supplies to the soldiers and then throw himself on the king's

mercy. The sutler, completely fooled, did just that. The king, enjoying the prank, gave him a pension and forgave Jack.

Shortly after that escapade Jack fell in with a captain who forced Jack to help him get rich by throwing dice. Jack, tiring of his subservience to the captain, persuaded the officer that the best means of getting ahead in the army was to turn spy and seek out information valuable to the king. The gullible captain, entering the French lines, was discovered by the French and almost killed before he was sent hustling back to the English camp.

The campaign over, Jack found himself back in England once again. When the peacetime duties of a page began to pall, he left the king's household and turned soldier of fortune. After crossing the English Channel to find some means of making a livelihood, he reached the French king too late to enter that monarch's service against the Swiss, and so he traveled on to Münster, Germany. There he found John Leiden leading the Baptists against the Duke of Saxony. He observed a notorious massacre, in which the Baptists were annihilated because they refused to carry the weapons of war into battle. After the battle Jack met the Earl of Surrey, who was on the continent at the time.

Surrey, having been acquainted with Jack at court, was glad to see the page and confided to him his love for Geraldine, a lovely Florentine. Surrey proposed that Jack travel with him to Italy in search of the woman. Jack, having no future in sight, readily consented to accompany the earl.

Jack and Surrey then proceeded southward out of Germany into Italy. As they traveled Surrey proposed to Jack that they exchange identities for a time, so that the nobleman could behave in a less seemly fashion. Jack, pleased at the prospect of being an earl, even temporarily, agreed.

Upon their arrival in Venice, on the way to Florence, they were taken up by a courtesan named Tabitha, who tried to kill the man she thought was the Earl of Surrey, with the true earl as her accomplice. Surrey and Jack, turning the tables on her, caused her and her pander to be executed for attempting to conspire against a life. In turning the tables, however, Jack came into possession of some counterfeit money. When they used the coins, Jack and the earl were seized as counterfeiters and sentenced to death.

While languishing in prison, Jack met Diamante, the wife of a goldsmith who had imprisoned her because he suspected her of infidelity. The page made her his mistress after assuring her that thereby she revenged herself on the husband who thought little of her chastity.

After a few weeks Jack and the earl were released through an English gentleman who had heard of their plight and had secured the efforts of the poet Aretine to prove to the court that Tabitha and her procurer had been the real counterfeiters. Aretine also saw to it that Diamante was released from prison to become the mistress of Jack once again. Within a few weeks Diamante's husband died of the plague. Jack married Diamante and, in view of his new fortune, decided to travel.

He left the Earl of Surrey in Venice, but the pleasure of bearing the nobleman's title was so great that Jack kept it. After some time Surrey heard that there was another earl by the same name and went to investigate. Learning that the double was Jack, Surrey forgave him, and they started once again on their interrupted trip to Florence. Upon their arrival the earl, wishing to do battle to prove his love for Geraldine, issued a challenge to all the knights and gentlemen of the city. The tourney was a great success, with Surrey carrying off all the honors of the day. After that event Surrey and Jack parted company. Jack, still accompanied by Diamante, went on to Rome.

There they lived with Johannes and Heraclide de Imola. During the summer Signor de Imola died of the plague. Shortly after his death and before his corpse could be removed from the house, bandits broke in and raped Heraclide de Imola and Diamante. Jack, overpowered by the bandits, was unable to help the women. Heraclide killed herself after the attack. When police broke into the house they blamed Jack for what had happened. He was unable to clear himself because the only other witness was Diamante, whom the bandits had kidnaped.

A banished English earl, appearing in time to save Jack from the hangman's noose, produced witnesses to show that one of the bandits had made a deathbed confession clearing the page of any part in the crimes. Released, Jack went in search of Diamante. While searching for her he fell through an unbarred cellar door into the house of a Jew, and there he found Diamante making love to an apprentice. The Jew, roused by the noise of the fall and Jack's anger at Diamante, came into the cellar and accused them both of breaking into his house and corrupting his apprentice. Under the law, they became the Jew's bond servants. Jack was turned over to another Jew, the pope's physician, to be used in a vivisection.

He was saved from that horrid death when one of the pope's mistresses fell in love with him and used her influence to secure his person for herself. Diamante also fell into the woman's hands. Jack and Diamante, keeping their previous relations a secret, hoped in that way to be able to escape from the house. One day, when the woman went to a religious festival, they escaped, taking with them as much loot as they could carry.

Traveling northward, Jack went to Bologna, where he saw a famous criminal executed. The assassin, Cutwolfe, had confessed to murdering the bandit who had led the assault on Heraclide de Imola and Diamante months before. Moving on into France, Jack found the English armies once again in the field and returned to King Henry's service.